D1237051

Understanding and Preventing Teacher Burnout

"Burnout" was first investigated in the 1970s as a crisis of overextended and disillusioned human service workers. But the nature of the syndrome has changed with the evolution in the nature of human service professions. The current experience of burnout is lived out in a more difficult social context, with human service workers struggling harder for social credibility and job security. For instance, through the greater demands on their time and energy, many teachers are being pressed to do more work with fewer resources, while receiving fewer rewards and less recognition of their efforts. Psychologically, they run the risk of experiencing more emotional exhaustion and a sense of alienation from their work lives.

A prime objective of this volume is to provide new perspectives and a deeper understanding of the nature, conditions, and consequences of burnout, notably in the teaching profession. To do this, the contributions review the most recent research in the field, describe a "research agenda," and provide an "action agenda" designed to prevent the incidence of burnout in the workplace.

Roland Vandenberghe is currently Dean of the Faculty of Psychology and Educational Sciences of the University of Leuven. He is also Chair of the Center for Educational Policy and Innovation.

A. Michael Huberman is Professor in the Faculty of Psychology and Education at the University of Geneva.

Understanding and Preventing Teacher Burnout

A Sourcebook of International Research and Practice

Edited by

Roland Vandenberghe
A. Michael Huberman

CAMBRIDGE
UNIVERSITY PRESS

PUBLISHED BY THE PRESS SYNDICATE OF THE UNIVERSITY OF CAMBRIDGE
The Pitt Building, Trumpington Street, Cambridge, United Kingdom

CAMBRIDGE UNIVERSITY PRESS
The Edinburgh Building, Cambridge , UK   http: //www.cup.cam.ac.uk
40 West 20th Street, New York, NY 10011-4211, USA   http: //www.cup.org
10 Stamford Road, Oakleigh, Melbourne 3166, Australia

First published 1999

Understanding and Preventing Teacher Burnout has been
published with the support of the Johann Jacobs Foundation.

Printed in the United States of America

Typeface Palatino 10/13 pt.   *System* QuarkXPress™ 4.0 [AG]

*A catalog record for this book is available from
the British Library.*

Library of Congress Cataloging-in-Publication Data
Understanding and preventing teacher burnout : a sourcebook of
   international research / edited by Roland Vandenberghe,
   A. Michael Huberman.
      p. cm.
      ISBN 0-521-62213-1 (hb)
      1. Teacher – Job stress.   2. Burn out (Psychology) – Prevention.
   3. Teaching – Psychological aspects.   4. Stress management.
   I. Vandenbergh, Roland.   II. Huberman, A. M.
   LB2840.2.U531999
   371.102′01′9 – dc 21   98-40330
                                                      CIP

ISBN 0 521 62213 1 hardback

Contents

Contributors

Barbara M. Byrne, School of Psychology, University of Ottawa, 145 J.J. Luissier Street, Ottawa KIN 6N5, Canada

Peter de Heus, Department of Social and Organisational Psychology, Wassenaarseweg 52, NL-2333 AK Leiden, The Netherlands

Barry Farber, Department of Clinical Psychology, Teachers College, Columbia University, 525 W. 120th Street, New York, NY 10027, USA

Isaac A. Friedman, The Henrietta Szold Institute, 9 Columbia Street, Jerusalem 96583, Israel

Patricia Graham, Graduate School of Education, Harvard University, Monroe C. Gutman Library, Appian Way, Cambridge, MA 02138, USA

A. Michael Huberman, Faculty of Psychology and Educational Sciences, Université de Genève, route de Drize, 1277 Carouge, Genève, Switzerland

Geert Kelchtermans, Center for Educational Policy and Innovation, K.U. Leuven, Vesaliusstraat 2, B-3000 Leuven, Belgium

Michael P. Leiter, Faculty of Science, Acadia University, Wolfville, Nova Scotia BOP 1X0, Canada

Kenneth A. Leithwood, Department of Educational Administration, Ontario Institute for Studies in Education, 252 Bloor Street West, Toronto, Ontario M5S 1V6, Canada

Willy Lens, Department of Psychology, K.U. Leuven, Tiensestraat 102, 3000 Leuven, Belgium

Christina Maslach, Department of Psychology, University of California at Berkeley, 3210 Tolman Hall, #1650, Berkeley, CA 94720-1650, USA

Lynne Miller, University of Southern Maine, 103 Bailey Hall, 37 College Avenue, Gorham, ME 04038, USA

Jennifer Nias, University of Plymouth, Faculty of Arts and Education, Douglas Avenue, Exmouth, Devon EX8 2AT, United Kingdom

Bernd Rudow, Universität Herseburg, Sachsen-Anhalt, Germany

Ralf Schwarzer, Freie Universität Berlin, Institut für Arbeitsorganisation und Gesundheitspsychologie WE-10, Habelschwerdter Allee 45, D-141915 Berlin, Germany

Thomas Sergiovanni, Radford Chair of Education and Administration, Trinity University, 715 Stadium Drive, San Antonio, TX 78216, USA

Peter Sleegers, Institute for Teacher Education and Teacher Training, Katholike Universiteit Nijmegen, P.O. Box 9103, 6500 HD Nijmegen, The Netherlands

Mark A. Smylie, College of Education, University of Illinois at Chicago, 1040 West Harrison Street, Chicago, IL 60680, USA

Roland Vandenberghe, Center for Educational Policy and Innovation, K.U. Leuven, Vesaliusstraat 2, B-3000 Leuven, Belgium

Peter Woods, Open University, Walton Hall, Milton Keynes MK 7 6AA, United Kingdom

Figures

Tables

Foreword

This volume is the fifth in a series sponsored by the Johann Jacobs Foundation. It is intended to build bridges between the scientific community and the practitioners in the field about an issue that has assumed growing importance – the burnout syndrome of teachers and its nefarious effects on their pupils. The quality of the relationship between teachers and pupils is indeed one of the most rewarding features of the teaching profession; it is potentially also the most vulnerable one, especially when viewed against the backdrop of an ever more rapidly changing world that compels both teachers and pupils to learn how to adapt. Because burnout in the teaching profession is a phenomenon that knows no national boundaries, the Johann Jacobs Foundation convened from November 2 to 4, 1995, an international conference with more than 40 scientists and young scholars at its Communication Center at Marbach Castle on Lake Constance in Germany. This book provides a well-balanced overview of the work of the conference, with a special and purposeful "confrontation" between North American and European perspectives. The various chapters in this text are drawn from papers and commentaries presented at the conference, reflecting the intensive and fruitful discussions that characterized the event. Moreover, the book also offers suggestions for future research and the development of useful interventions. This is very much in line with the Foundation's goal of seeking to increase knowledge of what is needed to improve the circumstances affecting the lives of young people and of ensuring that such knowledge is made available to those in a position to act concretely on it. The book should therefore be of interest to all people concerned with the quality of education and the well-being of youth. It should be especially valuable to those who seek to innovate and invigorate our schools so that today's youth may, in the best sense of the word, be well educated for tomorrow's world.

Klaus J. Jacobs
Founder and Chairman
Johann Jacobs Foundation

Introduction – Burnout and the Teaching Profession

A. MICHAEL HUBERMAN AND ROLAND VANDENBERGHE

"Burnout" was first investigated in the 1970s as a crisis of overextended and disillusioned human service workers. Early interpretations centered on the collapse of the professional mystique; people entering these sectors presumably had developed unrealistic expectations on the basis of their training and general cultural background. Gradually, the problem was attributed more specifically to conflicts between caregivers' values for enhancing the lives of their recipients and limitations in the structure and process of human service organizations.

Unlike the classic, largely one-dimensional models of stress, the experience of burnout has been conceptualized in terms of three interrelated components: emotional exhaustion, depersonalization, and reduced personal accomplishment.[1] In terms of outcomes, burnout has been linked to decrements in both psychological and physical well-being and has been associated with various problem behaviors, both on the job and in the home.

The nature of the syndrome has changed as human service professions have evolved. For example, the current experience of burnout occurs within a decidedly different social context, with human service workers struggling for social credibility and fearing job insecurity. Changes in mandates, retrenchments, and more skeptical perceptions of the worth of human service professionals have all realigned responsibilities and professional demands; they have altered the meaning of work and its underlying exchange agreement between professionals and their organizations. For

---

1. This classification is now generally adopted by working researchers. It derives from the work of C. Maslach (USA) and her colleagues. Professor Maslach is a contributor to this volume. Emotional exhaustion refers to feelings of being emotionally overextended and depleted in one's emotional resources. Depersonalization refers to a negative, callous, or excessively detached response to other people – often the recipients of one's service or care. Reduced personal accomplishment refers to a decline in one's feelings of competence and successful achievement in one's work.

example, in his contribution to this volume, P. Woods claims that through the "intensification" of their work demands, teachers are being pressed to do more work with fewer resources while at the same time receiving fewer rewards and less recognition for their efforts. For B. Farber, this could be the start of a downward spiral leading to burnout. Given such feelings of inconsequentiality, teachers may come to believe that their efforts are disproportionate to their perceived effects. In his recent study, H. C. Cherniss (1995) underlines the sense of frustration and ineffectuality among teachers when their pupils do not make visible and significant improvements in a realistic period of time.

Burnout has long been recognized as an important stress-related problem for people who work in interpersonally oriented professions. In these occupations, the relationship between providers and recipients is central to the job, and the nature of the work (be it service, treatment, or education) can be highly emotional. Education is a prime example. Providing affective, instructional, and moral services to pupils of necessity makes emotional demands on the service providers.

These demands take place within a complex network of interactions. Some interactions are intensive (pupils, colleagues, principal); others are more remote, but they also have an impact on the quality of work-related interactions (parents, inspectorate, central administration). These more distant agents are characterized less by their social and emotional commitments to teachers' needs than by their high expectations, their sensitivity to public demands, and a greater emphasis on pupils' academic achievements. In the eyes of many teachers, these more remote agents in the educational enterprise take emotional energy but give little back.

On the other hand, close partners in the school setting itself are likely to be more supportive sources of emotional and professional sustenance. For example, the collegial network of peers facilitates the discussion of meaningful daily problems, where uncertainties and questions are accepted as an essential part of teaching. Skeptical colleagues, however, or those who are already burned out can have a detrimental effect.

Two other local "partners" affect emotional and social support. First, interested, hard-working, and high-achieving pupils can be preventive sources of undue stress and burnout. Conversely, unmotivated or undisciplined pupils are a prime source of emotional exhaustion. Another strong factor, as K. Leithwood and M. Smylie point out in this volume, is school directors or principals. They can create working conditions in which teachers feel both sustained and professionally rewarded, thereby avoiding some of the classic symptoms of burnout. They can also, however, function as administrative managers, taking no responsibility for affective or relational matters within the school.

Teaching, as a focus of this volume, shares with other human service professions a close relationship with recipients – in this case, with students. The quality of the relationship between teacher and pupils can be one of the most rewarding aspects of the teaching profession, but it can also be the source of emotionally draining and discouraging experiences. Because burnout has considerable implications for teachers' performance relative to pupils and colleagues – not to speak of teachers' own well being – it is a problem with potentially serious consequences both for the teaching career and, more fundamentally, for the learning outcomes of pupils themselves. This particular aspect – the effects of teacher burnout on *pupils'* behavior and outcomes – has been neglected in the "classic" and contemporary research literature.

Burnout also has important implications for the extent to which teachers can pursue important values through their work. To be rewarding, teaching must be meaningful. The opportunity to enact values pertaining to personal relationships, the learning process, or the actual content of the curriculum is part of the essential attraction of the teaching profession. In her contribution to this volume, J. Nias shows clearly that the enactment of values through such work as teaching requires a commitment to the work itself, the prerogative to make consequential decisions about that work, and control over important aspects of the teaching process. If parts of the job or its organizational setting – notably through conflicting expectations from within and without the institution – make it difficult for teachers to pursue their values, then burnout is more likely to occur. This experience may lead all too readily to alienation from a specific post or even to occupational withdrawal. In effect, the research reported in this volume suggests strongly that conflicting expectations, increased work pressure, impractical innovations, unsupportive school environments, and uumotivated or undisciplined pupils appear to affect a large number of the teaching force in both Europe and North America. This in turn leads to frequent absences, lowered commitment, episodic or prolonged illnesses, physical ailments, undue stress, and ultimately what has come to be known as "burnout." The last steps may well be high degrees of job dissatisfaction and ultimately, teachers leaving the profession.

This is not to say that burnout is endemic to the teaching career but rather that there are sources at the individual, institutional, and societal levels that can compromise career satisfaction: meaningfulness, successful execution, enduring commitment, professional growth through increased experience and the learning of new skills, caring relations with peers and pupils, and the balance between work and family life, to name some of the most important sources.

A Working Model of Teacher Burnout

A prime objective of this volume is to reflect and communicate a deeper understanding of the nature, conditions, and consequences of burnout in relation to the teaching profession. To crystallize the understanding and from there to arrive at a more "preventive" perspective, a working model might be a useful heuristic. The model shown here is taken from Chapter 19 ("A Research Agenda"), written by two researchers who have, in many ways, defined the contemporary field: C. Maslach and M. Leiter.

On the one hand, burnout is considered to be a factor contributing both to teachers' and students' behavior and experience. On the other hand, burnout is depicted as being influenced by multiple factors, ranging from qualities in the social environment to others in the school setting and in the specific nature of the work itself. Also critical are the personal characteristics of teachers and their pupils. This pattern is consistent with the current model of organizational health, which explains personal distress in terms of enduring conflicts between organizational factors and personal needs and aspirations. In this way, the roles and relationships of teaching can be tied conceptually to the ecology of the workplace and, beyond this, to such macro-analytic factors as social and economic conditions.

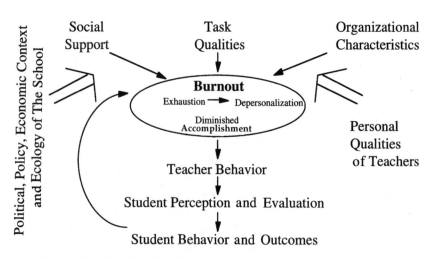

Proposed model of teacher burnout.

So far, empirical evidence in the teaching profession, as compiled and synthesized in this volume by B. Byrne (for North America) and B. Rudow (for continental Europe), supports the model shown above. In the burnout "process," *emotional exhaustion* occurs first and chains to increased *feelings of depersonalization*. *Reduced personal accomplishment*, the third classic component of burnout, develops more separately. This causal configuration connects to different factors in the school setting. Theoretically, certain work demands (overload, interpersonal tensions, role conflict, role ambiguity) predict exhaustion and depersonalization. Levels of personal control and social support are more closely linked to personal accomplishment. To this must be added such other school- and teaching-specific factors as class size, demographics, heterogeneity of pupils, pupils' aptitudes and sociocultural backgrounds, and the like.

More ominously, as shown in this volume, burnout is predictive of "minimalist" responses: lowered effort, involvement, and investment. So burnout could be inversely related to the frequency with which teachers respond encouragingly to students' accomplishments. Here, we encounter the research of W. Lens, whose contribution to this volume shows empirically how undue stress and resulting burnout take a heavy toll on the teachers' thoroughness of preparation and involvement in classroom activities. Also, teachers are likely to criticize pupils more as their levels of burnout increase. Students are then likely to change their perceptions of the teacher, their feelings toward the teacher, and their behavior in the classroom. At the end of the causal chain, then, we may see among pupils lowered self-perceptions of competence, intrinsic motivation, and ultimately, less initiative and less depth of learning. In the long run, the threat is consequential: pupils' disidentification with schooling. The ultimate consequences of teachers' reduced investment are thereby major in cases where our primary concern is with pupils' attitudes and performance.

Understanding and Prevention

The Leiter–Maslach model is parsimonious and conceptually compelling. Little research in the area of burnout, educational or otherwise, has looked beyond the personal characteristics of the "victims" themselves, the service providers, and the causal conditions contributing to their state of health. Fortunately, the most recent work has transcended the notion of burnout as a pathogenic condition residing within individuals and predisposing them to undue stress and resulting breakdown. That work has homed in on the organizational conditions associated with burnout. Some schools, for example, have higher rates of burnout than others, and those rates can be tied to working conditions in the school. Several of the principal authors in this volume (K. Leithwood, M. Smylie, P. Woods), in addition to authors of the attendant commentaries, have addressed this issue; several contributions have identified the most salient or intractable factors in the incidence of burnout, the alleviation of the contributing factors that matter most, and the specific workplace characteristics that can actually ward off the incidence of demotivation and exhaustion.

In the selection of papers and commentaries for publication after the Johann Jacobs Foundation Annual Conference, an attempt was made, on an international level, to take the "field" one step farther – that is, to focus on two critical issues. Both have been mentioned. One was the effect of burnout not only on teachers but also on *pupils*, those at the center of the educational enterprise. The second concern was the specific transformations in the workplace required for teachers to pursue meaningful and rewarding careers over the long haul. Burnout in teaching and in most human service professions is correlated with age; older teachers, with more than ten years' experience, are more at risk.[2] Because the profession is aging, and doing so at an *international* level, far more attention needs to be paid to career satisfaction, and more specifically, to the conditions that contribute to career satisfaction, such as professional development. Here, the work of the "Teachers College" School in the United States, in particular, of A. Lieberman, L. Darling-Hammond, and L. Miller, has been influential. The paper in this volume by L. Miller is an exemplar of the most recent applied work in this field. It is all the more instructive as it describes actual arrangements for career enrichment in teaching through the reorganization of the workplace and the provision of opportunities for professional growth through the career span.

Scope of the Volume

The volume has several facets. First, it reviews the most recent research in the field, especially the chapters by B. Byrne and B. Rudow. What is intriguing here is the "confrontation" between North American and European perspectives. The latter is represented by B. Rudow, whose research career includes work in both Eastern and Western Europe. B. Byrne has cast her

---

2.   This does not mean that the majority of teachers at mid-career experience burnout. Many, in fact, are more satisfied with their work situations, having attained seniority, better working conditions, and more realistic expectations, and they focus on the parts of their work they feel are most personally satisfying (Cherniss, 1995; Huberman, 1989a).

net within, but also beyond, North America to the United Kingdom and other European countries. In the commentaries to these chapters, more work from these countries (France, Switzerland, Dutch-speaking Belgium, Italy) is reported and analyzed.

Next, the volume combines analyses of burnout with the study of its contingencies and causal determinants. As mentioned earlier, these are the social-cognitive (R. Schwarzer and E. Greenglass) "workplace" or organizational factors shown in the model. Teaching and other social professions are compared (P. de Heus and R. Diekstra). In parallel, there is a more deliberate attempt to connect burnout in teachers to the self-perceptions and behaviors of their pupils.

Other perspectives are included: a narrative-biographical perspective (G. Kelchtermans), a social-psychological perspective (W. Lens and S. Neves de Jesus), and an historical account (P. Graham).

Several contributions move into the intersection of theory and practice. How does one reconfigure the workplace to create conditions that actually prevent incidents of burnout, not simply derive individual-level remedies once the problem has become acute? For example, I. Friedman describes the features of "healthier workplaces" by bridging between professional self-efficacy and professional demands. P. Sleegers addresses professional identity and school reform. What needs to be done here, and how realistic are such measures? Can they be generalized to large numbers of schools? If so, how? In these contributions, the bridge is from the conceptual to the practical, from understanding the nature of the problem to the architecture of actual reforms. The necessary components of that shift are described in detail by G. Kelchtermans and A. Strittmatter. In that regard, the inclusion of actual exemplars in this text is meant to reach beyond the research community to include decision makers, consultants, and administrators connected with the enterprise of schooling.

The Research Agenda

Finally, we have both a research agenda (C. Maslach and M. Leiter) and an action agenda (G. Kelchtermans and A. Strittmatter). The research agenda calls for more work on such crucial causal factors as work overload and role conflict while taking into account variables relating to class level (elementary, secondary), class size, number of pupils and classes, and heterogeneity of the student body (ethnicity, gender, linguistic differences, academic abilities, and socioeconomic background). The impact of teacher burnout on students, along with the converse influence, is another key item on the research agenda. Both call for predictions and correlations with the standard burnout measure, the Maslach Burnout Inventory (MBI), as developed by Maslach and Jackson (1986).

Other research priorities include the study of personal variables on the part of teachers (e.g., levels of intrinsic motivation, sociability, initiative, curiosity), along with work on coping patterns or coping skills. By encouraging or suppressing an "action-oriented" coping style among teachers, the work setting may have a significant impact on the personal qualities relevant to burnout (Leiter, 1991a). Everyday tasks also warrant further study. They may well bring to the surface role ambiguities or role conflicts (between instructional priorities, between administrators at different levels, between leadership or mentor roles, between the demands of parents and other constituencies) between life domains – the conflict between the job and family life (Huberman, 1989a).

We also need more precise information on the "work overload" factor that is often tied to burnout – not only its quantitative aspects but also its qualitative dimensions, such as demands on pupils' neglected academic skills; requirements for conflict management; and challenges for motivating pupils of different backgrounds, abilities, and interests.

In the "action agenda," much stock is placed in social support. What are the characteristics of collegial and supervisory networks that prevent or alleviate burnout? Will the new focus on teamwork and task interdependency break down the isolation that is often associated with burnout among seasoned teachers? Is the key factor here the *amount* of support or the *discrepancy between desired and actual support?*

As in the chapters of this volume, research agendas need to address the organizational characteristics associated with burnout. As noted earlier, some schools appear to have a very low incidence of burnout. Why? Is the key to be found in the decision-making environment? In the type and amount of professional prerogatives teachers may exercise in their teaching?[3] In attitudes, including their own levels of resignation or skepticism, among school administrators? Finally, the larger social context comes into play. If the environment is socially "toxic" (Garbarino, 1995), with extreme conditions of violence, poverty, or alienation, the impact on teachers would come through student behavior and performance.

In terms of priorities, the link between teacher burnout and student outcomes is of paramount importance. This relationship requires more precise

---

3. An important distinction here is between teacher autonomy (control at the classroom level) and teacher influence (control at the school level), both of which appear to contribute to career satisfaction.

conceptualization, operationalization of variables, research paradigms, and appropriate measures. Contextual variables need to be incorporated. We can move from there, or in parallel, to intervention studies. Methodologically, longitudinal designs would be powerful vehicles, especially if they confirmed the pattern of relationships identified in cross-sectional studies. Finally, the field is crying out for multiple measures. Self-reports, large-scale survey methods, and the administration of validated scales need to be complemented by qualitative research. This calls for more biographical work, for intensive observations over time in school settings, for extensive interviewing, for microlevel inquiries on pupil–teacher interactions and the dimensions of classroom and school climate. From these lines of inquiry may come the next generation of measures for understanding, alleviating, or actually preventing burnout.

The "Action" Agenda

G. Kelchtermans and A. Strittmatter start with the premise that the symptoms of burnout would be reduced in environments in which teachers experience professional growth, self-efficacy, and perceived success in their career progression. As a result, guidelines for action should center on opportunities for individual development, but mainly through the enhancement of organizational life. These guidelines, however, should not be separated from pupils' progression through the successive years of academic life.

The guidelines begin, however, at the top, where political and administrative authorities provide a general frame of goals, expectations, and standards. With this frame, schools would be given adequate autonomy to interpret or even modify such policies as a function of the local context. The premise here is that increased organizational autonomy, together with professional recognition, would provide requisite goals and expectations that are locally meaningful. Theoretically, this would lead to increased interpersonal trust and heightened instructional quality. Both would then correlate with lower incidences of burnout.

This would be the case, however, only if the necessary support and resources were made available. Expectations are hard to meet when the requisite means are lacking. Decentralizing responsibilities and withholding resources might lead to greater vulnerability to exhaustion. Autonomy over the *use* of resources (for materials, for training, for external counseling, for action-oriented research) is another key factor in the achievement of more fluid, autonomous school governance.

The action agenda centers on two further dimensions. One is the nurturing of an ethos of caring, one that can be collectively pursued, both toward pupils and among staff. The second dimension is career-long professional learning, less for individual skill enhancement than for collective problem resolution. Teaching is thus perceived as a cooperative task, governed by a culture of inquiry. The workplace then becomes the locus of ongoing professional learning, guided by principles of school-based development, adult learning, cooperative planning, ongoing evaluation, and active knowledge transfer within the school.

The notion of a culture of inquiry maps onto the school's perceived mission. The definition and negotiation of that mission constitute an important organizational process, one that reduces the type of role conflict and role ambiguity mentioned in the research agenda. The mission encompasses explicit commitments to pupils, staff, administrators, and external constituencies. Forging the mission is a public and collective enterprise, to which members of the school community commit – with exceptions, as in all establishments – and which, ideally, is perceived as meaningful and functional in conversations and transactions. Theoretically, this kind of contract – a psychological contract and a professional contract – should enhance teachers' sense of personal accomplishment – one of the key factors in preventing burnout. Similarly, outcome certainty is seen as facilitating teachers' self-efficacy through greater self-regulation and by providing concrete exemplars of having attained the school's goals (see R. Schwarzer and E. Greenglass, this volume). Here again, means for lowering the incidence of burnout are addressed in collective, organizational terms.

Another component of the action agenda has to do with procedures for ongoing evaluation (collective reflection on pupils' learning and on organizational operations within the school). This is often called an inquiry orientation for the improvement of local practices through greater understanding. Here, small-scale action research is the method of choice. Still another piece relates to shared leadership through the genesis of differentiated structures for decision making. There lurks a danger here, however, as noted in the chapter by M. Smylie: role overload leading to undue stress among school staff.

The foundation beneath the set of guidelines in the action agenda is that of teachers' collegiality and professional development. Collegial and collaborative cultures are more likely to reduce the incidence of burnout (see J. Nias and P. Woods, both this volume). They constitute a professional community. They can lead to increased learning and enhanced problem solving. Within schools, the hallmark of professional learning derived from collegiality would be collaborative instructional projects and collective school development projects. Collective problem solving would take similar forms (peer consulting groups, mutual observations, peer coaching). Taken together, these multiple forms of organizational inquiry and problem solving are designed to devolve governance to local levels, where they can be flexibly deployed. This, in turn, is meant to allow for a more collaborative and interdependent responsibility for the quality of school life, with the progression of pupils' learning at the core. Theoretically, at least, these guidelines address the classic symptoms of teacher burnout – essentially by moving beyond purely personal concerns and problems to the collegial level. The components are, however, admittedly demanding ones and presume that the strong individualism and departmentalism that characterize most schools can actually be transcended.

PART ONE. Teacher Burnout: A Critical Review and Synthesis

1. The Nomological Network of Teacher Burnout: A Literature Review and Empirically Validated Model

BARBARA M. BYRNE

"Burnout," a term originally coined by Freudenberger (1974) to describe healthcare workers who were physically and psychologically depleted, is now commonly associated with human service professionals such as teachers, nurses, social workers, police officers, physicians, and therapists. (For an historical review of the genesis of the burnout construct, see Maslach, this volume.) In broad terms, the idea represents a response to the chronic emotional strain of dealing extensively with others in need (Maslach, 1982a); to date, however, there is still no universally accepted definition of burnout (Dworkin, 1987; Farber, 1991a; Handy, 1988; Jackson, Schwab, and Schuler, 1986; Shirom, 1989). Even so, most empirical work in the area has embraced the three-component structure proposed by Maslach and Jackson, whose seminal validation research is now widely cited (for reviews, see Maslach and Jackson, 1984, 1986; Farber, 1991a). Based on findings of differential patterns of association between each component and other variables for diverse professional groups, Maslach and Jackson (1984, 1986; Jackson et al., 1986) emphasize that burnout should never be conceptualized as unidimensional; rather, it should be regarded as a multidimensional construct comprising three conceptually distinct yet empirically related facets: emotional exhaustion, depersonalization, and reduced personal accomplishment (see Shirom, 1989, for an alternative perspective).

For teachers, these three elements of burnout have been empirically validated at the elementary, intermediate, and secondary levels (e.g., Beck and Gargiulo, 1983; Byrne, 1991a, 1991b, 1993, 1994a; Friesen, Prokop, and Sarros, 1988; Friesen and Sarros, 1989; Gold, 1984; Iwanicki and Schwab, 1981; Jackson et al., 1986; Schwab and Iwanicki, 1982a, 1982b) and across gender for each of these teacher groups (Byrne, 1994b). According to Schwab and Iwanicki, teachers exhibit signs of emotional exhaustion when they feel that they can no longer give of themselves to students as they did earlier in their careers. They become depersonalized, developing negative, cynical, and

15

sometimes callous attitudes toward students, parents, and/or colleagues. They have feelings of diminished personal accomplishment when they perceive themselves as ineffective in helping students to learn and unmotivated in fulfilling their other school responsibilities. Overall, teachers who fall victim to burnout are likely to be less sympathetic toward students, have a lower tolerance for classroom disruption, be less apt to prepare adequately for class, and feel less committed and dedicated to their work (Farber and Miller, 1981). These symptoms can lead ultimately to increased neurotic and psychosomatic illnesses, absenteeism, and early retirement (see Rudow, this volume).

A literature review makes clear that teacher burnout is a function of the quality of worklife in the educational institution (Cedoline, 1982; Cunningham, 1982, 1983; Farber, 1991a). However, before the burnout problem can be resolved effectively, the syndrome must be thoroughly understood. In particular, construct validity work is needed to identify the nomological network (Cronbach and Meehl, 1955) of teacher burnout. From such research, we can assess the impact of (a) relations between burnout and other constructs with which it is empirically related (between-network relations) and (b) relations among the dimensions of burnout itself (within-network relations). Determination of a viable nomological network represents the first step in building a theory of burnout.

Unfortunately, methodological limitations of most burnout research have hindered theoretical development thus far (Einsiedel and Tully, 1981; Freudenberger, 1983; Gold, 1984; Handy, 1988; Jackson et al., 1986; Maslach and Jackson, 1984; Meier, 1983; Perlman and Hartman, 1982). Despite much empirical research linking the construct to other variables for various professional groups, findings have not been summarized into one conceptual framework that can be replicated and tested statistically. As a consequence, there is currently no established and empirically testable theoretical model of burnout.

The primary focus of this chapter is to address these construct validity issues by modeling the nomological network of teacher burnout as reflected in the international literature. Specifically, there are two purposes. The first is to review the burnout literature as it bears on the teaching profession worldwide. In particular, its international coverage represents research relative to at least five regions: Africa (Nigeria), the Middle East (Israel), Australasia (Australia, New Zealand), Europe (England, Finland, France, Ireland, Italy, Malta, Scotland, Sweden; for an extended review of the European literature, see Rudow, this volume), and North America (Canada, United States) as well as the British West Indies (Barbados). The second purpose is to establish, on the basis of this review, a salient nomological network of teacher burnout that can be modeled and tested statistically. Because of the methodological and space limitations of this chapter, it is impossible to elaborate on the ways additional or alternative constructs may be incorporated into the model; this remains the work of future research.

The construction of the model follows a three-stage strategy. The first is a brief description of early theoretical perspectives that have been linked historically to the concept of burnout. The second is a review of the empirical literature and a schematic summary of the findings. Last is a report of findings from a recent test of this model for Canadian elementary, intermediate, and secondary teachers (Byrne, 1994a).

Stage 1: Theoretical Perspectives on the Concept of Burnout

Ideally, the building of a theoretical model should be grounded in other related theories. The concept of burnout, however, has evolved empirically rather than theoretically, a course that may derive from its perception as a social problem (Maslach and Jackson, 1984). Nonetheless, its conception has been shaped by four somewhat overlapping perspectives.

The first of these is the *clinical perspective.* It is reflected in Freudenberger's (1974) approach to burnout, which addressed its etiology, symptoms, clinical course, and recommended treatment. For Freudenberger, burnout represented a state of exhaustion that resulted from working too intensely and without concern for one's own needs. The syndrome characterized individuals whom he perceived as paying a high price for an overzealous desire to help others.

The *social-psychological perspective* of Maslach and Jackson (1981) took a more research-oriented approach to the topic in attempting to identify work environmental conditions conducive to burnout. In particular, these theorists emphasized how role-related stress (caused, for example, by work overload) could lead a person to experience mental fatigue, the mechanistic treatment of clients, and perceptions of a diminished ability to succeed at his or her job. Maslach and Jackson labeled these three aspects of burnout emotional exhaustion, depersonalization, and reduced personal accomplishment, respectively. Whereas Freudenberger perceived burnout as precipitating even more effort on the part of the professional worker, Maslach viewed it as leading to worker withdrawal accompanied by a tendency to treat clients in a detached, dehumanized manner. (For variants of this theoretical model, see Golembiewski and Munzenrider, 1984; Leiter, 1988.)

Cherniss (1980b) also sought links between burnout and particular features of the work environment, but he did so from an *organizational perspective*. His interest lay in learning how organizations and their sociocultural environments affect a person's response to work. In contrast to Maslach's contention that emotional exhaustion, depersonalization, and reduced personal accomplishment are caused by organizational stressors, Cherniss argued that they represent three coping mechanisms used in reaction to stressful, frustrating, or monotonous work.

Finally, the *social-historical perspective* (Sarason, 1983) emphasizes the impact of society at large on the precipitation of burnout rather than the effect of the individual or the organization. Sarason pointed to current societal values embracing the philosophy of individualism over a sense of community as major catalysts in this regard. In particular, he argued that when social conditions are not conducive to personal concern for others, it is difficult to maintain a commitment to human service work.

Stage 2: Review of the Empirical Literature

As an aid to future efforts in developing a theory of burnout, we begin here by examining several variables shown empirically to be related to the construct as it bears on the teaching profession. In addition to acknowledging the important impact of several key background variables, researchers have posited that teacher burnout is a function of stressors engendered at both the organizational and personal levels (Cooper and Marshall, 1976; Farber, 1991a; Ianni and Reuss-Ianni, 1983; Iwanicki, 1983; Perlman and Hartman, 1982). An examination of this early literature shows how it bears on each of these factors.

Background Variables

Research investigating the importance of particular background variables on teacher burnout have shown the following to be worthy of further study: gender, age, years of experience, marital/family status, grade(s) taught, and type of student taught.

Gender. Except for the depersonalization facet, investigations of gender differences in teacher burnout have yielded inconsistent findings. Depersonalization, however, has appeared to be significantly higher for males than for females among elementary and high school teachers (Anderson and Iwanicki, 1984; Burke and Greenglass, 1989a; Byrne, 1991a; Greenglass and Burke, 1990; Ogus, Greenglass, and Burke, 1990; Russell, Altmaier, and Van Velzen, 1987; Schwab and Iwanicki, 1982a; Schwab, Jackson, and

Schuler, 1986). Whereas significantly higher levels of emotional exhaustion have been reported for female than for male human service professionals (Maslach and Jackson, 1981) and elementary and university educators (Byrne, 1991a), Anderson and Iwanicki (1984) found the reverse to be true; others have reported no significant gender differences (Maslach and Jackson, 1986; Russell et al., 1987; Schwab and Iwanicki, 1982a). Finally, significantly greater feelings of reduced personal accomplishment have been reported for female high school teachers (Anderson and Iwanicki, 1984), university professors (Byrne, 1991a), and human service professionals in general (Maslach and Jackson, 1981); Schwab and Iwanicki (1982a) and Russell et al. (1987) reported no significant differences for both elementary and secondary teachers.

In addition to these domain-specific studies,[1] three have examined gender differences related to the global construct of burnout, producing mixed results. Based on a sample of 884 Canadian elementary teachers, Long and Gessaroli (1989) reported that men, compared with women, exhibited significantly greater occupational stress and, ultimately, proneness to burnout. Likewise, Beer and Beer (1992), studying American elementary and secondary teachers of regular and special education students, found male high school teachers of special education students to exhibit significantly higher levels of stress than their female counterparts. In contrast to these studies, however, Capel (1992) reported no significant gender differences for a sample of 405 British elementary and secondary teachers.

Age. Age appears to be a very salient differentiating variable with respect to the emotional exhaustion component of burnout. Although young teachers have shown significantly higher levels of emotional exhaustion than their older colleagues (Anderson and Iwanicki, 1984; Maslach and Jackson, 1981; Russell et al., 1987; Schwab and Iwanicki, 1982a; Schwab et al. 1986), Byrne (1991a) found this to be so for university professors only. Findings are less consistent for the other two facets of the syndrome. Maslach and Jackson (1981) reported significantly lower perceptions of personal accomplishment for younger, compared with older, human service professionals; Byrne (1991a) reported similar findings for elementary and university educators. However, whereas Maslach and Jackson (1981), as well as Pierce and Molloy (1990), determined significantly higher depersonalization scores for their young respondents, Byrne (1991a) found no significant differences with respect to this dimension of burnout; Anderson and

---

1. Studies that focused on the three separate facets of burnout as defined by Maslach and Jackson (e.g., 1984), rather than on burnout as a global construct.

Iwanicki (1984), as well as Schwab and Iwanicki (1982a), reported no significant age differences relevant to either of these dimensions.

Finally, in an interesting study of cultural differences related to burnout for elementary and junior high school teachers in Italy and France, Pedrabissi, Rolland, and Santinello (1993) reported age to impact significantly on the depersonalization and emotional exhaustion facets, although the effects varied for each. Although levels of depersonalization for Italian and French teachers were significantly different before the teachers reached the age of thirty, these differences diminished after that age. In contrast, although there were no significant differences in levels of emotional exhaustion between the two cultural groups at the beginning of their careers (i.e., before age thirty), this differentiation materialized later in their careers (after age thirty).

Years of Experience. Years on the job would appear to be an important variable in terms of burnout; research findings are sparse, however, and generally show little support for this notion. From a global perspective, based on a sample of 844 Maltese primary school teachers, Borg and Falzon (1989) reported findings that teachers with more than twenty years of experience exhibited significantly higher levels of stress than their less-experienced colleagues. In contrast, however, Malik, Mueller, and Meinke (1991) found years of experience not to account for a significant degree of variance in occupational stress for a sample of 166 American elementary and secondary teachers. From a more specific perspective, Anderson and Iwanicki (1984) reported significantly lower levels of perceived personal accomplishment for teachers in the experience category of thirteen-to twenty-four-years, compared to any other group of teachers; no significant findings were reported for the facets of emotional exhaustion and depersonalization (see also Schwab and Iwanicki, 1982a).

Marital/Family Status. Findings related to the marital/family status variable are quite inconsistent. For example, Maslach and Jackson (1986) and Schwab and Iwanicki (1982a) reported no significant effect of marital status but a significant effect of family status on the incidence of burnout for elementary and high school teachers; respondents with children exhibited less burnout relative to all three aspects of the syndrome than those with no children. Byrne (1991a), on the other hand, found both variables to be nonsignificant for the same teacher populations. At a more specific level of analysis, Pierce and Molloy (1990) reported that elementary and high school teachers experienced lower levels of depersonalization than their childless counterparts; Russell et al. (1987) found married elementary male teachers to exhibit higher levels of personal accomplishment than both their female colleagues and all high school teachers.

Grade Level Taught. There is now substantial evidence in the literature that teacher burnout is more prevalent among high school than among elementary school teachers (Anderson and Iwanicki, 1984; Beer and Beer, 1992; Burke and Greenglass, 1989b; Feitler and Tokar, 1982; Schwab and Iwanicki, 1982a; Schwab et al., 1986). Furthermore, investigations of specific aspects of burnout have indicated that intermediate and high school teachers exhibit higher levels of depersonalization and lower levels of personal accomplishment than their elementary school counterparts (Anderson and Iwanicki, 1984; Russell et al., 1987).

Type of Student Taught. It seems reasonable to expect that certain types of students generate high levels of stress and frustration for teachers; typically, these students require extra attention, discipline, and/or special care (e.g., vocational, learning disabled). Anecdotal studies of teacher burnout have suggested that, based on intensity of direct contact with children, special education teachers are probably more vulnerable to burnout than regular teachers. Even so, research findings have been inconsistent. For example, Beck and Gargiulo (1983) and Bensky, Shaw, Grouse, Bates, Dixon, and Beane (1980) found that teachers of regular students experienced higher levels of burnout than teachers of children with learning disabilities; Olson and Matuskey (1982) found no significant differences between the two groups of educators.

In a recent study of elementary, intermediate, secondary, and university educators, however, Byrne (1991b) found that the type of student taught had an important impact on emotional exhaustion for high school teachers as well as on perceptions of personal accomplishment for both high school teachers and university professors. Specifically, she reported significantly higher levels of emotional exhaustion for teachers of students in the regular academic stream than for teachers whose classes were limited to vocational students. Interestingly, although high school teachers of regular academic students, on average, demonstrated feelings of reduced personal accomplishment compared with teachers of other types of students, the differences were not significant. At the university level, however, differences between professors who taught mainly graduate versus undergraduate students were highly significant; those teaching mostly graduate students clearly experienced a greater sense of personal accomplishment.

Organizational Factors

Both role conflict and role ambiguity have been identified as important determinants of burnout for teachers (see, e.g., Cunningham, 1982, 1983;

Kyriacou, 1987; Kyriacou and Sutcliffe, 1977a). Other contributing factors are work overload, poor classroom climate, low decision-making power, and little support from superiors and peers. Empirical research findings related to each of these constructs showed the following results.

Role Conflict. Role conflict represents the simultaneous occurrence of two or more sets of pressures such that compliance with one makes compliance with the other more difficult (Kahn, Wolfe, Quinn, Snoek, and Rosenthal, 1964). That teachers are increasingly confronted with conflicting demands is now well documented (e.g., Blase, 1986; Cedoline, 1982; Greenberg, 1984; Edgarton, 1977; Farber, 1991a; Iwanicki, 1983; Kyriacou and Sutcliffe, 1977a; Litt and Turk, 1985; McLaughlin, Pfeifer, Swanson-Owens, and Yee, 1986; Phillips and Lee, 1980). Common examples of role conflict for teachers are (a) quantity of work to be done and quality of work realistically possible within time constraints; (b) meeting the demands of overly large classes comprising students of diverse ability levels and meeting the needs of individual students; and (c) taking positive action in resolving student disciplinary problems and coping with negative or neutral support from administrators and parents.

Empirical findings have shown role conflict to be a critical factor in generating feelings of job stress and ultimately burnout among teachers (Bensky et al., 1980; Capel, 1992; Jackson et al., 1986; Pettegrew and Wolf, 1982; Proctor and Alexander, 1992; Tosi and Tosi, 1970; but see Burke and Greenglass, 1993 for an opposing finding). Studies investigating the multidimensional aspects of burnout have reported role conflict to be significantly related to the emotional exhaustion (Burke and Greenglass, 1995; Jackson et al., 1986; Pierce and Molloy, 1990; Starnaman and Miller, 1992; Schwab and Iwanicki, 1982b) and depersonalization (Jackson et al., 1986; Schwab and Iwanicki, 1982b) facets of the construct. In contrast to this research, Burke and Greenglass (1993) reported no significant impact of role conflict on the global construct of burnout.

Role Ambiguity. Role ambiguity is associated with a lack of clarity regarding a worker's obligations, rights, objectives, status, and/or accountability; other contributing factors include increasing complexity of tasks and technology and continued rapid organizational change (Farber, 1991a). Often cited by teachers as prime contributors to feelings of job stress are (a) unclear and inconsistent policies regarding student behavior, (b) required restructuring of curricula and pedagogical approaches in accordance with changing government mandates, and (c) the perception of being held in low esteem by students, parents, administrators, and the general public (Blase and Matthews, 1984; Cedoline, 1982; Farber, 1991a; Ginsberg and

Bennett, 1981; Holdaway, 1978; Iwanicki, 1983; Kyriacou and Sutcliffe, 1977a; McLaughlin et al., 1986).

Although Schwab and Iwanicki (1982b) suggested that role ambiguity may be less potent than role conflict, it has generally been reported as an important determinant of burnout (Bacharach, Bauer, and Conley, 1986; Bensky et al., 1980; Pettegrew and Wolf, 1982; Schwab and Iwanicki, 1982b; Tosi and Tosi, 1970). Empirical findings at the multidimensional level, however, are inconclusive. Although results are consistent in showing role ambiguity to be a significant predictor of reduced personal accomplishment (Pierce and Molloy, 1990; Schwab and Iwanicki, 1982b; Starnaman and Miller, 1992), they are mixed with respect to its prediction of the other two facets. Although findings from two studies (Burke and Greenglass, 1995; Schwab and Iwanicki, 1982b) found role ambiguity to be an important predictor of emotional exhaustion, Pierce and Molloy (1990) reported it to be a significant predictor of depersonalization. Finally, Friesen and Sarros (1989) reported the prediction to be nonsignificant.

Work Overload. Work overload comprises both quantitative and qualitative components (Cooper and Marshall, 1978a; French and Caplan, 1972). Quantitative overload involves too many demands and too little time in which to meet them adequately. Qualitative overload refers to job complexity, or work that is perceived as too difficult to complete satisfactorily. Teachers have consistently cited work overload as a major stressor in their job; important factors include excessive paperwork, oversize classes comprising students of heterogeneous academic abilities, imposed time constraints, and the need to teach courses that are outside their particular skill area (Blase, 1986; Borg, 1990; Borg and Riding, 1991a; Borg, Riding, and Falzon, 1991; Byrne, 1991a; Cedoline, 1982; Evers, 1987; Farber and Miller, 1981; Ginsberg and Bennett, 1981; Hiebert, 1985; Iwanicki, 1983; Jenkins and Calhoun, 1991; Kyriacou and Sutcliffe, 1977a; Lortie, 1975; Lutz and Maddirala, 1990; McLaughlin et al., 1986; O'Connor and Clarke, 1990; Okebukola and Jegede, 1989; Phillips and Lee, 1980; Proctor and Alexander, 1992; Sakharov and Farber, 1983; Weiskopf, 1980). Empirical testing of these aspects of perceived work overload by teachers has provided ample evidence that they contribute to teacher stress and burnout in general (Bensky et al., 1980; Borg and Riding, 1991a; Cichon and Koff, 1980; Cooper and Kelly, 1993; Jenkins and Calhoun, 1991; Kyriacou, 1987; O'Connor and Clarke, 1990; Olson and Matuskey, 1982; Pettegrew and Wolf, 1982; Proctor and Alexander, 1992; Smith and Bourke, 1992), and to emotional exhaustion in particular (Friesen et al., 1988; Friesen and Sarros, 1989; Lutz and Maddirala, 1990; Mazur and Lynch, 1989).

Classroom Climate. Classroom climate (i.e., environment) bears critically on teachers' attitudes toward teaching (Cross, 1987; Holdaway, 1978). Thus, it is not surprising that any erosion of this climate leads to job stress. In particular, student discipline problems, student apathy, low student achievement, and verbal and physical abuse by students are primary sources of teacher stress (Blase, 1986; Blase and Pajak, 1985; Bloch, 1977; Borg, 1990; Cedoline, 1982; Evers, 1987; Farber and Miller, 1981; Ginsberg and Bennett, 1981; Greenberg, 1984; Hiebert, 1985; Holland, 1982; Ianni and Reuss-Ianni, 1983; Iwanicki, 1983; Kyriacou, 1987; Lortie, 1975; Litt and Turk, 1985; Phillips and Lee, 1980; Sakharov and Farber, 1983; Weiskopf, 1980). Related empirical findings have identified student discipline, attitude, and abusiveness to be significant correlates of teacher burnout (Bacharach et al., 1986; Borg et al., 1991; Cichon and Koff, 1980; Holdaway, 1978; Olson and Matuskey, 1982; Punch and Tuettemann, 1990).

From a more specific perspective that decomposed both the misbehavior and burnout constructs, Hoerr and West (1992) found "common" misbehavior – the predictable, repetitive behavior that never causes alarm but that also never goes away – to be most strongly related to the emotional and depersonalization facets of burnout; "crisis" misbehavior was significantly related to depersonalization only.

From a review of the literature, it seems clear that student misbehavior is a major contributor to teacher stress around the globe. Findings from recent studies of 1,024 Nigerian (Okebukola and Jegede, 1989) and 710 Maltese (Borg et al., 1991) teachers, as well as from two national studies – one in Northern Ireland (the Rodgers Report [N.I.], cited in McGrath, Houghton, and Reid, 1989) and the other in Canada (Hiebert, 1985) – determined poor student attitudes and behavior to rank first as the primary stressor for classroom teachers. Likewise, a study of over 5,000 American and Canadian teachers revealed that 63 percent of teachers reported student discipline problems as the most stressful factors in their work environment (Kuzsman and Schnall, 1987). Indeed, these large-scale findings, together with those of Borg and Riding (1991a; Malta), Brenner, Sörbom, and Wallius (1985; Sweden), Fletcher and Payne (1982; United Kingdom), Laughlin (1984; Australia), Mäkinen and Kinnunen (1986; Finland), Payne and Furnham (1987; Barbados), and Phillips and Lee (1980; United States), clearly attest to the deleterious effects of student discipline problems on the well-being of teachers around the globe.

Finally, based on a study of 545 Maltese high school teachers, Borg and Riding (1991a) reported poor classroom climate, as a consequence of student misbehavior, to be more stressful for younger than for older teachers.

Also, in a study of 444 Barbadian high school teachers, Payne and Furn-ham (1987) found poor classroom climate to be more stressful for women than for men (see also O'Connor and Clarke, 1990, for Australian teachers in general).

Decision Making. Another major stressor for teachers is their lack of involvement in decisions that bear directly on the quality of their worklife (Bacharach et al., 1986; Blase and Matthews, 1984; Cedoline, 1982; Evers, 1987; Farber, 1991a; Ginsberg and Bennett, 1981; Iwanicki, 1983; Lortie, 1975; McLaughlin et al., 1986; Natale, 1993; Phillips and Lee, 1980; Ricken 1980). Participation in the organization decision-making process has emerged as a critical factor in maintaining worker morale, motivation, enthusiasm, self-esteem, and overall job satisfaction (French and Caplan, 1972) and in minimizing role conflict and ambiguity (Maslach and Jackson, 1984). That teachers in general are permitted minimal input into decisions that directly concern them (e.g., policy changes and implementation, cur-ricula changes, student disciplinary action) appears to bear importantly on their declining morale, job satisfaction, locus of control, and self-esteem (Cedoline, 1982; Farber, 1991a; Ginsberg and Bennett, 1981; McGrath et al., 1989; McLaughlin et al., 1986); over time, the cumulative effects lead to job stress and ultimately to burnout.

Social Support. Research on teacher burnout has been marked by frequent reference to the lack of support by administrators (Blase and Matthews, 1984; Dworkin, 1987; Evers, 1987; Farber, 1991a; Farber and Miller, 1981; Greenberg, 1984; Iwanicki, 1983; Kuzsman and Schnall, 1987; McLaughlin et al., 1986; Natale, 1993; Phillips and Lee, 1980; Ricken, 1980; Sakharov and Farber, 1983). To date, however, findings appear to be incon-clusive. Although some empirical evidence has determined a significantly positive relation between supervisory support and teacher burnout (Bacha-rach et al., 1986; Litt and Turk, 1985; Sarros and Sarros, 1992), Burke and Greenglass (1993) have reported no significant relation. Beyond aspects of supervisory support, however, there is now considerable evidence that peer support is instrumental in the diminution of job stress (see e.g., Cun-ningham, 1982, 1983; Farber and Miller, 1981; Maslach and Jackson, 1984). Nonetheless, at least one study (Cecil and Forman, 1990) has reported co-worker support to be ineffective as an approach to stress reduction in teachers.

Overall, explanations for this melange of findings for social support may have both a theoretical and a statistical rationale. Theoretically, findings suggest that social support may be a multidimensional construct in which various types of work-related social support facets bear differentially on the teacher stress process (Brenner et al., 1985). Clearly, more construct validity research is needed for better understanding of the theoretical structure of this construct (Thoits, 1982). Statistically, much of the confusion in the literature may derive from the different functions it is given in particular study designs. For example, some researchers have treated social support as an independent variable in the prediction of stress or burnout whereas others have used it as a moderator variable (Brenner et al., 1985).

Personality Factors

There is growing evidence that personality factors may explain why individuals in the same work environment, having the same supervisor, and possessing the same educational and experience backgrounds often respond differently to the same stressors (Bloch, 1977; Cichon and Koff, 1980; Farber, 1991a; Hubert, Gable, and Iwanicki, 1990; Ianni and Reuss-Ianni, 1983; Mayou, 1987). Two factors considered important in an individual's ability to withstand job stress are locus of control and self-esteem.

Locus of Control. Rotter (1966) postulated individual differences with respect to a belief in internal versus external control as influential in whether burnout occurs. Individuals who believe that certain events are a consequence of their own actions believe in internal control; those who view the events as being beyond their control, due more to fate, luck, or other people, demonstrate a belief in external control. Findings have shown increasing evidence that teachers who manifest external locus of control are more likely to suffer from burnout (Cedoline, 1982; Farber, 1991a; Kyriacou, 1987; Lortie, 1975; McLaughlin et al., 1986); thus, this variable has typically been of interest in discussions of teacher burnout. Only two studies (Lutz and Maddirala, 1990; Mazur and Lynch, 1989) were found that have directly tested the influence of external locus of control on aspects of burnout for elementary and secondary teachers; both reported a significant effect on the emotional exhaustion facet of the construct. Two related studies have examined connections between locus of control and components of burnout. Whereas Capel (1992) reported a correlation of .45 between external locus of control and emotional exhaustion, Lunenburg and Cadavid (1992) found a value of .15; moreover, Lunenburg and Cadavid reported correlations of .25 and −.29 between external locus of control and the depersonalization and personal accomplishment factors, respectively.

Self-Esteem. Several researchers have suggested that self-esteem is strongly related to burnout (Farber, 1991a; Hogan and Hogan, 1982; Ianni and Reuss-Ianni, 1983; Maslach, 1982a; Motowidlo, Packard, and Manning,

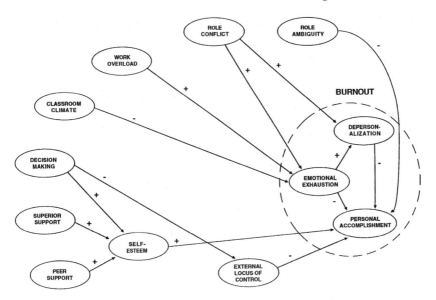

Figure 1.1. Summary model of teacher burnout derived from literature review.

1986). Because most people have a strong need for social approval, any event perceived as social rejection may also be perceived as stressful (Hogan and Hogan, 1982). Also, people who have little self-esteem are more threatened than others by rejection; therefore, they are more vulnerable to stress and burnout. Although anecdotal and review studies (e.g., McLaughlin et al., 1986; Phillips and Lee, 1980) have noted strong evidence of low self-esteem among teachers as a consequence of some antecedent factor (e.g., lack of support from administrators), followed by experienced job stress, only one study to date (Friedman and Farber, 1992) has empirically tested the relationship between self-esteem and burnout.[2] Based on a sample of 1,017 Israeli elementary teachers, Friedman and Farber reported a correlation of −.45 for these two variables. The researchers also determined self-esteem to be a significant predictor of burnout, but they suggested that the directionality is likely reciprocal.

Overall, this review of the literature has revealed considerable evidence that organizational and personality factors bear importantly on teacher burnout. A pictorial summary of these predictive relations is presented in Figure 1.1. Because some studies focused on burnout as a global construct

2. Of particular interest in this study, however, were the discrepancies between perceptions of teaching competence by self and significant others such as students, principals, and parents.

Table 1.1. *Breakdown of Demographic Data by Teaching Level*[a]

Variable	Elementary ($n = 1{,}242$)	Intermediate ($n = 417$)	Secondary ($n = 1{,}479$)
Sex			
Males	42.0	67.6	47.4
Females	58.0	32.4	52.6
Age			
20–29 years	7.9	5.5	4.7
30–39 years	19.7	19.2	20.6
40–49 years	51.3	55.0	49.3
over 50 years	21.1	20.2	25.4
Experience			
0–4 years	9.1	7.4	6.4
5–12 years	11.8	13.4	17.5
13–20 years	33.3	31.9	34.3
over 20 years	45.9	47.2	41.8

[a]Presented in percentages

whereas others were more specific in targeting the three facets of emotional exhaustion, depersonalization, and reduced personal accomplishment, burnout is modeled both unidimensionally and multidimensionally; the sign associated with each structural path represents the expected relational direction.

Stage 3: Test of the Summary Model

In the first study reported to have validated a postulated nomological network of teacher burnout empirically,[3] I (Byrne, 1994a) tested the model shown in Figure 1.1 for a sample of 3,138 (elementary, $n = 1{,}242$; intermediate, $n = 417$; secondary, $n = 1{,}479$) teachers from two large metropolitan cities in central Canada;[4] a descriptive summary is presented in Table 1.1. Little progress can be made in determining nomological links with other theoretically related constructs unless burnout is tested as a multidimen-

---

3. Although two other models of teacher burnout have been proposed (Harrison, 1983; Meier, 1983), their heuristic nature has precluded any statistical testing of their hypothesized structure.
4. Based on an initial randomly selected sample of 7,000, this represented a 45% response rate. Deletion of cases with ≥10% missing data (≥9 items) ultimately yielded final sample sizes of 1,203, 410, and 1,431 for elementary, intermediate, and secondary teachers, respectively.

sional construct (Friesen et al., 1988; Friesen and Sarros, 1989; Maslach and Jackson, 1984, 1986); therefore, all analyses were based on a multifaceted structure comprising the three related albeit distinguishable factors of emotional exhaustion, depersonalization, and reduced personal accomplishment.

Interpretation of the multidimensional model depicted in Figure 1.1 is straightforward, but some additional explanations are still in order. First, although studies of work overload and classroom climate have been limited largely to burnout as an all-encompassing construct, it was hypothesized that causal flow should be directed toward the emotional exhaustion factor only. Second, the original intent was that the variable of support would contain a single construct. However, preliminary analysis of the data revealed quite different response patterns to items measuring superior and peer support. On the basis of these findings, it was considered prudent to specify each as a separate construct. Third, although it is possible that some relations modeled here may be reciprocal, it was considered most appropriate to test such hypotheses through the comparison of alternately specified models – a task that went beyond the study described here. Finally, the within-network structure of burnout drew from the work of Leiter (1991a) in conceptualizing emotional exhaustion as holding the central position as it is considered to be most responsive to various stressors in the teacher's work environment (see also Friesen et al., 1988). As shown in Figure 1.1, emotional exhaustion was hypothesized as impacting positively on depersonalization but negatively on personal accomplishment; depersonalization was hypothesized to impact negatively on personal accomplishment.

In summary, the purposes of this initial search for a model of teacher burnout were fourfold: (a) to identify and test for salient organizational and personality factors contributing to burnout for elementary, intermediate, and secondary teachers; (b) to determine the pattern of causal structure for each teacher group; (c) to cross-validate this structure across a second set of independent samples; and (d) to test for the invariance of commonly specified causal paths across the three levels of teachers. All analyses were based on structural equation modeling procedures that allowed for the simultaneous testing of causal relations between organizational/personality factors and teacher burnout as well as their invariance across teacher groups (see Handy, 1988). (For further details about the sample, instrumentation, and analyses related to this study, readers are referred to Byrne, 1994a; for nonmathematical explanations and application examples related to structural equation modeling procedures, see Byrne, 1989, 1994c.)

A Summary of Findings

Comparison between the hypothesized and final models of causal structure related to multiple dimensions of burnout demonstrated remarkable consistency across the three teacher groups. Three common findings prevailed. First, of the fourteen causal paths specified in the hypothesized model (Figure 1.1), six were statistically significant for elementary, intermediate, and secondary teachers. These paths reflected the impact of (a) classroom climate on emotional exhaustion, (b) decision making on both self-esteem and external locus of control, (c) self-esteem and depersonalization on personal accomplishment, and (d) emotional exhaustion on depersonalization. Also worthy of note was the significant influence of peer support on self-esteem for elementary and secondary teachers. Second, two paths, not specified a priori (classroom climate→depersonalization; self-esteem→external locus of control), proved to be essential components of the causal structure for each teacher group; they were therefore added to the model. Finally, two hypothesized paths (role ambiguity→personal accomplishment; superior support→self-esteem) were not significant and were subsequently deleted from the model. A summary of causal paths relative to elementary, intermediate, and secondary teachers is presented schematically in Figures 1.2, 1.3, and 1.4, respectively; causal paths found to be common across the three panels are summarized in Figure 1.5.

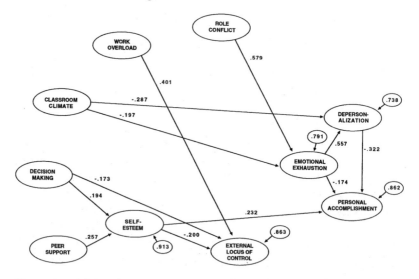

Figure 1.2. Validated model of burnout for elementary teachers. Values represent standardized estimates based on the calibration sample, with three outliers deleted ($n = 599$).

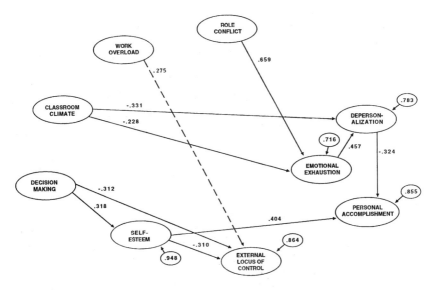

Figure 1.3. Final model of burnout for intermediate teachers. Values represent standardized estimates based on the calibration sample, with one outlier deleted (*n* = 204). Broken arrows and the estimates associated with them represent significant paths and values when based on the full sample (*n* = 410).

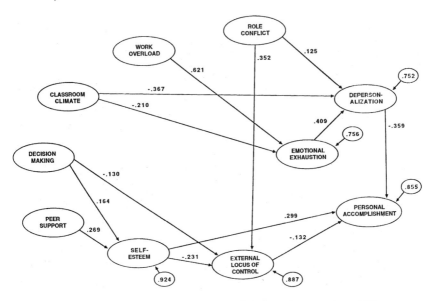

Figure 1.4. Validated model of burnout for secondary teachers. Values represent standardized estimates based on the calibration sample, with one outlier deleted (*n* = 715).

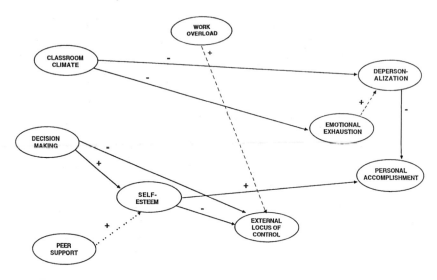

Figure 1.5. Common causal paths to burnout across elementary, intermediate, and secondary teachers. Solid arrows represent statistically invariant paths across all teacher groups. Broken arrows represent invariant paths across elementary and intermediate teachers, and the dotted arrow represents an invariant path across elementary and secondary teachers.

Overall, discrepancies in causal paths across teaching panels were small, the major difference appearing between teachers of high school students and those teaching at the lower grades. Specifically, four primary differences emerged; these involved the way in which work overload, role conflict, and external locus of control were linked to aspects of burnout.

Discussion

The following discussion is an attempt to link findings from this empirical test of hypothesized burnout structure to the extant literature as well as to the eventual impact on the teaching profession in general and the careers of elementary, intermediate, and secondary teachers in particular. Within the context of a nomological network perspective, the discussion is divided into between- and within-network construct relations.

Between-Network Construct Relations
Organizational Variables. Consonant with the international literature, *classroom climate* proved to be a major variable in the nomological network of teacher burnout. In addition to the hypothesized flow from classroom climate to emotional exhaustion, the impact of classroom climate on de-

personalization was strong and consistent across groups. These findings suggest that as the social climate of the classroom deteriorates, teachers become emotionally exhausted and develop increasingly negative attitudes toward their students and the teaching profession in general. In light of escalating class sizes, student apathy, and incidents of verbal and physical abuse by students, it is not surprising that teachers report student discipline problems as the most stressful factor in their work environment.

As hypothesized, *decision making* was another major albeit indirect determinant of burnout. Across all three teacher groups, this variable demonstrated a significant positive influence on self-esteem and a significant negative impact on external locus of control. It seems apparent, as noted over a decade ago by Lortie (1975), that the nonparticipation of teachers in making decisions that bear directly on their daily work environment leads to both a decline in self-esteem and strong feelings of external control by others. Over time, these effects take their toll, manifesting themselves first in job stress and ultimately, in perceptions of diminished personal accomplishment.

Although the variables of *role conflict* and *work overload* were also important components of the causal structure, their operation within the network differed considerably between elementary/intermediate and secondary teachers. Whereas *role conflict* triggered the response of emotional exhaustion for elementary and intermediate teachers, it stimulated the response of depersonalization for secondary teachers. Emotional exhaustion for the latter group stemmed from *work overload*, rather than *role conflict*.

A second intriguing comparison with respect to these two variables was shown by their influence on external locus of control; whereas elementary/intermediate teachers demonstrated stronger feelings of external locus of control when confronted with increased *work overload*, these feeling arose from perceptions of increased *role conflict* for secondary teachers. Why these four structural paths should be patterned differently but still be significant across elementary/intermediate and high school teachers is both interesting and curious.

One possible explanation for the discrepancy in perception of work overload may lie with the complexity of subject matter taught. Given the more advanced nature of course content at the high school level, these teachers may experience substantially more mental pressure in the preparation of lessons, construction of tests, and overall need to keep abreast of knowledge in their specialty area than do teachers of younger children; such stress is likely to be particularly debilitating for those in their early years of teaching. In contrast, work overload for elementary and intermediate teachers may manifest itself more in excessive paperwork and additional nonteaching tasks (e.g., recess supervision), resulting in perceptions that administrative and supervisory personnel in their work environment are in control, rather than the teachers.

Role conflict that leads to feelings of external locus of control for high school teachers may arise in this manner: Although these teachers perceive themselves as experts in particular subject areas, the curricula and teaching methods are largely dictated by government and/or school board administrative policies. For teachers of the lower grades, role conflict likely contributes to emotional exhaustion as a consequence of the multiple roles (e.g., teacher, guardian, nurse, counselor) necessarily played by these educators.

Of the two support variables in the hypothesized model, only *peer support* was found to make any significant contribution to causal structure. These findings suggest that the presence or absence of administrator support has little bearing on a teacher's self-esteem; of more importance is the support of the teacher's colleagues who share the same work environment.

Finally, findings from this study suggest that, within the teaching profession, the variables of *role ambiguity* and *superior support* do not operate as determinants of burnout (but see Maslach [this volume] regarding the importance of superior support in the nursing profession).

Personality Variables. Perhaps one of the most enlightening findings of the study of burnout structure was the prominence of personality variables within the nomological network. These results are the first to substantiate empirically the importance of personality factors that may, indeed, hold the key to why some teachers are more prone to burnout than others.

Of particular interest is the saliency of *self-esteem* across all three teaching groups. It seems apparent that *self-esteem* is a critical and controlling factor in the predisposition of teachers to burnout. In addition to having an important direct effect on perceptions of personal accomplishment, *self-esteem* appears to function as an essential mediator variable through which effects of environment-based organizational factors filter.

External locus of control was also found to be an important component of the nomological network, but why it was an important mediating variable for only secondary teachers in their perceptions of personal accomplishment is puzzling. One possible explanation may be the tendency for secondary teachers to equate success in the teaching profession with the acquisition of an administrative post that ultimately results in their exit from the classroom (see e.g., Byrne, 1991a). When this transition is slow to materialize, the teacher may begin to believe that the road is being blocked by other factors over which they have no control (e.g., department head evaluations, selection committee biases) rather than by their own abilities and skills.

Within-Network Construct Relations

As expected, emotional exhaustion appears to be the key element in burnout structure. Study findings revealed its highly significant impact on depersonalization which, in turn, had a moderately strong negative influence on perceptions of personal accomplishment; these effects were consistent across teacher groups. The hypothesized negative influence of emotional exhaustion on perceptions of personal accomplishment was small and limited to elementary teachers. In general, these findings support the notion that although emotional exhaustion provides the background within which teachers assess the people they serve (students, administrators, parents), its influence on their perceptions of their own personal accomplishment is modified by their sense of depersonalization within the teaching profession.

Conclusion

Findings from both the review of the international literature and the empirical study described above point to at least five important factors related to the nomological network of teacher burnout. First, the organizational variables of role conflict, work overload, classroom climate, and decision making, and the personality variable of self-esteem are critical determinants of particular aspects of burnout for teachers regardless of grade level taught; although external locus of control was also an important variable in its own right, its direct effect on perceptions of personal accomplishment was limited to secondary teachers. Second, the variable of support is evidently provider specific. Thus, to combine measurements of peer and superior support into a single construct serves only to mask the true effects of each in the causal process. Third, the three dimensions of burnout – emotional exhaustion, depersonalization, and reduced personal accomplishment – must be modeled as separate constructs; each is the target of particular predictors in the between-network structure, and each plays a specific role in the within-network structure of burnout. Fourth, although role conflict and work overload are important components of the burnout network, their causal patterns differ substantially for teachers of high school students and those teaching students at the lower grades. Finally, the variables of role ambiguity and supervisor support appear not to be causal links to burnout for members of the teaching profession.

Providing an interesting complement to these findings, Miller (this volume) has reported interim results from a school restructuring project in which administrators, teachers, and parents worked as a team to reduce teacher burnout. Their mandate was to address the issues of poor classroom climate, role conflict, work overload, and low decision-making power for teachers. Paradoxical findings have shown the elimination of burnout to be a less-than-simplistic task. For example, whereas improved classroom climate was found to be effective in reducing teacher stress, and increased decision-making powers for teachers heightened their sense of internal control and personal accomplishment, the revised decision-making role served concomitantly to intensify and augment feelings of emotional exhaustion associated with their teaching role. Miller concluded that burnout is both a complex and a resilient phenomenon, and she showed that, despite the best efforts and intentions of those involved in school reform, burnout simply does not disappear. (For an expanded discussion of school restructuring with a view to burnout reduction, see Leithwood, Menzies, Jantze, and Leithwood, this volume.)

One possibly major limitation associated with this review of the literature and thus the specification of the model tested is the postulated lack of discriminability among the constructs of stress, burnout, and depression (see e.g., Maslach, this volume; Rudow, this volume; Shirom, 1989). Three additional model misspecifications may derive from the failure to specify (a) reciprocal structural paths between self-esteem and burnout (see, e.g., Byrne, 1994a; Friedman and Farber, 1992; Maslach, this volume), (b) differential self-concept constructs that allow the measurement of discrepancies between the teacher's self-perception of his or her teaching competence and the teacher's perception of how significant others evaluate his or her competence (see e.g., Friedman and Farber, 1992; Maslach, this volume; Mazur and Lynch, 1989), and (c) constructs related to coping strategies (see e.g., Dewe and Guest, 1990; Sarros and Sarros, 1992; Seidman and Zager, 1991). Indeed, I strongly recommend that future construct validity research test at least one of these possible misspecifications in the nomological network of teacher burnout. Beyond these recommendations, the work of others (e.g., Leiter, this volume; Sleegers, this volume) points out the importance of taking into account the professional orientation of the teacher, the social organizational climate of the school, and the economic climate of the times in attempts to explain the onset of burnout more appropriately.

This chapter has reviewed the international literature related to teacher burnout. Based on this review, a summary model of its empirically derived nomological network was proposed and results presented relative to the initial testing and cross-validation of this hypothesized model for elementary, intermediate, and secondary teachers. As such, this model has provided a foundation on which to build a theoretical model of burnout. Future construct validity work is now needed to confirm or disconfirm these findings in the long and tedious pursuit of a sound and testable theory of burnout as it relates to the teaching profession.

2. Stress and Burnout in the Teaching Profession: European Studies, Issues, and Research Perspectives

BERND RUDOW

Introduction

Stress and burnout are phenomena that are becoming increasingly problematic. Whereas teacher stress has been an issue for some time, burnout is gaining importance. Being a social helper, the teacher is particularly affected by stress and burnout. The data on incidence of stress and burnout in the teaching profession show that in Western and Eastern countries, about 60% to 70% of all teachers repeatedly show stress symptoms and at least 30% of all teachers show distinct burnout symptoms (see Borg and Falzon, 1989; Brenner, 1982; Capel, 1992; Koleva, 1985; Kyriacou, 1980; Kytaev-Smyk, 1983; Müller-Limmroth, 1980; Temml, 1994).

Consequences of Stress and Burnout

This frequency is particularly serious because of the consequences. Stress and burnout have an influence on the following phenomena in particular.

Sickness Rate. The sickness rate of teachers is determined by neurotic and psychosomatic disorders (compare Rudow, 1995) in which stress plays a prominent role. Typical symptoms for burnout are fatigue, sleeping disorders, depression, and abuse of alcohol or drugs.

Absence. The sickness rate results in a high absence rate of teachers. However, we need to distinguish here between temporary and permanent absence. Temporary absence – short and repeated absences – occurs mainly in stress situations, often in the beginning phase of burnout. Continuous absences can be observed more in burnout phases.

Early Retirement. Burnout is a developing process, so highly distinct symptoms of performance weakness and fatigue do not generally appear until a person has spent fifteen to twenty years on the job. For example, in 1992, retirement occurred for 42.7% of all teachers sixty years old and 33.5%

of all teachers between sixty-one and sixty-two years of age in the state of Rhineland-Palatinate in Germany. (The legal age for retirement of German teachers is 65 years of age.) This means that three out of four German teachers did not reach the legal age for retirement. The numerous early retirements are a significant cost factor for the school systems in various states.

Teachers' Performance. It makes sense that stressed and burned-out teachers perform less well than others. Although the performance of a teacher is difficult to measure, one can assume that stressed teachers show more inappropriate actions (e.g., yelling at students in conflict situations) and cognitive misfunctions (for example, overlooking mistakes when correcting written tests) than nonstressed teachers. This means that the quality of teaching is adversely affected by teacher stress.

The Mood States. Stress and burnout are discernible at first in the teacher's change of mood. Continuous negative feelings appear in the progressive stages. These are, above all, job dissatisfaction, depressive moods, dullness, and the lack of drive.

Social Behavior of the Teacher. Because a relevant characteristic of burnout is the depersonalization between teacher and student, teacher and teacher, teacher and principal, and teacher and parents, interpersonal relations are impaired. Burned-out teachers lack involvement, charisma, and warm emotions when dealing with students. This affects learning behaviors and motivations as well as student discipline.

Research on Teacher Stress and Burnout in European Countries: A Literature Review

This section offers an overview of research studies in Europe. There are, however, two basic problems. (a) Studies on teacher stress and burnout are not stringently separated by their content. This is a conceptional problem. (b) This review applies mainly to the Scandinavian countries, England, and Germany. The approach to the literature from Eastern European countries is very difficult, given the relative lack of data. Therefore, the review is limited to studies from Russia (former Soviet Union) and the former GDR. I have focused on German, British, and Russian studies to complement the contribution by Barbara Byrne (this volume).

The following questions are dealt with in this review: Which theoretical concepts are at issue? Which empirical studies were conducted? Which variables were tested? Which empirical results were obtained? Which methodology was applied?

Theoretical Concepts

Relatively few studies about the theoretical aspects of stress and burnout can be found in the European literature. A theoretical model on teacher stress was first elaborated by Kyriacou and Sutcliffe (1978a) and later by Rudow (1990a, 1995). Both models consider stress as a process in which the appraisal of and coping with work demands play a central role. Personality characteristics as well as organizational factors and daily activity have an influence on this process.

The model on teacher stress by Worrall and May (1989) can be considered a partial expansion of the model by Rudow and Kyriacou and Sutcliffe. Whereas the concepts of Rudow and Kyriacou and Sutcliffe have a cognitive perspective for the most part, Worrall and May underline the affective and social-organizational perspective of teacher stress. The Worrall and May approach implies that the emotional status of teachers influences their cognitive appraisal of demands. The following types of stress affect emotional status:

1. Core stress – minor stress or daily hassles (e.g., when the overhead projector is missing for a lecture)
2. Ambient stress – the biographical life events or stress episodes (e.g., transfer to another school or continuous interpersonal conflicts) experienced by the teacher
3. Anticipatory stress – the unpleasant events anticipated by the teacher (e.g., an upcoming talk with the principal)
4. Situational stress – the present mood of the teacher
5. Retrospective stress – the way the teacher evaluates past personal stressful events or experiences

The teacher's emotional status, along with the mood created by this stress, is manifested by self-presentation: voice and body language (miming, movement, etc.), especially toward the students. The emotional status affects the interactions between teacher and students.

Rudow (1990a, 1995) incorporated stress and burnout into a working scientific stress–strain concept. He attempted to differentiate between stress and strain as well as to differentiate between those two and other phenomena, such as psychic fatigue and fear. His concept of stress and burnout relies on activity and action theory, which originated in East European psychology.

Empirical Studies of Stress

Among the numerous empirical studies of stress and burnout in the teaching profession, some relate to particular European countries. According to the German Knight-Wegenstein study (1973), for example 87.6% of 9,129 teachers felt overstrained. Brenner (1982) reported that 25% to 50% of Swedish teachers felt "stressed." Biener (1988) concluded that 60% of 325 Swiss teachers experienced high stress at work. English studies show fewer "stressed" teachers. Kyriacou (1980) found that 23.4% considered their job very or extremely stressful; Capel (1987) found the proportion to be 19%, indicating a medium level of stress. In Malta, 30% of 844 rated their job very/extremely stressful (Borg and Falzon, 1989). In Austria, a recent study found that 86% of female teachers questioned and 82% of male teachers were under stress (Temml, 1994). In the Soviet Union (Ukraine), 90% of teachers considered their job to be "very strainful" and 10% as "strainful" (Tomaschevskaja, 1978).

Few studies on burnout exist in Europe. There is, however, the German study by Kohnen and Barth (1990), who found 28% of 122 teachers to show no or only minor burnout symptoms, 43% with medium burnout symptoms, and 28.7% with severe symptoms. In a study in German special schools, Strassmeier (1995) found teachers in schools for learning impaired children and for children with behavior disorders to be far more affected by burnout than teachers in schools for mentally retarded children. Furthermore, more men than women teachers were affected. Middle-age groups were more frequently affected than young colleagues (under 30). No teacher older than fifty-nine had burnout symptoms in this study. In England, 37% of secondary school teachers and 25% of primary school teachers indicated that they would give up their job because of the stress, including perceived burnout (*Daily Telegraph,* 29 May 1989). In the United States, the reported burnout rates of teachers seem even higher. According to Pines, Aronson, and Kafry (1991), about 50% of all teachers wanted to give up their jobs. In a comparative analysis with the American study by Maslach and Jackson (1986), Barth (1992) found various degrees in the three burnout dimensions. The German teachers tested were less affected by emotional exhaustion than their American colleagues (23% to 33%). The differences in depersonalization are even more distinct. Only 8% of German teachers were severely "depersonalized" compared to 33% of the American teachers. Personal accomplishment was reduced for 40% of German and 35% of American teachers. Further empirical studies tested the variables affiliated with stress or burnout or affecting both stress and burnout. Concerning the determinants of stress and burnout, there is consensus that one should differentiate between personality and organizational activity variables.

Personality Variables. The following *personality variables,* which have a correlation with stress and burnout, should be included in studies of burnout.

1. *Self-consciousness* (self-control, self-esteem, self-confidence, etc.) has often been examined in the context of stress and burnout of teachers. Although various facets of self-consciousness have been operationalized, the empirical studies from Europe, North America, Australia, and Germany are consistent (see also Byrne in this volume). Studies of Australian teachers by Innes and Kitto (1989) and Pierce and Molloy (1990) show that self-consciousness – measured in terms of "hardiness" – is a considerable mediator variable for the relation between subjective strain and stress or burnout symptoms. For example, Pierce and Molloy (1990) found that teachers who consider their occupational demands (a) more a calling than a duty, (b) a challenge, and (c) internally controllable show a significantly lower burnout rate than teachers without these attributes. According to Mazur and Lynch (1989), teachers with a lower self-esteem show a significantly higher burnout rate, especially in regard to their performance. In a study from the former GDR, Buhr and Scheuch (1991) found that teachers with a higher self-control experience less stress.
2. Based on the Lazarus concept (Lazarus and Folkman, 1984), it makes sense to examine *coping styles* in conjunction with stress and burnout. Kyriacou and Pratt (1985) asked 127 English school teachers how they effectively cope with strain situations. The most frequent answers were trying to stay calm, sharing problems with others, keeping things in perspective, avoiding confrontations, praying, being well prepared, and relaxing after work. Grimm (1993) ascertained the following coping strategies, used by German teachers in stressful class situations:
   • Active search for solutions: analysis of the problem situation
   • Preoccupation and brooding, accompanied by guilty feelings
   • Repressive behavior: threatening pupils, using insults or punishments
   • Defense: negation of the stressful situation, distraction
   • Rationalizations or new interpretation of stressful situation, such as "see it positively"
   • Spontaneous change of teaching behavior without reflection on the situation
   • Escape: end the lecture, complain to the principal, or other tactic
   The results of this and other studies can be summarized as follows: active and palliative coping strategies in strainful situations help to lessen stress and burnout. Inactive, regressive styles (escape, negation, belittling, resignation, etc.) seem to bring on stress and burnout.
3. *Internal/external locus of control* is also examined frequently among the personality variables. Overall, empirical results show clear similarites across countries. Teachers with higher internal control show significantly lower stress and burnout symptoms (see details by Byrne in this volume).
4. Another relevant personality characteristic is *type A behavior,* which also has been examined in European studies. No significant correlations were found between type A behavior and the experience of stress (Rudow and Buhr, 1986). Orpen and King (1987) confirmed that finding with 42 Australian teachers. They discovered no differences between type A and type B behavior in teachers' reactions to emotional and physical stress. On the other hand, Buhr and Scheuch (1991) and Vogel, Scheuch, Naumann, and Koch (1988) found that teachers with distinct type A behavior show more neurotic and somatic disorders (caused by stress) than other teachers. The results obtained by Mazur and Lynch (1989) point in the same direction: significant positive correlations exist between type A behavior and burnout. No significant correlation existed between depersonalization and personal accomplishment.
5. Some studies examined *neuroticism* or temperamental characteristics in conjunction with stress reactions. According to Innes and Kitto (1989) and Wilson and

Mutero (1989), neuroticism is a significant predictor of stress in teachers. A study examining the correlation between temperamental characteristics on the one hand and fatigue and stress experience and neurotic and functional disorders on the other is particularly intriguing (Rudow and Buhr, 1986). "Strength or stability of the excitation of the nervous system," "strength of inhibition of the nervous system," and "mobility of the nervous system" were included in the design. These variables originated with the Polish psychologist Strelau (1983). The authors found significant correlations between chronic stress and fatigue and neurotic and functional disorders. The strength of nervous excitation or instability is especially striking as it shows a very significant correlation with all stress variables.

6. A personality variable relevant to burnout is *empathy*. In Mazur and Lynch's study (1989), it predicted emotional fatigue. According to Williams (1989), there is a significant correlation between empathy – higher in female teachers than among men – and (reduced) personal accomplishment, and emotional fatigue and reduced personal accomplishment.

Organizational Variables. The following *organizational variables* were examined in conjunction with stress and/or burnout in teachers.

1. *The possibility for actions and decisions* (cf. Hacker, 1986), a variable also examined in the teacher strain research, appeared in at least two studies of burnout. Rudow and Buhr (1986) found a significant and negative correlation between the opportunity to make decisions and chronic stress among teachers. Schubert (1983) discovered that 40% of teachers with numerous stress symptoms mentioned their restricted possibilities for action and decision making.

2. *Social support* has been examined relatively often. It shows a significant and negative correlation not only with stress but also with burnout. Social support assumes a buffering function between subjective strain and stress or burnout. This is reflected in the European literature (Brenner, Sörbom, and Wallius, 1985; Fletcher and Payne, 1982; Kyriacou, 1981; Leuschner, 1976; Mazur and Lynch, 1989; Schubert, 1983). These authors documented significant correlations between all three burnout dimensions, with low social support correlating with emotional fatigue.

3. Another organizational characteristic that has been examined in regard to stress and burnout is the style of *leadership* in school. The European literature produced results different from those obtained in other parts of the world. Whereas most studies found a positive correlation between stress and the teacher's perception of leadership style of the school principal (Blase, Dedrick, and Strathe, 1986; Brenner, 1982; Leuschner, 1976; Schubert, 1983), Mazur and Lynch (1989) did not discover a significant correlation between the principal's leadership and burnout.

4. The psychic *work overload* also affects teachers' stress and burnout (see Byrne in this volume). Based on Karasek's (1981) stress management model of strain, we can ascertain significant correlation between subjective strain and chronic stress. The correlation between overload and burnout was examined more frequently. According to Mazur and Lynch (1989), work overload is the prominent predictor for emotional fatigue; it does not relate to depersonalization and personal accomplishment.

5. *Role conflict and role ambiguity* have been analyzed in conjunction with burnout (see Byrne in this volume). According to Capel (1987), role ambiguity explains the biggest portion of variance of all burnout factors. The largest stressors for

English teachers proved to be role conflict and role ambiguity, according to a qualitative study conducted by Calderwood (1989). Mazur and Lynch (1989) found a significant correlation between role ambiguity and reduced personal performance ability or emotional fatigue as well as between role conflict and depersonalization or emotional fatigue.

6. Closely related to the role structure is perceived *responsibility*. According to a study by Mazur and Lynch (1989), this variable shows a significant positive correlation with all three burnout factors; the correlation between depersonalization and reduced personal performance ability is the highest.

Methodology of Empirical Studies

Few different methodologies have been used in studies treating teacher stress and burnout research in the Western European literature (D'Arcy, 1990; Kyriacou, 1987). A summary of relevant methodical issues reveals the following trends.

The largest portion of empirical studies, whether in Europe, North America, or Australia, are *cross-sectional studies*. Because stress and especially burnout are considered processes, these phenomena can be grasped in only limited ways through cross-sectional designs. Consequently, there is a need for more longitudinal studies (cf. Kleiber and Enzmann, 1990). For example, there seems to be no longitudinal study on stress or burnout in the teaching profession in Germany whereas there are several in Scandinavian countries (Brenner et al., 1985; Kinnunen, 1988, 1989; Mäkinen and Kinnunen, 1986).

One hundred eighty-seven teachers were examined over a period of fourteen months (April 1983 to May 1984) by Mäkinen and Kinnunen (the Finnish school year ends on May 31). The following stress variables were measured during the work week and the weekend: fear, depression, strain (subjective stress), sexual passivity, psychosomatic disorders, and drug abuse. In addition, the catecholamines (adrenaline and noradrenaline) were measured at the following times: total working time, lecture time, extracurricular working time, leisure time, and sleeping time. The results show a cumulation of stress reactions in the late fall, in November and December. The stress decreases from January until May, except for minor worsening in April (before Easter). When teachers feel better, the amount of adrenaline and noradrenaline they secrete decreases significantly. In addition, four time-related individual stress reaction patterns were found among the Finnish teachers. The first group displayed an increased amount of fatigue, depression, stress, and anxiety. The second group had stress reactions only during the first weeks of the fall semester. The third group had no stress symptoms throughout the entire fall semester, and the fourth group showed stress reactions only at the beginning and end of the fall semester.

Many studies on stress are conducted by means of simple *surveys*. Often, teachers report on "stress" based on a few items, sometimes on even one item. Complex stress feelings are thus being reduced to very few indicators. Also, most items have nothing to do with teaching. Whereas various measures of stress were developed in America (Farber, 1984; Fimian, 1988; Kremer and Hofman, 1985; Pettegrew and Wolf, 1982), valid measuring instruments do not yet exist in the German-speaking countries. This is not the case for burnout. At least German translations exist. The Maslach Burnout Inventory (MBI) (Maslach and Jackson, 1986) was translated and adapted by Barth (1992) into German. The standardization of the German version for teachers is still pending. The Tedium Scale (Pines, Aronson, and Kafry, 1983) was translated into German by Enzman and Kleiber (1989). It is presently being tested in a study on teachers in Rhineland-Palatinate in Germany (Rudow, 1996).

Subjective reports dominate in the stress and burnout research; extensive *physiological, biochemical, and immunological studies* are missing. There are several reasons for this. First, such measurements are very demanding. Second, they consist of a small "spot check." Third, although such measures are reliable, they often are not valid in regard to stress or even burnout; many individual factors, which are hard to control, can affect the results – for example, heart rate or blood pressure (compare Kyriacou, 1987). Despite these methodological restrictions, such studies also have advantages. (a) Stress and burnout are also manifested in somatic reactions. This means that physiological, biochemical, and immune reactions are relevant stress and burnout indicators. (b) Physiological, biochemical, and immune reactions are precise, recordable, and very reliable. (c) Physiological and biochemical reactions, such as blood pressure or EKG parameters, can indicate an objective health risk. Consequently, some European studies are particularly pertinent. Stress can be measured in terms of somatic data (see Table 2.1). In particular, several studies measured physiological parameters during individual teaching activities. For example, Bönner and Walenzik (1982) measured teachers' pulse frequency in several situations. The heart rate slowed down in aversive situations. When the pupils ignored the teacher's authority or offended him or her personally, the physiological stress reactions were strongest. Furthermore, psychoimmunological studies are very interesting. In Norway, Ursin et al. (1984) measured the plasma immunoglobulin (IgA, IgB, IgG, IgM) of chronic and acute stress in forty teachers. Among other things, they discovered that teachers with continuous

Table 2.1. *Physiological, Biochemical, and Immunological Studies on Teacher Stress*

Parameter	Type of activity/time	Author
Pulse rate	Activity types over a school day	Zeller (1975)
Heart rate, blood pressure, catecholamines	Total activity over a catecholamines	Scheuch, Schreinicke, Leipnitz, & Rudow (1978)
17-Oxycorticosterin catecholamines	Total activity over a school day and a school year	Karpenko (1975)
Pulse rate	Activity types	Bönner & Walenzik (1982)
Heart rate	Coping styles	
Catecholamines	Total activity	Brenner, Sörbom, & Wallius (1985)
Heart-blood-circulation parameter (blood pressure, heart rate, pulse rate, EKG, etc.)	Total activity over a school year	Scheuch et al. (1982)
Heart rate	Activity types and total	Naumann et al. (1985)
Blood pressure	activity over a school day	
Catecholamines	Total activity	Kinnunen (1989)
Immunoglobulins	Total activity	Ursin et al. (1984)

subjective stress in their job showed reduced IgM rates in experimental social stress situations.

Physiological, biochemical, and immunological studies are underrepresented not only in Europe but also worldwide in comparison with subjective teacher reports. They should be conducted more often, especially in conjunction with subjective teacher reports. These studies are especially suitable for the individual case analysis (see below) of stress and burnout in teachers, notably stress levels at a more advanced stage. It remains to be seen how worsening of the subjective states affect somatic processes.

The so-called objective measurements include behavior and performance characteristics. These are obvious indicators of stress and burnout (D'Arcy, 1990; Rudow, 1995). Indicators such as speech during classes (stuttering, loudness, pace), facial expression, rate of absence, level of sickness, and health awareness (alcohol and drug abuse) are all illustrations. To date, very few studies of these variables have been done in Europe, even though they would be excellent tools to complement subjective reports of stress and

burnout as well as the studies of physiological, biochemical, and immunological aspects.

Additionally, *causal determinations* of teacher stress and burnout should
be differentiated. Causes have been examined in terms of organizational
and personality variables; however, data on concrete causes of occupational
socialization (choice of job, training, job biography) and occupational activity (mission, conditions, social effects) of the teacher are missing. The
crucial question is which educational, systemic, and social conditions primarily cause stress and burnout. An interesting German study by Jehle,
Lebkücher, and Seidel (1994) addresses this question. One hundred twenty-
seven teachers named the following causes for job-related anxieties and
burnout:

1. Education at the university. Here, teachers emphasized insufficient preparation
   for praxis and insufficient training.
2. Parents who cede all responsibilities to the school.
3. Other perceived causes, including the high workload, teaching schedules, size
   of classes, the trend toward large and disorganized schools, the stress of job-
   related supervision.

Studying the causes of stress/burnout that arise from occupational socialization and teacher activity would be an interesting intercultural research
project.

Because burnout is an individual process, more attention should be devoted to empirical studies of *individual case analysis.* Thus, another needed
piece is biographies of teacher burnout (see Laughlin, 1984).

A methodological problem is the *intercultural comparison of epidemiological results* on teacher stress and burnout. Such comparisons are possible
only when the diagnostic methods are comparable and the demands on
teachers of different countries are known. The stress and burnout research
is limited to teachers' reactions. In addition to stress and burnout reactions,
the demands on teachers need more consideration. Demand analysis must
first determine the difference between teachers in European countries,
America, Australia, Asia, and Africa – for example, the school type. We are
not talking about *the* teacher, but teachers of different school types. In Germany, for example, we would need to distinguish between different school
types: high school (13th or 12th grade) (German: Gymnasium), primary
(German: Hauptschule), elementary (German: Grundschule), special (German: Sonderschule), and vocational school (German: Berufsschule). Job
demands and workloads, which affect stress and burnout, differ considerably from one school type to another.

Theoretical Conceptualization of Stress and Burnout

The differentiated conceptualization of stress and burnout implies a big problem. "Stress" is often used as a generic term for all kinds of "load" or "demand" or "strain." The word "stress" was in use in the seventies, and the term "burnout" appeared in the early/mid-eighties. Thus, one got the impression that burnout simply replaced stress. However, they are not the same; they need differentiated empirical research. An important issue is to determine the differences between and the commonalities of stress and burnout.

There are three theoretical approaches to conceptualizing stress and burnout (see Rudow, 1995): (a) work-related concepts of the load-strain sequence (Rohmert, 1984), (b) occupational-psychological action theory by Hacker (1986), and (c) activity theory by the Russian psychologist Leontjew (1982). Directly or indirectly, all three are based on the following model of the load-strain sequence, in which stress and burnout are considered to be relatively independent phenomena (see Figure 2.1). Rohmert's concept deals primarily with stress factors, strain, and their correlation. Stress (as an independent variable) results from the work task and the work environment in terms of their strain effect. The behavioristic tendency of this stress–strain concept is overcome in Hacker's action theory by elaborating the psychic regulation of the work activity. It results from intellectual, perceptual, and sensory-motor processes. The pedagogic competence of the teacher is determined primarily by the intellectual (planning, setting of goals, etc.) and perceptual processes (perception of the teaching situation, teaching methods, etc.) (Rudow, 1995). Thus, it is a pedagogic *activity* competence. The elaboration of the activity theory is based on the TOTE (Test-Operate Test-Exit) model developed by Miller, Galanter, and Pribram (1960) and the activity theory of Soviet psychology. Leontjew (1982) in particular developed the activity theory, thus making it of interest to the psychological stress research community (Kannheiser, 1983; Rudow and Scheuch, 1982). To his credit, he elaborated the dominance of the motives in the psychic regulation of the activity. This means that the motives not only have an "ignition" function for the activity, as in traditional theories, but they also determine the psychic activity. For example, the pedagogic activity and its effects on the teacher (stress, burnout, etc.) are determined by the teacher's motives.

Figure 2.1 shows the need to abandon the superconstruct "stress," whereby other strain reactions and consequences are conceptualized. A differentiation of the global stress concept is necessary. The relations among the individual strain reactions and consequences are outlined here.

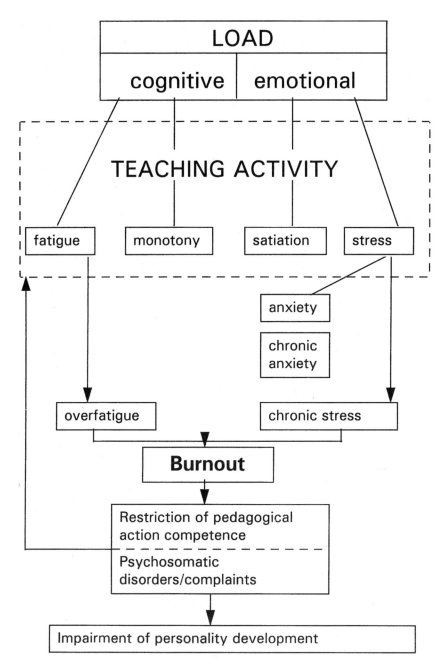

Figure 2.1. The model of negative strain reactions and consequences in teaching activity.

The description of the relationship between stress and burnout is particularly important as these two concepts are often confused. Fatigue and chronic stress are significant conditions of burnout. There is also a difference between stress and anxiety, words that are often used as synonyms. The model shows the relationships between stress and strain as well as personality development. This relationship becomes particularly transparent for burnout that as a crisis has a negative influence on personality development.

All factors that affect the teacher's educational activity are called *load* (German: Belastung). They include working tasks and working conditions. Working conditions are noise, discipline and pupils' motivation, teaching schedule, class schedule, and relationship with colleagues. *Strain* (German: Beanspruchung) is the result of the confrontation of subjective abilities and motives with objective work demands. As a consequence of permanent activity strain, there are reactions and consequences. *Strain reactions* occur temporarily and are reversible. *Strain consequences* are long term and only partially reversible. According to Leontjew (1982), strain reactions in the context of action can be considered as goal related and strain consequences in the activity context as motive related. One differentiates between positive and negative strain reactions and consequences. The strain reactions are positive when they improve the psychophysical action regulation; they are negative when they result in a destabilization of the psychophysical action regulation. Sense of well-being, emotional stability, job satisfaction, and the pedagogical action competence constitute positive strain reactions or consequences (see Rudow, 1995). Although the teaching profession bears positive as well as negative strain phenomena, these phenomena have been studied very little. Besides workloads, the following negative strain reactions and consequences are of interest.

Loads

Loads or stressors of the teaching activity have been well studied in Germany, England, Austria, and Switzerland. These studies produced more or less differentiated lists of load factors or stressors. The most frequently stated load factors are listed in Table 2.2. Behavior disorders of students, particularly manifested in discipline problems, constitute a major load factor. Shortage of modern equipment in school and classroom and the number of students (30 and more) also pose a problem for many teachers. Teachers often complain about the large portion of administrative tasks they must do. Noise in the school and classroom poses a psychic load on

Table 2.2. *Load Factors on the Teaching Profession*

Load factors	Authors
Behavior disorders of children	Krieger et al. (1976), Kyriacou & Sutcliffe (1978b), Wittern & Tausch (1980), Urban (1985), Temml (1994)
Deficient equipment in schools and classrooms	Knight-Wegenstein (1973), Gehmacher (1980), Elbing & Dietrich (1982), Wulk (1988), Temml (1994)
Large classes	Schuh (1962), Knight-Wegenstein (1973), Merz (1979), Häbler & Kunz (1985), Urban (1985)
Administrative tasks	Niemann (1970), Müller-Limmroth (1980), Häbler & Kunz (1985), Wulk (1988), Rudow (1990b)
Noise	Scheuch et al. (1978), Leuschner (1979), Wulk (1988), Knothe et al. (1991)
Working time	Saupe & Möller (1981), Häbler & Kunz (1985), Wulk (1988), Schäfer (1990)
Staff	Niemann (1970), Wittern & Tausch (1980), Gehmacher (1980), Cooper & Kelly (1993)
Leadership	Leuschner (1979), Urban (1985)
Teaching schedules	Barth (1992), Temml (1994), Merz (1979), Gehmacher (1980), Urban (1985)
Social class recruitment	Häbler & Kunz (1985), Wulk (1988), Pieren & Schärer (1992)
School reforms	Barth (1992), Temml (1994)
Occupational image	Niemann (1970), Merz (1979), Elbing & Dietrich (1982), Urban (1985)
Pay	Elbing & Dietrich (1982), Urban (1985)
Daily hassles	Gerwing (1994)

teachers. The noise level increases up to ninety-three decibels during breaks. Compared to other jobs, the working time is long. According to several studies, it ranges from forty-six to fifty-two hours per week (see Rudow, 1995). Problems among the teaching staff (rivalries, lack of cooperation and communication) are not conducive to a positive atmosphere. Another problem is authoritarian, noncooperative leadership in a school. In regard to teaching schedules, teachers complain about limits to their autonomy to structure classes. Also of pertinence is the large portion of foreign and emigrant students in many German and Swiss schools. School reforms imply structural, legal, and teaching schedule changes that psychically strain teachers. In public opinion polls, the teaching profession has an ambivalent image, one with which teachers are dissatisfied. The same applies to the low pay, which especially affects Austrian teachers. An interesting methodical approach to the qualitative analysis of subjective load was pursued by Gerwing (1994), focusing on daily hassles in the profession.

Psychic Fatigue and Overfatigue

Mental fatigue is an impairment of psychic functioning of a short or longer duration (ranging from a few minutes to several days). Normally, it can be compensated for by a recovery process. Chronic fatigue, however, is continuous; it can last up to several months. Mental fatigue is different from physical fatigue, which again is different from physical strain. Acute and chronic fatigue is manifested by performance impairment, a sense of feeling tired, and physiological reactions. Unfortunately, few empirical studies have been conducted on mental fatigue in the teaching profession. In the German literature one can find a few studies dealing explicitly with this phenomenon. The classic book on mental fatigue by Offner (1910) refers mainly to the teaching profession. More recent work has been conducted by Navakatikjan (1980), Scheuch et al. (1982), and Rudow (1986). These studies show that teachers often feel very tired. Corresponding symptoms can be observed, especially at the end of the school year and in older teachers, as measured by the feeling, performance, and physiological parameters. For example, the heart rate of Ukrainian teachers decreased at the end of the school year whereas their systolic blood pressure and pulse frequency increased and the amplitude of the T-point of the EKG decreased (Scheuch et al., 1982).

Monotony and Psychic Satiation

Monotony is a state of reduced psychophysical activity that can occur in nonstimulating situations during continuous cognitive and repetitious work activity. It is an "overdemand by underdemand" (German: "Überforderung durch Unterforderung"). Contrary to mental fatigue, which requires a recovery process, monotony can often be ended by changing to an interesting activity. Psychic satiation is a state of affective denial of a repetitious activity or situation.

Although the phenomena of monotony and satiation can occur in the teaching profession, no empirical studies have been done on these subjects to date. I believe this to be more a conceptional problem: corresponding empirical results are generally described as "stress" rather than as "psychic satiation."

Stress and Anxiety

Definitions of stress and anxiety are needed because "teacher stress" and "teacher anxiety" are used quite differently, even in scientific literature.

"Teacher stress" is the general term for negative emotions of teachers that are reflected in aversive demands to their work. This includes emotions such as anger, rage, aggressivity, irritation, frustration, disappointment, depressivity, and anxiety, in particular. Kyriacou (1987, p. 146) agrees with this conceptualization. The literature does not sufficiently differentiate between stress as a strain reaction and chronic stress as a strain consequence. Acute stress can occur in episodes lasting for one day of teaching up to about a week. Chronic stress can last for several months. It can be manifested in permanent anxiety, frequent sleeping disorders, repeated mistakes, and an increased physiological activation (high blood pressure, high pulse rate, etc.). Whereas the acute stress could be limited to a school day, chronic stress also affects the leisure time of the teacher. Most epidemiological studies on "teacher stress" do not say whether teachers were talking predominantly about acute or chronic stress.

In my opinion, "teacher anxiety" is a specific stress phenomenon. It is a negative emotional state that occurs when teachers perceive and evaluate a threatening demand or situation in their teaching activity. Often, action insecurity is involved. Teacher anxiety consists of two components: (a) emotionality and (b) worry. The first is an emotional component; the second one is cognitive.

As empirical studies on teacher stress were discussed above, some empirical studies on teacher anxiety are introduced here (for details see Jehle and Nord-Rüdiger, 1989). In Wittern and Tausch's study (1980), 51% of teachers questioned indicated problems of anxiety when dealing with students. Peez (1983) found in his questioning of 152 teachers that 14.6% often experience conflict-related anxiety, 11.3% have anxiety related to failure, and 3.2% suffer from separation anxiety. Based on other studies, 10% to 20% of teachers can be estimated to experience serious anxiety disorders. Nuding (1984) tried to study the separate components of "worry" and "emotionality" in 112 teachers. He obtained the following results: worry (49% of persons questioned) dominated among young teachers and was attributed to curriculum demands, the challenge of establishing one's authority in new classes, and the eventuality of classroom visits by evaluators (school leader, mentor, inspectorate). Elementary and primary school teachers (43% of teachers) showed the highest level of emotionality.

In a review of the German literature on teacher anxiety Jehle and Nord-Rüdiger (1989) found a dominance of theoretical discussions, sometimes of a speculative nature. There are no systematic empirical studies that exceed simple questions, descriptions, and case reports. The authors concluded that the German empirical research had barely studied teacher anxiety.

Burnout

Both "stress" and "burnout" are concepts that have not been defined accurately. The terms are often used as synonyms. Burnout needs to be defined as a specific quality so that it can be differentiated from other negative strain phenomena.

1. Burnout is a phenomenon that takes years or even decades to evolve. It is often a lingering process unnoticed or underestimated by the teacher. Burnout is thus in large part a function of years of employment. The syndrome typically does not show clearly until after fifteen to twenty years on the job.
2. The central descriptive characteristic or focal symptom of burnout is the physical, mental, and emotional exhaustion, whereby the emotional exhaustion prevails. Other important characteristics are depersonalization and lowered sense of personal accomplishment. Depersonalization is manifested by the teacher's perceiving the students as impersonal "material." Students' questions, problems, and concerns are considered with indifference, lack of interest, and cynicism. Performance weakness is primarily a consequence of chronic fatigue or exhaustion.
3. According to our concept, stress plays an important role in the burnout process. Exhaustion can be considered a consequence of repeated daily hassles. Disappointments in dealing with the students play an important role.

Which theories or concepts are appropriate to describe and explain the burnout syndrome? Primarily, there is the activity theory of Russian psychologists (Leontjew, 1982; Vasiljuk, 1984). Leontjew's psychological activity theory differentiates three activity moments in a hierarchical order: the *motive,* which determines the entire *activity;* the *goal,* which determines the *action;* and the *condition,* which determines the *operation.*

Full teacher activity is differentiated into individual actions, and the actions are divided into individual operations that are accomplished under certain working conditions. For instance, the main motive, which may determine the activity of a teacher, is to help weak students. Objectives are derived from it that determine his or her actions. These can be regular talks with these students, regular performance controls, talks with the parents, and so on. The conditions of the action execution, determining the individual operations, may be personality characteristics of the student (i.e., extraversion versus introversion), the distance to the student's home, and the parents' willingness to talk to the teacher.

The *purpose* is the most important category of activity theory. The purpose of an activity is the reflection of the relation between the action goal and the activity motive. Depending on their motives, the same actions may have different purposes (see Jantzen, 1987). This personal purpose determines the relationship of the subject to the object of the activity. Activity makes sense for the teacher when his or her activity motives and action goals correspond sufficiently. If this is not the case, the activity loses its purpose. For instance, if a teacher, whose main motive is to convey modern curricular content, must meet the curriculum requirements, forcing him or her to teach antiquated material, the activity becomes meaningless. If the teacher sets his or her pedagogic goals too high for the students, a loss of meaning may also occur.

Fulfillment of purpose or loss of purpose in teaching are manifested by typical emotions. In the case of fulfillment, job satisfaction and joy occur, and they reach their peak in the "flow" experience (Csikszentmikaliy, 1985). Loss of purpose results in disappointments, which, when frequent, can cause depressive moods, helplessness, and hopelessness.

Burnout can be described as a *crisis.* This is a stressful, continuous, changing process of the person that is characterized by destabilization of psychic action, regulation, or organization, together with destabilization in the emotional sphere, shown by severe mood changes, doubts, and disappointments. When central areas of the personality or more durable behaviors and feelings are affected, the phenomenon is considered a crisis (Vasiljuk, 1984), especiallly when the activity involves realization of motives. Even though the crisis begins as an occupational identity crisis, it will generalize to the entire self-concept of the teacher. It is then not only an occupational crisis. It can expand into a life crisis.

Which teachers are susceptible to burnout? In general only the teacher who is "burning" can "burn out." Teachers subject to burnout are those who are involved, devoted, and conscientious. Their involvement is determined by social caring and helping motives, which make up the personal purpose of the job. Such motives are, for example, "love for children," "working with people," "helping all weak students," "never being absent," "giving advice to helpless children," and so on. Helper motives, as opposed to pedagogical or subject-oriented motives, dominate in teachers who are susceptible to burnout. Corresponding action goals and high expectations are derived from these motives. The expectations include learning motivation, competencies, discipline, and the gratitude of the students. In the course of their careers, teachers realize that these high expectations cannot be fulfilled. As a consequence, they are disappointed when their expectations do, in fact, remain unfulfilled (see Hofer, 1986). This is a decisive point in the burnout process in how teachers cope with these disappointments and their causes (if they are aware of them) and how they adjust to the discrepancy between expectations of students and school life and actual student behavior and real school life. The relationship between stress and coping has been studied frequently, but the relationship between burnout and coping has not. "Coping" should be less related to direct actions and palliative strategies, as in the stress research (Lazarus and Folkman, 1984). Attention should be focused on intrapsychic aspects of coping – to the change of motives, value orientations, and attitudes. These are the processes of purpose generation. Overcoming the crisis means restoring the conformity between personal motives and action goals. If the teacher does not succeed, the crisis will grow. Note also that purpose fulfillment or loss depend not only on the teacher but also on the working tasks and conditions. These often restrict teachers in personally determining their action goals.

Burnout can be defined then by the following characteristics, which are conceptually and empirically different from the negative strain phenomena described above:

1. Burnout is an overlapping concept within the negative strain phenomena and thus assumes a key position in the gray zone between health and illness. It is overlapping as it unites symptoms of (chronic) stress, fatigue, job dissatisfaction, anxiety, and so on.
2. In comparison with psychic fatigue and stress, the burnout syndrome has another quality: Typical reactions occur in regard to stress or fatigue resulting from the discrepancy between environmental or perceived demands and individual competencies; burnout, however, affects the entire person. Emotions prevail that affect the core psychic health of the person such as depression, self-consciousness, doubts, depersonalization, exhaustion, or helplessness and hopelessness.
3. As compared to stress or psychic fatigue, burnout is a phenomenon of occupational socialization (see Kleiber and Enzmann, 1986). Normally, it evolves over the years and decades during occupational activity. It occurs as a crisis that constitutes at least a temporary stagnation or inhibition of personality development. Whereas stress or fatigue in the context of action has an episodic character, burnout in the context of activity has a diachronic character.
4. Burnout occurs in activities that increasingly contain socially interactive moments. Strictly speaking, it is a phenomenon of helping occupations, including the teaching profession. It can also affect professionals who frequently have social interactions, such as managers and policemen. Thus, burnout is a life crisis in which the professional's emotional relationship with the client plays a central role.

The activity-oriented description goes beyond the four theoretical perspectives on the burnout concept as described by Barbara Byrne (in this volume). It is a general psychological approach that can be applied to the clinical, social-psychological, organizational, and social-historical perspective.

Research Status and Implications

Research on teacher stress and burnout has had a long tradition in North America; it is far more embryonic in European countries, except for England. Consequently, one cannot talk about "typical" European research on teacher stress and burnout. Much more research is needed in Europe. However, not only traditional concepts originating from English-speaking countries should be looked at. It is necessary to try new approaches of theory, empiricism, and praxis. In conclusion, several suggestions are offered.

Based on the working scientific concept of the load-strain sequence, more attention should be devoted to the analysis of load factors in the teaching activity. Different, mostly simple concepts are presently available in load analysis (as discussed earlier in the chapter and in more detail in Rudow, 1995). Load analysis should be conducted within the context of activity so as to include pedagogical situations. Only two empirical studies have been done on this issue in Europe. Partial activities or actions of the teacher were analyzed for their cognitive and emotional load by Rudow (1990b). Another study was conducted by Ilmarinen, Suurnäkki, Nygard, and Landau (1991) in Finland. Important characteristics of the teacher activity as load factors were measured with the Work Scientific Survey, which is based on an activity analysis by Rohmert and Landau (1979). The study by Gerwing (1994) examining daily irritations in the teaching profession is also interesting.

Based on the load-strain sequence, the development of stress and burnout should be studied more within the context of defined loads. So far, little is known about the psychic load under which organizational, activity, and personality conditions lead to stress and burnout. A basic problem of empirical research is that, on the one hand, there are studies of load factors or stressors in the teaching profession and, on the other hand, there are separate, numerous studies on the stress and burnout phenomena. The relationship between load factors and stress or burnout can be examined only by means of longitudinal studies that measure the short-term and long-term effects of some well-defined load factors.

Another important task is to measure the occurrence of stress/burnout in teachers of individual European countries. The existing epidemiological findings on the frequency of stress or burnout in the teaching profession are not comparable; they are based on different theoretical definitions or concepts and they use different, mostly simple, reporting methods. The data on the occurrence of stress/burnout in teachers in Germany, England, Switzerland, and Austria are typically the product of approximate ratings, rather than of exact empirically verified data.

Also, they may give a wrong impression of the psychophysiological effects of the teaching activity. Although it can be assumed that the occurrence of stress and burnout is relatively high, the phenomena should not be dramatized in a spectacular way, as is the case in German magazines (i.e., *Der Spiegel*, 1993, no. 24; *Stern*, 1994, no. 19). Aside from negative emotions, teachers also experience positive emotions such as joy, satisfaction, or happiness. There are not only anxious, stressed, or burned-out teachers but also contented teachers. This balance should be considered more in the epidemiological as well as the entire teacher strain research.

Stress and burnout research are economically relevant. Both phenomena have a significant influence on health and performance. However, little is known about the impact of stress or burnout on pathogenesis, especially on the development of psychic health disorders and sickness. There are many cross-sectional studies with significant correlations between teacher stress and psychic and psychosomatic symptoms (i.e., Kyriacou and Pratt, 1985); but we know very little about the actual influence of stress and burnout on the development of such symptoms. Only longitudinal studies can measure the occurrence (frequency and degree) of stress/burnout in relation to the development over time of psychic and psychosomatic disorders and illness.

The intercultural teacher stress research, especially in European countries, should not only measure the frequency of stress or burnout in teachers but also examine the cultural conditions, school systems, school types, and student clientele. These are also important determinants of psychic demands and loads of teachers. A survey of these specific conditions of the teaching profession, which possibly have an impact on stress and burnout, requires interdisciplinary cooperation between psychologists, pedagogues, sociologists, and occupational scientists.

The theory of psychic regulation of activity and action should be used for the conceptualization of stress and burnout in the teaching profession. This theory goes beyond the transactional stress-coping concept of Lazarus et al. (Rudow, 1992, 1995). Stress and burnout can be examined in a more differentiated way based on this theory. This approach involves both theoretical and empirical analysis and recognizes the need to differentiate among the individual concepts of load-strain sequence (stress, burnout, fatigue, monotony, job dissatisfaction, alienation, depressivity). From an empirical point of view, it is necessary to examine the working tasks and conditions of teachers that result in psychic strain and thus constitute essential sources of stress, psychic fatigue, and burnout (Hacker and Richter, 1984). The activity-oriented analysis of teacher stress and burnout is a genuinely European, even East European, approach – one that goes back to the Russian and East German psychology. It could complement the predominantly empirically oriented (North) American teacher stress research that currently exists.

3. Teacher Stress in a Time of Reform

MARK A. SMYLIE

These are tough times to be a teacher. The nature and organization of the job make teaching inherently difficult. Teachers face new challenges and opportunities from increasingly diverse and needy student populations. Demands on teachers to develop new knowledge and skills and perform new tasks are increasing rapidly. So too are expectations for school and teacher performance and accountability. Taken together, the characteristics and conditions of teaching present increasingly stressful situations for teachers, situations that may have positive or deleterious consequences for them and for their work with students.

This chapter has several related purposes. The first is to explore the primary sources and consequences of stress in teachers' work. A second purpose is to analyze the ways that recent educational reforms may introduce new stress into their work. A third purpose is to assess the implications of stress in work and change for teachers. I begin my analysis with a conceptual and theoretical overview of psychological stress in the workplace, focusing particularly on organizational sources and consequences of stress. This overview draws primarily on literature from social psychology, organizational and industrial psychology, and organizational studies. I follow this discussion with a brief review of the research on work-related sources of stress for elementary and secondary teachers. Then, I turn to the issue of stress in change. After a general discussion, I analyze two current, contrasting types of reforms as sources of stress for teachers: (a) standards and assessments, and (b) teacher leadership development.

The issue of work-related stress generally, and stress in teachers' work particularly, is viewed by most of the literature as problematic. Although

I thank the following persons for their helpful comments and suggestions on an earlier draft of this chapter: Michael Huberman, Roland Vandenberghe, Christina Maslach, Michael Leiter, and Judith Little. I also wish to acknowledge the assistance of Marietta Giovannelli in identifying and reviewing a substantial portion of the literature cited in this chapter.

the literature acknowledges the possibility that stress may have positive outcomes, its orientation is primarily toward understanding the negative consequences of stress for workers and their job performance. Little attention has been paid to the potentially productive consequences of work-related stress. So too has much of the literature painted workers generally, and teachers specifically, as passive or reactive in their relationship to stress. Stress is something to be responded to, managed, coped with, or avoided. It is not portrayed as something actively sought or proactively challenged, and certainly not as something created purposefully. Finally, much of the literature on change views change as stress inducing, not stress reducing. Very little research examines the potential of change to alleviate sources of stress.

As it is in large part a review of the available literature, this analysis reflects these predominant perspectives of stress as negative, of teachers as reactive, and of change as stress inducing. By remaining within this frame of the literature, however, we are left with an incomplete picture of stress in teachers' work lives and the role of stress in change. Therefore, I conclude this chapter with a brief exploration of the more positive aspects of stress in teachers' work and with an assessment of individual and organizational implications.[1]

Stress in the Workplace

The literature defines psychological stress in several different but related ways, each grounded in a person–environment–interaction perspective. Cherniss (1980b) contends that environments impose certain demands on individuals at the same time that individuals attempt to influence those en-

---

1.   There are three important aspects of workplace stress that I do not examine in any detail. The first has to do with the wide range of individual and cultural factors that can mediate a teacher's perception and interpretation of a situation as stressful (see Barley and Knight, 1992; Freudenberger, 1977; Lazarus, 1966; McGrath, 1983; Van Harrison, 1978). With the exception of an individual's preparation and perceived capacity to deal effectively with potentially stressful situations, I leave the discussion of these factors to others. The second aspect has to do with developmental considerations (see Cherniss, 1980b; Latack, 1989; Lazarus, 1966; Lazarus and DeLongis, 1983). While I refer briefly to the issue of stress in work role transition, I also leave to others the discussion of how different phases of adult and career development may affect teachers' perceptions of and reactions to stressful aspects of work and the workplace. Third, to understand fully the nature and function of workplace stress, one must approach the problem systemically (Sarason, 1982). This means that to understand teachers' work-related stress, one must also explore its broader personal, organizational, social-cultural, and professional fields (see also Meyer and Rowan, 1977). With acknowledgment of needed attention to these contexts, and with cognizance of space limitations here, I confine my analysis specifically to the workplace.

vironments to conform to the individuals' needs and values. Stress results from an imbalance in this interaction, an imbalance perceived to be detrimental by the individual. Similarly, French and his colleagues (1974) define stress in terms of a "goodness of fit" between an individual and the environment. Accordingly, stress can result from a lack of fit between the needs, goals, and abilities of the individual on one hand and the resources or demands of the environment on the other (see also Katz and Kahn, 1978; Van Harrison, 1978). Lazarus (1966) portrays stress as a derivative of conditions that are perceived to disrupt or pose risk to individuals' personal or social values or to their conceptions of meaning and order. In yet another view, McGrath (1983) argues that stress may result from an environmental situation perceived as presenting a demand that threatens to exceed the person's capabilities and resources for meeting that demand.

These definitions suggest that virtually any physical, psychosocial, or cultural factor in an environment or any event that requires coping or adaptation can act as a stressor (Barley and Knight, 1992; Katz and Kahn, 1978). The level of stress experienced depends in large part on how the person perceives and interprets the environmental factor (Cherniss, 1980b; Lazarus, 1966; Winnubst, 1984). According to Selye (1971), the stressfulness of a situation depends on how individuals perceive the demands and opportunities of that situation in relation to their needs and goals. It also depends on how individuals perceive their abilities to deal with those demands and opportunities in ways that are consistent with their needs and goals (McGrath, 1983). Therefore, a condition of work may be considered stressful to the degree that it is perceived to risk or threaten something of need or value to an individual, a risk beyond the individual's perceived capacity to avoid or abate.

General Sources of Stress

The literature points consistently to several general conditions of work that are potential sources of stress. One condition is role conflict. Role conflict is defined as two or more sets of inconsistent, conflicting role expectations experienced simultaneously by an individual (French and Caplan, 1972; Kahn, Wolfe, Quinn, Snoek, and Rosenthal, 1964). Work roles may contain internally contradictory expectations (McGrath, 1983). Mattingly (1977) illustrated this form of role conflict well by contrasting the client care and custodial-managerial aspects of child care employees' work. Work role expectations may also conflict with an individual's preferences, goals, and values (Kahn et al., 1964; Van Harrison, 1978). Finally, an individual may experience conflict between the expectations of different roles, such as family roles and work roles (McGrath, 1983).

A second condition of work associated with stress is role ambiguity. Ambiguity involves lack of clear, consistent information regarding rights, duties, tasks, and responsibilities (Kahn et al., 1964). Role ambiguity is generally associated with vague organizational goals, role definitions, and expectations for performance. It is associated with uncertainty concerning what a person must do to perform his or her role effectively (Cherniss, 1980b; McGrath, 1983). Ambiguity may result from a lack of opportunity to experience task completion and closure and from an inability to see immediate or direct effects of one's work (Freudenberger, 1977). Role ambiguity may arise when experiences of success are inconsistent and seemingly random (Mattingly, 1977).

Another source of workplace stress are constraints on individual autonomy and control over one's work and work environment (Lazarus, 1966). While being "in the organization" restricts individual freedom generally (Cooper and Marshall, 1978a), prescribed pace and methods of work may impose specific constraints on individual discretion and control (Katz and Kahn, 1978). Rigidly structured work and bureaucratic interference (e.g., standard operating procedures, politics, and paperwork) may reduce perceived autonomy (Cherniss, 1980b; Maslach and Pines, 1977). Such troublesome work situations are generally experienced as more stressful if individuals believe they cannot influence the onset or duration of these situations (Latack, 1989; Sutton and Kahn, 1987).

Yet another source of stress is workload. Generally, stress is associated with overload – that is, the perception that one must to do more of a difficult task than time permits (Sales, 1969). Overload has quantitative and qualitative dimensions. Quantitative overload refers to amount and pace of work to be done. Qualitative overload refers to characteristics and difficulty of the work to be done (French and Caplan, 1972).

Several aspects of quantitative overload have been associated with stress. One aspect is task load or the sheer number of tasks for which one is responsible. Another aspect concerns high expectations for task performance. Task load and performance expectations become particularly potent stressors when they interact with time constraints. Long, excessive, and inconvenient hours, deadlines, and pressure to work quickly may increase levels of stress (Cooper and Marshall, 1978a; Katz and Kahn, 1978; McGrath, 1983).

Several aspects of qualitative overload are also related to stress. Stress has been associated with task complexity, difficulty, and simultaneity. Tasks carrying requirements that exceed the performance capabilities of the individual are particularly stressful (McGrath, 1983). So too are tasks that require individuals to think about and deal with multiple situations at the same time (Greenberg, 1984; Mattingly, 1977). Tasks that require individuals to process large amounts of information with great speed and intensity and to make large numbers of decisions (often major decisions) within limited periods of time may be stressful (Freudenberger, 1977; Katz and Kahn, 1978; Mattingly, 1977). Other sources of stress may be tasks that are performed within the public view of clients, peers, and supervisors, and tasks that require an individual to serve as a model for others (Katz and Kahn, 1978; Mattingly, 1977).

The literature suggests that work involving responsibility for other people creates additional potential for stress (Cherniss, 1980b; Katz and Kahn, 1978). Responsibility for others may heighten expectations for job performance and emotional availability (Freudenberger, 1977; Mattingly, 1977). It may also raise the stakes for effective performance (Cooper and Marshall, 1978a; Winnubst, 1984). Client load – that is, the number of individuals for whom one has care and responsibility – and long hours spent working with clients may raise stress (Maslach and Pines, 1977). Stress may increase if clients and the people with whom one works are of a different race or culture (Freudenberger, 1977; Lazarus, 1966). It may also rise if clients and co-workers are difficult to work with, resistant, or not as motivated, cooperative, or grateful for assistance as expected (Cherniss, 1980b; Freudenberger, 1977). Finally, stress may increase if clients pose threats of physical or psychological harm (Mattingly, 1977).

The effects of workload are usually considered in terms of overload, but underutilization can also be an important source of workplace stress. Stress can emanate from tasks that evoke few of an individual's overall skills and abilities; that require little responsibility; or that lack variety, challenge, and intellectual stimulation (Cherniss, 1980b; Cooper and Marshall, 1978a; Katz and Kahn, 1978). The effects of underutilization can be exacerbated when tasks that require relatively few skills also impose heavy demands on the individual for time, effort, and emotional involvement.

Related importantly to the issue of workload, particularly overload, is lack of preparation or perceived lack of capacity to perform (Sarason, 1985; see also Bandura, 1986). Stress can result when individuals are, or feel that they are, ill equipped to deal with problems in their area of work responsibility (Cooper and Marshall, 1978a). It can also derive from self-doubts and insecurities about one's competence to act effectively and to meet others' expectations (Cherniss, 1980b; Lazarus and DeLongis, 1983).

A last source of workplace stress is relations with supervisors and co-workers. Stress has been associated with tension, irritation, and disagreement with peers and supervisors (McGrath, 1983; Winnubst, 1984). It has also been associated with lack of opportunity to interact with these individuals (Cherniss, 1980b; Katz and Kahn, 1978; McGrath, 1983). Finally, lack of communication with and lack of social-emotional support from co-workers and supervisors have been found to intensify stress from other sources, particularly job overload (Cherniss, 1980b; French et al., 1974; Katz and Kahn, 1978).

The Matter of Threat

To understand why these conditions of work may be stressful, look at perceived threat (Lazarus, 1966; McGrath, 1983). In theory, stressful work conditions may, in real or perceived terms, threaten individuals' psychological needs and values. Among the many needs and values held by individuals, three general psychological needs are particularly germane to this analysis. One of these psychological needs is to establish and maintain order, rationality, and meaning for what individuals may perceive as a vague and inchoate environment (Berger and Luckman, 1966; Weick, 1979). A second need is for agency, particularly self-determinism and instrumentality (Bandura, 1986; Deci and Ryan, 1985). A third need is for accomplishment, especially achievement of valued goals (Locke, 1968; Van Harrison, 1978).

Theoretically, role conflict may challenge the values, orientations, and identities that individuals have developed to give order and meaning to their work, their work environments, and their place in those environments. It may threaten accomplishment through overload, creating additional and contradictory demands on scarce resources available to the individual (e.g., knowledge, skill, effort, time). Ambiguity may blur the relationship between an individual's efforts and the outcomes of those efforts. It may also obscure the goals and technologies necessary for accomplishment in work. Loss of autonomy and self-determinism may suggest to an individual that the outcomes of work are attributable to external forces rather than to one's instrumentality. A diminished sense of agency may serve as a performance disincentive, negatively affecting individual accomplishment (see Bandura, 1986).

Lack of preparedness and capacity (real or perceived) may also reduce both the perceived possibilities for instrumentality and the accomplishment. Perceived lack of preparedness may suggest to an individual that he or she lacks the knowledge and skills necessary for agency. A diminished sense of agency may reduce effort and therefore accomplishment. Beyond a diminished sense of agency, actual lack of knowledge and skills may reduce the real and the perceived possibilities of goal accomplishment.

Lack of supervision and support reduces individuals' access to important sources of information and motivation. It reduces the feedback available to individuals for assessing their accomplishments and the relationship of their efforts to those accomplishments. It reduces knowledge available about how an individual's work relates to the broader goals of the organization. It also reduces knowledge available to an individual about how specific tasks may be accomplished.

Consequences of Work-Related Stress

The literature suggests that work-related stress can have positive or negative consequences. A certain amount of stress is thought to be necessary to motivate performance and induce change (Cherniss, 1980b; Lazarus, 1966). On the other hand, excessive stress is considered deleterious (Van Harrison, 1978; Winnubst, 1984). Because stress is phenomenological in large part, making generalizations about the types, amounts, and intensities of stressors that lead to positive or negative outcomes is extremely difficult. One could argue, for example, that the same condition of role ambiguity that spurs creativity and growth and satisfies the need for personal autonomy for one person could lead to conservatism, isomorphism, and a loss of meaning and agency for another.

The literature indicates that the perceptions and consequences of stress depend importantly on personality and on developmental and cultural considerations (Barley and Knight, 1992; Katz and Kahn, 1978; McGrath, 1983), factors beyond the scope of this analysis. The literature also indicates that the perceptions and consequences of stress depend on an individual's real and perceived capacity to deal effectively with that stress. An individual's ability to deal with stressful situations, reactively or proactively, may have as much to do with whether the consequences of stress are positive or negative as the type or intensity of the stress itself.

Generally, then, we would expect the most negative consequences to occur under conditions in which stress exceeds an individual's capabilities to mediate it. In these circumstances, work-related stress could lead to varying levels of psychological tension and frustration. The literature suggests that in its most excessive forms, stress can lead to "job burnout," a psychological state of failure and exhaustion (Freudenberger, 1974). Maslach and Jackson (1984) summarized the primary manifestations of burnout as emotional exhaustion, depersonalization of clients, and feelings of reduced personal accomplishment. Others have identified more specific symptoms. Cherniss (1980b), for example, associated job burnout with increased apathy, negativism, cynicism, pessimism, and fatalism about work. He further associated it with decreased motivation, effort, and involvement in work and with preoccupation with one's own comfort and welfare on the job. Cherniss indicated that burnout may also lead to loss of concern for and irritability toward clients, treatment of clients in a detached and mechanical manner, and a tendency to rationalize failure by blaming clients or blaming "the system." Finally, Cherniss added that burnout may result in loss of creativity, growing rigidity, and resistance to innovation. Lazarus (1966) concluded that excessive stress can lead to fear and anxiety, anger, guilt and depression, physiological problems, and impairment of skills, cognitive functioning, and social behavior. These aspects of burnout can readily compromise an individual's job performance and the quality of service provided clients (Cherniss, 1980b; Freudenberger, 1977; Maslach and Pines, 1977; Mattingly, 1977).

Stress in Teaching

Many of the sources of workplace stress outlined earlier in the chapter are found in the nature and organization of teachers' work. The examination of stress in teaching begins here with a brief overview of the conditions of teachers' work, followed by a discussion of the empirical evidence concerning the consequences of stress in teachers' work. This literature focuses primarily on the negative consequences of stress, specifically burnout and other psychological and physiological problems. Very little research has examined its more positive aspects, a subject explored at the conclusion of the chapter.

The Conditions of Teachers' Work

Teaching is inherently prone to stress. It has been characterized historically by role conflict, ambiguity, and overload (Lieberman and Miller, 1984; Lortie, 1975; Waller, 1932). Teachers are asked to assume multiple and often contradictory roles, including, among other things, providing academic instruction; maintaining order in the classroom; attending to the social and emotional well-being of students; and meeting sometimes conflicting expectations of students, administrators, parents, and the community (Heck and Williams, 1984). Teachers must often reconcile the different demands of school, district, state, and national policies. They are often bound by decisions in which they have had little or no input. As a teacher in Woods' (1989a) study of stress suggests, one of the most significant challenges teachers face is to manage the "built-in schizophrenia of the job" (p. 90).

The primary setting of teachers' work – the classroom – has distinctive properties that are potential sources of stress (see Doyle, 1986). Classrooms are crowded places in which many people with different preferences and abilities must use a restricted supply of resources to accomplish a broad range of social, institutional, and personal objectives. They are places where many things happen at once, at a very rapid pace, with unexpected turns, and in view of many people. In addition to these classroom conditions, the goals of teaching are often vague and conflicting (Lieberman and Miller, 1984). The knowledge base and the strategies that teachers could use to achieve these goals are uncertain. The effects of teachers' work with students are often difficult to detect (Lortie, 1975). A teachers' impact on students may not be readily apparent for a very long time. Furthermore, teachers frequently work in isolation from other teachers, receive little feedback concerning their performance from administrators and colleagues, and experience few meaningful opportunities for ongoing professional learning and development (Smylie, 1989).

As indicated in the introduction to the chapter, teachers now face new and complex challenges arising from changing student populations (Pallas, Natriello, and McDill, 1995) and heightened expectations for performance and accountability (Firestone, Bader, Massel, and Rosenblum, 1992). Teachers must navigate the ambiguities of "postmodern" shifts in social, political, economic, and cultural relations (Hargreaves, 1994). They must contend further with concurrent challenges to long-standing, taken-for-granted knowledge, assumptions, and values concerning teaching and schools as institutions. Taken together, these general conditions and current challenges present potentially stressful situations for teachers, situations that may have deleterious consequences for them and for their work with students.

Consequences of Work-Related Stress for Teachers

The nature and organization of teachers' work contain many of the same sources of stress identified in the social-psychological and organizational literature. A developing body of empirical research provides some evidence concerning the relationships of these work-related sources of stress to burnout and other stress-related problems for teachers.[2]

Role Conflict. Several studies have found significant relationships of role conflicts in teachers' work to elements of burnout – emotional exhaustion, depersonalization of students – and to general psychological tension and anxiety among teachers (Byrne, 1994a; Cedoline, 1982; Greenberg, 1984; Jackson, Schwab, and Schuler, 1986; Schwab and Iwanicki, 1982b). This research finds these problems specifically related to the multiple and conflicting expectations in teachers' jobs (i.e., teaching academic subject matter and attending to students' emotional and social needs). It also finds these problems associated with conflicts between job expectations and teachers' personal values and orientations toward teaching (see also Heck and Williams, 1984; Woods, 1989a). General psychological tension and anxiety have also been associated with differences between what teachers were prepared by preservice teacher education to do and what they are expected to do in their jobs by their employing schools and districts (Dworkin, Haney, Dworkin, and Telschow, 1990).

Role Ambiguity. Several studies have found positive relationships of role ambiguity to anxiety and physiological problems among teachers (Bacharach, Bauer, and Conley, 1986; Greenberg, 1984). Other studies have found role ambiguity associated with emotional exhaustion, depersonalization of students, and teachers' lack of feeling of personal accomplishment (Capel, 1989; Schwab and Iwanicki, 1982b). Unlike the findings concerning role conflict, the evidence concerning role ambiguity is not altogether consistent. For example, Byrne (1994a) found that role ambiguity was not related significantly to emotional exhaustion, depersonalization, or reduced sense of personal accomplishment among teachers.

Constraints on Autonomy. Several studies have found that perceived lack of control and sense of powerlessness are related to tension, frustration, and anxiety among teachers (Dworkin et al., 1990; Woods, 1989a; Yee, 1990). Similarly, other studies have found that teachers with stronger external locus of control are more likely to experience tension and frustration in work and feel less personal accomplishment than teachers with stronger

2. The findings of the empirical research are difficult to synthesize and interpret, first, because of conceptual confusion between stress as a source of psychological and physiological problems and those problems as consequences of stress. The matter is further complicated by the use of significantly different and often vague and ambiguous definitions and measures of stress and stress-related problems across the literature. Although doing so is somewhat awkward, I report the findings of this literature in terms of the conceptual and operational definitions of variables used in individual studies rather than by some common, overarching definitions.

internal locus of control (Capel, 1989; Dworkin, 1987). Bacharach and his colleagues (1986) found that high routinization in work was associated with high levels of anxiety and physiological problems among elementary teachers (but not secondary teachers). Their study also found these problems greater among elementary teachers who wished to have more opportunities for participating in school-level decision making than were currently available. However, Byrne (1994a) found no relationship of teachers' actual levels of participation in decision making to emotional exhaustion, depersonalization, or loss of sense of personal accomplishment.

Overload. Much attention has been paid to quantitative and qualitative overload in teachers' work. The literature suggests that teachers' responsibility for children is inherently stressful (Cedoline, 1982; Greenberg, 1984; Sarason, 1985). The act of teaching is highly interpersonal and rests substantially on teachers' sense of care and compassion. It calls for teachers to expend much effort and to give in far greater proportions than they receive (Heck and Williams, 1984; Yee, 1990).

Several studies identify specific aspects of classrooms that relate to tension, anxiety, and burnout. One aspect is class size or the total number of students for whom a teacher has responsibility (Bacharach et al., 1986; Byrne, 1994a; Jackson et al., 1986). Research suggests that the problems of a teacher's client load may be mediated in several ways. First, the actual number of students that teachers teach may be less a factor in tension and anxiety than teachers' perceptions that that number is too great for them to teach effectively (Bacharach et al., 1986). Second, the problems of student load may vary depending on the grade level and the characteristics of the students (Jackson et al., 1986).

Several studies indicate that beyond class size, unpredictable and poor student behavior are associated with tension, anxiety, and role alienation (i.e., felt meaninglessness and powerlessness in work) generally and with emotional exhaustion and depersonalization of students in particular (Bacharach et al., 1986; Byrne, 1994a; Dworkin, 1987). Student apathy, opposition, and verbal and physical abuse of teachers are also associated with teacher frustration, anxiety, and burnout (Byrne, 1994a; Woods, 1989a). The evidence concerning student academic ability and performance is less clear. For example, Bacharach and his colleagues (1986) found greater anxiety and physiological problems among teachers of high-ability students. Byrne (1994a) found heterogeneity in student ability associated with emotional exhaustion among secondary teachers and low student achievement related to emotional exhaustion and depersonalization among both elementary and secondary teachers. Finally, Dworkin (1987) and Woods (1989a) point to racial differences and cultural conflict between teachers and students as a source of role alienation, frustration, and anxiety.

Professional Preparation and Support. The literature also identifies lack of professional preparation and inadequate opportunities for learning and development as sources of stress-related problems for teachers (Cedoline, 1982; Sarason, 1985; Woods, 1989a). It marks principal support as an important mediator. Generally, the research indicates that positive and supportive relationships with principals are negatively associated with anxiety, stress-related illness, and burnout among teachers (Bacharach et al., 1986; Dworkin et al., 1990; Jackson et al., 1986). However, a discrepancy between the preferred and perceived role of the principal has been found to be positively related to teachers' felt alienation (Dworkin, 1987). The few studies that have examined peer support find generally weak or indirect relationships to teachers' sense of professional accomplishment (Byrne, 1994; Jackson et al., 1986). Peer support appears unrelated to other problems of work-related stress examined here (e.g., Dworkin et al., 1990). This may be because teachers' professional interactions tend to be geared toward general social and emotional support rather than toward addressing specific aspects of work, which may be the principal sources of stress (Lieberman and Miller, 1984; Little, 1990b). Indeed, the professional norms of privacy, egalitarianism, and autonomy that characterize many schools may actually mitigate against the types of classroom-oriented, instructional-focused, problem-solving collegial interactions that may help teachers deal more productively with sources of stress in their work.

Stress in Reform

The literature discussed thus far focuses on the general sources of work-related stress for teachers. In addition, the literature identifies change as another potential source of stress. Change can exacerbate stressful conditions already associated with teachers' work and it may introduce new sources of strain. Conversely, as discussed at the end of the chapter, change may be a source of relief from work-related stress.

Change as a Source of Stress

The literature on change in organizations suggests that change can create a number of potentially stressful conditions (Bolman and Deal, 1991). Change can introduce new roles and performance expectations that conflict with other roles an individual is expected to perform (Brett, 1980; Latack, 1989;

Louis, 1990). Change can also introduce new uncertainties and ambiguities about organizational goals, the roles of individuals in the organization, and the knowledge and skills that are required to perform new roles (McGrath, 1983).

Change can create feelings of incompetence (Bolman and Deal, 1991). In work role transitions, for example, change may challenge the confidence individuals have in the appropriateness and adequacy of their knowledge, skills, and response repertoires (Nicholson, 1984). Change can also lead to quantitative and qualitative overload as individuals attempt to keep up with changing technologies and standards for performance (Cooper and Marshall, 1978a).

Change can evoke a sense of powerlessness. It can threaten individuals' discretion and ability to influence their work environments (Lazarus, 1966; Nicholson, 1984). Indeed, changes involving specification and standardization, while acting to reduce ambiguity, may challenge and diminish individual autonomy and self-determinism (Winnubst, 1984) – and inability to influence the onset and duration of change may itself increase the amount of stress experienced by an individual (Sutton and Kahn, 1987).

Finally, change may evoke stress by challenging the beliefs, values, attachments, and assumptions that create personal order and meaning in an organization (Bolman and Deal, 1991; Schein, 1985). It may disrupt the pursuit of individual goals (Lazarus, 1966; Lazarus and DeLongis, 1983; Weick, 1993). Change involves cognitive and emotional challenge, loss, and redefinition (Bolman and Deal, 1991; Lewin, 1935; Schein, 1969). It means letting go of the old and learning the new.

The literature on educational change suggests how change can create potentially stressful situations for teachers (Fullan, 1991). Several studies indicate that change can lead teachers to question their own capacities and competencies (Elmore and McLaughlin, 1988; Guskey, 1984). Change can evoke a wide range of concerns among teachers that relate to their personal role in the change, their ability to meet the demands of the change, the strategies necessary to implement the change, and the likely effects of the change on their students and on other aspects of their work (Hall and Hord, 1984). The literature also suggests that change can present overload and role conflicts to teachers (Elmore and McLaughlin, 1988; Purnell and Hill, 1992). Innovations most often create new demands on teachers' time. Current daily demands are rarely reduced proportionately. Old programs and ways of doing things are almost never discarded for new (Cohen, 1990; Elmore, Peterson, and McCarthy, 1996). Thus, teachers may confront a dilemma of choosing between overload – trying to accommodate daily demands, old programs and practices, and innovations – and role conflict, reallocating time between current demands and innovations. Finally, change can challenge the beliefs, assumptions, values, and patterns of practice that define school culture and lend meaning and sense to teachers' work (Rossman, Corbett, and Firestone, 1988; Sarason, 1982). To help explain change as a source of stress among teachers, two examples of educational reform are offered next. These are being developed and implemented concurrently – standards and assessments and teacher leadership development.

Standards and Assessments

In recent years, new efforts have been made in the United States and in several European countries, including Belgium, the Netherlands, and Great Britain, to develop centralized systems of performance standards and assessments. These systems, whether targeted at schools or at teachers as individuals, seek to improve performance by identifying common goals for student learning and specific standards for student outcomes. They may also identify standards for school delivery systems – that is, for the instructional processes and allocations of resources that create opportunities for students to learn (Porter, 1993). Typically, these systems contain indicators and assessment processes (e.g., standardized tests, alternative assessments) and may be accompanied by common curriculum guidelines and student course-taking and promotion requirements.

Little research is available on the most recent of these initiatives, however, when one looks across the few studies that exist and the findings of earlier studies of similar centralized curriculum and testing policies, the sources of stress these reforms present to teachers become apparent. The studies indicate that standards and assessment policies can lead to substantial role conflicts for teachers and threaten their sense of control in their work. In one example, Archibald and Porter (1994) studied math and social studies high school teachers in American states with centralized curriculum policies (i.e., curriculum guides, centralized textbook adoptions, standardized student testing). They found that teachers in districts with lower curricular centralization generally felt more personal control over the subject matter they taught and methods they used to teach it than did teachers experiencing greater centralization. Teachers in districts with greater curricular centralization felt less control over content but believed they still maintained some control over pedagogy.

Dunham (1992) noted similar threats to individual teacher autonomy and self-determinism in his study of the United Kingdom's Education Reform Act of 1988. He found that the implementation of a standardized national curriculum and testing system spawned a sense of powerlessness among teachers. In addition, Dunham discovered that the national curriculum and testing system presented substantial role conflicts for teachers, pitting the reform's values of performance, efficiency, and academic achievement against teachers' values of care and investment in the broader cognitive, social, and emotional development of students. The system suggested a shift in the orientation of teachers' roles from professional to employee. Further, the reform presented problems of overload. Teachers had to find ways to deal with increased paperwork, meeting schedules, and administration of student assessments. They often cited as problematic the increased pace of activity, their lack of preparation to implement the new curriculum and testing system, and the lack of time to reflect on and adjust to the reforms (see also Silvernail, 1996).

Case studies of the California Mathematics Curriculum Framework reveal similar sources of stress on teachers, particularly around role conflict (Cohen and Ball, 1990; Peterson, 1990; Wiemers, 1990; Wilson, 1990). These cases portray teachers confronted with incompatibilities between their beliefs and values concerning teaching and learning and the goals and orientations of the Framework. The examples illustrate conflicts between the expectations for student learning contained in the state curriculum and those expectations held by parents and local communities. Finally, the cases cite conflicts between the Framework and district policies and indeed between the Framework and the state's own preexisting student testing policies. These cases further reveal teachers' sense of overload, inadequate preparation and professional development, and lack of administrative and peer support to implement the reform.

Studies of centralized testing programs reveal similar sources of stress among teachers. For example, Black's (1994) study of national assessments in England and Wales reveals several role conflicts for teachers. The tests created tensions between teaching in response to testing demands and teaching what teachers thought was important for their students to learn. They also created tensions between subject matter–centered work reflected in the tests and pupil-centered instructional practices that, according to Black, had been emphasized among teachers for years. This study pointed to a reduction in teachers' autonomy – first, as they felt a need to move away from teaching what they thought was important for their students toward what the tests measured, and second, as they saw the standardized test results supplanting their professional judgments in administrative determinations of student progress (see also Silvernail, 1996).

Studies of state-mandated student testing in Arizona and Missouri reveal similar problems with increased role conflict and loss of self-determinism (Smith, 1991; Zancanella, 1992). In addition, Smith (1991) pointed to the problem of underutilization. Teachers in her study believed that the centralized tests reduced their ability to experiment with new ideas and adapt curriculum and instruction to meet the specific needs of their students. They believed their work was being "deskilled," preventing them from using knowledge and abilities they possessed that might further promote student learning. The themes of role conflict, loss of autonomy, and overload also appear in earlier analyses of centralized curriculum and testing programs in the United States (see Darling-Hammond and Wise, 1985; Madaus, 1988; Wise, 1979).

Teacher Leadership

The second type of educational reform discussed here involves developing new leadership roles for teachers. The most prevalent of these work redesign initiatives have taken the now familiar forms of career ladders; lead, master, and mentor teacher roles; and participative decision making. Teacher leadership initiatives have been developed widely throughout the United States as well as in Australia, Canada, Great Britain, New Zealand, and Spain. In contrast to the regulatory orientation of centralized standards and assessment policies, teacher leadership initiatives are oriented toward the development of teachers' professional knowledge and skills and the discretionary exercise of local expertise in problem solving and school improvement.

The literature points to several sources of stress associated with these new leadership roles (Smylie, in press). It identifies role conflict as a significant issue. Role conflict may result from differences between teacher-leaders' expectations for their new roles and the actual leadership activities they perform (Smylie and Denny, 1990; Wasley, 1991). Conflict may also arise from incompatible internal goals of work redesign initiatives and from overlap between the new roles and prerogatives of teacher-leaders and the traditional roles and prerogatives of administrators (Henson and Hall, 1993; Smylie and Brownlee-Conyers, 1992; Troen and Boles, 1992; Wallace and Hall, 1994).

One of the greatest sources of role conflict in teacher leadership concerns tensions teachers feel between their roles as classroom instructors, working with students, and their roles as teacher-leaders, working with other teachers and administrators (Bird and Little, 1983; Kilcher, 1992; Smylie and Denny, 1990; Wasley, 1991). Another significant source of role conflict comes from discrepancies between the expectations and activities of teacher leaders and the expectations, rules, and obligations that define the professional cultures of schools. New teacher leadership roles may challenge the norms of privacy, autonomy, and egalitarianism that govern teachers' professional relationships (Griffin, 1995; Smylie, 1992; Troen and Boles, 1992; Wasley, 1991). These challenges may have a "chilling effect" on the performance and outcomes of teacher leadership roles, independent of others' actual support of or opposition to these roles.

New teacher leadership roles may also foster role ambiguity. Studies of lead and master teachers and career ladder programs point to uncertainties concerning leadership responsibilities and how to perform them (Hart and Murphy, 1990; Kilcher, 1992; Trachtman, 1991; Wasley, 1991). Studies of participative decision making often reveal confusion concerning what types of decisions can be made, who can make them, and how those decisions ought to be made. Several studies find that the uncertainties of these new roles blur the professional identities of teachers, raising questions in the minds of teacher-leaders about whether they are teachers or administrators or something altogether different (Ainscow and Southworth, 1994; Kilcher, 1992).

Another source of stress associated with new teacher leadership roles concerns loss of individual autonomy and control. Several studies of career ladder programs suggest that teachers are concerned that career ladder evaluations could constrain their classroom discretion (Kauchak and Peterson, 1986; Smylie and Smart, 1990). In addition, studies of participative decision making indicate that individual teacher autonomy may be substantially reduced as collective decision making and group accountability increase (Odden and Odden, 1994; Smylie, Lazarus, and Brownlee-Conyers, in press).

One of the most common conditions of teacher leadership development found in the literature is overload. Several dimensions of overload seem particularly stressful. Studies of virtually every type of teacher leadership role point to increases in the amount, the variation, and the complexity of teacher-leaders' responsibilities (Bird and Little, 1983; Chapman and Boyd, 1986; Fay, 1990; Henson and Hall, 1993; Kilcher, 1992; Trachtman, 1991). They also point to the problem of time. Teachers who assume these roles generally report that there is not enough time to fulfill their new responsibilities, particularly if these roles are added to their regular classroom responsibilities. The lack of time may lead to role conflicts, particularly among leadership, administrative, and classroom responsibilities. In addition to the problems associated with increased responsibilities and time constraints, new leadership roles often give teachers responsibility for the care and development of other teachers or for making decisions on their behalf. Both conditions may place pressure on teacher-leaders to perform their roles according to the expectations of others, to make the best decisions possible, and to avoid criticism and alienation from their colleagues (Smylie, Brownlee-Conyers, and Crowson 1991; see also Weiss, Cambone, and Wyeth, 1992).

These conditions point further toward relationships with teaching colleagues and administrators as a potential source of stress. The literature indicates that teacher-leaders often anticipate and experience tensions and conflicts with their fellow teachers (Henson and Hall, 1993; Smylie and Denny, 1990; Smylie and Smart, 1990; Trachtman and Fauerbach, 1992; Wasley, 1991). These tensions and conflicts may arise from differences in expectations held by teacher-leaders and their colleagues. They may also arise from issues of differential status and influence as well as the threats teacher-leaders pose to other teachers' privacy and autonomy. The issues of differential status and influence seem particularly germane in relationships between teachers who are involved in participative decision making and teachers whom they presumably represent (Hallinger and Hausman, 1994; Weiss et al., 1992).

Tensions may also arise in relationships between teacher-leaders and their administrators. These tensions are generally associated with conflicts between expectations for teacher-leaders' roles and administrators' roles (Henson and Hall, 1993; Smylie and Brownlee-Conyers, 1992). This literature suggests further that lack of administrator support of these new roles complicates their development and compromises their function (Bryk, Easton, Kerbow, Rollow, and Sebring, 1993; Firestone, 1977; Malen, 1994; Smylie and Brownlee-Conyers, 1992; Trachtman, 1991; Troen and Boles, 1992).

Finally, teacher-leaders point to lack of preparation as a source of problems in their new roles. Lead and master teachers often report that poor preparation, particularly in the areas of communication and collaboration with colleagues and administrators, restricts the development and performance of their roles (Smylie and Denny, 1990; Wasley, 1991). Likewise, mentor teachers generally express a need for additional knowledge and skills to work successfully with their proteges (Feiman-Nemser and Parker, 1994; Manthei, 1992). Lack of training in decision making processes and in the content of decision areas are often cited by teachers and administrators as an impediment to successful participative decision making (Capper, 1994; Chapman and Boyd, 1986; David and Peterson, 1984).

Contradictions in Reform

These two examples of reform – standards and assessments and teacher leadership development – represent very different approaches to change: The former is bureaucratic and the latter is professional (Firestone and Bader, 1992; Rowan, 1990). Each contains specific sources of stress for teachers. In addition, these reforms illustrate the prospects of compounded problems as teachers experience multiple and conflicting demands for change (Elmore and McLaughlin, 1988).

In the United States, educational policy concerning teachers' work has developed over the past fifteen years in now familiar phases or waves (Darling-Hammond and Berry, 1988; Firestone et al., 1992). The first wave was oriented primarily toward centralization, specification, standardization, regulation, and accountability. The second wave, emerging in the mid-1980s, was oriented more toward decentralization, development of local capacity for improvement, and teacher professionalism. As the second wave began to swell, the first did not subside. The contradictions between the first and second waves are well portrayed in the concurrent development of standards and assessments policies and teacher leadership development initiatives. The implementation of both types of reforms creates a problem of conflicting demands for teachers. They find themselves in a position in which they must balance "all manner of contrary tendencies" (Cohen and Ball, 1990, p. 334). The result may be an exponential increase in stress from heightened ambiguity, role conflict, and overload as well as increased potential for burnout and other problems associated with that stress.

Another View of Stress in Teachers' Work

By and large, the existing literature focuses our attention on the negative consequences of work-related stress and stress in change. As I noted in the introduction to the chapter, this affords half the picture. We are reminded that stress in work may also have positive consequences. We are also reminded that change may be stress-reducing as well as stress-inducing. These possibilities are explored briefly below.

Sources of Stress in Learning and Motivation

The very conditions that have been identified as sources of problematic stress in work may also be impetuses for more positive outcomes, such as learning and motivation. For example, theories of adult learning consistently suggest that learning begins with ambiguous situations that present dilemmas, problems, or felt difficulties (e.g., Brookfield, 1991; Merriam and Caffarella, 1991). Argyris and Schon (1978) argue that learning in organizations takes place under conditions of surprise or nonroutine circumstances that require heightened attention, experimentation, and determination of sources of problems. Learning occurs as individuals confront and alter taken-for-granted assumptions to reframe problem situations. Jarvis (1987) also argues that the impetus for learning comes from conflict between personal "biographies" and current experience. When conflict, or threat, is perceived, individuals will seek to reestablish balance by testing and possibly revising their biographies to accommodate new experiences (see also Louis, 1990).

Across these and other theories of adult learning and learning in organizations, a common picture emerges (Smylie, 1995). Learning is thought to begin with perceptions of discrepancy, challenge, and ambiguity. It then proceeds to self-doubt and search for new information and then to reconceptualization and development of new understanding and meaning.

Similarly, theories of motivation point to several aspects of work that may be sources of both stress and inducement for performance and improvement (see Miskel and Ogawa, 1988; Mitchell, Ortiz, and Mitchell, 1987). For example, in one of the most widely accepted theories of motivation in work, Hackman and Oldham (1980) argue that the motivating potential of work is associated with three crucial psychological states: (a) meaningfulness of the job; (b) experienced responsibility for work outcomes; and (c) the degree to which an individual knows how well he or she is performing the job. According to this jobs characteristics model of motivation, the significance of the tasks one performs to others (e.g., clients and co-workers) and to the overall effectiveness of the organization is key to establishing meaningfulness of work. So too is the extent to which the job is challenging and calls for skill variety in its performance. Sense of personal accomplishment for the results of work performed is the essence of experienced responsibility.

As I have argued throughout this chapter, ambiguity; challenge to one's knowledge, skills, and assumptions; task significance and the stakes associated with one's performance; demand for the use of multiple skills; and personal accountability have each been identified as potential sources of stress that, when experienced in excess, may have deleterious consequences for teachers and their work. Yet at more moderate levels, these conditions may promote learning and motivate performance. What moderate and excessive levels mean would likely depend on the individuals concerned and their particular circumstances. Still, the potential for positive outcomes from these sources of stress is apparent.

Change as Stress-Reducing

Similarly, the stress-inducing nature of change depends importantly on the nature of the change itself and on the individuals who experience it. It is distinctly possible that certain types of change would produce little additional stress and, indeed, would work to alleviate sources of deleterious stress in teachers' work. Although little has been written about this side of change, new programs and policies can be imagined that might clarify teachers' roles, thereby reducing role conflict and ambiguity, or that might redistribute and reassign teachers to tasks (and indeed to students), thereby reducing qualitative and quantitative aspects of overload. One can also imagine new programs and policies of teacher professional development that would prepare them better for their work.

Likewise, change need not introduce conflicts with teachers' values and assumptions. Change can bring work more closely in line with individuals' value systems, thus alleviating a source of potentially deleterious stress. For example, teachers who believe they should play a major role in crafting programs and policies that affect their work with students and who suffer stress from the lack of opportunity to play such a role (see Conley, 1991) may have that source of stress reduced or eliminated by the introduction of participative decision making in their schools.

Stress and Teacher Agency

The literature on work-related stress shows clearly that the consequences of stress are the result of an interactive and interpretive process. At the same time, the literature portrays individuals as mostly reactive to stress or as subjects that stress works on. Not much attention is paid to the notion of agency in the individual's relation to stress.

Certainly, there are some teachers who assume a reactive posture to stress, some who seek to manage it or cope with it, and some who seek to avoid it. However, there are teachers who actively pursue stressful conditions in which to work, such as those who wish to teach in low-achieving, inner-city schools (see Dworkin, 1987). There are also others who choose to meet stressful situations head-on, to anticipate them, and to master them. These are teachers who are problem finders and problem creators, not just problem solvers. These teachers are proactive in their own professional learning and development and in improving their practice, not merely re-active to problems that present themselves.

Finally, teachers may be the initiators of change, not merely the subjects of it (Fullan, 1991). Some teachers are pioneers who actively seek change, who venture intentionally into ambiguous and potentially stressful new situations (J. W. Little, personal communication, November 2, 1995). These are individuals Yee (1990) calls "high-involvement" teachers. Yee charac-terizes them as teachers who seek to exert influence and control over their teaching environment, who want and seek professional stimulation and professional growth opportunities. They do not wait for things to happen to them.

Conclusions and Solutions

What does all this mean? We may reasonably conclude that stress is an en-demic part of teachers' work and that it may or may not accompany spe-cific reforms aimed to increase the effectiveness of their work. We may also conclude that burnout and other psychological and physiological prob-lems may be associated with particularly stressful aspects of work and re-form. Yet, while we may conclude that conditions of teaching are stressful and that excessive stress may have deleterious consequences, it is difficult to determine the extent of the problems or the damage actually caused by stress in teachers' work and reform. Indeed, I have argued that it is not (or should not be) a foregone conclusion that stress in work and change leads inevitably to problems. Stress in work and in change may have quite pro-ductive consequences. Whether the results of stress are positive or nega-tive has much to do with the nature, source, and intensity of stress, as well as the individual's interpretation of and agency in relation to it.

The State of Stress in Teaching

Evidence on the "state of stress" in teaching is scant and inconsistent. Of the research drawn on for this analysis, some studies report relatively low levels of perceived stress and related psychological problems among their sampled teachers. For example, Bacharach and his colleagues (1986) re-ported very low average levels of anxiety and stress-related physiological problems among their statewide sample of teachers in New York. Capel (1989) also reported low mean scores on measures of burnout in her sam-ple of secondary teachers in England. Similarly, Schwab and Iwanicki (1982b) reported relatively low scores on two elements of burnout – emotional exhaustion and depersonalization – in their statewide sample of teachers in Massachusetts. However, they reported moderately higher scores on a third element of burnout – lack of personal accomplishment. Levels of experienced stress and teacher-reported stress-induced illness were relatively higher among the central city teachers sampled by Dworkin and his colleagues (1990); however, it is difficult to tell whether these levels were alarmingly high.

Likewise, there is some evidence to suggest that reforms containing additional sources of stress for teachers may actually do little harm and may indeed induce positive change. For example, Archibald and Porter (1994) found that despite a felt loss of personal control over subject matter and pedagogy, teachers' sense that they could be effective with students did not diminish with curricular centralization. Similarly, Cohen and Ball (1990) indicated that the teachers in their case studies appeared little troubled by the ambiguities, role conflicts, and loss of control associated with centralized curriculum and testing. These researchers explained their finding with evidence that teachers were able to exercise enough agency to reshape the new curriculum according to their own values and capabilities. Further, Smylie's (in press) review of the literature on teacher leadership found evidence that these new roles may have positive effects on the commitment, satisfaction, knowledge, and skills of teachers who assume them. According to findings from the most rigorously designed longitudinal studies, teacher leadership may have positive consequences for school climate, classroom instruction, and student learning.

On the other hand, despite the potential of stress for positive consequences and despite teachers' ability to confront sources of stress productively, there are indicators of significant trouble in the teacher workforce. The findings of a recent national survey conducted by the U.S. Department of Education (1993) revealed that approximately 40 percent of American teachers expressed various degrees of dissatisfaction with their workloads, the resources that were available for them to perform their jobs, the support they received from their administrators, and the procedures that were used to evaluate their work. Half the teachers in the United States were dissatisfied with the amount of influence they had over school and district policy, and nearly three-quarters were dissatisfied with how their work was viewed by the general public. In longitudinal analyses of membership surveys, the National Education Association (NEA) (1992) found that the proportion of teachers who said that they would enter teaching again fell from 74 percent to 59 percent between 1971 and 1991. The proportion of teachers who said they would not choose teaching again rose from 12 percent to

22 percent. The NEA reported that in 1991 nearly 40 percent of its member teachers were either undecided about whether to remain in teaching, wanted to leave teaching as soon as they could, or planned to continue teaching only until something better came along.

It is difficult to know the extent to which these troubling indicators are attributable to the stressful conditions of teachers' work or to the myriad of other personal and contextual factors that may affect teachers' work-related attitudes and behaviors (Meyer and Rowan, 1977; Sarason, 1982). Nevertheless, the theory and research on stress in the workplace suggest that at least the potential for problems is great and deserves our attention.

Addressing the Problems of Stress

The literature is replete with suggestions for addressing the problems of stress in teachers' work (e.g., Cedoline, 1982; Dunham, 1992; Greenberg, 1984). Many of these suggestions aim at increasing the individual's capacity to manage or cope with stress. There is some evidence that counseling, training, and other efforts to enhance individuals' coping abilities may bring some temporary relief (Lazarus, 1966; Winnubst, 1984). However, the effectiveness of these strategies is quite limited. They seek to reduce the psychological threats imposed by the characteristics and demands of work primarily by altering the individual's perceptions and interpretations of them. They do little to alter the stressful characteristics and demands of work that may be the geneses of the threats. Their use, therefore, may be helpful but insufficient to prevent or remedy effectively the problems of stress in teaching.

As I have suggested throughout this chapter, stress in teachers' work may best be thought of as a social and organizational issue as well as an individual psychological issue. It calls for social and organizational solutions (Cherniss, 1980b; Winnubst, 1984). The objective is not to eliminate stress from teachers' work, even if that were possible. It is to keep stress in balance and channeled to induce performance and improvement (see Cherniss, 1980b; McGrath, 1983; Van Harrison, 1978). Several recommendations to achieve this objective are outlined next.

One place to start is to audit the work of teachers to identify potentially problematic sources of role conflict, ambiguity, and overload. An audit of work should be aggressive and accompanied by an examination and clarification of goals for schools and assumptions of schooling. Institutional goals and individual roles and assignments (e.g., the students, grade levels, and subject matters teachers are assigned to teach; extraclassroom responsibilities, etc.) must be realigned with an eye toward disentangling and redistributing potentially conflicting roles among teachers, administrators, and other school personnel. Present allocations of time and other resources required for work must similarly be assessed and adjusted.

The responsibilities of teachers should be newly articulated, not as routinized or standardized tasks but as professional duties linked closely with the achievement of broader institutional goals, such as student academic learning. Local discretion should be encouraged in the performance of these duties as an exercise of individual and collective agency. Teachers may be held accountable for behaviors and outcomes consistent with their professional duties, not for compliance with specific task procedures.

Teachers must play a genuine, not symbolic, part in this process of restructuring work. Their involvement may provide substantive expertise; however, there is little evidence that teacher participation in decision making results inherently in higher quality decisions (Smylie, in press). At minimum, their involvement is important for addressing the issue of agency and for developing individual and collective responsibility and accountability. Teacher participation is also necessary to address the intentional, built-in ambiguities associated with pursuing work restructuring from the perspective of professional duty. Teachers would need to play an important role in determining the meaning and obligations of professional duty for their individual schools and districts.

Finally, restructured work must be built on a new foundation of opportunities for professional learning and development for teachers. I have argued that lack of preparation and lack of supervision and support may become sources of problematic stress for teachers. The literature on professional development of teachers indicates that feedback about work and opportunities for learning and improvement are woefully inadequate for many teachers (Smylie, 1989). Theories of adult learning and organizational performance point to the importance of developing workplaces as learning communities (Argyris and Schon, 1978; Senge, 1990; Smylie, 1995; see also Sarason, 1990). In schools, these communities would encourage and support ongoing, collective, collaborative opportunities for teacher learning. Learning would be focused on the performance of teachers' professional duties and the achievement of institutional goals. By their collective nature, these opportunities would give teachers access to others' expertise and experience. At the same time, linkages would be made to external sources – such as other schools, professional organizations, and universities – to provide teachers with additional opportunities for learning.

Developing learning communities in schools may help address several issues. They could promote a collective focus on institutional goals, professional duties, and individuals' roles in the school organization. They could provide the knowledge, skills, and feedback teachers need to fulfill their responsibilities. Furthermore, these communities could provide needed social support and accountability mechanisms as incentives for performance. As teachers' work is being restructured, the developing learning communities could begin to address the problems of role conflict, ambiguity, lack of autonomy, overload, and lack of preparation and support in teachers' work.

In closing, remember that these and other admittedly ambitious social and organizational solutions may themselves contain the seeds of stress. They represent fundamental changes in the organization of teachers' work and workplaces. They may create new and perhaps unanticipated problems. For example, Bacharach and his colleagues (1986) remind us that specification aimed at reducing stress associated with ambiguity may *increase* stress associated with role conflict and loss of autonomy (see also Winnubst, 1984). Efforts to enhance teachers' knowledge and skills may create new role conflicts and ambiguities and challenge teachers' prevailing knowledge, beliefs, and confidence in their practice (see Guskey, 1984; Hall and Hord, 1984). Increased involvement in decision making, while addressing problems of agency, may lead to role conflicts and overload (Smylie, in press). Finally, efforts to enhance supervisory and collegial support may conflict with prevailing norms of privacy, autonomy, and egalitarianism that define and govern teacher and administrator prerogatives and working relations (Little, 1990b; Smylie and Brownlee-Conyers, 1992).

It seems important, then, to approach solutions to the problems of teachers' work-related stress thoughtfully, problematically, and strategically, in full anticipation that addressing one source of stress may exacerbate another. It also seems important to recall the importance of approaching the problem of teacher stress systemically, perceiving the teacher as an active agent. Various solutions, whether they are aimed at enhancing individual coping capacity or redesigning work and workplaces, may best proceed from understanding more about the relationships between teachers' work; their broader personal and professional lives; and the larger social, cultural, and institutional contexts of teaching.

4. Teacher Burnout:
A Critical Challenge for Leaders of Restructuring Schools

KENNETH A. LEITHWOOD, TERESA MENZIES,
DORIS JANTZI, AND JENNIFER LEITHWOOD

\99u?

*The highest reward for a person's toil is not what is received for it, but
what he/she becomes by it.*
                                                            – Anonymous

Burnout is a label used to define the stress experienced by those who work
in interpersonally intense occupations subject to chronic tension (Cunningham, 1983), such as teaching. This form of stress manifests itself as a state
of physical, emotional, and cognitive exhaustion that produces feelings of
alienation, indifference, and low self-regard (Huberman, 1993b). The most
commonly used instrument for assessing burnout, the MBI (Maslach Burnout Inventory; Maslach and Jackson, 1981), defines it in terms of three dimensions: emotional exhaustion, depersonalization, and a reduced sense
of personal accomplishment.

Symptoms of burnout are both organizational and personal. Organizational symptoms include increased absenteeism, performance decline, poor
interpersonal relations with co-workers and, in the case of teachers, with
students (Cunningham, 1983). At a personal level, teachers who experience
burnout are less sympathetic toward students, are less committed to and
involved in their jobs, have a lower tolerance for classroom disruption, are
less apt to prepare adequately for class, and are generally less productive
(Blase and Greenfield, 1985; Farber and Miller, 1981). Perhaps even more
germane to school restructuring is the evidence, reviewed by Cunningham
(1983), that teachers experiencing burnout tend to be dogmatic about their
practices and to rely rigidly on structure and routine, thereby resisting
changes to those practices.

Clearly, these symptoms are anathema to most current school restructuring efforts. To be successful, these efforts require, for example, increased
levels of commitment to school goals (Fullan, 1993); greater sensitivity by
teachers to the diverse needs of their students and an expanded, more
flexible instructional repertoire (Murphy, 1991); and more collaborative

working relationships with fellow teachers (Lieberman, Saxl, and Miles, 1988) as well as with students and parents (Connors and Epstein, 1994). Although the effects of burnout undermine the success of school restructuring efforts, the conditions in which teachers involved in restructuring often find themselves provide fertile ground for the development of burnout. These are conditions that may further exacerbate the effects of an already stressful job. The percentage of the teaching population experiencing such stress at any given time is estimated to range from 15 percent to 45 percent (e.g., Friedman and Farber, 1992; Leach, 1984; Schlansker, 1987; Tuettemann and Punch, 1992).

Beyond "business as usual," however, restructuring requires teachers to adopt new and ambiguous roles outside the classroom, roles that often bring teachers into conflict with the traditional roles of school administrators. Engagement in these roles places considerable demands on their time and often leads to feelings of work overload. Many teachers also experience considerable stress as their expectations for how restructuring will proceed confront a far less ideal reality (Conley, 1993; Louis and King, 1993; Prestine, 1993). This is so especially for those exceptionally enthusiastic teachers who are often among the first to implement new practices associated with restructuring (Huberman, 1993b). These conditions are typically viewed as powerful contributors to teacher burnout (e.g., Byrne, 1994a; Cunningham, 1983; Milstein, Golaszewski, and Duquette, 1984).

Sustaining and institutionalizing school restructuring initiatives appears to depend in no small measure on preventing burnout as a result of teacher participation in such initiatives. The study reported in this chapter sought to contribute to this goal by developing a conception of the types of leadership practices that influence teacher burnout and a defensible explanation of the relationships between such practices and teacher burnout. Our point of departure was a model of "transformational" school leadership, developed and refined in the context of a series of studies on forms of leadership that contribute to restructuring success (e.g., Leithwood, 1992, 1994; Leithwood and Steinbach, 1993). The model is derived from both theoretical and empirical work outside of education (e.g., Bass, 1985; Burns, 1978; Podsakoff, MacKenzie, Moorman, and Fetter, 1990). Roberts introduces the concept of transformational leadership as follows:

> The collective action that transforming leadership generates empowers those who participate in the process. There is hope, there is optimism, there is energy. In essence, transforming leadership is a leadership that facilitates the redefinition of a people's mission and

vision, a renewal of their commitment, and the restructuring of their systems for goal accomplishment. (1985, p. 1024)

A two-stage, data-driven strategy for developing a model to explain teacher burnout was used in this study. Stage 1 consisted of the formulation of an initial model to explain burnout, which included leadership and its relationship with burnout; this was based on a review of empirical literature. Stage 2 refined the initial model in response to analyses of an original data set.

Stage 1: Initial Model Development from a Review of Literature

Central to stage 1 of the study was the review of a relevant set of empirical studies to answer four questions:

- What factors other than leadership ought to be included in a defensible explanation of teacher burnout?
- What specific leadership practices are significantly related to teacher burnout?
- What is the relative importance of school leadership as a factor in explanations of variation in teacher burnout?
- How do leadership and nonleadership factors interact to explain variation in teacher burnout?

Method

Studies of teacher burnout used for model building were identified in two steps. After a preliminary search on the general topic of teacher burnout, a second search was carried out limiting the relevant sources to published, empirical studies conducted within approximately the past decade (1984 to the present, with one study published in 1983). Each of the eighteen studies selected for the final analysis had to have investigated leadership as one of the variables. In some of these studies, leadership was a central focus of the research; in others, it was a component of one or several more inclusive variables such as "social support" or "participative decision making." Data search sources included the ERIC and Educational Index databases along with a follow-up of the studies listed in reference sections of papers identified in those databases.

Methodological characteristics of the eighteen studies are summarized in Table 4.1. Subjects for whom data were collected included elementary teachers in two studies, secondary teachers in four studies, elementary and secondary teachers in eight studies, special and general educators in one study, former special educators in one study, school counselors in one study,

Table 4.1. *Methodological Characteristics of Eighteen Empirical Studies of Teacher Burnout*

Author	Subjects	Sample size	Sampling method	Data collection procedures
1. N. Benson & P. Malone (1987)	K-12 teachers	311	Not reported	Survey: unnamed
2. J.J. Blase (1984)	Elementary and secondary teachers (enrolled in graduate schools of education)	202	Selected	Combined survey and interview technique Survey: Teacher Stress Inventory
3. J.J. Blase (1986)	Elementary, junior high, and senior high school teachers (enrolled in graduate schools of education)	149 77 166	Selected	Survey: Teacher Stress Inventory
4. J. Blase, C. Dedrick, & M.Strathe (1986)	Elementary, junior high, and senior high school teachers (enrolled in graduate schools of education)	71 31 60	Selected	Survey: Leader Behavior Descriptions Questionnaire
5. J.S. Brissie, K.V. Hoover-Dempsey & O.C. Bassler (1988)	Elementary teachers	Teachers = 1,213 Districts = 8 Schools = 78	Participation requested of districts and of schools	Surveys: • Maslach Burnout Inventory • Teacher Stress Scale • Teacher Opinion Questionnaire
6. B.M.Byrne (1994a)	Elementary, intermediate and secondary teachers	1,242 417 1,479	Random sample	Surveys: • Maslach Burnout Inventory • Teacher Stress Scale • Classroom Environment Scale • Internal-External Locus of Control Scale • Self-Esteem Scale

Table 4.1. (cont.)

Author	Subjects	Sample size	Sampling method	Data collection procedures
7. C. Cherniss (1988)	Special educators, principals, teacher aides, ancillary staff (of schools for severely retarded children)	23 2 5 13 Schools = 2	Selected	Surveys: • Maslach Burnout Inventory • Supervisor Behavior Observation Scale
8. O.W. Cummings & R.L. Nall (1983)	School counselors	Teachers = 31	Random sample	Survey: • School Leadership Inventory • Self-reported rating of burnout; • Semantic differential scales
9. I.A. Friedman (1991)	Elementary teachers	Teachers = 1597 Schools = 78	Random sample	Combined survey and interview technique Survey: • Maslach Burnout Inventory Interviews
10. M. Huberman (1993b)	Secondary teachers	160	Stratified random	• Locus of control • Modified version of Maslach • Semantic differential
11. P.C. Littrel, B.S. Billingsley, & L.H. Cross (1994)	Special educators and general educators	385 313	Random sample of special educators; general educators nominated	Survey: • Unnamed followed by telephone interview of 15% of nonrespondent special educators
12. P.J. Mazur & M.D. Lynch (1989)	Senior high school teachers	Teachers = 200 Schools = 9	Volunteer selected	Survey: • Modified version of Maslach Burnout Inventory
13. J.M Platt & J. Olson (1990)	Former special education teachers	76	Random selection from list of former special education teachers	Survey: • Unnamed

Table 4.1. (*cont.*)

Author	Subjects	Sample size	Sampling method	Data collection procedures
14. D.W. Russell, E. Altmaier, & D. VanVelzen (1987)	Elementary and secondary teachers	313	Stratified random sample	Surveys: • Unnamed surveys • Social Provisions Scale • Maslach Burnout Inventory
15. J.C. Sarros & A.M. Sarros (1992)	Secondary teachers	Teachers = 491 Schools = 229	Random sample	Surveys: • Unnamed (a social support instrument) • Maslach Burnout Inventory
16. B. Schlansker (1987)	K-12 teachers	169	Selected	Survey: • Schlansker Supports Value Inventory
17. S.M. Starnaman & K.I. Miller (1992)	Elementary and secondary teachers (number who did not indicate grade level)	93 75 14	Stratified random sample	Surveys: • Maslach Burnout Inventory • Survey of Organizations • Job Description Index • Organizational Commitment Questionnaire • Unnamed questionnaire (Pettegrew & Wolf, 1982)
18. E. Tuettemann & K.F. Punch (1992)	Full-time secondary teachers	574	Random sample	Survey: • Unnamed survey incorporating the General Health Questionnaire

and special educators, principals, teacher aides, and ancillary staff in the final study. Sample sizes ranged from 31 to 3,138 participants. The individual was used as the sampling unit in each of the studies. Sampling procedures were random in seven of the studies, and selected in five. For the study involving special and general educators (Littrel, Billingsley, and Cross, 1994), special education teachers were selected randomly, and general educators were nominated by them. Two studies were volunteer selected, and one study selected a random sample from a list of former special education teachers. With respect to design, thirteen of the eighteen studies used survey methods exclusively to collect data. One of the studies combined a survey with a self-reported rating of burnout, and semantic differential scales. The final three studies used a combination of survey and interview methods.[1]

All the studies used burnout or a close proxy as the dependent variable. The study results were analyzed by coding the independent variables in relation to one of three major categories (described later in this chapter). A voting method (total number of positive, negative, or not significant relations reported among variables) was used to assess the strength of the evidence supporting a positive or negative relationship between each independent variable and teacher burnout (Glass, McGaw, and Smith, 1984). The small number of studies reporting evidence about any single variable and the theory-development aim of the review (Cooper, 1984), along with the inclusion of a significant proportion of qualitative studies, made inappropriate and/or prohibited the use of more sophisticated, quantitative, meta-analytic synthesizing techniques.

In the remainder of this section, answers are summarized to the four research questions based on a synthesis of results from the eighteen studies. Our answer to the last of these question takes the form of a model for explaining variation in teacher burnout.

Factors Other than Leadership Explaining Teacher Burnout

Tables 4.2 and 4.3 describe two categories of nonleadership factors – personal and organizational – identified as influencing burnout in the eighteen studies. Also used as conceptual organizers in many of the studies reviewed,

1. The eighteen studies used for model building were conducted in K-12 settings, whereas model testing was carried out with data from teachers in community college settings. There are significant differences in these two institutional contexts, the effects of which on explanations of burnout remain to be determined. The unknown effects of these contextual differences on the results of our model testing and on the application of our results to K-12 settings is an important limitation of this study.

Table 4.2. *Personal Variables Influencing Teacher Burnout*

Variables contributing to burnout	Evidence
External locus of control	6, 10
Teacher gender (high proportion of males)	9, 15, 18
Teacher age (older)	9, (14), (15)
Teacher education (lower)	9
Teacher experience (more)	9
Feelings of being trapped in teaching	10
Problems in personal life	10
Type A personality	12
Anomia (sense of meaningless and alienation)	12
Variables Reducing Burnout	
Perceptions of teaching efficacy	5, 10, 18
High self-esteem/ self-concept	6, 10, 12
Feelings of intrinsic rewards from teaching	5
Internal locus of control	6, 10, 12
Teacher gender (high proportion of females)	9, 15, 18
Teacher age (younger)	9, (14)
Teacher education (higher)	9
Teacher experience (less)	9

those categories encompass all the specific, nonleadership factors influencing burnout identified in the studies.

The left-hand column of each of these tables lists the specific factors included in each category. Factors identified as contributing to burnout are listed in the top section of each table and those reducing burnout appear in the bottom section. These are sometimes different variables (top and bottom) and sometimes simply different conditions of the same variable. The location and phrasing of a variable is a direct reflection of the results of the study that reported it.

The right-hand column of each table identifies, by numbers keyed to Table 4.1, studies that provided evidence of the variable being "significantly"[2] related to burnout. A number in parentheses identifies a study that explicitly tested a relationship but reported nonsignificant findings.

Personal Factors. Table 4.2 includes a total of seventeen different factors explicitly identified in the studies reviewed: nine of these exacerbate, and eight reduce burnout. Each of these specific factors appears to fit within one of four subcategories: demographic characteristics, general personality factors, psychological traits, and motivational disposition. The first two

---

2. We use this term in the standard sense of statistical significance for quantitative studies as well as in reference to strong relationships reported in qualitative studies.

Table 4.3. *Organizational Variables Influencing Teacher Burnout*

Variables contributing to burnout	Evidence
Student misbehavior (discipline, absence, apathy)	3, 6, 10, 6, 12, 13, 18
Work overload, excessive paper work, pupil load	12, 18
Isolation	3, 10
Overdemand (reduced time for instruction)	3
Underdemand (excessive job specification)	3
External pressure for change	5, 10
Organizational rigidity	(6), 12, 17
Role conflict, ambiguity	18
Inadequate access to facilities	9
Orderly, rigid use of physical facilities	9
Hierarchical administrative structure	10, 12
Lack of support	12
Excessive societal expectations	18
Variables Reducing Burnout	
Support of friends, family, and colleagues	16, 5, 6, 12, 14, 15, 18
Sharing professional experience	16
Recognition leading to advancement	16
Having an influence on decisions	16, 1, 5, 6, 18
Job security	16
Access to support personnel	16
Adequate physical facilities	16
Relaxed, flexible use of physical facilities	9
Flexible administrative structure	9
Reduced workload	10
Allowance for changing assignments	10
Clear job expectations	12

of these subcategories are largely unalterable; the remaining two can be altered. As the right column of Table 4.2 indicates, the amount of evidence supporting the contribution of each personal factor to teacher burnout never exceeds three studies. For ten of the seventeen factors, support is provided by only one study.

With respect to *demographic characteristics,* burnout is marginally less likely with younger, female teachers. It is also less likely for teachers with very little and quite extensive (more than twenty-four years) experience. Length of teacher experience alone has not been shown to influence burnout. Demographic characteristics typically explain little of the variation in teacher burnout.

With respect to *general personality* factors, burnout is less likely for teachers with personalities that avoid the extremes of competitiveness, impatience, and striving for achievement. In reference to *psychological traits,* teachers with an internal locus of control and a strong sense of purpose in their professional and personal lives (the opposite of "anomie") are less likely to experience burnout. Finally, the *capacity beliefs* of teachers, part of a larger set of motivational conditions discussed later, influence the likelihood of burnout. Teachers with high levels of self-esteem and positive self-concept as well as high levels of professional self-efficacy are more resistant to burnout.

Organizational Factors. Table 4.3 lists thirteen organizational factors identified as increasing, and twelve factors as reducing the likelihood of teacher burnout. These specific factors can be grouped together into one of three clusters: job demand (or pressure), social support, and organizational support. Of the twenty-five organizational factors cited in Table 4.3, evidence of a significant relationship with teacher burnout is limited to only one study for seventeen of these factors. Student misbehavior is identified as contributing to burnout in the largest number of studies naming a single factor (six studies). Having the support of friends, family, and colleagues, and having an influence on decision making in the school are identified most frequently as reducing burnout (seven and five studies, respectively).

In relation to *job demand,* burnout is less likely for teachers who do not have excessive demands on their time and/or energy, do not have to deal with constant and severe student misbehavior, and do not experience serious role conflict and ambiguity. Burnout is also less likely for teachers who do not experience significant pressure from others to change their practices and who do not perceive excessive societal pressure for change.

With respect to *social support,* burnout is less likely for teachers who: receive such support from friends, family, and colleagues, have opportunities to share professional experiences, and who do not experience feelings of professional isolation. Burnout also is less likely for teachers who receive recognition for their efforts and achievements.

Organizational support conditions reducing the likelihood of burnout include opportunities to change assignments or types of work, and to work within flexible, nonhierarchical, administrative structures. Access to adequate physical facilities that can be used in flexible ways and access to support personnel (also a form of social support) reduce the likelihood of burnout as does having an influence on decisions and job security.

Leadership Practices Explaining Variation in Teacher Burnout

Table 4.4, using the same format as Tables 4.2 and 4.3, includes specific leadership practices identified in the studies reviewed as significantly as-

Table 4.4. *Leadership Variables Influencing Teacher Burnout*

Variables contributing to burnout	Evidence
Expectations of teachers (unclear, high, perceived as unreasonable)	3, 2, 9, 12
Extensive emphasis on student achievement	9
Inconsistent behavior/expectations	3, 2
Nonparticipative decision style	3, 2
Failure to provide essential resources	3, 2
Lack of follow-through	3, 2
Lack of knowledge (curriculum, childrens' needs)	2
Poor teacher evaluation	2
Indecisiveness	2
Lack of administrative support	2, 13
Favoritism	2
Harassment	2
Authoritarian leadership style	8
Lack of trust in teacher's professional adequacy	9
Variables Reducing Burnout	
Providing support/consideration (general)	3, 5, (6), 7, 10, 12, 14, 15, 16, 17
• emotional	11, 3
• appraisal (recognition, feedback, standards)	11, 3, 14, 16, 18
• instrumental (direct assistance)	11, 16
• informational (access to knowledge)	11
Modest emphasis on student achievement	9
Value integration with staff and assisting others	9
Style: high level of structure and consideration	4
Participative leadership style	8, (12), 17

sociated with teacher burnout. Although almost always treated piecemeal in the studies reviewed, these factors, as a whole, incompletely reflect many aspects of a "transformational" model of school leadership demonstrated to be useful in school restructuring contexts (e.g., Leithwood, 1994; Leithwood and Jantzi, 1990; Leithwood, Tomlinson, and Genge, in press). With conceptual roots in research outside schools (Burns, 1978, and Bass, 1985, for example), eight dimensions of leadership practice currently define the meaning of such leadership.

Three of the eight leadership dimensions involve purposes or direction setting. The first concerns *vision;* this is behavior on the part of the leader aimed at identifying new opportunities for his or her school and developing (often collaboratively), articulating, and inspiring others with a vision of the future. The second dimension entails fostering the acceptance of *group goals* by promoting cooperation among staff and assisting them to work together toward common goals. None of the leadership factors associated with burnout reflect these first two dimensions of transformational school leadership.

The third direction-setting dimension involves *high performance expectations*. This is behavior that demonstrates the leader's expectations for excellence, quality, and/or high performance on the part of staff. Burnout factors associated with this dimension include excessively high expectations of teachers, emphasis on student achievement, and poor teacher evaluation.

Three of the eight transformational leadership dimensions are focused directly on the emotional and cognitive capacities of people, usually teachers. *Modeling* consists of behavior by the leader that sets an example for staff to follow and that is consistent with the values espoused by the leader. Burnout factors associated with this dimension include inconsistent behavior, lack of follow-through, favoritism, and harassment.

Providing individualized support, another emotionally oriented dimension of transformational leadership, includes behavior by the leader that indicates respect for individual members of staff and concern about their personal feelings and needs. Encompassed by this dimension are the burnout factors: low levels of (structure and) consideration, failure to provide essential resources, failure to provide administrative support, lack of trust in teachers' professional adequacy, and lack of several different types of "support" based on the House and Wells (1978) taxonomy (emotional, appraisal, instrumental, and informational). *Providing intellectual stimulation* is the third people-oriented leadership dimension. This involves challenging staff to reexamine some of their assumptions about their work and to rethink how it can be performed. One burnout factor is encompassed by this dimension – lack of knowledge on the leader's part.

Transformational leadership also entails *building a productive school culture* by encouraging collaboration among staff and assisting in the creation of a widely shared set of norms, values, and beliefs consistent with continuous improvement of services for students. The burnout factors valuing integration of staff as well as staff assisting one another weakly reflect practices associated with this dimension. Finally, transformational school leadership includes helping *structure* the school to enhance participation in decisions, creating opportunities for all stakeholder groups to participate effectively in school decision making. This dimension encompasses burnout factors identified as nonparticipative leadership style, authoritarian leadership style, and low levels of structure (and consideration).

All leadership factors identified by the eighteen studies are readily subsumed within the dimensions of our model of transformational school leadership. By far the most support is available for factors associated with *providing individualized support* (eleven studies). *Holding high performance expectations* (four studies) received the next largest amount of support. These results may be interpreted as helping to clarify the particular nature of the contribution that some dimensions of transformational leadership make to its overall effects.

In most cases, however, burnout factors do not capture the full range of intentions and practices for the dimension to which they relate. Furthermore, there is no reflection in the burnout factors of the first two dimensions of transformational leadership concerned with direction setting. One may argue that this is hard evidence of their impotence in relation to burnout. Results from the qualitative studies that directly asked teachers to identify leadership practices that reduced or promoted stress (Blase, 1984, 1986; Blase, Dedrick, and Strathe, 1986; Cherniss, 1988) would seem to support this interpretation. In the case of the quantitative studies, however, their piecemeal approach to leadership may have resulted in these dimensions of leadership simply being overlooked.

The Relative Importance of Leadership Factors

Review of the eighteen studies suggested that leadership factors may have been underestimated in explanations of teacher burnout. First, many of the specific organizational factors (e.g., organizational rigidity, hierarchical administrative structure) along with some of the alterable personal variables (self-efficacy) are either as easily conceptualized as leadership factors or are unarguably influenced by leadership factors. In particular, distinctions made between organizational and leadership variables often appear to be arbitrary. All but three of the fifteen variables identified in Table 4.3 as contributing to burnout (student misbehavior, pressure for change, and excessive societal expectations) could be considered direct or indirect products of leadership/administrative practice. Indeed, some aspects of student misbehavior (those influenced by the development and systematic application of discipline policy, for example) and change (e.g., the initiation of various "improvement" efforts by a principal) might be viewed in this way also. Similarly, among the twelve variables reducing the likelihood of burnout, only support of friends, family, and colleagues and sharing professional experience seem independent of administrative practice.

A second reason for suspecting that leadership factors may have been underestimated is that a very high proportion of the eighteen studies that included leadership factors in their design reported significant associations between such factors and teacher burnout. Only Benson and Malone (1987) and Byrne (1994a) failed to report such results.

These reasons notwithstanding, the associations reported between leadership and burnout are more variable and often weaker than associations reported between burnout and both organizational and personal factors. Aside from inevitable variation in results due to differences in research methods, these uneven and weak associations may be a function of researchers' confounding leadership and (especially) organizational variables in some studies (e.g., Mazur and Lynch, 1989) and redistributing leadership effects across factors not conceptualized as leadership in other studies (e.g., Russell, Altmaier, and Van Velzen, 1987). Given these possible explanations, there is ample justification for the inclusion of a robust and comprehensive model of leadership in our own model of teacher burnout.

A Model for Explaining Variation in Teacher Burnout

Figure 4.1 summarizes the factors and the relationships among those factors making up a model for explaining variation in teacher burnout growing out of the review of the eighteen studies described earlier. The three major categories of factors associated with burnout reflected in the studies are incorporated in this model. In reality, these factors undoubtedly are related in much more interactive ways than Figure 4.1 indicates; but the strictly linear simplification of such relations is a heuristic guide for initial empirical exploration of the model.

Personal factors are conceptualized as mediating the effects of both leadership and organizational factors. This is consistent with the conclusion that Byrne (1994a) drew from her data about both self-esteem and locus of control variables. In our model, unalterable personal factors have been eliminated, primarily because we were interested in factors subject to intervention. In addition, one of these subcategories (demographic) explained little variation in burnout in the eighteen studies (see Russell, Altmaier, and Van Velzen, 1987, and Brissie, Hoover-Dempsey, and Bassler, 1988, for example).

Not included among alterable personal factors in Figure 4.1 is the subcategory, *psychological traits*, defined in the studies reviewed by anomie and locus of control. In the Figure 4.1 model, anomie (usually defined as a sense of meaninglessness and feelings of alienation) was considered to be an aspect of burnout rather than a factor contributing to burnout. Locus of control was reconceptualized, after Bandura (1986), as an aspect of self-efficacy.

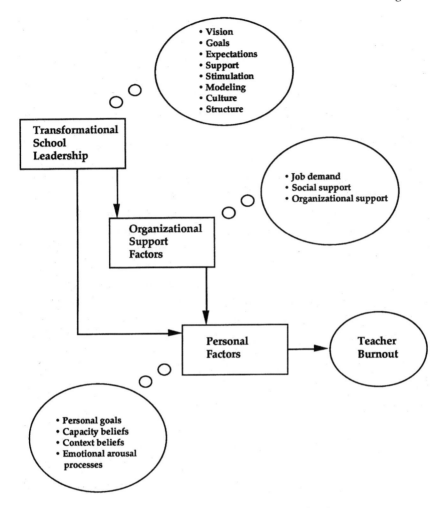

Figure 4.1. A model for explaining variation in teacher burnout.

With these changes, all personal factors in our model are subsumed by a comprehensive, social cognitive theory of human motivation (Bandura, 1986; Ford, 1992). According to this theory, self-concept, self-esteem, and self-efficacy give rise to *capacity beliefs*, beliefs about one's personal ability to cope with the challenges one is facing. A second context belief concerns the support one will receive from the environment in which one is working. Our model reconceptualizes the subcategories *job demand* and *social support* from the organizational category of variables as beliefs about the relative supportiveness of one's context for successfully meeting the demands of one's job, a personal rather than organizational set of factors.

In addition to these two sets of beliefs, a person's motivation, according to this social cognitive theory, is influenced by personal goals, especially judgements about their achievability, and the amount of change their achievement would entail. Finally, this theory also identifies as motivating (especially in the short run) positive rewards, sources of satisfaction, and excitement experienced from day to day: These are *emotional arousal processes*. Neither personal goals nor emotional arousal processes were included in the studies of teacher burnout that we reviewed. Nevertheless, our own prior research has demonstrated significant direct or indirect relations between transformational leadership and each of these four motivational conditions: It has demonstrated, as well, significant effects of such conditions on the success of school restructuring (Leithwood, Jantzi, and Fernandez, 1994). This is warrant, we believe, for including the full set of motivational conditions in our initial model for explaining teacher burnout.

Figure 4.1 not only predicts that the effects of both leadership and organizational factors will be mediated by personal factors but also that the effects of leadership on personal factors will be both direct and indirect (through organizational support factors).

Stage 2: Refinement of the Model from Analyses of an Original Data Set

The second stage of the study was intended to answer three questions beyond those addressed in stage 1:

- Does our model account for a significant proportion of the variation in teacher burnout?
- Is it possible to demonstrate empirical support for the mediating role of personal factors suggested by our model?
- Can our theoretically based claim that previous studies have underestimated leadership effects on teacher burnout be supported empirically?

With respect to each of these questions, we also considered what additional refinements to the model were warranted and what further research would be helpful.

Method

A secondary analysis was performed on a set of survey data originally collected for different although related purposes (Menzies, 1995). These data were requested from all 555 teachers in the business, technology, and health faculties of three community colleges within a three-hour driving radius of Toronto. Three hundred and thirty-one teachers (60%) responded to the survey. For the present study, individual survey items were selected from the original instrument that matched conceptually the factors in our model. A total of seventy-two items were organized into eight scales, one for each of the categories and most subcategories in our model. Because all variables were measured using teachers' responses to the same survey, results of the analysis are susceptible to same-source bias.

SPSS was used to calculate means, standard deviations, scale reliabilities (Cronbach's alpha), and Pearson product-moment correlation coefficients. Path analysis was used to determine the relationships among the factors in our model. This technique allowed for testing the validity of causal inferences for pairs of variables while controlling for the effects of other variables. The LISREL VIII analysis of covariance structure approach to path analysis and maximum likelihood estimates (Joreskog and Sorbom, 1989) was used to test the model.

Table 4.5 includes the means and standard deviations of responses to all items and for the scales measuring each of the factors in the model. Also reported in this table are the reliabilities measuring internal consistency for each scale. Table 4.6 indicates the correlations among all factors in the model.

Figures 4.2 and 4.3 report the results of testing a general as well as more detailed version of our model of teacher burnout using LISREL. These models are refinements of the model described in Figure 4.1, made after a review of the correlations among the full set of factors reported in Table 4.6. LISREL is intended to be used strictly to test theoretically defensible models specified a priori. However, because we viewed this as a theory refinement rather than a theory-testing exercise, we violated this intention, following the lead of the data more than would be considered defensible otherwise. For example, the relationship between organizational factors and burnout was created as a means of finding a model that would fit the data. Then we set out to find an adequate theoretical explanation.

Amount of Explained Variation in Teacher Burnout

With a Goodness of Fit Index (GFI) = .99, Adjusted Goodness of Fit Index (AGFI) = .94 and a chi-square = 4.33 (1 degree of freedom; df), the model in Figure 4.2 is an acceptable fit to the data. The three sets of factors treated as independent variables in Figure 4.2 combine to explain a total of 30 percent of the variation in teacher burnout. Leadership and organizational factors together explain 43 percent of the variation in personal factors. And leadership alone explains 33 percent of the variation in organizational factors.

Table 4.5. *Respondents' Mean Ratings for Scales and Items (N = 331)*

	Mean	S.D.
Leadership		
Leadership Mean (Reliability = .923*)	3.13	.81
1. The goals and vision for our department are determined by our department as a whole.	3.23	1.38
2. The faculty and Chair together determine the vision and goals for the department.	2.96	1.36
3. It's easy to admire my Chair, who is honest, open, and fair.	3.43	1.27
4. Our Chair spells out expectations and constraints.	3.18	1.19
5. There is participatory decision making in our department, whereby the Chair usually consults faculty on important issues.	3.12	1.30
6. The Chair takes action on uncommitted teachers.	2.26	1.17
7. My Chair gives me informal feedback on my successes and failures.	2.90	1.29
8. There is sufficient accountability in our department.	2.67	1.25
9. My Chair gives me feedback on what I am doing well and where I might improve.	2.94	1.33
10. The feedback I get contributes to my growth as a teacher.	3.16	1.29
11. I feel appreciated and respected by my Chair.	3.63	1.17
12. My Chair formally meets with me to set and review professional goals.	2.38	1.21
13. I feel I am listened to and have influence in my department.	3.81	1.13
14. My Chair encourages ongoing teacher collaboration for implementing new programs and practices.	3.44	1.19
15. Our Chair is in touch with faculty and understands their problems.	3.09	1.30
16. I could rely on my Chair to be impartial and just if I had a conflict with a student.	3.59	1.25
17. I have a positive attitude toward my Chair.	3.58	1.23
18. I have a positive attitude toward the administration.	2.92	1.26
Organizational Factors		
Factor Mean (Reliability = .728)	3.19	.50
1. I often feel students put in as much effort as I do.	1.98	1.06
2. I have learning opportunities such as professional development in my subject area.	3.59	1.20
3. I have opportunities to learn new teaching techniques.	3.74	.99
4. I'm teaching motivated students.	3.24	1.17
5. Students are very supportive of me.	4.18	.80
6. There is a good feeling of give and take in our department; it's more like a team with the Chair just facilitating our actions.	2.94	1.34
7. I am certain about my job security.	2.97	1.41
8. Few students in my classes are hostile or disruptive.	3.11	1.32
9. I have adequate everyday resources like overheads.	3.57	1.20
10. I have adequate up-to-date equipment.	2.65	1.33
11. Financial cutbacks have not affected class sizes or workload.	1.52	.76

Table 4.5. *(cont.)*

	Mean	S.D.
12. I have freedom and flexibility, within a structure, over my teaching.	4.28	.78
13. In our college, teachers have a genuine voice (not just lip service) in collegewide decisions.	2.15	1.16
14. There is no gap between the way I do my job and how I would like to do it.	2.68	1.27
15. My students are great; I like them and think most are responsible.	4.17	.83
16. Many students are worthy of my respect.	4.26	.83
Motivational Conditions (Reliability = .888)	4.09	.38
Personal Goals (Reliability = .735)	3.47	.86
1. Our department has a vision and specific department goals.	2.98	1.37
2. The overall direction in my department is compatible and not overly controlling.	3.32	1.26
3. I support the college goals and work toward them.	3.80	.88
4. I support the department goals and work toward them.	3.86	.91
Capacity Beliefs (Reliability = .812)	4.52	.38
1. I feel knowledgeable and capable in my subject specialty.	4.52	.69
2. I know I am doing a good teaching job.	4.40	.67
3. I know that my teaching is helping students succeed.	4.41	.65
4. I feel professional.	4.40	.76
5. What we teach here is worthwhile and of value to students and society.	4.46	.75
6. I care about how I teach and try to be a good teacher.	4.83	.37
7. Student success is important to me.	4.69	.50
8. I am proud to be a teacher.	4.48	.63
9. I am happy to be a (subject) specialist.	4.42	.73
10. I made an appropriate decision in choosing my profession.	4.59	.67
11. It's important to me that students grow and develop intellectually.	4.53	.57
Context Beliefs (Reliability = .806)	3.76	.55
1. Colleagues help me do a good job.	3.80	.94
2. Some colleagues are also friends.	4.16	.80
3. My colleagues sometimes tell me I am doing a good job.	3.89	.86
4. Our program teachers work as a team with friendly collaboration.	3.53	1.15
5. In our program area we collaborate on curriculum development for existing and new courses.	3.79	1.02
6. In our department/program area most teachers just get along and work together.	2.77	1.23
7. In our department we work together on program and course improvements.	3.84	.98
8. I get recognition for doing a good job and this motivates me to achieve more.	3.15	1.24
9. If I have a problem with a course, I know I'll solve it with the help of colleagues.	3.37	1.17

Table 4.5. *(cont.)*

	Mean	S.D.
10. I have many friends in my department.	4.47	.74
11. I really feel I fit in, and don't want to leave this college.	3.96	.99
12. I have a positive attitude toward my colleagues.	4.13	.68
13. I am proud to be working at this college.	4.01	.90
Emotional Arousal Process (Reliability = .716)	4.48	.44
1. Positive feedback from students motivates me to increase my teaching effort.	4.51	.70
2. I am greatly motivated by seeing students learn.	4.68	.51
3. I feel successful when students give me a positive feedback.	4.42	.64
4. When I see *the light bulb go on,* knowing that a student is learning, it excites me.	4.54	.58
5. I enjoy being with students and get along well with them.	4.49	.52
6. Student feedback about how good I am at my job is very important.	4.24	.78
Burnout (Reliability = .784)	3.54	.75
1. I have enough time to prepare for classes thoroughly.	3.18	1.26
2. I don't face insurmountable problems, such as ever-changing course material and new courses.	3.40	1.24
3. I am able to keep up-to-date in my field.	3.76	1.06
4. I do not feel burned out.	3.35	1.34
5. My workload is fair.	3.43	1.29
6. I do not feel a lot of stress because I can keep up-to-date.	3.74	1.13
7. It is not difficult to keep up-to-date in my field of expertise.	3.16	1.25
8. I have a positive attitude toward my job.	4.34	.87

*Cronbach's Alpha

All regression coefficients are significant but range from being weak (between personal factors and burnout, .15), through moderate (leadership to personal factors, .30, and organizational factors to burnout, .44), to strong (leadership to organizational factors, .58). In this model, leadership has a combined direct and indirect effect on burnout of .34, organizational factors of .50, and personal factors of .15.

The model developed to this point explains almost a third of the variation in burnout among community college teachers included in the sample. Although the largest proportion of the variation remains to be explained, the power of this model compares favorably with the small number of other models for which comparable information is available. Surprisingly, only two of the eighteen studies reviewed in the first stage of our research (Brissie, Hoover-Dempsey, and Bassler, 1988; Byrne, 1994a) provided this critical information. Byrne's model explained up to 29 percent of the variation

Table 4.6. Correlation Coefficients for Factors in the Model

	Organizational factors	Personal factors	Personal goals	Capacity beliefs	Context beliefs	Emotional arousal processes	Burnout
Leadership	.58**	.55**	.70**	.17**	.56**	-.06	.26**
Organizational factors		.61**	.56**	.40*	.56**	.04	.53**
Personal factors			.64**	.72**	.89**	.41**	.42**
Personal goals				.23**	.55**	-.05	.25**
Capacity beliefs					.41**	.51**	.37**
Context beliefs						.13**	.40**
Emotional arousal processes							-.01

*p < .05; ** π < .01

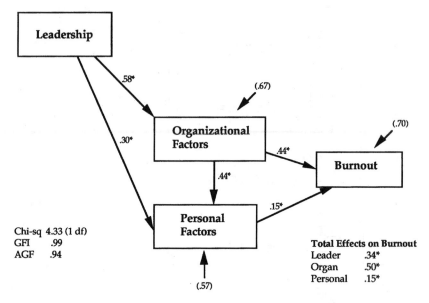

Figure 4.2. First empirical exploration of a model for explaining variation in teacher burnout.

in teacher burnout; the model developed by Brissie et al. explained about 44 percent.

Unlike most other models, ours is limited to potentially alterable factors. It seems reasonable to conclude, then, that teacher burnout is significantly *created by* and *ameliorated through* factors over which those in the school organization have some, or considerable, control; furthermore, this seems largely to be the case whatever personal predispositions teachers bring to their work. For these reasons, the practical significance of future research on teacher burnout seems to depend, to a considerable degree, on developing and testing the explanatory power of models composed of alterable variables, seeking out the most potent of those variables, and inquiring about how best to influence their condition.

The Mediating Role of Personal Factors

Results of testing a more detailed version of the model are presented in Figure 4.3. This model, also a good fit with the data (GFI = .97, AGF = .91, chi-square = 34.95, 9 df), assesses the independent effects of each of the four personal factors on burnout; it also examines the effects of leadership and organizational factors separately on each of these factors.

Of the four personal factors, teachers' context and capacity beliefs are

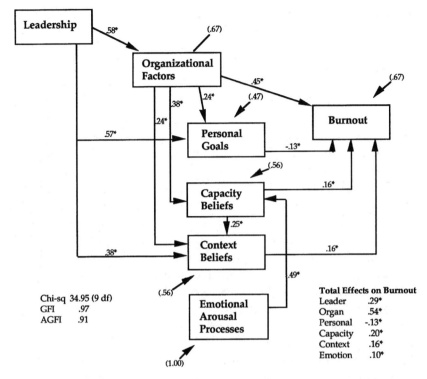

Figure 4.3. Second empirical exploration of a model for explaining variation in teacher burnout.

weakly but significantly and positively related to burnout (coefficients of .16 in each case). Personal goals is related weakly but negatively to burnout (–.13). Capacity beliefs has the largest total effect on burnout (.20) followed by context beliefs (.16) and indirectly through capacity beliefs, emotional arousal processes (.10).

Both leadership and organizational factors have moderate to strong effects on teachers' context beliefs and personal goals with coefficients of .24 for both in the case of organizational factors, and .38 and .57 in the case of leadership factors. Organizational factors also have moderate effects on capacity beliefs (.38) and the largest total effects on burnout (.54).

This evidence is in distinct contrast with Byrne's findings. In summing up the most consequential aspects of her study, she argued for the prominence of personal factors, in particular self-esteem, which acts as "a critical and controlling factor in the predisposition of teachers to burnout" and which "functions as an essential mediator variable through which the effects of environment-based organizational factors filter" (1994, p. 567). As

Figures 4.2 and 4.3 indicate, personal factors in our model lag behind both leadership and organizational factors in their total effects on teacher burnout.

It is tempting to explain away these differences as, for example, a function of the two samples: K-12 teachers in Byrne's study and community college teachers in ours. There is some justification for this explanation, but it ignores an important conceptual issue largely unaddressed by models of burnout other than our own and Byrne's. This is the constructed nature of both leadership and organizational factors. It is not the objective condition of such factors that influences burnout. It is the teacher's personal judgement of those conditions. So the same objective school structures, for example, may be interpreted by one teacher as overly rigid, thereby reducing choices for action and contributing to stress. Another colleague will view the same structures as providing the clarity and discretion needed to respond comfortably to the challenges of the job.

If teacher burnout depends on such a constructed reality, as surely it must, then models of burnout ought always to locate personal factors as mediators of the external environment, however that environment is construed. This means that, in the case of our own work, the model arising from our review of the literature (Figure 4.1) is correct in its assertion about the place of personal factors. Our LISREL-influenced models (Figures 4.2 and 4.3) may be telling us that the specific factors we conceptualized as organizational factors in this study might better be conceptualized as an extended set of context beliefs. This line of reasoning ought to be tested in subsequent research.

The Underestimated Effect of Leadership on Teacher Burnout

The total effects of leadership on burnout were .29 in our empirical study, considerably more than personal factors and substantially less than organizational factors. These are effects of leadership, largely realized through organizational factors. In direct opposition to claims arising from Byrne's (1994a) study, for example, this evidence further fuels our suspicion that prior research has underestimated leadership as a factor in the creation and amelioration of teacher burnout, likely because of inadequate conceptualization and measurement. Our results, however, are the outcome not just of measuring aspects of leadership derived from any coherent view but of using a transformational conception demonstrated, through previous inquiry, to have influence on most of the personal and organizational factors included in the model explaining burnout (Leithwood, 1994; Leithwood, Tomlinson, and Genge, in press).

The significant effects on teacher burnout suggested by our data still seem likely to underestimate the power of leadership, however, because of our inability to construct, from the available data set, adequate measures of each of the dimensions of transformational leadership. Instead, a single scale was constructed to represent such leadership, one largely composed of individual survey items reflecting each of the dimensions of transformational leadership. This means, for example that the one dimension most frequently identified in prior research as strongly related to burnout, *individualized consideration*, had little influence on the explanatory power of the leadership construct in our burnout model. Subsequent research should include robust measures of all dimensions of transformational leadership, as well as testing the relative contribution of leadership practices identified in qualitative studies such as those reported by Blase and his colleagues (1984, 1986). And to be consistent with our earlier argument about the constructed nature of organizational factors, subsequent research should more precisely define leadership variables as "perceptions of leadership" on the part of teachers. A modest-size literature describes how such perceptions are formed (e.g., Jantzi and Leithwood, 1995).

Conclusion

This chapter began with a worry about the fate of significant and potentially useful efforts at school improvement, efforts often given the label "restructuring." Although initiatives traveling under this label are quite diverse, typically they share in common an implicit expectation that teacher-implementors are prepared to develop new capacities and will be committed to making the often poorly specified restructuring initiatives work in real schools and classrooms. Clearly, teachers who are already burned out are unlikely candidates for such a challenge. And the conditions created by restructuring initiatives can exacerbate tendencies toward becoming burned out.

In response to this worry, we attempt to understand better the alterable conditions giving rise to or ameliorating teacher burnout, especially the influence of leadership This was done, as a first stage, by reviewing a selected body of empirical studies in which leadership was explicitly included among a larger set of independent variables. A tentative model for explaining variation in teacher burnout was the principal outcome of this first stage. Included in the model were three independent constructs: personal factors, leadership, and organizational factors. We refined the model in a second stage of our work, by examining the contribution of these constructs to teacher burnout using a secondary analysis of data originally collected for another, related purpose. Results of this stage indicated significant direct and indirect effects of the independent constructs on teacher burnout.

In conclusion, we return to each of the independent constructs in the model. After briefly reiterating how each was conceptualized and measured, we initiate what will need to be a much more elaborate consideration of the model's theoretical relationships with one or more of Maslach and Jackson's (1981) three dimensions of burnout: *emotional exhaustion, depersonalization, reduced sense of personal accomplishment.* Then we point to some promising directions for future research.

Personal Factors

Of the three independent constructs in the model, two have strong conceptual roots. One of them, *personal factors*, is defined by four variables that together offer a compelling account of human commitment and motivation (Bandura, 1986; Ford, 1992). These variables, including personal goals, capacity beliefs, context beliefs, and emotional arousal processes, further our understanding of burnout as a psychological state created by teachers most directly through their choice of features in their environments to notice and their evaluations of those features.

According to this conception of personal factors, the chances of *depersonalization* theoretically are increased – for example, as teachers assess the goals of their organizations and find them to be incompatible with their personal professional goals. When teachers judge as inadequate their own capacities to respond to the challenges they face, they are likely to experience a reduced sense of *personal accomplishment;* this also may result if teachers believe that the support available to them from other members of their organization (context beliefs) is less than they need. And when teachers find little in their day-to-day work to stimulate their excitement and enthusiasm (emotional arousal processes), the chances of experiencing *emotional exhaustion* may increase.

Evidence provided by the empirical portion of the present study offered significant but weak support for these theoretically plausible relationships. One limitation of that evidence was its treatment of burnout, for measurement purposes, as a unidimensional phenomenon. This limits our ability to understand the extent to which the four separate variables defining the personal factors construct have varying effects on separate dimensions of burnout. A promising follow-up to the present study, then, would be research that incorporates into its design the measurement of all three dimensions of burnout and the examination of the contribution of each of the four personal factors variables.

Leadership

The *leadership* construct is defined by a coherent pattern of practices intended to transform both the capacities and commitments of organizational members coming into contact with them. Shamir, House, and Arthur (cited in Shamir, 1991) argue that

> [transformational] leaders increase the intrinsic value of effort and goals by linking them to valued aspects of the followers' self-concept, thus harnessing the motivational forces of self-expression, self-consistency, specific mission-related self-efficacy, generalized self-esteem, and self-worth. (p. 92)

A reduced sense of *personal accomplishment* seems an especially likely outcome of, for example, transformational leadership practices that assist members in clarifying their collective goals. In the absence of such clarity, it is easy to imagine teachers having difficulty in evaluating their own progress, becoming discouraged by the continual debate about just what goals schools ought to achieve, and becoming uncertain about the value of those goals they have chosen individually to pursue. As another example, leaders' efforts to provide feedback to teachers about their work and to reward them for successful practices and for taking the risks associated with efforts to improve their practices also seem likely to enhance teachers' sense of personal accomplishment. Such contingent rewards may ameliorate a lowered sense of personal accomplishment by reducing the uncertainties teachers frequently have about the relative merit of their work, due partly to the typical isolation of that work from the scrutiny of other adults (Hargreaves and Macmillan, 1995).

Transformational leadership practices, as these examples suggest, theoretically ought to have a potentially powerful ameliorating effect on teacher burnout by enhancing teachers' sense of personal accomplishment. The significant indirect effect of leadership on teachers' capacity beliefs in the present study provides modest empirical support for this potential. Similarly, Hipp and Bredeson (1995) report significant correlations between several dimensions of transformational leadership and teachers' self-efficacy.

In contrast, the theoretical effects of "holding high performance expectations," a leadership dimension often included in transformational models, may be to exacerbate teachers' sense of *emotional exhaustion*. However, this is likely to be contingent on, for example, the situation in which those practices are experienced and the state of teachers' existing expectations for themselves. Future research would do well to assess the contribution to variation in teacher burnout of the separate dimensions of transformational (or other) leadership practices. Their effects may be very different.

Organizational Factors

Specific variables defining the *organizational factors* construct in our model, unlike the other two independent constructs, were not based on any coherent theory. However, in light of evidence indicating that the total effects of this construct on teacher burnout were almost twice as strong as the effects of other constructs, this is a part of the explanation of variation in teacher burnout critically in need of further work.

The practical question to be addressed by such work concerns organizational designs that minimize members' chances of experiencing burnout. Furthermore, it seems reasonable to assume that reduced probability of burnout will be a by-product of working in organizations that clearly value, make direct use of, and provide many opportunities for the further development of their members' capacities and to their commitments to the collectively held goals of the organization. Such organizations are designed to increase members' sense of personal accomplishment by providing them with opportunities to become increasingly competent at what they do. By specifically developing both collective and public commitments through, for example, shared decision-making structures, such organizations also encourage personal investment in the work and success of the organization (Duke, 1994), the antithesis of *depersonalization*.

Is there an existing organizational design that meets these criteria? We believe that conceptualizing schools as "learning organizations" holds considerable promise, although this perspective could not be explored empirically with the data available for this study. A learning organization may be defined as

> a group of people pursuing common purposes (and individual purposes, as well) with a collective commitment to regularly weighing the value of those purposes, modifying them when that makes sense, and continuously developing more effective and efficient ways of accomplishing those purposes. (Leithwood and Aitken, 1995, p. 41)

Organizational learning (OL) has been defined as "the process of improving actions through better knowledge and understanding" (Fiol and Lyles, 1985, p. 803).

As yet, research evidence directly useful in identifying the conditions that give rise to organizational learning in schools is quite limited, although much has been written about other types of organizations from this perspective (e.g., Senge, 1990; Watkins and Marsick, 1993). We draw on the results of our own recent inquiry, however, to illustrate the nature of these conditions (Leithwood and Aitken, 1995; Leithwood, Jantzi, and Steinbach, 1995). In this work, conditions influencing organizational learning in the school (aside from leadership) have been associated with five aspects of the school's design, including its visions and mission, culture, structure, strategies for improvement, and policies and resources.

School *vision and mission* are associated with organizational learning when they are clear, accessible, and widely shared by staff. To have this association, a school's vision has to be perceived by teachers as meaningful; it also has to be pervasive in conversations and decision making throughout the school. These conditions have the potential to enhance teachers' sense of personal accomplishment.

School *cultures* foster learning when they are collaborative and collegial. Norms of mutual support among teachers, respect for colleagues' ideas, and a willingness to take risks in attempting new practices are all aspects of culture that teachers associate with their own learning. Some teachers indicate that receiving honest, candid feedback from their colleagues is an important factor in their learning. Teachers' commitments to their own learning appear to be reinforced by shared celebrations of successes by staff and a strong focus on the needs of all students. Collaborative and collegial cultures result in informal sharing of ideas and materials among teachers that foster organizational learning, especially when continuous professional growth is a widely shared norm among staff. *Depersonalization* seems unlikely in the context of these conditions. These conditions also provide the social support that helps reduce teachers' *emotional exhaustion*.

School *structures* supporting professional learning are those that allow for greater participation in decision making by teachers. Such structures include brief weekly planning meetings, frequent and often informal problem-solving sessions, regularly scheduled professional development time in school, and common preparation periods for teachers who need to work together. Other structures also associated with learning are the cross-department appointment of teachers and team teaching. When decisions are made by staff through consensus, something easier to do in smaller schools, more learning appears to occur. The physical space of schools has some bearing on teachers' learning when it either encourages or discourages closer physical proximity of staff. Such structures are likely to have indirect effects on teacher burnout through, for example, their contribution to the development of shared cultures.

Clarifying short-term goals for improvement and establishing personal, professional growth goals are school *strategies* that aid teachers' learning. This learning is further assisted when school goals and priorities are kept current through periodic review and revision and when there are well-designed processes for implementing those specific program initiatives designed to accomplish such goals and priorities. Schools foster organizational learning when they are able to establish a restricted, manageable number of priorities for action and when there is follow-through on plans for such action. These conditions ought to enhance the chances that teachers will experience a strong sense of personal accomplishment.

Sufficient *resources* to support essential professional development in aid of teachers' initiatives is a decided boost to their learning. Within their own schools, teachers use colleagues as professional development resources, along with professional libraries and any professional readings that are circulated among staff. Access to rich curriculum resources and to computer facilities help teachers' learning, as does access to technical assistance (consultants, etc.) for implementing new practices. Access to community facilities also can help teachers learn. Through their influence on teachers' context beliefs, these conditions seem likely to increase opportunities for teachers to experience a sense of personal accomplishment. Insufficient resources also may lead to a sense of frustration, thereby contributing to emotional exhaustion.

Further research will undoubtedly add to and refine this set of conditions, but purpose for summarizing them here is to illustrate the type of organization we think would likely minimize the burnout of its members by *design*. A promising direction for future research, then, would be to define the *organizational factors* construct in our model in terms of conditions influencing organizational learning and empirically inquire about their individual and collective effects on teacher burnout.

The constructs in our model offer complementary perspectives on the explanation of burnout. In each case, the constructs have been defined by variables that assume the prevention of burnout depends on teachers being and perceiving themselves to be increasingly successful at their work. This in turn breeds commitment and increases the likelihood that useful school restructuring initiatives will receive the treatment they deserve.

5. Intensification and Stress in Teaching

PETER WOODS

A Sociological Perspective on Teacher Stress

Teaching is generally reported to be a very stressful occupation (Borg and Riding, 1991b; Borg, Riding, and Falzon, 1991; Galloway, Panckhurst, Boswell, Boswell, and Green, 1987; Kyriacou and Sutcliffe, 1977b, 1978a, 1979; Laughlin, 1984; Solman and Feld, 1989). In recent years, in some parts of the world at least, the problem seems to have grown worse (Manthei and Gilmore, 1994). This fact in itself suggests, as Durkheim (1970) showed with regard to suicide, that stress is as much a social and historical issue as it is a psychological one. It is, in short, a multilevel and multidimensional phenomenon, requiring a number of theories of different kinds for full comprehension rather than one all-embracing theory or model. In this chapter, I examine some of the sociological factors behind the increases at micro, meso, and macro levels. The micro refers to social factors within the teacher's biography and person; the meso is related to institutional and other middle-range factors; the macro deals with wider forces deriving from global trends and government policy. The interaction between the three is the field on which teacher experiences are played out.

To study this interaction, I bring together two approaches that I believe have particular relevance: interactionism and some recent formulations about "deprofessionalization" and "intensification" of teachers' work derived from theories of the labor process. The latter provide a view of how recent macro developments bear on stress, the former on how they are actually experienced by teachers, and how we might conceptualize those experiences. I begin from a view of stress that sees its immediate cause in many cases as

the maladjustment of two or more factors that normally might be

For their helpful comments on a previous draft of this chapter, I am grateful to Michael Huberman, Roland Vandenberghe, Nick Hubbard, Bob Jeffrey, and Geoff Troman.

expected to work in harmony. It is not just pressures, therefore, which some teachers might actually need in order to function; nor problems, which are a necessary part of a professional's job. An alternative view is of the "ordinary" course of events as one exhibiting a dominant climate of harmony among a number of key variables, such as teacher and pupil interests; government, local and school policy; school climate; the demands made on teachers; the resources to meet them, and the rewards to be gained from meeting them. A potentially stressful situation is set up when a teacher's personal interests, commitment or resources not only get out of line with one or more of the other factors, but actually pull against them. The classic case is having too much work, plus a strong moral imperative to do it, and not enough time and energy within which to do it. A variant on this basic theme is being pressed to do more work, given fewer resources with which to do it, and then receiving no reward or recognition, and worse, perhaps censure, when it is nonetheless accomplished. An everyday nightmare teachers face is losing at the last minute a restorative free period and being asked to take a difficult class for an absent colleague. In all of these instances there are elements grating against each other. (Woods, 1989a, p. 84)

As a teacher told Gerald Haigh (1995, p. 3), "You have to believe, in this business, that you are making things better and moving things on. If that particular spark is not there – if something happens that makes you think things are going the opposite way – it can be a very destroying occupation."

The incidence of such disjunctures is likely to rise during the "intensification" of teachers' work. Intensification is a worldwide development affecting all professionals, as several other chapters in this volume attest. The theory of intensification (Apple, 1986, 1988) derives from Larson's (1980) discussion of the proletarianization of educated labor. The argument is that as advanced capitalist economies seek to maintain and promote efficiency, the sphere of work narrows, high-level tasks become routinized, and there is more subservience to the bureaucratic whole. In the classroom there is more for teachers to do, including a proliferation of administrative and assessment tasks. There is less time to do it in, less time for re-skilling and for leisure and sociability, and few opportunities for creative work. There is a diversification of responsibility, notably with a high level of specification and direction, and a separation of conceptualization in long-term planning and policy making (others) and of execution (teachers). There is a reduction in quality of service as corners are cut to cover the ground. According to this view, teachers have little or no choice but to carry out the dictates of others. In this mode, they are technicians rather than professionals (Schön, 1983). They have become de-professionalized and de-skilled as their work has become increasingly intensified. The economic depression of the late 1980s and early 1990s brought on crises of accumulation and legitimation that gave an emphatic boost to these developments (Apple, 1988). Technical control processes impinged further on the curriculum. Centralization, standardization, and rationalization became the norm in policy circles. By 1992, there were some areas in the United States where "it has been mandated that teachers must teach *only* that material which is in the approved text book" (Apple and Jungck, 1992, p. 20).

Clearly, this is not a single, all-inclusive, deterministic development. There are contrary tendencies occurring at the same time leading to enhanced professionalism, such as the "action research" and "teacher-researcher" movements (Carr and Kemmis, 1986; Elliot, 1991; A. Hargreaves, 1994; Stenhouse, 1975, 1985; Woods, 1989b). Fullan (1991, p. 16) acknowledges the influence of intensification, but also notes the countervailing force of what he calls "restructuring," which

> usually involves school-based management; enhanced roles for teachers in instruction and decision-making; integration of multiple innovations; restructured timetables supporting collaborative work cultures; radical reorganization of teacher education; new roles such as mentors, coaches, and other teacher leader arrangements; and revamping and developing the shared mission and goals of the school among teachers, administrators, the community and students.

There is also, usually, a considerable gap between macro trend and micro practice, allowing room for negotiation and adaptation (Ball and Bowe, 1992). I therefore consider some successful adaptations to intensification before going on to examine less successful cases, in the process trying to identify some of the conditions that apply.

I have taken England and Wales as a case study in these developments. Elsewhere, of course, experiences may have been different, though again, evidence from other chapters in this volume indicate similarities with a number of other countries. But I would argue that the English/Welsh experience has much to tell us about stress in general and may suggest theoretical and conceptual constructions that have common currency. They are a critical case, for there has been a rapid rise here in the incidence of stress and burnout in recent years. Using the reason of poor health, 5,549 teachers under the age of 60 retired in 1993–1994, compared with 2,551 in 1987–1988 (Macleod and Meikle, 1994) – more than a 50 percent increase. Furthermore, the situation appears to be getting worse. In the first three months of 1995, 2,000 applications were made for early retirement on health grounds, twice as many as for the same period in 1994. This figure, of course, does not include those who chose to retire early for other reasons (which may have included a measure of ill-health or anticipation of it) or those who remain in teaching but earnestly wish to leave. In a survey of 430 schools in ten local authority areas, Smithers (1989) found a deeply discontented profession, with one in three teachers feeling "trapped," and wishing to "escape." The late 1980s and early 1990s saw the phenomenon of "escape committees" – groups set up unofficially or officially with union sponsorship to help teachers "escape" the profession. The situation is even worse for headteachers. The National Association of Headteachers says four out of five heads are opting for early retirement and that its officers are dealing with enquiries from members who feel burned out in their forties (Fisher, 1995). Further, there is evidence that teachers in some respects have been worse off than other professions at risk. Travers and Cooper (1993), for example, report that

Teachers, as compared with other highly stressed occupational groups, experienced lower job satisfaction and poorer mental health. . . . Teachers were found to be reporting stress-related manifestations that were far higher than . . . other comparable occupational groups.

The increase dates from the Education Reform Act of 1988, which introduced a National Curriculum for the first time, new forms of standardized assessment, a restructuring of schools on a major scale. Evidence is easily found from research done on the effects of the National Curriculum in English primary schools to support the intensification thesis. What for some was "a dream at conception" turned into a "nightmare at delivery" (Campbell, 1993). Clearly there has been massive work overload, a loss of spontaneity, and an increase in stress; the sense of "fun" and caring human relationships have receded in some classrooms; quantification has replaced qualitative evaluation; bureaucracy has burgeoned; some teachers feel that they have lost autonomy and control in the curriculum; and accountability has become a matter of threat (Campbell, Evans, Neill, and Packwood, 1991a; Campbell and Neill, 1990; Osborn and Broadfoot, 1992; Pollard, 1991, 1994; Pollard, Broadfoot, Croll, Osborn, and Abbott, 1994). Teachers fear further intrusion into pedagogy (see, for example, Dadds, 1992; Drummond, 1991). The new inspection system, set up in 1992, seemed to some to represent an attempt by the government to police the system and to set up a kind of Foucauldian surveillance, thus reducing the traditional degree of negotiability in the implementation of policy (Ball, 1994). Some argue that the way teachers think and feel has also been exploited. They have been caught in the "trap of conscientiousness" (Campbell, Evans, Neill, and Packwood, 1991b), doing their best to meet the prescribed targets but compromising the quality of learning and their own health. Their inability to meet them all aggravates the "guilt syndrome" (Hargreaves and Tucker, 1991). If they do manage to meet them and celebrate their accomplishment, this may only be "misrecognized professionalism" (Apple, 1988; Densmore, 1987). That is to say that teachers may feel more professional through mastering the range of technical criteria and tests accompanying the changes, whereas in reality this skill is yet another example of "the administrative colonization of teachers' time and space" (Hargreaves, 1990, p. 318).

Possibly, however, this may be only a passing phase of a wider event. What has been happening in the English and Welsh educational system in recent years may be a status passage (Glaser and Strauss, 1971). Status passages as events have their own stress-producing aspects. Van Gennep (1960) conceived of three main stages of status passages: separation, transition, and reincorporation. The legislation of the later 1980s and early 1990s sought to "separate" the system from that of the 1944 Education Act and of the hugely influential Plowden Report of 1967 – a system characterized by partnership in control, professional autonomy, equality, and child-centered teaching methods. The new system, guided by the "market" philosophy of the Thatcher administrations, saw an increase in centralization and government control, an emphasis on the consumers and "parent choice," heightened teacher accountability, a prescribed National Curriculum and standardized national assessment, a drive for more traditional teaching methods, and a growth of managerialism. The system is still in the "transitional" phase, one that Turner (1969) argues is typically characterized by "marginality" or "liminality." One is "neither here nor there, but in-between" (p. 95). There can be much confusion; fear of the unknown; nostalgic hangings-on to the past; much experimentation, some leading to false trails. There is a sense of rapid, uncontrollable change, in itself a major stress inducer, involving "change-on-change beyond the control of most teachers" (Cox, Boot, Cox, and Hanson, 1988), leading to "innovation fatigue." In status passages attended by politics, as in education, there will be an aura of conflict and struggle. In short, the transition phase can induce anomie, a situation in which "the rules and standards by which an individual is accustomed to live are rendered irrelevant by changing circumstances" (Worsley, 1977, p. 484). A teacher with some thirty years' experience provides an example of personal experience of anomie:

One of the main reasons I threw in the towel (i.e., resigned) was that the job was no longer the one for which I had trained and which I had enjoyed. When the praise changes almost overnight to criticism, when you are told that what you are doing and *know* works is all wrong, but are not told how or why or even given any hints as to how you should improve, demoralization swiftly follows. I was no longer convinced, as I had been up to about 1985, that I knew what I was doing, that I was doing it well, and that the children were benefiting. (Hawes, 1995)

How long does a liminal phase last? This is difficult to say. There is some evidence (for example, Osborn, 1995) that teachers are gradually adjusting to the changes, a trend assisted to some extent by the steady departure of dissatisfied teachers and the arrival of new recruits trained in the new system. Others (for example, Campbell and Neill, 1994a) feel that some features, such as a long working week, have now become the norm. In any event, not all teachers are experiencing stress. Many are coping, with varying degrees of success. Some continue to enjoy and find fulfilment in their work (Pollard et al., 1994). I consider first, therefore, as a comparative base, some features of "accommodation" – that is, successful adaptation to the changes – before going on to some prominent features of nonaccommodation – the seedbed of stress and burnout.

Accommodation

Four major kinds of accommodation were revealed in our research. They are contestation, appropriation, strategic action, and re-alignment.

Contestation

In contestation, teachers resist the changes. This involves active opposition to some significant part of requirements. It induces strong feelings, with a heartfelt desire to reverse the requirement. There is a marked tone of defiance, fight, and struggle. The struggle is likely to be keen and lengthy – the school is unable to "appropriate" or "incorporate" the changes in question in any large measure for the moment, but it does have certain resources to keep it going. The resistance has substance and is not merely "noise." Such resistance is not total. There may be equally strong support for other changes. However, the mood is a prevailing one and the resistance is motivated by strong principles, which are consistent through both opposition and support. In one multiethnic primary school, the resistance was not addressed to the idea of a National Curriculum as such. Parts of it met with the teachers' approval, though, like most other teachers, they felt there was too much of it, it was subject to too rapid change, and it was inappropriately assessed (Pollard, 1992, pp. 111–112). Rather, their objection had to do with which children had access to it. The rationale for their support of such a curriculum was that all children were "entitled" to certain basic provision, but in the 1988 National Curriculum, they felt that some were "more entitled" than others. They saw it as ethnocentric and monolingual, with young learners who spoke English as a second language at a considerable disadvantage. The curriculum therefore directly contravened the values that were at the heart of their teaching and provided their strongest motivation. Resistance took the form of re-articulation of the philosophy and principles on which their teaching was based. Even so, while there was a spirit of fight and even, on occasions, a triumph, at bottom they felt their position was precarious (see Woods, 1995). In itself, resistance is not sufficient. It has to lead to something of substance.

In other research (Woods and Jeffrey, 1996), we have noticed some teachers developing a new professional discourse in reaction to the managerialist, technicist discourse permeating the new system. They legitimated and reaffirmed their own preferred, child-centered teaching approach by extolling its virtues, reviewing evidence of its successes, and comparing unfavorably the new objectives-type model with their own reliance on process. They used a number of strategies to cope with the attempted "colonization" of their time and space (Hargreaves, 1990), such as morally undermining the demands made on them and using a range of resources (such as students) to help secure their ends. They redefined "accountability" – one of the key symbolic concepts of the managerialist discourse – by labeling the new imperative "heavy duty accountability" and attacking the credentials of those to whom they were accounting while restating their view based on their own notions of professionalism. They also articulated solutions – ways they had found of reaching a happy medium, or striking a balance between the new demands and their own aspirations. Here also, however, despite mental clarity, there was considerable emotional confusion, marked by loss of confidence and feelings of guilt. The sense of guilt derived from a profound feeling of moral and social responsibility. In consequence, teachers were beset by a number of tensions that were almost impossible to resolve. For example, one felt that she could still teach in the style she wished, but "you feel guilty about doing it, because you feel that you're not doing the other things that you should be doing." If you do those, however, "it's eroding what children want to do, what they enjoy, how they learn through their experiences." This is a classic stress syndrome, for "it's like you're being pulled in different directions."

Appropriation

Successful contestation leads to appropriation. Another school in my research – Coombes – had successfully appropriated the National Curriculum into their own preferred approach, though not without difficulty. This school had won several awards for the development of its grounds, which serve as an integrating force for the curriculum. Against their instincts they had felt the need to engage in politics of their own, notably in forming alliances – with parents, governors, the local community, and local inspectors. In so doing, they had formed their own power base. It is possible to have "weak" and "strong" appropriations. In the former, there might be misrecognition of some of the signals as discussed earlier. Appropriation is strong where the curricular adaptation is genuine and where the school ethos is reinforced, not modified. With regard to the curriculum, Bernstein (1975) has argued that a collection-code curriculum (consisting of compartmentalized contents, as in the National Curriculum) cannot be reconciled with an integrated curriculum (as at Coombes), as the two reflect basic societal differences in the distribution of power and principles of social control. However, the control situation is not entirely clear-cut. Although the government has increased its powers in recent years at the expense of all other participants in education, there are still sites of struggle, of which the school is one. The continuous refinements to the National Curriculum since inception are testimony to the effectiveness of opposition. The situation is, therefore, unstable. Bernstein argues that if an integrated code is to be accomplished, there must be "some relational idea," consensus about it, a clear connection between the idea and the knowledge to be coordinated, and probably multiple criteria of assessment (p. 109). Coombes meets these terms, exploiting the current instability around their relational idea of the environment, which is "far more than just a combination of programmes of study extracted from science and geography. It also encompasses moral, cultural, spiritual, political, aesthetic and emotional dimensions. It touches on all aspects of our lives" (Wheatley, 1992, p. 30).

As for the ethos, Coombes is generating a focus of power from below, that involves a notion of "power with" rather than "power over" (Kreisberg, 1992). This is a strength based on "relationships of co-operation, mutual support and equity" (Bloome and Willett, 1991, p. 208). Foucault (1980) has argued that power is a force that "produces things, induces pleasure, forms knowledge, produces discourse" (p. 119). In a case such as Coombes, the seat of power is the school ethos, established, compelling, legitimated, and permeating every moment of the day. Individuals draw from it to sustain and develop themselves; they also contribute to it, thus consolidating and developing its power. Power is enforced through discourse – through the new articulation, and through continual reminders such as, "That's what it's all about." It would be a mistake to underestimate the power of the state or to deny that in some respects teachers' work *has* become intensified. The collective resistance of teachers throughout the profession is required if the general structures and policies are to be changed or modified. It was such resistance that led to the concessions made by the government following the Dearing review (1994). Into the spaces opened up by collective action, individual schools such as Coombes can work to develop their own power base and make their own appropriations.

Even so, however, some who are attempting to do just that are balancing on a knife edge. An example is a lower-school headteacher in our research whom we described as a "composite head" (Boyle and Woods, 1995). She has developed her own form of leadership in the face of the changes. In contrast to many accounts of headteachers, which report their practice in the form of typologies or bimodal polarities (for example, as "leading professional" or "managerial executive"), we report a headteacher who has made a comprehensive, multivaried role for herself, despite conflicting elements within it, which reaches across the standard dimensions. This was her way of meeting statutory requirements and staying true to her own beliefs. The chief characteristic of her role is a universalism, evidenced in her self-expression through teaching and her omniscience, orchestration, omnipresence, and controlled collaboration with her staff. She accomplishes this difficult task through objectifying the problems, taking time out, using "resistance humour," and with the aid of a number of personal qualities, including her love of her job and of her children, her stance as a "professional mother," and her motivation through feelings of guilt. The role of the headteacher is seen to be complex, full of conflicts and contrasts, and irreducible to a polarized position. Rather, there is adaptation to particular circumstances that produces a composite form of leadership. This may be seen as a form of successful appropriation, but throughout the interviews in which she recounted this to us, she punctuated her comments with "It's hard . . . it's very hard."

Strategic Action

When teachers are under pressure, they may resort to coping strategies (Hargreaves, 1978; Pollard, 1982). At one extreme, teachers employ survival strategies in which survival (getting through the day, week, term, year, with mental and physical health intact) becomes the main aim, rather than teaching the children. Various survival strategies have been noted in schools in difficult circumstances, including negotiation, fraternization, ritual and routine, absence or withdrawal, and occupational therapy (Woods, 1979). Some teachers may be marking time, waiting for the liminality to pass, a kind of strategic compliance (Lacey, 1977), going along with things for the time being but hoping they will soon change; other are moonlighting – directing the best of their energies and creativity elsewhere, simply holding down their teaching post for instrumental reasons, or undertaking "parallel careers" (Nias, 1989). Still others may "personally adjust" (Becker, 1977) – that is, alter their own values, beliefs, and actions to align with the changes, persuading themselves that the changes are for the best.

Realignment

If personal adjustment happens on a large scale, there may be a system-wide realignment. In other words, if the reforms are successful in ushering in a new technical-rationalist age in education, many teachers will become little more than technicians, operating a prescribed National Curriculum in stipulated ways, their work closely monitored by the national inspectorate. Others will become "managers," working the system to good effect and deriving considerable intrinsic rewards from their endeavors. Such a system, with such compliance, is almost proof against stress and burnout. Put another way, if "official" definitions of "good teaching" prevail – and these invariably put the emphasis on "personal qualities" – securing an effective teaching force is a matter of selection, training, and, if necessary, screening out. There is no room for stress in such a scenario for teachers are kept within the government tramlines (see Troman, 1996).

    Although these have been presented as ways of avoiding stress, the first two involve considerable risk and the second two are not available to teachers with firm convictions that run counter to the prescribed changes. The next section explores in more detail the factors that, for many teachers, make accommodation difficult.

Nonaccommodation

There are personal and situational factors behind the growing incidence of teacher stress and burnout, given the background of intensification and the government policy of marketization.

Personal Factors

Commitment. Not all teachers are equally committed to teaching nor in the same way. We have identified vocational, professional, instrumental, and political forms of commitment (Sikes, Measor, and Woods, 1985). Teachers may have some or all of these to varying degrees. I would argue that teachers at most risk of stress are those with strong feelings of vocation, those who care strongly about their work and their students (see also Rudow, this volume). For these, the personal "self" is inextricably bound up with the teacher role. They cannot switch off at the end of the school day to another life and another persona. Teaching is an essential part of their identity (Nias, 1989). So much is this the case that if suddenly deprived of opportunities to exercise their preferred mode of teaching, they may experience a form of "grieving for a lost self" (Nias, 1993b). These teachers may be very self-determined and expert at self-renewal, but for highly committed teachers, selves can be easily "ruined" (Woods, 1995). This is because they "cannot help but get their sense of personal worth mixed up with their professional competence" (Haigh, 1995, p. 3). Coping strategies and personal adjustment are not on their agendas. They continue to strive after perfection, following their own self-imposed demands in circumstances where others are making contrary demands (Osborn and Broadfoot, 1992). Consequently, they are easily damaged (Radnor, cited in Haigh, 1995, p. 3). A teacher comments:

> You lay yourself bare. You are not thinking of protecting yourself, because that's counterproductive – every fibre is going for the progress of the child, and that makes you vulnerable so that the slightest flick hurts so much. (p. 4)

Haigh quotes another example of a teacher who was the subject of a parental complaint, which was later shown to be unjustified. What was important was "the devastating effect it had on him, not just as a teacher, but as a person with a private life and a set of emotions" (p. 3). The teacher said afterward, "I now doubt my ability right across the board. I dread each day. I'm left with a legacy of low self-esteem. They've stolen a period of my life, and I feel terribly hurt by that."

A teacher in our research illustrates again the wholesale emotional commitment some make to their work, leaving no room for political infighting:

> You just come in and do it and go, don't you? It still seems quite interesting that before not too long I will have spent twenty five years in teaching and it just seems ludicrous that one's burning so hard and so bright after twenty five years. After twenty five years one should

be honed and it should be skilled and effortless as if you were watching a kind of blacksmith after twenty five years or you were watching a potter after twenty five years. They wouldn't be putting such strain on their heart or such emotional strain into what's happening. I mean it's almost like sulphur burning, isn't it? It's frightening and it's getting more difficult and we're giving more to children. I don't think the way that I teach is physically or emotionally the easiest way to do it. I don't think it is the most cost effective way of doing it. (Woods and Jeffrey, 1996, p. 30)

Another skilled, successful teacher would welcome a little more praise for things well done and less blame for things that lie outside teachers' control:

Stress is not merely the effect of working hard. Many people, myself included, have worked many hours a day for many years. Stress is caused by feeling bad about oneself and constantly being made aware of one's inadequacy even though one is actually quite good at the job. (Richardson, 1995, p. 67)

Career and Role. Teaching used to be a secure job – a job for life. That used to be one of its attractions, a benefit to set against the relatively poor material rewards. This is no longer the case. There has been what one ex-teacher describes as an "explosion of insecurity." A series of budget reductions in recent years has led to a large number of redeployments and redundancies (and a concomitant growth in class size and use of teaching assistants) to add to the early retirements. Just as selves can be ruined, careers can be "spoiled" (Goffman, 1968). There is, or used to be, a career structure, with a notional idea of progression for aspiring teachers. For many, this provides a framework for their working lives. It becomes part of their present and future selves. At any particular time, the career structure presents opportunities for some, frustration for others. A generation ago, a teacher might expect to progress through various positions of responsibility to, perhaps, a middle or senior management post. There were never enough of these posts to go around among the aspirants, and "mid-life crises" around the age of forty were not uncommon (Sikes et al., 1985). This is not to say that these posts were not demanding but that in the way of things in bureaucratic organizations, status carried its own in-built protection to some extent. Now, however, status is not enough, and these posts, which used to attract hundreds of applicants, are not wanted. Readvertisements are running at a high level (Smithers, 1989). The top of the career structure has evidently become blocked off even for many of those who formerly might have expected advancement. Bell (1995, p. 11) comments that some teachers now feel that they are so bruised by constant changes which have to be implemented at a speed, allowing no time for reflection, that they have probably lost their sensitivity to the processes of re-creation. A worrying number make it clear they no longer wish to be promoted.

This is not so much a matter of salaries as conditions. As Fisher (1995, p. 12) reports:

Many teachers are less than anxious to leave their classroom to occupy a power vacuum. Deputies who might once have considered themselves automatic promotion prospects withdraw from the fray. They say they're put off by money as well as stress. 'The difference in salary wouldn't keep me in Paracetamol I'd need', says one deputy who will avoid the headaches of ambition. 'Why should I take on all that aggravation for 10% more money? . . . I've looked at a lot of heads and I don't want to end up like them'.

Those in such positions become subject to feelings of inappropriateness and/or inadequacy as the nature and demands of the job have changed. The headteacher's role in particular has changed radically from that of "leading professional" to one of "chief executive" in the "scientific corporate management" structures that are being introduced in the increasing drive for efficiency, with their implications for depersonalization, top-down management structures, and division of labor between heads and their staffs (Ball, 1990). One headteacher who had retired early told me that he felt the role was becoming depersonalized, and he feared for his own self-development, which was a necessary part of his teaching:

It had gone beyond the point where it was being used to challenge the person further within the context of their own personal development, and was making demands on them that would ultimately have a clone-like effect, a stereotyping effect, that I felt I needed to resist quite strongly. (Woods, 1995, p. 153)

Also, as Evetts (1994) has shown, by no means all teachers, especially women, are aspiring in this particular way. Nias (1989), for example, has pointed to the virtue of lateral careers for some of the women teachers in her sample and has urged that a more flexible definition of careers be available to men also, "whose morale and enthusiasm might also be revived by the opportunity sometimes to move sideways (or out) as well as up" (p. 76). As it is, some may feel constrained to go along with promotion beyond even their own expectations and wishes. Such a one was Geoff, who, though not fully qualified, because of staffing and financial pressures was asked to take over as head of modern languages when the previous head left. Before that, he was "head of year" – "a pastoral job which I enjoyed. I thought I'd found a niche for myself." With the arrival of the GCSE (General Certicate of Education) and the National Curriculum,

> things began to change very rapidly in modern languages teaching, almost daily. I suppose I felt inadequate. I couldn't persuade myself I had the qualifications, the experience or the ability that the post needed. . . . I was very conscious of the fact that I had to get things right to give the students in my care the best possible chance of success. I never felt entirely confident with my own French and these exams were being taped before going off to be monitored. In effect, I was on public display. (Mersh, 1991)

After three nervous episodes of a stress-related mental disorder, Geoff went for stress management counseling and decided to leave teaching. His case shows how those who experience stress so often blame themselves rather than the social factors that precipitate the crisis:

> The problem was within me and my own perception of me, what I did and the way I did it. I realise now that I had always been prone to anxiety. People have always told me I under-estimate myself, play down my strengths and emphasize my weaknesses. (Mersh, 1991)

An ex-headteacher who had recently suffered burnout, after reading this chapter, commented on the theme of guilt:

> I do believe this is a central theme. It is certainly a feeling which I consistently experienced as a teacher and as a head and it is a feeling which stays with you. It is very much part of the continuous contestation (because I think that is what it feels like) between what one feels one should be achieving in the job and the attempt to maintain the self. The sense of guilt becomes stronger as one increasingly feels that one is no longer able to achieve what one sees as necessary, thus putting the self under strain. . . . We (i.e., heads) feel that we are the ones who should be capable of adapting to what we see as necessity and to perform accordingly. If we fail, we naturally have to take the personal responsibility for that failure. This is particularly true in relation to our responsibilities towards children whom we would view as especially vulnerable to the consequences of our failures. (Anonymous)

Others may hold a different concept of career, one that in structural terms shows a horizontal rather than vertical progression (Hughes, 1937), guided more by considerations of maximizing the intrinsic rewards of teaching. Here, too, for some, the future has become blocked off as those kinds of opportunities have declined. If times are hard, some consolation might be found in the hope of future prospects. Where those are curtailed, the difficulties are greater. To the question of "what am I doing?" is added "where am I going?" compounding the sense of anomie.

Those most at risk in these respects are teachers in mid-career to late mid-career. They have been socialized into those kinds of expectations. It is too early for them to retire, and it is difficult for them to move to other jobs or professions (Smithers, 1989). They are stuck. Younger teachers trained within the National Curriculum are less at risk in this respect. Their notions of career and outlook on the future have the National Curriculum and other changes as their baseline. This is not to forget that teachers in their first year often do have a hard time (Hanson and Herrington, 1976). Nor that young teachers can rapidly become disillusioned. A twenty-eight-year-old teacher, after five years of teaching, was "almost scared to do anything creative in case I fall foul of the law. . . . I'm feeling overworked, under-valued and almost burned out. If this is how I feel at 28, what will I be like at 45?" (Cusack, 1993, p. 7).

Values

Teaching is a matter of values. People teach because they believe in something. They have an image of the "good society." So do politicians. The reforms of the late 1980s and early 1990s in England and Wales were informed by the policies of the "New Right" applied in a systematic way (Ball, 1990; Quicke, 1988). These, curiously, amalgamated two contradictory tendencies. One argued that the education system was wasteful and lacking in enterprise. It suffered from being dominated by educationalists – the producers – and the balance of power should be tilted toward the consumers – the parents. If pupils were rigorously tested in a compulsory and standardized way at certain key points, the results published, and parents given a choice of where to send their children, the bad schools would soon be driven out. At the same time, others felt there should be more control and prescription in education. They attacked "progressive" teaching methods, linking them to "falling standards." There should be emphasis on the basics and on cultural heritage as opposed to new forms of knowledge, and teachers should be made more accountable. The new system was to be policed by a new, more frequent and regular mode of inspection under a new agency.

Where teachers are in sympathy with these ideas, their work and careers may well receive a boost. Such was the case with a group in one school identified by Mac an Ghaill (1992), whom he called the "New Entrepreneurs." Where teachers are opposed, they have difficulty adjusting to new roles and new work patterns. Many primary school teachers do subscribe to different values from those of the "New Right." These teachers prefer a different model of good teaching, one based on child-centered principles. Core features are full and harmonious development of the child, a focus on the individual learner rather than the whole class, an emphasis on activity and discovery, curriculum integration, and environmentally based learning (Sugrue, 1992). There is also an emphasis on "caring" and studied attention to the emotional aspects of learning. The very nature of these beliefs, apart from their standing in opposition to government policy and preference, makes teachers vulnerable. As one primary head told me, "As teachers wanting to be tender to others and have that tenderness returned to you . . . we are exceedingly thin-skinned . . . and that makes it easy for people to injure you" (Woods, 1995, p. 85).

In a survey of teachers who had left or who were on the point of leaving the profession (Walsh-Harrington, 1990, p. 27), one "just couldn't cope any longer, the emotional demands of the job were exhausting." Another "would come home emotionally drained, unable to give my own children the attention they deserved." An ex-teacher told Croall (1995, p. 7),

> The head felt we shouldn't get emotionally involved with the children, that we should stay behind the barrier of authority, that a more informal relationship left you in no-man's land. He also said that if we were 100 per cent dedicated it was too much like hard work, and we would burn ourselves out. But I'm not that kind of person.

A daughter writes an open letter to her father, burned out after 30 years' teaching:

> You are a giving, sensitive and caring person and until recently you have been able to channel your qualities to a large degree into your job. People like you always get exploited because you don't put a price on what you give to others. . . . Teaching is being restructured in a way that stifles your ability to care for and stimulate your students . . . but also prevents you attending to yourself. ("Dear Dad," 1993, p. 2)

It has not helped such teachers that they have been subjected to a "discourse of derision" in the national media directed toward their pedagogy and their achievements (Wallace, 1993). The polemical rhetoric of politicians and the press lambasted teachers in the early 1990s, engendering a "moral panic" over educational standards and teaching methods and swamping rationality (Woods and Wenham, 1994). Not for the first time, teachers were the scapegoats for national decline. One "no longer feels that one is doing a job that society values" (MacFarlane, 1989, p. 19). This was the major factor in Walsh-Harrington's (1990) survey of ex-teachers. Morale within the profession sinks lower; guilt levels rise (A. Hargreaves, 1994). All the pressures are on them to find new roles within teaching; but this would be a betrayal of all that they believe in. Unable to proceed forward or back, they develop feelings of anomie and loss of confidence. The central element in this, according to Rose (1962, p. 545) is that

> life is meaningless. This entails a sense of worthlessness, a loss of motivation, a belief in one's inability to achieve anything worthwhile. . . . The result is a persistent psychological beating of the self with a circular intensification of the process. Soon the individual is no longer able to control his feelings of anxiety and depression.

To recover, Rose goes on, the individual needs to develop a positive attitude toward the self and

> must *do* those things which are in accord with his own values and which reflect the values of some social group that he rates highly. He must be able to congratulate himself occasionally and receive congratulations from esteemed others. (p. 548)

The ex-headteacher who experienced burnout comments,

> This is a recurrent problem among headteachers. The position of being a head leads to a form of isolation which precludes the opportunity for assurance. One can get that assurance from other headteachers but the new managerialism has tended to breed a culture of cope or bust.

(See Nias, Chapter 13, for further commentary on "values.")

Situational Factors

A number of situational factors, notably school and neighborhood characteristics, teacher culture, and pupil characteristics, appear to be relevant.

School and Neighborhood Characteristics. There are certain objective indices, such as level and size of school, though no data are available on the latter. With regard to school level, one could argue that teaching in a school for children four to seven years old involves less pressure than teaching in one for children eight to twelve years old, and certainly much less than teaching in a school covering the whole age range of four to eleven years. The reasons are not only that the full age range schools are larger but also because test results have to be published for students at age eleven, and this is seen as a critical juncture in the pupils' career, affecting their movement to secondary school.

Second, school ethos is likely to be as significant in producing stress as it is in encouraging school effectiveness (Rutter, Maugham, Mortimore, and Ouston, 1979 ; Mortimore, Sammons, Lewis, and Ecob, 1988). History of the school, for example, certainly seems to be a factor in successful adaptation to the National Curriculum (Ball and Bowe, 1992), especially when the school was successful with previous curriculum reform. As noted earlier, there might also be a strong "relational idea" (Bernstein, 1975) that serves to integrate the curriculum and unite the staff. Alliances are important, as where a school has established a strong role within the community, earning passionate support from all involved (Woods, 1995), or is a member of a consortium of schools, linked in mutual support.

Third, the area that a school serves is of crucial importance. Those serving deprived areas, for example, not only have to minister to a large number of intractable social problems, but until recently have had their results compared with other schools without any compensation or value added. Inevitably, they rank toward the bottom of the lists, appearing to the world at large as failing schools, even though they may have had uncommon success on their own terms. This ranking is a double blow for the staff, as shown here:

> In the first year that league tables were published, my school's intake measured at the age of 13 had 73 per cent of pupils with a reading age below their chronological age but, by the time they were 16, 27 per cent had achieved grades of A-C in GCSE (General Certificate of Secondary Education) English. This is something to celebrate; instead we were the "worst" school in the area. To come bottom in the league, even if only in one's own local education authority, is to feel not only failure but the threat of impending closure. The sense of failure afflicts the students as well as their teachers. (Richardson, 1995, p. 63)

Teacher Culture

D. H. Hargreaves (1994) argues that a "new professionalism" is emerging, characterized by a shift in the values and practices of teachers and a synthetic relationship between professional and institutional development. Significant developments in the changing teacher culture, he claims are a move from individualism to collaboration, from hierarchies to teams, from supervision to mentoring, from inservice training to professional development, from authority vis-à-vis parents to contract. D.H. Hargreaves (1994, p. 426) asserts,

> Older teachers who found the changes too stressful took early retirement; those remaining now divide into those who increase stress by

trying to persist with the old structures and culture and those who are, sometimes reluctantly and painfully, generating a more collaborative culture built on new social structures.

Hargreaves points the way to the need for more "collaborative cultures," and where these are genuine – that is to say democratic, antihierarchical, where the motive force comes from the group – there is a good record of educational success (Nias, Southworth, and Yeomans, 1989) and of successful political resistance (Woods, 1995). However, A. Hargreaves (1994) has identified the phenomenon of "contrived collegiality" – enforced collaboration from above in the interests of managerialism rather than the interests of the group. Such collaboration can only contribute to the alienation of individuals opposed in principle to such developments. D. H. Hargreaves seems to attribute the onset of stress to individuals' reluctance to change; and indeed, when teachers prove totally intractable at a time of rapid social change, they must accept some responsibility. In other cases, one might argue that the responsibility lies with those promoting some of the changes and/or to policies of resource, which affect provision and levels of inservice training. Whatever the case, teacher culture certainly seems to be in transition. As one of the anchors in a teacher's life, one of the major securities, and one of the chief resources for defining the teacher's self, change can be profoundly disturbing for teachers who have enjoyed success and established ways of achieving it through long and arduous endeavor within the prevailing teacher culture.

Pupils. In general, in situations where teachers otherwise feel pressured, the one thing that keeps them going is their relationship with the pupils (Campbell et al. 1991a; Walsh-Harrington, 1990) and dedication to the cause of their needs. But there are some fearsome tales of deteriorating behavior among pupils, to such an extent that it has driven some teachers out of teaching (see also Rudow, this volume). Croall (1995, p. 6), for example, interviewed an ex-teacher who taught at a deprived inner-city school:

> Over the three years I was there I became exhausted, drained, depressed and cynical. . . . Some of the children's problems were horrendous. In every classroom we had three or four who were living in extreme poverty or very difficult family circumstances.

Overcrowding, parental abuse and/or neglect, malnutrition, overwork in the home were rife.

> These conditions obviously affect the children's behaviour in school. They were unable to concentrate and unwilling to work, they disrupted others, and they were constantly seeking attention because they were so emotionally needy.

Other testimony has strains of a "blackboard jungle":

> Kids mill about, walking in and out of the room. If you try to interrupt their conversations they turn on you. Sporadic fights break out. Someone is kicking, pinching, stealing, lighting matches. Textbooks, scarce now, are ripped up, chucked around. While the girls comb their hair and put on mascara, the boys play cards, flick catapults and pass cigarettes to each other. In front of me I see pornographic cartoons . . . where French verbs should be. (Owen, 1990, p. 25)

Women teachers may be subjected to more direct sexual harassment (Lock, 1986; Mahoney, 1985). Male teachers are not immune, though they do not appear to be as distressed by the experience (Dubberley, 1988).

The causes of pupil deviance are complex. Arguably, however, some of the major factors are trends associated with developments in society at large, which have seen the decline of the inner cities, and for some people, have brought long-term unemployment, poverty, and the destruction of the family. Pupils and their teachers are living out the consequences of this in some of our schools.

The Experience of Intensification

To illustrate some of these points further, I offer two examples. The first is a statement from a letter to the educational press; the second is a comparison arising from my recent research (Woods, 1995). I conclude with a note about "life after burnout."

A "Shameful Time for Education"

Under this heading, the following letter appeared in the educational press:

> I have 34 years' teaching experience including three headships and am one of those who this year contributed to the 47 per cent increase in early retirement of headteachers and deputies. I have given my time and most of my life to helping children to learn. For the last three or four years, I wasted my experience and time responding to government changes, minimising their worst effects, protecting children, fighting for special needs' integration, reassuring anxious and confused parents, encouraging demoralised staff and moving mountains of paper. I didn't work longer hours, but so many of the hours I worked were of no real value to the education of children. I retired before I became ill, leaving a school which I had opened eight years earlier and which I still loved. . . .

My husband also retired early from a headship after supporting parents who made an informed stand against Standard Assessment Tests.[1] The anxiety and pressure caused by his determined and heroic stand against these badly flawed tests made him very ill, and he decided to bring a long and outstanding career to a close. We know that between us we have deprived our schools of the knowledge built up over a total of 60 years and the remaining 10 years we could have both worked through.

Our careers had been exciting, rewarding, demanding. But we recognized that because we constantly put children's needs before government rulings, we could no longer carry on. (Ball, 1994, p. 21)

This example illustrates several features of the analysis: This is clearly an experienced and successful teacher who has held several positions of responsibility. She was very dedicated to her work and to her pupils and had strong emotional attachment to her school. The huge waste of time for no educational benefit is the classic "grating" stress-inducing effect. It is tinctured with the hallmark of intensification – burgeoning administration and bureaucracy. Her husband demonstrates the risks attached to resistance. Typically, there is a suggestion of self-blame ("we have deprived our schools . . ."). There is an indication of the strong intrinsic rewards they used to derive from teaching, but in the end, the clash of values between them and the government made their positions untenable.

Scheduled and Unscheduled Status Passages

In some recent research (Woods, 1995), I met two primary headteachers who both retired early, for similar reasons. However, one experienced burnout, the other did not. The reasons for their leaving feature prominently in this article – intensification of work, fundamental changes in the headteacher role, strong commitment, clash of values, loss of intrinsic rewards and external appreciation, sense of an assault on the self, a growing feeling of isolation, anomie and alienation, and a system out of control. But whereas one (Peter) chose to leave teaching almost in a spirit of triumphalism ("I hope my retirement is not perceived as somebody abandoning ship. Rather, it's transferring from one ship to another ship that's going rather more in the direction that I want to go" [Woods, 1995, p. 171]); the other (Dave) suffered burnout. It is impossible to say conclusively why

---

1. These are mandatory tests for all children at certain key stages, much disliked by teachers for, in their opinion, being worthless and time-consuming. Since 1994, as a result of teacher action, the tests have been restricted to the core curriculum subjects.

there should be this difference, but there are some suggestive factors in their backgrounds that may have contributed.

Peter had a lifelong history of marginality. As a schoolboy, he had alternated between the invariably alienating formal world of the school and the "real" world of the countryside. He considered the latter a far more meaningful learning environment. In his teaching, he worked to reproduce similar effects of naturalism and authenticity, the joy of discovery, holistic and integrated learning. Ironically, the teaching high point of his career came with the publication of a book (*Rushavenn Time*) written by a children's author together with a group of pupils from his school in 1988 – the same year of the Education Reform Act instituting the National Curriculum and restructuring the system (Whistler, 1988). Peter came to show most of the features of nonaccommodation discussed earlier, though not others. Crucially, he was at a career point in his later fifties when he could contemplate a legitimate, scheduled move into retirement. He had been a successful head for a number of years. After the high point of *Rushavenn Time*, he began to see his school career, in the light of the changes, on a downward curve. Then, the "side bets" (Becker, 1960) – those life factors that usually force teachers to keep going whether they want to or not – changed to make the option of retirement even more of a possibility. His wife, also a teacher, offered herself for voluntary redundancy at her school, which had to lose a teacher, and she was subsequently awarded a disability pension; his mother died, leaving him a house and a small legacy. Thus he had no money worries and he was able to undertake the passage into retirement jointly with his wife. Further, he was motivated by a vision that was wider than the school. He came to recognize that his "self" needed "rescuing." Because of his lifelong history of marginality, this self was invested in a broader concept of learning that was not always best served by the institution of school. He positively looked forward, therefore, to recapturing some of the magic that he had experienced as a boy, though now with the advantages a lifetime of teaching had given him. There is a continuity here, therefore, and a sense of progression to new heights.

Dave had a more conventional career. He was also a younger man – in his late forties and at the height of his career. He had been a head for five years. He had a young vibrant staff in his lower school, for children four to nine years old, where the needs of the children, many of them from minority ethnic groups and who could speak little English when they arrived, were great. He held strong principles and championed their cause, so ill-served by the National Curriculum, speaking of the need to "fight back." This in itself, as noted earlier, made him vulnerable. As he commented

Where you're trying to transform national orders to actually fit the needs of your pupils . . . in the context of a single school that's a very fragile process, and one perhaps that can be knocked down very easily. (Anonymous)

Beyond this, the intensification pressures created "a shout for help . . . towards 'how are you going to help me with today's situation,'" and turned his work into a struggle for survival. He became submerged under reports and policy statements, found no time for reflection, was forced to make key decisions in a hurry. The headteacher role had changed so much that

I was beginning to feel a dinosaur. . . . The type of thing I was having to do in administration was taking me away from some of the ideals that I got into the job for. I felt that the kind of person they were looking for was somebody completely different. I was not the kind of headteacher that they needed or wanted. (Woods, 1995, p. 177)

After a long period of illness, Dave applied for early retirement on the grounds of ill-health. Crucial differences between his case and Peter's were his younger age, which made the legitimate status passage of retirement unavailable to him; the associated side bets, which counted on his continuance in teaching – all this constituting a kind of entrapment as mentioned earlier; his rising achievement curve, which meant that more was at stake; the particular needs of the children at his school, whom the reforms hit more starkly; the high-risk strategy of resistance to some of the measures. All of these produced even more of the classic "grating" effect between need, aspiration, and accomplishment.

Beyond Burnout

Burnout might be regarded as one of the products of the liminal stage of unscheduled status passages. There is no awareness of an "anticipation" phase in these cases. The person is unprepared, and all the expectations are that one will continue in the role. Socially, however, the stress-inducing factors multiply, disjunctures occur and deepen, the self becomes more and more damaged and is precipitated against its will into liminality. But if liminality has its darker, confused, disorienting side, it also has a brighter, revelatory one. For it is not uncommon for those who go through such an experience to rebuild the fractured self, or even to emerge with a newfound self in the "reincorporation" phase, launched on a new career either in or outside teaching. Millard (1995), having related the factors that forced his early retirement at age fifty-two, hopes it will be a time that "will prove to be early *retyre*ment. New treads are badly needed and . . . I can't help feeling that I still have miles to go before I sleep!" Geoff has set up business as a consultant in stress management. "I've moved on to a new phase in my life," he said. The ex-headteacher of thirty-four years' experience is currently "trying to raise public awareness about the parlous state of an education system controlled by ministers who consistently show ignorance of children as learners" (Ball, 1994, p. 21). Dave is studying for a postgraduate degree, researching the problems of, and provision for, young bilingual learners and acting as a consultant for local schools. Peter is also writing and researching and has been prevailed on to undertake some supply teaching. Helping one teacher with a National Curriculum project titled "The Romans" – a topic in which he has specialist knowledge – he has rediscovered the zest that went into *Rushavenn Time*.

Conclusion

I have taken a particular sociological perspective to examine a critical case study in the production of teacher stress and burnout to reveal factors that may well have general relevance. This has shown a complexity of factors operating at a number of levels. At the micro level, there are factors concerning teacher commitment, values, career and role, and factors concerning ability and willingness to change or adapt. At the meso level, there are factors to do with type of school, school ethos, neighborhood, and teacher and student cultures. At the macro level, there is the intensification of teachers' work and its particular manifestation at national level in government policy. However, intensification cannot account for everything that occurs in schools or educational changes in process, and I have noted the existence of powerful contrary forces. In fact, teachers may experience feelings of enhanced professionalism and stress at the same time. What pushes them in one direction or the other, one might argue, is the particular conjuncture of other factors that apply, and the balance between intensification and professionalization, as mediated perhaps through national policy. In the case study considered here, the balance has been shifted over the last decade from professionalization and toward intensification, and there has been an increasing incidence of stress. It may be that over the next decade, the balance will shift back again. In that event, we might expect stress and burnout to diminish. It is equally safe to say, however, that given the number and complexity of other factors, it will remain in some shape or form an attendant feature of teachers' lives. It is an inevitable concomitant of the job.

6. Reframing Teacher Burnout in the Context of School Reform and Teacher Development in the United States

LYNNE MILLER

In this chapter, I intend to reframe the discussion of teacher burnout within the context of current school reforms in the United States. I've divided the work into two sections. The first presents an overview of school reform in the United States since the publication of *A Nation at Risk* by the National Commission on Excellence in Education in 1983. It begins with a brief history of recent school reforms and describes their salient features and foundations. It then explores what this all means for teachers as individuals and as members of a profession.

In the second section of the chapter, I look at the implications of these changes for the concept of teacher burnout. I draw heavily on Byrne's (1994a; and this volume) model to frame the discussion. To ground my thinking in real, rather than imagined and idealized schools, I present a case study of one high school that is now in its fourth year of reform. Central High, a "good" suburban school, represents many of the shifts in teaching, school organization, and teacher learning that are discussed in the first section of this chapter. It offers a rich opportunity for thinking concretely about the implication of reform for teacher burnout.

The Central High School case helps to reframe the organizational variables related to burnout in important and occasionally unexpected ways. It also leads to insights about how professional development can serve as a buffer against some of the causes of burnout.

Current School Reform in the United States

The current movement for school reform in the United States can be traced to 1983 with the publication of *A Nation at Risk*. This small volume had a large impact. Building on American fears about the loss of economic security and world prominence, the report argued that American schools were so dysfunctional that they appeared to be created by an enemy power. The

139

report recommended that schools work harder at doing the very things they had been doing for some time. Mandates and directives for more courses, more tests, more standards, more controls, and more requirements dominated the policy arena. New laws governing teacher certification, school curriculum, and student assessment were promulgated by almost all the states within a very short time. This legislated approach has come to be known as the first wave of school reform. Its emphasis on controlling inputs and measuring a narrow range of student outcomes supported the long-held view that schools were like factories. Based on industrial values of bureaucratic efficiency, the factory model of schooling had framed public discussion of schools and how to improve them for most of this century. This tradition continued into the first wave of reforms.

An important challenge to this long-established view came a scant three years later with the publication of *A Nation Prepared: Teachers for the 21st Century* (1986). Researched and written under the auspices of the Carnegie Foundation, this monograph focused on the culture of the school. It paid special attention to the role of teachers rather than to issues directly related to student achievement. The report argued for a new teacher professionalism, expanded teacher roles, and teacher-initiated and teacher-led reforms. The linchpin of proposals to improve teaching was the establishment of a National Standards Board to identify and recognize highly accomplished teachers. The Carnegie Report initiated what has been called the second wave of school reform in the United States and was taken seriously by educational professionals and their associations. Its call for more teacher participation in decision making and the institution of site-based management promoted reforms that gave teachers a new voice in the operation of their schools. The Carnegie report presented an alternative to the factory model of schools. It advocated treating schools as professional organizations where teachers, working together as colleagues, could shape their own work lives and transform the school as an organization.

The Carnegie Report offered a fresh starting point for the discussion of schools, teaching, and the goals of education. Its clear focus on teachers was decidedly different from previous discourse that had emphasized structures and incentives and paid scant attention to the people who were supposed to carry out the recommended mandates and policies. However, whereas the report was effective in opening conversation, it did not motivate a movement toward comprehensive school reform. What was missing from the Carnegie analysis was a clear vision of what school experiences should be for students. The necessity of focusing on student learning was eloquently presented by Sizer in *Horace's Compromise* (1984). Sizer offered a powerful critique of teaching and learning in American high schools and suggested remedies for change. He wanted to rethink the school from the perspective of students. He emphasized not only the content of an education but the processes of learning as well. This emphasis on student learning and new forms of instruction and assessment has been termed the third wave of school reform. It views schools as "centers of inquiry" (Schaeffer, 1967) where investigation and understanding are the central tasks of the organization.

Taken together, the second and third waves of reform present an ambitious agenda for changing schools. This change affects both students and teachers. For students, schools become places where they learn to "use their minds well" (Sizer, 1984), engage in rigorous intellectual work, demonstrate their learning to high standards, and function as members of democratic communities. For teachers, schools become work organizations that promote professionalism, foster colleagueship, and ensure that the teacher voice is heard in decisions that affect the learning and development of their students as well as the conditions of their own work. The move from factory schools to this new vision of schooling is no small undertaking. To make the shift from one form to another, educators engage in building the foundation for reform. Among the building blocks for this foundation are these elements (adapted from Lieberman and Miller, 1990):

1. *Rethinking curricular and instructional efforts to promote quality and equality for all students.* This is the cornerstone of reform; it implies a systematic questioning of all current instructional practices and a willingness to modify and in some cases to eliminate basic beliefs about what learning is and how it can be promoted. Practices such as sorting children by age into grade levels, grouping students by ability, organizing the curriculum into academic disciplines, and assessing student achievement by paper-and-pencil tests come under careful scrutiny in an effort to ensure that all students learn at a high level of achievement.
2. *Rethinking the structure of the school.* Changes in instructional practices require a change in how schools are organized and administered. Specifically, the role of the teacher comes under close scrutiny. This often results in the alteration of how teacher time is used, a change in how teacher education and development is provided for, and the development of new training opportunities in the areas of decision making and conflict management.
3. *Thinking simultaneously about restructuring environments for student learning and for teacher development.* Often, in discussions of school reform, means and ends become confused. For example, school-based management and new decision-making structures are effective means of empowering teachers; but the empowerment of teachers is not an end in itself. It is a means toward achieving more effective learning environments that directly benefit students. This notion of dual benefit, that teachers and students are both served by the transformation of schools, is critical. Educators who attend to both sides of the student/teacher equation help ensure that the changes they make are more than illusory.
4. *Making connections outside the school.* Although individual schools are capable of

making significant change, they are always vulnerable when they work in isolation. When teachers learn to form alliances with one another and with institutions and people from outside their usual boundaries, they increase their knowledge base and their effectiveness. Partnerships, networks, and coalitions offer the potential for exploring new possibilities, exchanging ideas and practices, and comparing experiences, and insights.

5. *Welcoming the increased and changing participation of parents and the community.* Traditionally, parents and community members have been left out of professional debates on school reform and the major reform efforts. Educators are often accused of using language that is inaccessible to the public and of embracing new ideas because they are trendy and bring high status. Because the current reform movement is moving far beyond mere "fiddling" with programs and procedures, teachers committed to fundamental change also work to develop the disposition and skills to involve their local communities in reform.

What Reform Means for Teaching and Teachers

Teachers involved in reforming and restructuring their schools are engaged in two enormous projects. They are reinventing school and they are reinventing themselves. The conditions they face are very different from those they experienced in the factory model schools where they first learned their jobs and forged their professional identities. Writing ten years ago, Lieberman and Miller (1984) identified some of the norms, expectations, and conditions of teaching under these conditions. Among them were these: (a) Teachers developed a highly individual and personal style of teaching that was forged in isolation from colleagues, based on trial and error, and sought to resolve some of the central contradictions endemic to teaching on their own. (b) Teachers depended almost exclusively on their students as the source of feedback, rewards, and indications of success. They lacked the collegial interaction and feedback that other professionals took for granted. (c) Teachers were never sure that their teaching was resulting in learning. They acted out of a blind faith that their planning and actions would hit the mark. The assessments they designed for their classes may have provided the basis for assigning grades, but not for evaluating learning. (d) Teachers worked from a weak knowledge base. There was no professional consensus about what was basic to teaching, what was understood about learning, and what evidence was acceptable for demonstrating knowledge. (e) Teachers were confronted with goals characterized by vagueness and that often were in conflict with each other. Were teachers supposed to impart skills or enrich lives? Serve a social agenda or focus on academics? Educate everyone or concentrate on those with the most promise? There was little clarity about what they were supposed to do and for what they were to be held ultimately responsible. (f) Teachers spent a disproportionate amount of time establishing control norms in their individual classrooms. They acted on the assumption that control preceded instruction and they spent much energy enforcing rules and keeping discipline. (g) Teachers lacked professional support. Sarason, along with his colleagues, captured this best when he wrote, "Teaching is a lonely profession" (Sarason, Levine, Goldenberg, Cherlin, and Bennett, 1966). There was little time and opportunity for colleagues to meet together, talk about their practice, learn from each other, and watch each other work. In effect, teaching in factory-like schools was dominated by norms of "individualism, isolation, and conservatism" (Fullan and Hargreaves, 1988).

The current reforms require a different kind of teacher and a different kind of profession from the one Lieberman and Miller (1984) described more than a decade ago. Based on more recent observations and interviews in reforming schools, Lieberman and Miller (forthcoming) have recast the conditions of teaching and identified six shifts that teachers are making in their work. They are from individualism to professional community, from teaching at the center to learning at the center, from technical work to inquiry, from control to accountability, from managed work to leadership, and from focus on the classroom to focus on the whole school. Below, each shift is described.

From Individualism to Professional Community. Teachers in reforming schools are moving away from the individualism, isolation, and privatism of traditional schools in favor of new norms of collegiality, openness, and trust (Little, 1981; McLaughlin and Talbert, 1993; Rosenholtz, 1989). Working jointly to deal with problems of curriculum and teaching helps to begin this transition. Teachers come together in teams or as whole school staffs to decide on common goals, develop integrated programs of study, craft shared assessments, and examine student work. There is time set aside for planning together, teaching together, and talking together. Peer observation and consultation contribute to a shared professional culture in which risks are encouraged, mistakes acknowledged, and learning scrutinized.

From Teaching at the Center to Learning at the Center. The shift from "What do I do as a teacher and transmitter of knowledge?" to "How can I plan with others for what *students* do as learners?" means that, in effect, student work determines the agenda for teacher work. Teachers report that they do not plan their curriculum from abstract goals or from objectives divorced from the realities of their classrooms. Rather, they "plan backward" from outcomes and assessments of actual students (MacDonald 1991). Planning begins with an examination of student work: samples of writing, problem solving, logical thinking, and creative arts are collected and analyzed as a first step in building designs for learning. Rather than focusing exclusively on how teachers teach (collaborative learning, direct instruction, questioning strategies, etc.), educators focus as well on how students learn as the springboard for teaching.

From Technical Work to Inquiry. Teaching, under the conditions of reform, becomes less the collection of skills or the mastery of techniques and more the intellectual work that engages its participants. Teachers pose problems, seek solutions, raise questions, and find answers; they create knowledge and use it. Systematic inquiry, research, and reflection stand at the core of teachers' work in restructuring schools. Like their students, teachers are engaged in a process of continual learning.

From Control to Accountability. In schools that are reforming, the public display of student achievement and accomplishment replaces classroom management as the measure of teacher effectiveness. In this way, accountability for student learning becomes more important than accountability for student behavior. Instead of working to establish norms of control, teachers work to establish norms of learning to which they hold students and themselves accountable.

From Managed Work to Leadership. When learning norms become central, the teaching role expands. Teachers refer to themselves as designers, musical conductors, coaches, and leaders as ways of recognizing the new power relationships that are being established in classrooms. This redefinition of power carries over to the whole school as well. In the same way that teachers shift control to enhance student learning, principals and other administrators diffuse power to enhance school development. Teachers report new responsibility for areas that were traditionally reserved for administrators – instruction, assessment, rules and procedures, and major decision making.

From Focus on a Classroom to Focus on a Whole School. Teachers, in adjusting the boundaries of their work, find that the classroom is, as always, an important venue – but not the only one. As they work together to forge a professional community, they move from solely individual concerns about *my* classroom and *my* students to concerns about *our* school and *our* students. Accountability for student learning expands from the classroom to the school as all adults assume responsibility for the learning of all students. Teachers begin to think of the culture of the whole school and how to develop and support it. They engage in conversation about what the school stands for, how it should be organized and governed, and how it is fulfilling its mission. They also extend themselves beyond their schools to expand their thinking and strengthen their resolve.

These six shifts speak to a reformulation of teaching and a reframing of issues that surround the profession. In the next section, one of these issues – the phenomenon of teacher burnout – is explored more deeply.

Teacher Burnout and School Reform

Two questions frame this discussion of teacher burnout and school reform: (a) How are the variables identified with burnout (Byrne, 1994a, p. 95) enacted in a reforming school? (b) Does a reforming school provide mechanisms for mediating teacher burnout? To aswer these questions, we examine a single case study. The case involves an American high school that has advanced from a factory model of schooling to one representing the "third wave" of school reform.

In the pages that follow, the case study school is described and analyzed against the variables associated with teacher burnout. Mechanisms that mediate burnout in the school are then identified and discussed. Finally, conclusions about the connections between school reform, teacher burnout, and mediating influences are drawn, with an eye toward further research.

Central High School

Central High School is located in a suburb of a large city in the Northeast of the United States. It enrolls 402 students with 38 staff members and two administrators. The school serves a predominantly white middle-class population. About 15 percent of the students come from blue-collar families; a very small percentage of students live below the poverty line. More than 75 percent of its graduates go on to postsecondary education. In many ways, Central High School typifies the suburban educational dream. It is highly rated among its peers; its graduates go on to selective colleges and universities; its students score above national and state norms on all standardized tests; and it has won designation as a National School of Excellence. Yet, with all this success, the Central High School staff decided that it wanted to take a critical look at itself and make substantial changes in how it did business. As one teacher explained,

> I think the people on the inside knew that a lot of the standards of being a good school were pretty superficial. There were some cracks in the facade plus the drum beats from the outside where people were talking about reform and change triggered a lot of ideas. . . . Being the best of an archaic model of education is not good enough and so Central is willing to dive into the deep when it doesn't really have its strokes down. (Murphy, 1995, p. 82)

The school staff met over an academic year in small and large groups and hammered out a statement of beliefs that they could all agree to. The statement resonates with the basic principles of school reform advocated by second and third wave reformers.

Central High School

BELIEFS THAT GUIDE OUR RESTRUCTURING

WE BELIEVE THAT . . .
1. All students can and must learn.
2. In determining what things all students should know and be able to do, we should look to the world of work and commerce for standards that will enable our students to be economically competitive after high school. Use of the world of work for benchmarks or performance will result in higher standards.
3. If we believe that all students can and must reach these higher standards of mastery and learning, we must alter our teaching strategies and classroom organizational patterns so that students of all learning styles and abilities do in fact attain these higher standards.
4. In order to determine to what degree students of different learning styles and abilities have progressed in the attainment of these standards, we must search for alternative and authentic methods of assessing student progress.
5. Although they may learn in different ways, girls are just as capable as boys of mastering math and science concepts and skills, and boys are just as capable as girls of mastering language arts skills.
6. All students, college-bound and no-college bound, should feel that they belong at Central High School.
7. If all of this is to happen, traditional school relationships will change – students and teachers will relate differently. Teachers and administrators will relate differently. Teachers and parents will relate differently, etc. . . .

Central High School staff have put these beliefs into practice by instituting a variety of changes in the school's program and organization. Among the changes are (a) the introduction of an adviser/advisee system in which all staff meet daily with eight to ten students to discuss student issues; (b) the addition of a sixty-hour community service requirement for graduation; (c) new programs focusing on students who have traditionally failed in the school program; (d) restructuring of the school schedule from eight classes of forty-five minutes per day to four classes of ninety minutes per day; (e) the hiring of a technology coordinator and the infusion of computers into the curriculum; (f) the establishment of a new governance structure in which faculty make most educational decisions in consultation with the principal; (g) the institution of grade-level teams and learning area groups to replace the traditional departmental structure; (h) the establishment of a school improvement team composed of faculty, students, and parents to facilitate communication and goal attainment, to manage conflicts, and to develop a shared vision for the school; and (i) the phased elimination of traditional final examinations and their replacement by performances, demonstrations, and projects.

These changes brought with them shifts in the conditions of teaching, many of them resonant with those described by Lieberman and Miller (1984). A sense of professional community pervades the school. There is team planning and team teaching, joint assessment of student work, and continuous structured conversation about the direction of the curriculum and the kind of knowledge it promotes. Teachers are involved in numerous committees where they make and remake policy, discuss students and their work and design appropriate interventions, develop standards and guidelines for evaluation, and reflect on their practices and the successes and failures of the school. The teachers continue to hone their technical skills but they focus the bulk of their energy on questioning, problem solving, and systemic inquiry about practice. Discussions at faculty meetings focus on learning and teaching issues rather than discipline procedures. Information is transmitted through memos so that meeting time can be spent in conversation and productive work. The school has stopped ringing bells to signal the end of classes and does not require hall passes of students or assign teachers to monitoring duties. A core group of teachers has assumed a leadership role in the school whereas most others participate in the various committees and task forces that are continually emerging.

Reframing the Burnout Variables at Central High School

Central High School is a living example of the third wave of school reform as practiced in the United States. It represents reforms in both the organization of the school and the organization of teaching. As such, it provides rich ground for examining the phenomenon of teacher burnout in the context of U.S. school reform. Relying on the organizational variables that

Byrne (1994a; see also this volume) associates with teacher burnout (classroom climate, decision making, role conflict, and work overload), this section analyzes Central High School and its interaction with the burnout syndrome. Below, each organizational variables is discussed as it applies to Central High School in particular and to reforming schools more generally.

Classroom Climate. Byrne concluded that "as the social climate of the classroom deteriorates, teachers become emotionally exhausted and develop increasingly negative attitudes toward their students and the teacher profession" (1994a, p. 665). She cites class size, student apathy, and verbal and physical assault as examples of deteriorating classroom climate. The challenge of a changing social climate has been recently explored by McLaughlin and Talbert (1993). They found that teachers who responded either by holding fast to traditional teaching methods or by lowering standards and expectations experienced feelings of frustration, disengagement, and burnout. On the other hand, they found that teachers who made changes in their teaching and who were supported in these changes by their colleagues experienced a greater sense of accomplishment in their work. At Central High School, we see a faculty that is struggling to respond to students by adapting teaching practices. A dramatic example of this adaptation is the new group of ninth graders who entered the school in the fall of 1995. The class came with a reputation of being problematic. Their junior high school teachers characterized them as undisciplined and lazy, with lower skill levels than previous students. When the two science teachers who had constructed a new ninth grade course based on the demonstration of specific learning outcomes faced these students, they encountered a moral dilemma.

> I'd catch myself siding with the kids. I'd watch them and I'd almost say, "If you just do this, I'll pass you with a D." But my co-teacher and I didn't say that. Instead we made it clear to them that we had high expectations and that we would meet them more than half way. We said, "If you don't do this level of work, you will not graduate. We believe you can do it. We can all do it together." It was a profound encounter for them as well as for us. (Lieberman and Miller, in press)

There are other indications that school climate has undergone considerable change at Central High School and that, as a result, it does not add to teacher stress. As noted previously, Central High School is remarkable in its tranquility. As the attention of faculty has focused more on issues of learning and teaching, there is less time or effort expended on concerns about discipline and control. The organizational variable of school climate at Central not only has different connotations from traditional schools; it has different effects. It serves to reduce teacher stress.

Decision Making. Byrne found that at all grade levels, teachers reported that lack of participation in decision making had a negative influence on their personal accomplishment and led to burnout.

It seems apparent, as noted over a decade ago by Lortie (1975) that the nonparticipation of teachers in decisions that bear directly on their daily work environment leads both to a decline in self-esteem and to strong feelings of external control by others. Over time, these effects take their toll manifesting themselves first in terms of job stress and ultimately in perceptions of diminished personal accomplishment. (1994a, p. 665)

We would expect to find in reforming schools that changing teacher roles and responsibility would give teachers more authority and a new sense of power in decision making. This is very much the case at Central High School where teachers are involved in all the major committees that make school decisions. Teachers express feelings of empowerment, renewed energy, and importance. "We feel that we are part of something new here, that might set the standard, that is pioneering, breaking new ground" (Murphy, 1995, p. 76).

They view themselves as being respected and acknowledged by the administration and the larger community as well. "I think that people truly believe that they're going to be supported and if their plan makes sense it can be implemented. I think it is an awakening or realization that we really, really can do things differently if we want to" (Murphy, 1995, p. 76). On the negative side, increased involvement in decision-making also leads to emotional exhaustion and frustration. As teachers continue to shoulder the same responsibility for classroom teaching and in addition, assume new roles as leaders and decision makers, they find themselves overextended in ways that detract from their total performance. At Central High School, there is a rumbling of discontent about the effect of being involved in decision making. These are complaints of overload.

I sometimes wonder how long we can keep our energy up and continue to change. Many of us are approaching fifty; I'm not sure we can continue to work this hard with no relief in sight. Because it looks like the changes get more complex and we have to spend more time figuring things out and making changes. (Fieldnotes, Miller, 1994)

Huberman (1993a) found that teachers who had been engaged in school reforms for a large part of their careers left teaching with a sense of dissatisfaction. They "felt that the time and effort expended on ambitious attempts to change ongoing practices had essentially exhausted and embittered them, given the few concrete results they observed" (Huberman, 1993a, p. 205). There is certainly the danger that greater involvement in decision making may have this unintended consequence in schools like Central High.

Role Conflict. Role conflict is understood as "the simultaneous occurrence of two or more sets of pressures such that compliance with one makes more difficult compliance with the other" (Byrne, this volume). Central High School's agreed-on belief statement, its widely shared conception of teaching and learning, and its adaptations to student needs all serve to reduce conflict about the role of the teacher. However, the very nature of the reforms at Central creates new sources of conflict about the teacher role. There is a contradiction between the new ways teachers want to teach and the old expectations of teaching.

There are three major sources of this conflict at Central. The first has to do with content versus process/coverage versus mastery concerns. As teachers place more emphasis on the *how* of learning, they have tended to place less emphasis on the *what* and this goes against the grain for many. As one teacher said,

> I haven't resolved the guilt of not covering content the way I did a few years ago. I would like to say that I have and on my better days I know that I'm doing the right thing but emotionally, it's so hard. I don't think it's a control thing; it's just a deeply ingrained sense that certain things need to get done. (Murphy, 1995 p. 124)

The second conflict has to do with meeting expectations from the world outside the school about evaluation of students. Because Central is known for having its students attend the nation's most selective colleges, it must comply with the established norms of reporting student progress. This produces substantial stress for teachers who are bent on establishing new assessments and alternative ways to demonstrate knowledge and skills.

> What ticked me off was going to all of that trouble of new methods of assessment of student achievement and I wasn't allow to put a Pass on the report card. All of a sudden for computer reasons or transcripts or honor roll I had to put a number on there. (Murphy, 1995 p. 128)

Finally, teachers experience conflict with parents and the community. Though supportive of reforms in general, parents often are not as amenable to reforms that affect their children in particular. This causes considerable stress for teachers who are convinced they are on the right track. One teacher noted,

> I think the demands of the community are more dangerous than any-

thing from inside because I think there's a desire to sort of be on board at the same time community members aren't quite informed. There's a fragility around what's happening. They may bring pressure on us at the same time we are trying to get through some fairly dicey ideas (Fieldnotes, Miller, 1995).

The experience of teachers at Central High School provides a cautionary note about the impact of changing teacher roles. On the one hand, teachers feel more clarity about their mission as teachers within the context of their own professional community. On the other hand, these teachers experience increased stress about their roles in terms of the more traditional expectations of the external community. In many respects, teachers are dealing in "dual currencies" (Lieberman and Miller, forthcoming). This not only increases their stress but it also impacts the way they view their workload.

Work Overload. Work overload is defined as "too many demands and too little time in which to meet them adequately . . . job complexity, work that is perceived as too difficult to complete satisfactorily" (Byrne, 1994a, p. 649). As indicated above, workload appears to be increasing under the conditions of school reform. At Central High School, it is often the case that the shifts in teaching that the school promotes bring with them new and increased levels of complexity and stress. As one teacher reported,

I guess if I had to identify the most stressful thing about this [it] is that it is such hard work to take these huge global ideas . . . and trying to bring them down to something that will operate in the classroom. I think that's been really hard. I want to tell you that change is really stressful and I'm sure it is for everyone. But for those of us who are obsessive/compulsive, it's really stressful (Fieldnotes, Miller, 1995).

In addition, increased demands on teachers' time in decision making leads to feelings of exhaustion. A teacher heavily involved in leading the reform efforts noted,

I feel overwhelmed right now. I think some of it may be the implementation dip but I also wonder if there is a sort of an exponential growth with restructuring. I find one thing leads to another to another to another like doors in a hallway. And once you get started you can't really go back. And so that is indicative to me as someone who is trying to handle restructuring around here and how some of us are feeling. On the one hand you do the best you can with it. . . . You know there are some days when I wake up in the morning and nostalgically wish for the old days but I could never go back. (Murphy, 1995, p. 134)

In terms of work overload, it appears that the demands of new forms of teaching, coupled with the expectations for increased involvement in decision making, increase stress for the very teachers the reforms are designed to help.

In summary, it appears that the third wave reforms have influenced each of the four organizational variables as they are being enacted at Central High. Classroom climate and participation in decision making have changed in ways that support personalization and a sense of accomplishment and have the potential to decrease burnout. Decision making, in particular, promotes a sense of internal control over events and policy and a heightened sense of self-esteem, two important mediators of burnout (Byrne, Chapter 1). In the area of decision making, however, the reforms are a double-edged sword. Whereas more teacher involvement builds a sense of accomplishment and personal investment in the organization, it also adds to the teacher workload, thereby increasing the demands of the job and the likelihood of exhaustion. The increased workload for teachers and the tension that results from trying to be two kinds of teacher at the same time also add to the complexity and difficulty of the job. These factors have the potential to enervate rather than energize the teaching staff.

What we find at Central High School, then, is an untraditional teaching staff in an untraditional school that is, ironically, facing some conditions that are traditionally associated with teacher burnout. The changed conditions surrounding classroom climate seem to lessen the potential of burnout in that domain; however, the changes in decision making, role conflict, and work overload are not so clear-cut or consistent. More specifically, the variables of role conflict and work overload have the potential to increase the risk. As noted previously, the variable of decision making has the potential simultaneously to reduce and increase stress on the job. The twenty-one teachers at Central High School surely work under different conditions from those encountered by their counterparts in factory-model schools; yet those very conditions have the potential to exhaust its most enthusiastic proponents.

Buffering Against Burnout

It is the case, however, that the faculty at Central High School are not enervated; they are energized. They are stressed; but they are not burned out. Teachers at the school will say, "Sorry, my plate is full," and then proceed to load their plates some more. Central High School helps us to see the possibility for maintaining high standards for students, increasing demands on teachers, and still maintaining a stable school environment. There are many explanations for this turn of events, but this analysis looks at the variable that was most frequently mentioned by teachers and most carefully documented by the school's leadership team. That is professional development.

Central High School initially depended on the use of external consultancies and workshops for its professional development. Teachers had numerous opportunities to attend national conferences and to hear local presentations by recognized experts in the areas of curriculum, instruction, and assessment.

It's amazing the number of times that people got to hear (Bill) Spady, (Ted) Sizer, and (Grant) Wiggins. I think we had more opportunity for this sort of professional development than any other district. People started to refer to these people pretty regularly. We read their articles and discussed them. That made a difference. (Murphy, 1995, p. 76)

As teachers became more engaged in putting in place the ideas they had heard, they tempered their enthusiasm for this externally driven form of teacher learning.

The theoreticians clarify theory; they don't clarify practice. We're in the middle of solving an important problem. We began by listening to outside experts. They had some good ideas. But quite truthfully, the further I got into this, the clearer it became that they have nothing to tell me now. We all have to do the work. We're the experts about practice. (Lieberman and Miller, in press)

Central High staff began to turn inward and to develop new kinds of learning opportunities for themselves within the boundaries of the school. These occurred during the school year and on school time.

The new forms of professional learning that Central High devised took many forms. Two examples stood out; they were frequently referred to by teachers in discussions of professional development. These were curriculum work and grade-level teams. Curriculum work involved all the teachers in the school in districtwide committees organized by learning or content areas. Each committee had members from each of the grades in the district (K-12) and was led by a teacher who was recognized for his or her knowledge and skill in the discipline. The committees were charged with developing broad learner outcomes for the district and for establishing grade level standards that answer the question: What does this mean for a second grader, fourth grader, eighth grader, and so on? The opportunity to meet across grade levels and to focus on issues related to the content of the curriculum has had dividends for teachers they didn't expect.

It has been such a rich experience. I've never worked with a second grade teacher before and it made me think differently about learning in the subject I teach. It's the first time I saw my teaching as a continuation of something that went before it and as a foundation for what comes next. (Fieldnotes, Miller, 1995)

The work of the committees took place during seven release time days during the academic year. Five of these were contracted release time days for the whole district and two additional days were given for each learning area to meet as it sees fit.

Like the curriculum committees, the grade-level teams involved every teacher at Central High. Unlike the committees, however, they did not involve teachers from outside the school. The purpose of the teams was to provide time for teachers to talk about students and student issues across the disciplines and within a grade level. For instance, the ninth grade team consisted of teachers of English, math, science, history, art, and foreign language who taught ninth graders as part of their load. The teams served students by coordinating their schedules and monitoring their workloads; they served teachers by providing structured time and opportunity to look closely at students and to develop an understanding about what goes on in other classes and in other areas. One English teacher noted,

As a result of being on the team, I now know what my students are learning in math and other areas. I know what assignments they have and how they are doing. Most important I get to learn about them as individuals and as learners and this helps me teach them in my own subject. (Fieldnotes, Miller, 1995)

Time for the grade-level team meetings was built into the weekly school schedule. Every Wednesday morning, there was a delayed start for students. This provided one hour and fifteen minutes of time for teachers to meet and talk about students. The only rule governing the time was that teachers not work individually; they had to meet together either as a whole team or in pairs and trios.

In addition to working together inside their school, Central High School staff became actively involved in a regional school/university partnership. The school joined the partnership during the second year of its reform effort. Teachers came to the partnership because it offered a connection to the university and because it presented opportunities for talking with other high schools and learning from them. Two high schools were particularly helpful to the Central teachers who made numerous site visits to learn more about student assessment. In addition, Central High School was selected as a demonstration school for the partnership, which meant that the school acquired additional resources for its work and had structured opportunities to compare its progress with that of other schools.

Teachers at Central credited the partnership with giving focus to their work and with helping them see the problems that occurred in the implementation of large-scale reforms.

When I heard what Porter High School was doing in social studies, I was both intrigued and horrified. I saw them getting so much into process that they didn't spend much time teaching the content. It made me realize how we are all walking that line between process and content and talking to Porter made me realize there were limits to how far I wanted to go. We had some deep discussions in our department about this after the visit with Porter. (Fieldnotes, Miller, 1995)

In addition, teachers acknowledged the support and relief they got from interacting with people from outside their own school.

It's so refreshing to hear other people's horror stories and to realize that you're not the only one experiencing all of this, that other people are tired and frustrated and that you're not alone. Sometimes, we just break out in laughter when we compare notes. Having a sense of humor is essential in this business and being able to laugh at yourself along with other people is a ticket to sanity. (Fieldnotes, Miller, 1995)

Finally, the Central High teachers commented on the power of partnership in learning to renew and energize them in their work.

Some days I would just drag myself to a partnership event wondering why I was adding one more thing to my plate. But after a good discussion, a nice dinner, and some time away from the school, I would drive home feeling like I had more energy and new excitement about ideas. (Fieldnotes, Miller, 1994)

The Elements of Time and Community

There appear to be two key elements in professional development at Central High School that help mediate exhaustion. These are (a) time to learn during the school day and (b) the support of a professional community.

Professional learning, built into the teaching day rather than being an "add-on," became a dimension of teaching. Teacher work was defined more broadly than simply instructing students. It included professional learning and development as well. When teachers had the opportunity to learn skills and examine beliefs on the job, their time was no less full, but became more productive. The curriculum committees and grade-level teams at Central were good examples of this kind of teacher development.

Professional communities provided another buffer against burnout. Little and McLaughlin (1993, p. 6) characterize effective professional communities as having three dimensions. The first is "interaction" expressed as the distinction between strong and weak ties occurring in "collaborative culture" where there are clear and demonstrable links to classroom practice. The second dimension is "inclusivity" of teachers' collegial groups that underscores the importance of multiple reference groups. The third dimension is "expressed as orientation and combines aspects of teachers' value dispositions and depth of expertise."

These dimensions were present in many of the professional development experiences of teachers at Central High School. The curriculum committees and grade-level teams promoted strong ties that were secured by common operating beliefs and practices. Memberships in the local partnership provided a variety of reference groups for teachers. It also served as a safe place to try out new ideas. Apart from the school, but connected to it, the partnership helped energize people by presenting fresh perceptions and support for inventiveness and risk taking. The professional community that the partnership created provided relief from the daily stresses teachers experienced in their home schools. It also mediated exhaustion by providing an arena where energy was recharged and commitments renewed in the company of friends. Along with time for teachers to learn, professional communities reduced stress and countered the forces of exhaustion that threaten all schools.

Conclusion

This chapter explored how the variables of teacher burnout are reframed within the context of American school reform. Using one case study as a reference point, the author concluded that although all the burnout variables were altered in a reforming school, this did not have the effect of reducing exhaustion among teachers. Rather, new sources of stress were uncovered.

Remarkably, the additional stress did not lead to increased burnout. Various forms of professional development, which took place both within and outside the boundaries of the school, served as buffers against burnout and provided teachers with the energy and support they needed to sustain themselves and the reform efforts in which they were engaged.

Connections between school reform, professional development, and teacher burnout are worthy of study and consideration beyond the limits of one case study. If school reform is to take hold, it must rely on the enduring commitment and determination of teachers. An understanding of how professional development can support change and mediate burnout emerges here as an important topic for further inquiry and research.

PART TWO. Teacher Burnout: Perspectives and Remedies

7. Inconsequentiality – The Key to Understanding Teacher Burnout

BARRY A. FARBER

A Hypothetical Experiment

Imagine an experiment. The subjects are a group of professionals, mostly female. They are subject to the following conditions: They receive limited pay; have limited contact with other adults during a six-hour workday; have no access to phones and almost no privacy; and are responsible for the emotional, social, and intellectual welfare of large groups of children. They are regarded by society as necessary but also only marginally competent. They are expected to engender considerable growth in virtually every child they work with, even those whose parents have failed them. Individuals with no training in their field routinely review and critique their work.

The experimental manipulation: Society begins to grant these individuals somewhat better pay; there is a serious movement toward affording these individuals a greater voice in decisions that affect their work; and government as well as industry begins supporting efforts to create alternative means to do the work more creatively and efficiently. However, the experimental manipulation includes several other conditions as well: The public's expectations for success rises dramatically, and the criteria used for judging success also become more stringent with a greater emphasis placed on standardized tests; in fact, the public begins to believe that these individuals are not performing adequately unless every child in their charge is performing at an average level or higher. Furthermore, public sentiment shifts such that most of the subjects in this experiment now become responsible for all sorts of kids sharing the same space – kids with different abilities, kids who are physically challenged, kids who are emotionally handicapped, kids who are learning disabled. And a few more conditions are instituted as well: One is that society enacts legislation in just about every state such that these professionals not only have to do their daily work with children but have to fill out an enormous amount of paperwork as well. Another condition is that more and more local communities veto tax increases that would pay for technology (computers, for example), support services, and more space – all of which would, of course, make these individuals' jobs easier.

The research question: As a result of the experimental conditions do these individuals, these teachers, feel more or less burned out than they did previously?

Of course, this is essentially what is occurring worldwide for teachers: Granted a bit more respect and a bit more money, they are nonetheless asked to do more and more with less and less. Moreover, they are getting little or no relief from the keenest stress of all – the intensive daily work with students. This is the work that not only provides the greatest source of difficulties and frustration but also the greatest potential source of gratification. For some teachers, the stress of classroom work is so great that they are unable to experience sufficient rewards from their teaching. Feeling deprived in this manner, some teachers will cut back on their efforts and psychological investment in order to balance the equation. They, of course, ultimately experience even fewer rewards and the downward spiral of burnout begins.

Does the research question, then, have an answer? Not an empirical one, but based on the assumption that teacher burnout is basically caused by feelings of inconsequentiality – of feeling that one's input is disproportionate to the perceived output – teachers are no less burned out today than they were five or ten years ago before these "experimental" conditions were put into place. Many teachers still feel that they are giving far more than they are getting. Those rewards that would make the most difference – that would make teachers feel more important, more gratified, less inconsequential, and less prone to burnout – are those that are closest to the source of their work: their everyday interactions with their students. The further away the rewards, the less is their impact, the less their power to attenuate stress. That is, while teachers may well appreciate acknowledgment from afar (say, for example, from board of education members who praise their work) or may feel gratified by the opportunity to share in decision making, these rewards only minimally alter the phenomenology of work. Put another way: If where teachers spend most of their time – the classroom – remains fundamentally unaltered (or too dramatically altered) and fundamentally unrewarding, then other changes, as well intentioned as they may be, are not likely to have an enduring effect on a teacher's vulnerability to stress and burnout.

In sum, the experiment that is occurring now, often referred to as the "teacher reform movement," has, for many teachers, increased their sense of power and engendered a greater sense of belonging in their school; nevertheless, for many, the reforms have failed to increase their sense of making a difference in the lives of their students. Indeed, given that teachers' expectations of job satisfaction may have risen as a consequence of anticipating the benefits of certain of the changes noted above, some feel especially embittered by conditions in the classroom that have remained fundamentally unaffected by recent reforms. Unfortunately, but hardly unexpectedly, the problem of teacher burnout remains a significant one for too many teachers worldwide.

On Woods's Paper, "Intensification and Stress in Teaching"

Woods's description of the nature of teacher burnout – of teachers being pressed to do more work, given fewer resources, and then receiving little reward or recognition for their efforts – is quite consonant with the idea that the essence of this phenomenon lies in the notion of "inconsequentiality." On the other hand, Woods's sociological perspective on burnout – as heuristically valuable as it is – does not seem sufficiently "experience near" for me. That is, despite my agreement with Woods that a multitude of stressors impinge on the teacher and that these stressors may be ordered according to certain sociological criteria, the essence of teacher burnout, as I see it, lies in a teacher's ultimate *psychological* sense of feeling inconsequential. Regardless of where the stressors emanate, burnout occurs when teachers feel that their efforts are disproportionate to the anticipated rewards and that further efforts cannot be justified or tolerated. (This is consistent with the feeling reflected in the letter from a teacher that Woods quotes in Chapter 5, this volume.) Several corollary principles follow from this assumption:

1. That a given teacher's sense of inconsequentiality is generally a result of stressors found at one specific sociological level rather than an aggregate of all three. That is, mild to moderate stress at each of Woods's three levels (micro, meso, macro) may well be tolerable whereas intense stress at one level and virtually none at the other levels may be sufficient to trigger the burnout process.
2. Similarly, that whereas for most teachers the primary source of stress lies within the immediate work environment (e.g., a chaotic classroom), for other teachers stressors found at the institutional level (e.g., lack of autonomy) or even wider political level (e.g., an inflexible, mandated curriculum) may be experienced as more salient. That is, teachers are not likely to be equally affected by stressors at each of the three levels; some are relatively immune to one type of stressor but quite vulnerable to another type.

3. That vulnerability to different types of stressors is based on both temperamental and situational factors. That is, a combination of predisposition (e.g., a teacher's emotional or physical strength) and situation (e.g., the frequency and intensity of bureaucratic interference; size and composition of class) determines which types of stressors most strongly affect any given teacher and the extent to which these stressors will incapacitate the teacher.

4. Similarly, that based on both temperamental and situational factors – that is, on both nature and nurture – teachers will manifest different types of stress-induced reactions. Some teachers will react to excessive stress by working harder and harder until exhaustion sets in (classic burnout as described by Freudenberger); other teachers (most, in fact) will react by cutting back on their efforts and commitment (what I have called "wornout").

5. That treatment strategies should be tailored both to the source of the stressors (the levels at which they occur and their exact nature) and the specific type of burnout manifested (i.e., the frenetic, overcommitted classic burnout type versus the emotionally depleted wornout type). Ideally, the treatment of teacher burnout proceeds by (a) identifying the sources of stress and attempting as much as possible to either lessen their intensity or increasing the individual's capacities to cope with them; and (b) working psychologically with the individual (through psychodynamic, cognitive-behavioral, or other means) to restore a balance in the input–output equation. Individuals who overcommit to teaching, to the exclusion of all else, inevitably feel taken advantage of by the system; conversely, individuals who dramatically cut back on their commitment to work rarely engender sufficient rewards to make teaching seem worthwhile.

Several other related issues and propositions may be noted briefly as well. For example, it seems intuitively correct that treatment for teacher burnout should be individually tailored to the specific etiology and symptoms of the disorder, but research on intervention has lagged far behind conceptual efforts in the field and thus has not been able to inform treatment approaches. We simply do not know which type of strategies work best with which kinds of individuals suffering from which kinds of stressors with which types of symptoms. In this regard, though, it is important to note that this level of specificity is lacking in the treatment of virtually all psychological disorders.

It may be further hypothesized that recent efforts to understand teacher burnout have been subject to political and social shifts such that certain stressors (i.e., the broad class of variables related to student attitudes and behavior) have been conspicuously neglected. This is not to say that researchers or theoreticians have been explicitly discouraged from examining these variables; rather, the lens shaping leading educators' perceptions of schools no longer permits student behavior to play a prominent role in explaining the ills or failures of education. To a great extent, the current Zeitgeist, at least in the United States, holds that students are victims – of poor teaching, of neglected schools, of a noncaring society – and to suggest that students, at least in some cases, are part of the problem, is to "blame the victim." Of course, one often hears a very different account from teachers themselves; many suggest that regardless of whether students have been victimized by society (and many teachers are quite sympathetic to this reality), schools and teachers nevertheless are often significantly affected by the behavior of even a few difficult students.

This reluctance to focus on student behavior as a variable in either educational outcome or teacher burnout has arguably led to some positive outcomes. Certainly, in the past, educational failure has too often been reflexively attributed to the inadequacies of students (the "deficit model" of the child), exonerating the teacher from assuming his or her responsibilities for educating all children. Moreover, this phenomenon seemed especially prevalent in urban schools. As a consequence, the push toward understanding special student needs and creating more flexible and individualized educational programs was effectively delayed for far too long. Thus, teachers and schools are now being held accountable for the education of all students, regardless of where these students "began" or the difficulties they may pose.

On the other hand, the presumption that educational outcome (e.g., performance on standardized tests) is unaffected by socioeconomic and psychological characteristics of students feels unreasonable, even absurd, to many teachers. Too often, this presumption feeds into teachers' perceptions of inconsequentiality – in this case, the sense that even hard-earned but small improvements (for example, in reading scores) will be viewed by others (principals, boards of education, the media) as insufficient, as an indication of failure. The point is that a teacher's tendency to feel inconsequential is facilitated by the failure of others to judge his or her efforts in the context of how difficult the task may actually be. As Woods notes, there is an essential unfairness in judging teachers in difficult schools on the same scale as those who teach in more favorable circumstances. In short, society's insistence on "no excuses" for teachers has perhaps hastened the overdue work on finding ways to educate children who were previously neglected, ridiculed, and deprived of opportunities; nevertheless, this trend, when taken to the extreme, has also hastened the departure of many talented teachers from school systems and has, for many others, engendered a kind of demoralization and diminished caring that we now term burnout.

Is stress, then, as Woods contends, "largely a social issue"? There are at least two reasons I believe this is not so.

1. Although the forces (stressors) impinging on a person may be construed as "social" in nature, these stressors are necessarily mediated by an individual's psychological makeup – the way he or she constructs the world. Note, for example,

the case of Geoff (see Woods, Chapter 5, this volume) "who, though not fully qualified, because of staffing and financial pressures was asked to take over as head of modern languages when the previous head left." According to Woods, Geoff's case "shows how those who experience stress so often blame themselves rather than the social factors that precipitate the crisis." It is true that social factors precipitated this crisis, but it is also true that Geoff's inability to turn down an inappropriate position – what I would term a psychological difficulty – played an equal part in precipitating his crisis. In addition, the fact that Geoff had "always been prone to anxiety" surely affected his subsequent vulnerability to work-related stress. Moreover, Woods himself implicitly acknowledges such psychological factors in later noting how teachers who are "thin-skinned" are vulnerable to the emotional demands of teaching.

2. The experience of stress is intensely psychological. Not only are stressors appraised by individuals but the experience (phenomenology) of stress varies considerably from individual to individual, even those encountering similar stressors.

As a final note in regard to the notion of "stress as a social phenomenon," I noted in an earlier paper (Sakharov and Farber, 1983) that there are problems in attributing teacher stress and burnout to capitalism. (Human service workers such as teachers function as their own tools and means of production; they are not alienated from their work in the usual sense. In addition, burnout often affects the most caring and most involved of teachers.) Similarly, there are, I believe fundamental problems in attributing disruptive student behavior to "trends associated with late capitalism." Although it is difficult to argue with the notion that capitalism inevitably leaves some at the bottom of the financial heap and that, in turn, poverty leads to massive social problems, it is also undoubtedly the case that poverty does not directly lead to disruptive behavior. Indeed, just as the majority of economically disadvantaged adults do not engage in criminal behavior, the vast majority of economically deprived school children are not disruptive. Clearly, a myriad of other factors mediate between poverty and disruptive behavior, including family structure and values, the nature and quality of peer relationships, and the nature and quality of schooling.

On Remediating Teacher Stress and Burnout

Teachers can resist the process of burnout and reaffirm a sense of consequentiality in several ways. One way, as Woods notes, is through resistance (contestation) to inane administrative fiats. The teachers alluded to in Woods's paper "legitimated and reaffirmed their own preferred, child-centered teaching approach," essentially ignoring administrative demands that, if heeded, would have lessened these teachers' sense of professionalism and undermined the personal meaning inherent in how they did their work. According to Woods, this strategy worked to a certain extent, although it also led to teachers feeling torn between their duties to their students and to their administrators. However, note that this approach to consequentiality (or similarly, union activities through which teachers feel empowered) can rarely be as effective in remoralizing teachers as those efforts that more immediately affect the student–teacher relationship, specifically in directions that lead to greater probability of student learning and hence, teacher gratification.

In a similar vein, I agree with Woods's ideas regarding the importance of social support, community, and collaborative cultures. All attenuate the impact of stress. However, note also that, to some extent, these valuable support structures often contribute to stress in subtle and often unacknowledged ways. Teacher support systems, for example, whether informal or formal, tend to focus on the difficulties, even the "impossibility" of teaching, thus tacitly reinforcing a sense of victimization. Even collaborative systems of governance that are intended to empower teachers inevitably exclude some teachers from power and increase the stress of those near the top of the power structure.

What teachers know more than anybody else is just how difficult it is to spend six hours a day with a room of full of children dependent on a single adult for knowledge, nurturance, advice, support, structure, group cohesion, and equitable distribution of attention. Moreover, not only are these children more than ever likely to be diverse in their backgrounds and abilities, but society's demands for a teacher to meet the individual needs of these children is likely to be stronger and more insistent than ever. Although I have argued elsewhere (Farber, 1991a) that teachers expect stress from their work and that the primary problem for teachers is a lack of sufficient rewards – I would also argue that for many teachers, the current level of distress in the classroom essentially precludes sufficient rewards and that the out-of-classroom rewards afforded by teacher reform acts, while in some ways laudable, are insufficient to balance the considerable and often overwhelming stress of daily classroom work.

As noted earlier, it is the student–teacher relationship that offers the greatest opportunity for stress as well as the greatest opportunity for reward and gratification. Thus, teacher reform, even those policies that facilitate teacher empowerment, will ultimately come up short if changes fail to increase the probability of teachers' feeling gratified by and successful in their efforts. Teachers, like all other people, need to feel wanted, important, and in some ways unique. They need to have these needs affirmed by those with whom they live and work.

8. Turning Our Schools into a Healthier Workplace: Bridging Between Professional Self-Efficacy and Professional Demands

ISAAC A. FRIEDMAN

Reports from many Western countries indicate that teachers claim to suffer from problem-laden schools; many are seriously considering giving up teaching as a career, and a substantial proportion actually do so every year. School principals too are experiencing difficulties in their schools and are considering leaving their position and the profession. For teachers and principals, then, teaching is a stressful occupation, and since unmediated stress may lead to burnout, schools are not a very healthy place to work. Burnout, commonly perceived as a sense of emotional exhaustion, lack of accomplishment, and a negative attitude toward service recipients, may manifest in cynicism and skepticism, withdrawal, and eventually, by the professional's quitting the job or the profession (Farber, 1991a; Friedman, 1993).

Ideally, the detection of the sources of stress and the antecedents of burnout should be grounded in related theories. Because the concept of burnout has evolved empirically rather than theoretically (Maslach, Chapter 12), a theory of burnout is not to be found in the literature, although several models of burnout have been formulated and tested.

Cherniss (1993) suggested that professional self-efficacy, as defined by Bandura (1989), can play an important role in explaining the etiology and amelioration of burnout. He argued that in applying the term "self-efficacy," we need to recognize that it is professional self-efficacy (the professional's beliefs in his or her abilities to perform in professional work roles) that is most relevant and important. He suggested that professional self-efficacy includes three different domains of professional role performance. These are (a) *task:* the technical aspects of the professional role, (b) *interpersonal:* the person's ability to work harmoniously with others, particularly recipients, co-workers, and immediate supervisors, and (c) *organizational:* beliefs about one's abilities to influence social and political forces within the organization.

Burnout in "Front-Line" Professionals and Teachers

The literature provides simple as well as complex causative models of burnout emphasizing the relationship between the individual, the organization, and the society. It also distinguishes between personal or personality factors and factors relating to the workplace. With regard to the personality factors, the almost universal consensus is that the individuals most likely to burn out are those who are sensitive, humanistic, dedicated, idealistic, inclined to take interest in others, and introverted (Bloch, 1977; Edelwich and Brodsky, 1980; Freudenberger and Richelson, 1980). However, with regard to the work-related antecedents of burnout, a long list of organizational factors were drawn up for many different occupations; some of these are applicable to almost all human service professions whereas others are unique to a particular occupation. For example, almost all human service professionals face ambiguity at work (expressed in lack of clarity regarding the employee's rights, responsibilities, social status, objectives, and measurement of successful performance); inter-role and intra-role conflicts (expressed as conflicting or inappropriate demands on the employee), and role overload. In addition, they complain of long working hours, feelings of isolation, too little authority, demanding clients, lack of understanding and support from the public for their professional difficulties, heavy caseloads, inadequate training, management indifference, or general indifference to their work (Byrne, 1994a; Farber, 1984; Kahn, 1974). Organizational aspects of burnout specific to schools were also investigated in several studies (Friedman, 1991).

The search for causes of burnout in the teaching profession has identified certain specific work-related features that were summarized by Farber (1991a) as follows: student violence, classroom discipline and apathy; overcrowded classrooms; mainstreaming; unreasonable or unconcerned parents; public criticism; public demands for "accountability"; excessive paperwork; loss of autonomy and sense of professionalism; lack of a promotional opportunities; isolation from other adults and the lack of a psychological sense of community; involuntary transfers; inadequate preparation; administrative insensitivity; bureaucratic incompetence; and deficiencies in the physical environment.

Managerial and School Principal Burnout

Compared with rank and file employees, the issue of burnout among managers, and especially school principals, has so far received only scant attention from researchers (Whitaker, 1992). This gives rise to the question: Do principals burn out? The answer, regretfully, is too often affirmative. Neville (1981) indicated that managers experience occupational hazards such as burnout because, by the very nature of their work, they face serious organizational and administrative problems, scarce resources, role ambiguity, and role conflict. Besides the common stressors existing among administrators or managers in industrial organizations, school principals are exposed to stressors stemming from the educational and learning environment (Begley, 1982). In the teaching profession, compared with the teacher, the principal's role is much wider and more varied and includes dealing not only with personnel and pupils, but also with long- and short-term administrative issues. The school principal is also considered to be a service provider but in a way that is quite different from the teacher. Martin and Willower (1981) suggested that the principal's workday is far less organized and planned than that of a teacher. The principal is required to complete a larger number of assignments and is subject to far more interruptions. In their comparison of teacher and principal roles, Welch, Meideros, and Tate (1982) emphasized the principal's isolation at work; problematic relations with teachers, students, and parents; and the special position occupied by the principal within the school's organizational structure. In comparison with teachers, home and work conflict was found to be a major stressor among school principals, particularly among female principals (Blitz, 1988). Friedman (1995a) suggested that in spite of its seeming complexity, school principal burnout is, in fact, made up of two components: (a) experiences (weariness or discontent) and (b) the focus (internal or external) of those experiences. These two components may be combined in four ways: internally focused experiences – (a) self-dissatisfaction and (b) exhaustion; externally focused experiences – (c) deprecation of others, and (d) aloofness. Based on this conceptualization, a scale to measure school principal burnout was developed (Friedman, 1995b). Sarros (1988) concluded that, like teachers, school administrators are exposed to stress and burnout, but they manifest different experiences and reactions to burnout.

Studies of the causes of school principal burnout point to the following key factors: (a) heavy workload, (b) relations with staff, (c) resource management, (d) local education authorities, (e) lack of support and need to solve conflicts, (f) working conditions and job responsibility (Borg and Riding, 1993; Cooper and Kelly, 1993; Gmelch, 1983; Kelly, 1988; Wilson and Otto, 1988).

In a study of 850 elementary and secondary school principals, the author studied the impact of certain common school work stressors and coping strategies on principal burnout and suggested a burnout prediction model, based on these variables (Friedman, 1995c). Drawn from Cherniss's (1993) classification of professional self-efficacy domains, the school stressors studied were these:

1. *Task:* Overload – work and responsibility
2. *Relations:* (a) with teachers – difficulties with teachers; (b) with parents – overdemanding parents, and (c), with administrative staff – difficulties with administrative staff
3. *Organization:* Collegiality – support and cooperation among those functioning in the school (teachers, team members, students)

Specifically, the scale to measure school–work stressors contained five subscales as follows: (a) *Work and Responsibility Overload* ("I don't have sufficient time to complete all my assignments as a school principal"; "During a day's work I face far more problems and crises than I can handle"; (b) *Difficulties with Teachers* ("Many teachers are disobedient – coming late, not showing up in meetings"; "Many teachers do not cooperate with one another"); (c) *Overdemanding Parents* ("Parents approach me or my teachers with claims and demands as if they are our 'bosses'"; "Parents are rude in their relations with me or my teachers"); (d) *Difficulties with Administrative Staff* ("I have to chase the janitor or the handyman to fix something at school"; "I have to interrupt my own work to personally monitor the school cleaning staff"); and (e) *Collegiality* ("Teachers comply willingly to my requests to conduct extra activities in their classes"; "During a day's work I find time to encourage a teacher facing problems and help him or her out").

The coping strategies studied were the following:

A. *Problem-Focused Strategies:* (1) *Vigilant resolution* (careful consideration of stressful events, situations, and problems, followed by decisive resolution); (2) *Avoidance* (evading stressors or problems); and (3) *Seeking advice* (usually from outside sources).
B. *Emotion-Focused Strategies:* (1) *Relaxation and physical exercise;* (2) Diversions (finding compensatory, outside activities, hobbies etc); (3) *Self-encouragement,* and (4) *"Battering ram"* (trying to ignore the difficulties and the stress, and just pushing on).

In the burnout prediction model, the 12 work-stressors and coping strategies variables were included in a multiple regression equation in which a burnout score served as the dependent variable. The results of the calculations are summarized and displayed in Table 8.1. The squared semipartial (part) correlation (abbreviated SSP) served as a measure of the variable's effect size.

Based on the data in Table 8.1, only five of the twelve variables in the

Table 8.1. *Multiple Regression Analysis of Burnout Scores on Job-Stressors and Coping Strategies, School Principals (N = 821)*

Work stressors and coping strategies	R	R^2	β	t	p	Semi-partial correlation^2
	.74	.55	—	—	—	—
A. *Task*						
Work & responsibility overload	—	—	.16	5.45	.00	0.02
B. *Relations*						
Difficulties with teachers	—	—	.25	7.73	.00	0.03
Overdemanding parents	—	—	.22	7.50	.00	0.03
Difficulties with administrative staff	—	—	.01	0.25	.80	0.00
C. *Organization*						
Collegiality	—	—	−.19	−6.43	.00	0.02
D. *Coping*						
Vigilant resolution	—	—	−.22	−8.57	.00	0.04
Self-encouragement	—	—	−.07	−2.88	.00	0.00
Avoidance	—	—	.07	2.88	.00	0.00
Diversion	—	—	.05	1.84	.07	0.00
Relaxation & physical exercise	—	—	−.03	−1.33	.18	0.00
"Battering ram"	—	—	.02	0.96	.53	0.00
Seeking advice	—	—	.01	0.25	.80	0.00

regression equation contributed significantly to predicting school principal burnout. Listed here in descending order of their contribution to predicting principal burnout, they were (a) Difficulties with Teachers (SSP = 3.46%); (b) Overdemanding Parents (SSP = 3.24%); (c) Vigilant Resolution (SSP = 4.24%); (d) Collegiality (SSP = 2.37%); and (e) Work and Responsibility Overload (SSP = 1.72%). The variables Self-encouragement and Avoidance had statistically significant regression coefficients ($p < .01$), which means that they were above zero, but the effect size of their unique contribution to the prediction of burnout was insignificant. The contribution to predicting school principal burnout made by the remaining variables (four coping strategies and one work-stressor category) was statistically not different from zero (see Table 8.1). Altogether, 55 percent (54% adjusted) of the variability in school principal burnout was predicted by the scores of the twelve work-stressors and the coping strategies. Those principals who reported a high occurrence of disturbing problems (involving teachers, unresolved conflicts with parents, time, work and responsibility overload) are in fact admitting their difficulties or even their inability to govern their environmental demands.

From the findings in this study, it emerges that principals who cannot exercise control over these environmental demands are more likely to burn out. On the other hand, competent principals, able to diagnose a problem and focus their efforts on disentangling it, are less likely to burn out. These findings, therefore, provide support for the hypothesis relating school principal burnout to principals' perceived professional self-efficacy being challenged or unsustained by recipients. The most important predictors of burnout were those variables categorized under the "relations" domain (difficulties with teachers, overdemanding parents), the "organization" domain (collegiality), and the "task" domain (overload). Vigilant resolution, although measured in this study as a coping strategy, can be categorized as a managerial skill and respectively classified under the "task" domain.

Approaches and Strategies for Mitigating Teacher Burnout

A number of intervention strategies for mitigating teacher burnout and programs aimed at dealing with stress in teaching have been presented in the literature in recent years. Kyriacou (1987), Dunham (1983), and Gmelch (1983) suggested that one way of distinguishing among burnout intervention programs may be based on the orientation and purpose of the designed treatment: (a) direct action – programs dealing directly with the causes of burnout, and (b) palliatives – programs involving indirect treatment of burnout, focusing on techniques for alleviating tension or fatigue. Direct action programs, which involve dealing with the extant sources of pressure, may, in the context of teaching, include limiting the number of pupils per class, making classes less heterogeneous, changing the curriculum with a view to increasing pupils' motivation, and so on. Palliative techniques are based on the assumption that stress is an actuality that must be lived with, but nevertheless they try to ease its emotional and physical manifestations. Palliative techniques may be divided into two categories: (a) *mental techniques,* which focus on altering the teacher's perception of her or his environment and circumstances ("putting things in their right perspective", trying to "look on the bright side," "see the humor in a difficult situation," using positive imagery, etc.), and (b) *physical techniques,* such as relaxation, exercise, workshops on pursuing a healthy lifestyle.

Undoubtedly, dealing directly with the causes of stress is preferable to offering palliative solutions, as the action taken directly addresses the sources and origins of the pressure source. If a direct intervention succeeds, the stress is removed and no further substantial action need be taken. However, direct action interventions face several important impediments. First, direct action is not always possible, either because of perplexities involved in identifying sources of stress or because the identified stressor may be difficult to deal with. Second, according to some studies, teachers tend to believe that burnout is a result of their own failure to cope with stress and therefore regard burnout as their own fault (Schwab, 1983) or as a personal failure (Cedoline, 1982). Therefore, inducing teachers to pursue a direct action to avoid stress or to prevent pressures may be more aggravating than consoling to them. Hence, palliative programs and approaches focusing on the emotions and symptoms accompanying burnout rather than on the environmental elements causing it may commonly seem more favorable. Approaches involving palliatives seem more advantageous also because they are easier to apply and, more important, attain quicker results.

A second way of distinguishing among burnout treatment programs is by the level of intervention – that is, whether the intervention occurs on the individual level (teacher) or on the organizational level (school). There are quite a few rationalizations for mitigating stress through the organizational level rather than through the individual one. First studies carried out in Israel showed that work-related stressors account for a significantly higher percentage of burnout in employees than sociodemographic or personal factors (Etzion, 1984; Ezrahi and Shirom, 1986. Second, there is evidence that organizational-level interventions are likely to be more effective than interventions at the individual level. Milstein and Golaszewski (1985) indicated that change on the individual level has limited effectiveness as it focuses specifically on the manifestations of stress and ignores the need to change stressful aspects of life in the organization. Instead, focus should be directed at the organizational level in which the school as a whole can act to reduce pressure on teachers: (a) through changes in the administrative procedures and style; (b) by devising organizational rules and working conditions designed to reduce pressure in schools; (c) by acting to raise the morale of "apathetic" teachers; and (d) by recruiting parent support. Furthermore, Shinn and Morch (1984) emphasized that many causes of stress lie beyond the employees' control; therefore, individual coping strategies are likely to be less effective than organizational strategies involving groups of employees. They also found that group coping, or coping programs initiated "from above," contributed a great deal to employees' positive attitudes toward their work and to their sense of job satisfaction. This is be-

Table 8.2. *Schematic Description of a Comprehensive Strategy for Mitigating Teacher Burnout*

Focus of treatment	Individual level (teacher)	Organizational level (school)
Tackling the sources of stress	Training teachers to cope with stressful situations; instruction on causes of burnout; developing and improving teacher's leadership ability, problem solving, and conflict resolution.	Reducing degree of polarization in the classroom; reducing number of pupils per class; changing teacher's work plan or teaching plan.
Treatment of symptoms of stress	Workshops on easing stress; support and assistance groups; holidays; inservice training.	Creating a supportive atmosphere in the school; opening channels of communication; involvement in decision making; developing a positive and open organizational climate.

cause employees sensed that their employers really cared. Moreover, it appeared that interventions directed toward improving working conditions (e.g., job enrichment, improved communication, low-conflict interactions) were more effective than interventions directed toward individual aspects of the employee (e.g., intervention designed to increase one's tenacity or for relocating focus of control). Mechanic (1974) concluded that many work-related stressors may not be successfully circumscribed by individuals and only combined organizational efforts may prove effective in restricting them.

Direct action programs combined with palliatives can be employed either on the individual or the organizational level, thus forming a comprehensive approach. A schematic description of a comprehensive strategy for dealing with teacher burnout is shown in Table 8.2. An inclusive inventory of practical activities leading to a reduction or prevention of burnout can be found in Friedman and Lotan (1993).

A third distinction between the various burnout prevention and treatment approaches is between interventions designed to prevent burnout and those whose aim is to halt existing burnout. The first involves preventive programs, which can be taught in teacher training colleges and in other contexts for teacher training.

Preventive programs can be effective for non-burned-out teachers at any point in their career. Most intervention programs aim to ease existing burn-out, in which case the program is regarded more as "treatment" for reducing stress in teachers experiencing a moderate to high degree of burnout. In addition to allowing recuperation, these programs are intended to prevent recurring burnout.

Prevention is more effective and less expensive than treatment and therefore the importance of prevention should be emphasized. Furthermore, dealing with people already burned out requires very substantial efforts before recognizable results are obtained. Preventive intervention should be varied and tailored to different groups of teachers: an orientation program for new teachers, which is based on providing them with information on personal coping techniques and about working in a complex organization; inservice training and support groups. Findings clearly indicate that young teachers experience a greater sense of emotional exhaustion than their older colleagues (Friedman and Lotan, 1985; Korshavn, 1991; Schwab and Iwanicki, 1982b). Therefore, young teachers as a group may be classified as high risk in terms of burnout, and its early prevention is important. Cherniss (1991) found that teachers who had "recovered" quickly from stress early in teaching were those who had worked in schools offering a high level of support, especially from experienced colleagues. During their first year in teaching, new teachers sought out experienced colleagues for advice, information, and feedback, and those that found such mentors enjoyed an easier passage through this early stage.

Conclusion: How to Establish Healthier Schools?

Healthier schools can be achieved by, first, enhancing teachers' sense of professional self-efficacy, and second, by improving organizational environment. Based on existing studies, a healthier working environment for teachers at school can be established by taking action on the following four levels. The level of primary importance involves *relationships between teachers and pupils* (Friedman, 1995d). Friedman and Krongold (1993) indicated that pupils seem to need to receive warmth from their teachers and feel that teachers should offer them guidance, advice, and assistance in solving personal as well as learning problems. They expect teachers to relate to them not only as their students, but also, and more important, as individuals with feelings, needs, and difficulties. Even during classes, pupils expect the teacher to treat them with warmth and friendship. Teachers too appear to prefer a warm relationship with pupils and perceive expressions of closeness from their students as signs of personal and professional esteem.

Therefore, in addition to having the obvious professional teaching skills, creativity, and originality, teachers must be equipped with skills to help them in their classroom leadership role – in particular, those skills involving the "social" aspect of classroom life (ability to create class solidarity, support, and nurturing the group's sociability). Promoting this aspect of teaching during early training or inservice training may assist the teacher in overcoming work-related stress.

The second level is that of the *school climate and culture* (Friedman, 1991). This level involves improving the sense of community at school and augmenting the teacher's sense of professionalism. The teacher should not feel anxious about a noisy classroom or of having to initiate new methods of teaching. Principals should provide the kind of support that reduces the effect of existing environmental stressors. This support should essentially be directed at increasing the teacher's autonomy and sense of job satisfaction. The principal can take steps to boost teaching staff morale by allowing them, for example, to implement ideas that bring about success and encouraging them to tackle tasks or areas in which they perform well.

The third level on which a healthy working environment for teachers can be built is by *making parents active partners in the teaching process* and by increasing their involvement in solving problems linked to class discipline. It is advisable to have teachers and parents meet to discuss problems of homework, discipline, and regulated TV hours. These activities are aimed at raising parents' awareness of teaching objectives, developing greater understanding of what is happening in the school, and encouraging a willingness to get involved in attaining these goals. Principals can take the initiative in gaining recognition from parents, relevant authorities, and the public at large for the unique conditions in which teachers work; they should communicate a clear message of respect and appreciation of the teachers' work to the world outside the school.

The fourth level is focusing on *improving the school principal's managerial skills*. A particular emphasis should be laid on those abilities that may assist in creating a more positive climate, in achieving better cooperation among teachers. In addition, principals should be equipped with stress-reduction techniques known to reduce pressure.

9. Teaching Career:
Between Burnout and Fading Away? Reflections from a Narrative and Biographical Perspective

GEERT KELCHTERMANS

In this chapter, I look at teacher stress and burnout through the lens of my narrative-biographical research on teacher development (Kelchtermans, 1993a; 1993b). In their retrospective narrative accounts of career experiences, teachers often mention periods of strain, disturbing events, or frustrating situations with stressful effects. I use "stress" in a broad sense, referring to all these aspects of the teaching job that are experienced by teachers as frustrating, dissatisfying, or demotivating. Although I realize that some "stress" might operate positively (e.g., as an extra stimulant to reconsider and eventually change one's teaching practice), my use of the term in this chapter always implies the negative connotation of the word. "Burnout" is seen here as an advanced position on the stress continuum, showing the three facets distinguished by Maslach and Jackson: emotional exhaustion, depersonalization, and reduced personal accomplishment (Maslach and Jackson, 1984; see also Byrne and Maslach, this volume). In the discussion about the strict conceptual definition of stress and burnout, this is a pragmatic stance, one that focuses on the subjective meaning of these phenomena: the way they are "lived" by the teachers themselves.

This chapter thus has its theoretical roots in the phenomenological and symbolic interactionist tradition (e.g., Blumer, 1969). Stressful events are situations that are subjectively experienced by the teachers as negatively affecting their self-perception and their professional performance. The narrative and biographical approach can further be characterized as "interactionist," "contextualized" and "narrative":

- *Interactionism:* Notably, this is the symbolic interactionist construct holding that people's behavior centers around the subjective interpretations and meanings they give to specific contexts (Blumer, 1969).
  Stress and burnout are therefore to be studied from the meaning they have for the people who experience them and, in the case in point, who suffer from them.
- *Contextualization:* In the biographical perspective, people's actions and thoughts are situated in a specific context. This context includes not only the sociocultu-

ral and organizational environment people are living in but also their specific biographical/historical backgrounds. *Stress and burnout for teachers are to be situated in and understood from the specific time and space in which they are experienced.*

*   *Narrative:* Storytelling can be a very powerful way to understand teachers' experiences in their temporal-spatial context (Carter, 1993). In effect, their narrative accounts reflect how situations and events became meaningful to their professional thinking and behavior.
    Narratives about experienced stress and burnout, as well as about (successful) coping with them, can allow for an in-depth understanding and offer perspectives for effective coping.

My first set of comments focuses on the thesis that the influence of sociological factors on teachers' motivation (or demotivation) and stress is mediated through individual teachers' interpretations. Second, I elaborate on the biographical perspective and its contribution to our thinking about stress and burnout. My final reflections concern the question of successful coping with endemic stress in teachers' work.

Macro-Factors Through the Micro-Perspective

"Intensification" Versus Professionalization

Teacher stress and burnout are complex, multidimensional phenomena resulting from the interaction between individual teachers and their *work environment.* This environment not only includes the classroom and local school context but should also be widened conceptually to include factors at the macro level: educational policies, sociohistorical factors, and others. Several authors in this volume broaden their analysis beyond the "meso" level of school organization. Smylie and Miller situate their analysis in the macro context of major educational reforms (first and second reform waves). Woods concludes that teaching has become more stressful during the last decade, from a sociological perspective. His analysis focuses on the trends of "intensification" and "deprofessionalization" on the job. In my opinion, these trends are mainly linked to the first reform wave, characterized by a "factory" model of schooling, with its industrial values of bureaucratic efficiency, input control, and central tests and standards for the measurement of an essentially narrow range of student outcomes (Miller, this volume). "Thatcherism" and "Reaganomics" constitute its larger political and macroeconomic background.

However, Woods also evokes an opposite trend toward professionalism. The developments inspired by the so-called second reform wave encompass new efforts for teachers' professional development. "Empowerment" and "restructuring" are key words in this perspective. Woods illustrates this by pointing to the growing appreciation for action research and the teacher-as-researcher movements. As Smylie observes, however, the appearance of the second reform wave did not lessen the influence of the first. Moreover, the coexistence of both reform waves and the underlying concepts, he argues, although incompatible, accentuates the stressful aspects of the contemporary work environment in schools.

Illustrations from Flemish Teachers and Schools

Both tendencies, intensification and professionalization, can be observed in Belgian/Flemish schools. For example, the constantly increasing demands and expectations toward schools and teachers appear to "intensify" teaching (e.g., Elchardus, 1994). Society still expects education to contribute significantly to the solution of social problems, such as prevention of AIDS and drug abuse, multicultural education, equal opportunities (including gender issues), moral education, prevention of child abuse, and so on. New curricula or teaching materials are supposed to be implemented. Parents with professional careers expect schools to baby-sit their children before and after school.

Many of these demands and expectations are experienced by teachers as improper to their tasks. Teachers often complain that they are expected to provide a kind of social service, but are not recognized in their specific professional work. Another complaint is that they are expected to take over educational tasks that were traditionally assumed by the parents, such as developing children's social attitudes and skills, and their moral and religious education. Often, this goes even further, to reeducating pupils whom their own parents judge as unmanageable.

The stress on teachers is well illustrated by the answers Flemish primary and nursery teachers give when asked to typify their job situation metaphorically. In one study, a significant number of respondents chose images that evoke the heavy workload and the open-endedness of the job (Kelchtermans and Vandenberghe, 1991). Some illustrative examples: a Don Quixote fighting windmills; a prophet in the desert, lonely in his calling; a human computer in which society invests its changes and expects productivity at high levels. It's hard to survive in the jungle of constantly changing demands and methods. Sometimes teachers feel like a foot mat: Everybody passes by it and wipes his or her feet.

In this last metaphor, as in others, teachers contrast increasing demands with the *lack of professional recognition*. In spite of their efforts to cope with the multiple and changing demands and duties, teachers often feel under-valued by parents, school administrators, and society in general. Quite of-ten, they refer to the image of a dogsbody:

- A principal writes: "I am everybody's slave: slave of the parents, the inspectorate, the school board and the Ministry of Education with its piles of paper."
- A teacher in mid-career commented: "We are society's fools. Pupils answer back; parents take their children's stories more seriously than what a teacher has to say; society does not value your work and cynical colleagues mock your commitment to cope with it all."
- A young teacher feels like "a soldier in the trenches. You're shot at from all sides, without seeing the enemy or being able to defend yourself."

The loss of social prestige in teaching thus seems to constitute an im-portant demotivation (Depaepe, De Vroede, and Simon, 1993). I observed that male primary school teachers in particular often felt frustrated in mid-career. They had made their career choice with an image in mind of the well-respected teacher in the local community. This image no longer cor-responds to social realities.

Throughout these narrative or metaphorical accounts also recurred the theme of *vulnerability and powerlessness.* Teachers felt "attacked" but "de-fenseless," as functionaries and executors of decisions or interests beyond their control. Clearly, these sentiments contribute to experiences of stress or eventual burnout, accompanied by a feeling of deprofessionalization (Kelchtermans, 1993a, 1996).

However, the opposing trend was also present. Flemish educational pol-icy makers have been active in the 1990s in launching structural measures, which – although induced by economical incentives of budget control – are justified by concern for educational quality and teachers' professionality. This policy centers around the concepts of "decentralization" and "re-sponsibility" of the local school through greater local autonomy in matters of curriculum choice, classroom practice, and internal organization. Inser-vice training facilities and educational consultancies have been established to support efforts to improve educational quality. In principle, this decen-tralizing trend in educational policy actively promotes professionalization and opportunities for professional learning and development. In practice, however, this policy operates as a double-edged sword (Miller, Chapter 6): In the experience of many teachers and principals, these new responsibili-ties weigh heavily, inducing uncertainties or even threatening professional self-images or school cultures. These feelings are further intensified by the paradoxical mixture in a political discourse of budget control on the one hand and a concern for quality improvement on the other. Thus, although the trends of both intensification and professionalization can be observed in Flemish education, the first trend appears to dominate teachers' day-to-day experience.

The research literature, including the studies presented in this volume, indicate that most teachers do not experience high levels of stress or burnout. Nor is the majority demotivated or insufficient. The media, however, could easily convince one otherwise. Teachers' stress and burnout get much media attention. They make for a good story and guarantee high "viewer figures." At the same time, they can contribute to unwitting generalizations of darkness and doom threatening future generations because teachers are no longer functioning properly. The large group of teachers, who appear to work with commitment, competence, and satisfaction, is thus offended by this image. Because there is still limited empirical evidence in many countries about the actual scale of stress and burnout among teachers, one should remain very circumspect, at the risk of negatively affecting teachers' levels of commitment, motivation, and professional satisfaction; they are already being put to the test (cf. Nias, 1996a).

Determinants Versus Perceptions

In the discussion about stress factors or burnout determinants at the different levels of national or regional policy (macro level), the school organization (meso level), or the classroom (micro level), it is obvious that there is no direct linear or causal effect on teachers' thoughts and actions. Whether certain situations, events, or workplace conditions result in problematic stress and burnout generally depends on the way they are experienced by the teachers. In other words, determinants of stress and eventual burnout are mediated through the perceptions of the teachers. As Byrne writes: "Teacher burnout, albeit a function of the educational work environment, weighs more heavily with teachers' perceptions of, and attitudes toward, that environment" (Byrne, 1991a, p. 668).

Stress and burnout manifest themselves as psychological, emotional, subjective, and experiential phenomena. They appear in teachers' self-perceptions and occupation situations. In her biographical study of successful innovative teachers, Schönknecht (1997) came to the conclusion that "objectively" present stress does not determine teacher burnout. Burnout depends on the way teachers perceive stressful situations and the coping strategies they use to deal with them (p. 111).

In discussions about teacher stress and burnout, a central place should be given to teachers' *meanings* and *experience*. Perceptions and interpretations of actual (stressful) job situations depend heavily on one's personal and professional life history. In other words, stress and burnout should also be understood from teachers' career development. This more dynamic emphasis is a central focus for a more biographical perspective.

Teachers' Selves, Their Biographies, and the Incidence of Burnout

Several potential – and negative – stress factors have been identified and analyzed in other chapters of this volume. Whether, when, and why these factors effectively cause the negative pressures, strain, demotivation, or eventual burnout for a specific teacher remains elusive. Let us consider how teacher stress and burnout can be better understood from a biographical perspective.

An Exemplary Case: Marc

In his career story, Marc, a fourth grade teacher in mid-career, recalls a "nervous breakdown" when he was in his early thirties. This experience marked the end of what he calls the first phase in his career: "searching, experimenting and working hard to get external recognition." During these first ten years he had worked hard to attain a feeling of professional competence that would be publicly acknowledged by the principal, colleagues, and parents.

His own experiences in primary and secondary school had not provided him with a positive self-concept. On the contrary, during his years in secondary school, he became aware of social class differences: of the "sons of lawyers and doctors," but also of teachers alluding to his working class background and "pushing him aside." "As a little boy I was completely defenseless to that." Feelings of self-doubt, fear of failure, and insecurity played an important part during Marc's teacher training. He remembered the only three teacher educators who positively contributed to his self-esteem: "They made me feel I was somebody, that I counted as a person."

In his first year of teaching, Marc had interim appointments in ten different schools. In retrospect, however, he evaluated this experience positively. Working in different schools helped him to develop a more realistic view of life and work in Flemish primary schools. Moreover, his short stays in these schools provided more freedom to experiment with different teaching strategies. He knew that if he "messed things up," he could leave the school shortly. This attitude made him more relaxed and helped him concentrate on coping with the day-to-day demands.

Marc's second year of teaching took place in one school but ended in conflict and misunderstanding with parents, colleagues, and the principal. The next year he got a job in the school where he is now working. His first contact with the principal, however, was shocking. He was asked bluntly how he – a young, inexperienced teacher – had the gall to apply for a job in such a highly regarded school. As the school needed an extra teacher and the school board appreciated Marc's voluntary commitment in the local youth movement, he still got the job. Struggling with the problems of a beginning teacher, increased by his personal and professional uncertainties as well as by a demanding and critical principal, Marc had a difficult start. However, things improved the following year when the principal asked him to experiment with a new teaching method for mathematics. From then on, he found his principal – although still demanding – to be a competent supporter. "That man gave me a whole lot of self-confidence and that was an enormously stimulating experience." The principal's judgments of Marc's work were severe, but he was also explicitly valued for the positive aspects. As Marc noted, "That was exactly what I needed at that time." After several years, the principal asked Marc to take over the first grade. "That again was a very hard change to make. But again I got a lot of support from that man." From Marc's account, the principal stimulated him and helped with concrete methodological or practical questions. He insisted that Marc take his time to deal with the challenges of teaching a first grade. That year, Marc spent much time studying learning problems and remedial teaching strategies, dealing with the specific needs of several children. Gradually, his work began to run more smoothly and – of great importance to Marc – he got positive feedback from the parents.

During his fourth year in the first grade, Marc had a class of thirty-two pupils, among whom six had learning and behavior problems. Together with other health problems (kidney stones, problems with his back), the stress of working with this difficult group "finished me off." He had to recuperate at home for several weeks. Thereafter, he found that he lacked the energy to renew his full commitment in the job.

This sick leave had become for Marc a time of self-reflection and reconsideration of his work as a teacher.

The Biographical Perspective on Teachers' Professional Development

As illustrated in Marc's case, teachers evolve throughout their careers: in their actions in the class with pupils; in their relationship with principals, colleagues, and parents; in their "thinking" about themselves, their teaching, and their role as teachers. We call this "professional development": a lifelong learning and developmental process resulting from the interactions between teachers and their professional environment (Kelchtermans, 1993a, 1993b). To better understand this process, experienced teachers' career stories or professional biographies were collected and analyzed: narrative, retrospective accounts of career experiences, through semistructured, biographical interviews, which stimulate autobiographical self-reflection (see Kelchtermans, 1994).

Professional development not only affects teachers' ways of coping with occupational demands but also their understandings and representations of schools and teaching. In other words, teachers develop a *personal interpretive framework*, a lens through which they perceive, give meaning, and act. The analysis of the career stories revealed two important and interwoven domains in this personal interpretive framework. First there is a set of conceptions about themselves as teachers: *the professional self.* A second domain is the *subjective educational theory,* the personal system of knowledge and beliefs about teaching.

This perspective thus indicates that teachers' actual behaviors and perceptions are embedded in their *personal history* (Carter, 1993, p. 7), which implies in turn that teachers' thoughts and actions can only be understood properly as the result of learning processes throughout their career, as subjective histories of learning.

The fragment from Marc's story also exemplifies the *contextualization* in the biographical perspective: Teachers and teaching are approached in their context, in both its spatial and its temporal dimension. For example, Marc's first confrontation with the principal takes on its full meaning only when it is placed against Marc's uncertainties from previous experiences during his induction, even during his days as a pupil. Thus, actual teacher behavior is contextualized both in the teacher's life history and in his or her professional environment (organizational; sociocultural). As Goodson (1984) states, biographical research should "constantly broaden the concern with personal truth to take account of wider sociohistorical concerns, even if these are not part of the consciousness of the individual" (p. 139). Marc's story reveals the pervasive influence of socioeconomic (class) differences on pupils' self-esteem when they are not only played off by other pupils but also by teachers. It exemplifies the important role schools have in children's socialization through middle-class values and norms. By situating teachers' "stories of action" in a broader theory of context, they become life histories with the potential for a deep understanding of the lived experience of schooling (Goodson, 1995). The biographical perspective thus allows for the study of teacher stress and burnout and their determinants as embedded in a specific constellation of time and space.

Critical Incidents and Phases: Stressful Challenges

Marc's nervous breakdown is a good example of what Sikes, Measor, and Woods (1985) call a critical phase or critical incident. Critical incidents are "key events in an individual's life, and around which pivotal decisions revolve. They provoke the individual into selecting particular kinds of actions, which lead in particular directions" (p. 57).[1] Critical phases are periods in teachers' lives with pervasive changes, challenges, or important decisions. "Critical" means here "distinctive, having a strong personal meaning." Teachers see themselves as forced to reconsider their teaching practices and professional selves. These experiences carry an intense emotional load and are often experienced as stressful and threatening. If successfully coped with, however, they constitute opportunities for learning and development. In this connection, Sikes et al. (1985) use the concept of counterincidents: events from which the teacher feels that he or she had successfully coped with challenges or difficulties (p. 63).

Although critical phases and incidents are not always as dramatic as Marc's breakdown, they typically have an important impact on teachers' professional selves and their subjective educational theories. Marc, for example, mentions two changes in his personal interpretive framework:

- The teacher is only one factor among many others in determining pupils' learning outcomes. So, don't blame yourself if you don't achieve all the results you strived for.
- Healthy survival in teaching demands a careful balancing of both commitment and distance. "I shouldn't constantly drive at maximum speed. If I want to keep my engine running, it is necessary to slow down regularly and to avoid pushing the limits all the time." Most important to him was learning not to take situations in the classroom too personally and to build some emotional distance into his professional commitments.

1. See also the work in Germany by Filipp and associates on "kritische Ereignissforschung" (critical incident research) (Filipp, 1990; Ulich, 1987). Denzin (1989) uses the concept of "epiphany" in a similar way to refer to "those life experiences that radically alter and change the meanings persons give to themselves and their experiences" (p. 125). Epiphanies alter the fundamental meaning structures a person's life; their effects may be positive or negative (Denzin, 1989, p. 14).

Other examples of critical phases that emerged in our study are the induction phase (initial years in teaching); periods of externally imposed educational innovation; parenthood and the education of one's own children; and periods of physical or psychological problems.

The meaning of those critical phases for individual teachers, however, will differ. To Marc, the frequent changes of schools during his induction period meant a "safe" opportunity for exploring his work and experimenting with it. Other teachers might experience the same working conditions as provoking insecurity and uncertainty.

Categories of critical incidents may include experiences that raise doubts about one's professional competence; the experience of decrease in social status; or the loss of beloved persons.

In teachers' career stories we also found what we called "critical persons": people who have a significant impact on one's personal interpretive framework. Examples are principals, teacher educators, or others who positively or negatively influence a given teacher's opportunities for personal and professional growth. In essence, these are positive or negative role models (Kelchtermans, 1993a), such as the supportive teacher educators and the principal in Marc's case.

In teachers' career stories, critical incidents, phases, and persons (and eventual counterincidents) constitute moments of *narrative condensation*. They reveal the complex interactions between teachers and their personal goals, norms, and values on the one hand and contextual demands on the other. Successful coping with those incidents implies not only efficient actions and social strategies but also changes in professional self and subjective educational theory. In analyzing the meaning and impact of potential stress factors, these are useful heuristic tools; "they reveal, like a flashbulb, the major choice and change times in people's lives" (Sikes et al., 1985, p. 57).

A Differentiated View of a Teacher's Professional Self

To a limited degree, teaching is a matter of technical skills and content knowledge; therefore, the person of a teacher is equally important. "The ways in which teachers achieve, maintain, and develop their identity, their sense of self, in and through a career, are of vital significance in understanding the actions and commitments of teachers in their work" (Ball and Goodson, 1985, p. 18; also Nias, 1989). This idea was integrated in my analysis of teachers' professional biographies and resulted in the development of a differentiated concept of professional self, which in turn might contribute to a more appropriate, integrative, and in-depth understanding of teacher stress and eventual burnout (Kelchtermans, 1993a, 1993b). The analysis of teachers' professional self resulted in the distinction of five components:

- *Self-image* (descriptive component): Who am I as a teacher?
- *Self-esteem* (evaluative component): How well am I doing my job as a teacher? In Marc's case, this was a continuing issue of personal concern.
- *Job motivation* (conative component): What motivates me to keep going in my job? Marc mentions the support by the principal, recognition by pupils and parents, and student outcomes as especially important motivating factors.
- *Task perception* (normative component): What must I do to be a good teacher? In Marc's task perception, continuous professional learning, notably by experimenting with new teaching methods and materials, had an important place.
- *Future perspective* (prospective component): How do I see my future as a teacher and how do I feel about it? For example, after having been a first-grade teacher for ten years, Marc felt that he started "to fly on automatic pilot" and feared getting stuck in routines. This awareness reminded him of a supervisor he had known during his training. That man's situation had always been an example of what Marc wanted to avoid for himself (a negative, critical person). These factors motivated him to change grade levels and to develop new career perspectives as a fourth-grade teacher.

In this differentiated concept of professional self, self-esteem can be understood as the subjective balance between a teacher's self-image and his or her task perception. Task perception refers to the teacher's "personal professional programme": the personal goals and norms to be achieved or respected throughout one's work. As illustrated in Marc's case, these goals and norms develop in the course of a career. However, if the discrepancy between teachers' self-image and their task perception becomes too wide, it will negatively affect their job satisfaction and motivation, as a consequence, it can cause undue stress. In Marc's story, this struggle to develop positive self-esteem is the thread running through his first career phase. The struggle not only concerns competence in contending with "objective" job demands but also with the internal processes of keeping one's personal professional programme sufficiently realistic. In other words, positive self-esteem is a matter of not only positive feelings but also the *content* of one's task perception and one's perceived capacity for dealing successfully with those demands.

Task Perception: Between Personal Values and External Demands

In coping with the social demands made on schools, a teacher's task perception is crucial. It constitutes the filter through which external demands and expectations are perceived, judged, and eventually assumed. Moreover, the task perception is a dynamic mental process that changes as a result of actually contending with evolving demands.

Task perception is linked to teachers' occupational commitment. Woods (this volume) argues that "teachers at most risk of stress are those with strong feelings of vocation. For them, the personal 'self' is inextricably bound up with the teacher role." The more teachers commit themselves to their job, the higher become their demands for their own performance and the greater the risk that they cannot meet their self-imposed standards. Nias makes the same observation about teachers who are highly committed, with a strong "caring" ethos (Nias, 1989). Keeping a realistic balance between their commitments and task perceptions, on the one hand, and the demands of school and classroom, on the other, constitutes a lifelong tension for teachers, as illustrated in the example of Marc.

Closely linked is a teacher's locus of control, especially concerning student outcomes. Because this variable is used as an important indicator of the quality of teachers' work, the way teachers attribute the causes for those outcomes is highly relevant to their job motivation. Here again, balancing internal and external locus of control is a task for teachers throughout their careers. Of course, student outcomes are only partially determined by instruction. Equally or sometimes more decisive are personal factors (motivation, perseverance, etc.) or social factors that are often very hard to influence or change. This creates an ambivalence. Teachers with high internal locus of control may experience high job satisfaction when student outcomes are good. On the other hand, when pupils' learning outcomes are poor, they may tend to blame themselves and feel frustrated and ineffective. Teachers with high external locus of control often ascribe student outcomes to factors beyond their efforts and often beyond their control. In some cases, this might negatively affect their feelings of professional competence ("I can't make a difference") and thus have a depressing effect on their motivation and eventually on their sense of self-esteem.

These findings stress the importance of teachers' interpretive interactions with their work environment, or more generally, the need to assess the interplay between personal (biographical) and contextual factors. Thus, increased stress and the risk of burnout can come not only from external locus of control but also from high levels of internal locus of control.

Coping Strategies

Not all teachers experience problematic stress. For example, Smylie (Chapter 3) concludes that "stress is an endemic part of teachers' work. . . . Yet, while we may conclude that conditions of teaching are stressful and that excessive stress may have deleterious consequences, it is difficult to determine the extent of the problems or the 'damage' actually caused by stress in teachers' work." In spite of the endemic stress in their job, most teachers cope more or less successfully with multiple demands. In this final part, I want to highlight some of these coping strategies from the perspective of teachers' professional development. For example, recent research at the University of Leuven in Belgium centers on the understanding of teachers' motives for using "conservative" coping strategies (Clement, 1995; Clement and Vandenberghe, 1997; Kelchtermans, 1993a; Vanoost, 1994; Vandenberghe and Vanoost, 1996). These findings support the idea that providing opportunities for professional growth and development in schools is important for educational quality and for the prevention of demotivation and burnout (Kievit and Vandenberghe, 1993; Little, 1993).

Parallel Careers

Much literature on educational innovation has highlighted teachers' and schools' resistance to externally imposed reforms (e.g., Sikes, 1992). This attitude merits closer attention. For example, Gitlin and Margonis (1995) recently argued that there is often good sense in teachers' resistance to reforms (Gitlin and Margonis, 1995). Blase (1988) ascribes many teachers' "conservative orientation" to their feelings of "vulnerability." Teachers often feel that they have no or only limited control over measures that have consequences for their own particular working conditions and practices. For Blase, this vulnerability might account for teachers' eagerness to keep the status quo (Blase, 1988). This can be illustrated by our finding about the central importance in teachers' career stories of a "lifelong assignment," which assures a tenured position as a civil servant (Kelchtermans, 1993a). In practice, this means that it is almost impossible for a teacher to get fired. Furthermore, it is a widespread custom in Flanders – at least in nursery and primary schools – for teachers to stay in the same grade level throughout their careers. In other words, structural and cultural working conditions may well contribute to a more conservative orientation. However, close analysis of teachers' career stories reveals still other motives and variations behind this trend to conservative educational perspectives and practices.

We observed the phenomenon of "parallel careers" (Nias, 1989) among male and female teachers (Kelchtermans, 1993a). Female teachers mainly referred to their parallel career as a mother and a housewife. For male teachers, these careers were sometimes "paid jobs" (e.g., freelance journalist, librarian), but in most cases, they were voluntary, "leisure-time activities": a board member of a local sport club, a jazz musician, and organizer of festivals. These activities appear to be highly motivating and satisfying, but they are possible only as long as teachers' occupational situations remain unaltered. Typically, teachers do not mention financial gain as an incentive for those activities. Rather, there are other benefits. A first benefit is contacts and collaboration with adults. This is a compensation for (primary and nursery) teachers' day-to-day work with young children. This balance of working with adults and children often helped teachers "to stay sane."

Another benefit of parallel careers is the enhanced social status teachers can get from it in the local community (e.g., as manager of the soccer club). The prestige is important; male respondents emphasized their frustration about the decrease in social status of their work and its negative influence on their satisfaction and motivation.

In a sense, the parallel career illustrates teachers' constructive coping with occupational demands. On the other hand, there is the risk that these job-external benefits become more rewarding than the intrinsic satisfactions of teaching, thereby leading to greater commitment to the parallel career than to teaching. More important, however, is the understanding of teachers' coping strategies: why they are chosen and what they signify. For example, parallel careers might be a constructive way of dealing with typical stress factors in teaching – for example, compensation for "infantilization" or spending the main part of the day with young children. The difficult question here is this: At what point does this strategy become counterproductive to teachers' professional commitment and to the quality of their work?

Leaving Teaching

In a recent study, Flemish primary school teachers who had voluntarily left teaching were compared with their colleagues who stayed (Vanoost, 1994; Vandenberghe and Vanoost, 1996). The analysis showed that four factors clearly differentiated leavers and nonleavers: sense of routine, lack of possibilities for promotion, relationships with colleagues and the principal, and the presence or absence of new challenges. "Leaving" teachers felt "stuck" in their careers, with no stimulation for continuing commitment and no opportunities for professional development. The threat of routine, the promotionally flat career, and the lack of intrinsic challenges led those teachers to conclude that this career did not offer sufficient opportunities for the development of their capacities. Among this subsample, relations with colleagues and with the principal were evaluated negatively; a supportive, collegial network was perceived as lacking in the schools.

Interestingly, several possible reasons for leaving teaching that were featured in the research literature turned out in this study not to differentiate meaningfully between leavers and nonleavers: the level of the wages, the social recognition and job status, and professional efficacy.

A disquieting conclusion of this study was that many of the teachers leaving education were talented, highly committed, and motivated, as if the "good ones" had left for lack of perspectives for their personal and professional self-development.

"It's Better to Burn Out, than to Fade Away" (Neil Young)

I conclude with this provocative, intriguing quote from the singer, Neil Young (although he probably didn't have teachers in mind). If, in fact, "leavers" are often good teachers who burned out in a frustrating job situation, can we judge their decision to leave as a positive coping strategy? In effect, are they stepping out to find new perspectives and opportunities for their own development? On the other hand, many teachers who stay in teaching – for whatever reasons – try somehow to "survive" in their job (Yee, 1991). They may fade away by developing minimal commitment, conservative attitudes toward innovation, or reluctance to take on ambitious challenges (see also Huberman, 1989b, p. 47). For example, Firestone and Pennell (1993) argue that the reduced commitment of burned-out teachers negatively affects pupils' learning outcomes. On the other hand, dynamic teachers, who commit themselves fully to their job, run a greater risk of burnout (cf. Smylie, Chapter 5). Would we prefer this profile to that of minimalistic survivors, who vanish in the web of daily routines?

How then do we improve the quality of life in schools to keep stress within manageable limits and avoid burnout? There is clearly no simple answer to this question. Generally, however, for teachers to "keep burning" at an acceptable and constructive level, schools must be places to live, learn, develop one's capacities, and work with commitment on valued projects. This is beneficial not only for teachers but also for pupils.

Promising possibilities and perspectives in this respect can be found in the literature on "teacher empowerment" and "restructuring schools" (see also the chapters in this volume by Miller, Smylie and, more indirectly, Leithwood and colleagues). Deeper insights into the interplay between teachers' professional development, their teaching practices, and their working conditions are still needed, as well as a more thorough understanding of successful restructuring projects. An example is the work of Clement (1995; see also Clement and Vandenberghe, 1997) on teachers' collegiality. Following work by Little and Hargreaves, Clement's study provides a balanced view of the tensions between teacher autonomy and collegiality in the workplace, on the one hand, and professional development on the other. Collegiality is clearly not the ultimate panacea for school problems.

Given the importance of teachers' personal interpretive framework for their day-to-day work, and given the turbulent sociohistorical environment they work in, teachers' *self-reflective attitudes and skills* are of crucial importance in establishing contextualized learning opportunities. Teachers' professional selves and subjective educational theories will have to be reflected on, and shared through dialogue. Teachers' storytelling or other forms of narrative exchange would constitute good starting points for explicit and in-depth reflection. The themes of stress, demotivation, and eventual feelings of burnout could, for example, find their place here with authenticity.

At the school level, forms of *collaborative practitioner research (action research)* could also provide a platform for exchanging ideas and conducting joint work. In this context, several researchers have emphasized the importance of the (micro)political, the moral, and the emotional dimensions of teaching and teacher development (Hargreaves, 1995; Little, 1993; Kelchtermans, 1996). The thesis here is that schools can be rich, dynamic environments in which teachers can acquire the flexibility and competence to deal with new challenges. In such stimulating environments, both teachers and pupils might sing along with Neil Young, "Rock 'n' roll is here to stay. . . . It's better to burn out than to fade away."

10. A Psychosocial Interpretation of Teacher Stress and Burnout

WILLY LENS AND SAUL NEVES DE JESUS

Teacher burnout is a very broad concept with several different aspects. It includes stress, professional dissatisfaction, absenteeism, low professional involvement, and the wish to leave the profession. In more severe cases, it may even lead to emotional exhaustion and depression (Esteve, 1992). Also for Rudow (this volume), "burnout is an overlapping concept... it is overlapping as it unites symptoms of (chronic) stress, fatigue, job dissatisfaction, anxiety." He notes that the terms "burnout" and "stress" (more specifically "distress") are used as synonyms. Teachers who have professional problems and who cannot cope in an efficient way with those problems experience distress (Pithers and Fogarty, 1995). Burnout results from continuously experiencing distress (not eu-stress). It is always negative. Maslach (1993; this volume) developed a multidimensional model defining "burnout as a psychological syndrome of emotional exhaustion, depersonalization and reduced accomplishment."

Woods (this volume) discusses the introduction of the Education Reform Act of 1988 in the school systems of England and Wales and the subsequent steep increase in the number of teachers applying for early retirement because of health reasons. He uses it as a case study that may tell us a lot about "theoretical and conceptual constructions that have common currency" regarding teachers' stress (and burnout). Also, when looking at stress from a psychological or a psychosocial point of view – as we want to do, rather than to consider it as a social or sociological phenomenon as Woods does – it is indeed possible to derive from the specific England/ Wales case more general underlying psychological processes leading (or not) to stress, burnout, and demotivation among teachers. Illustrating this is the main goal of the chapter.

First, we would like to make a few remarks. Not only teachers but also many other social professionals who work in close relationship with other individuals or groups of individuals show burnout. Also in other jobs, in private companies and public institutions, many people suffer from distress, demotivation, and burnout. Maslach's first studies of burnout did not even include teachers.

It is also important to keep in mind – as Woods does – that not all teachers experience stress. There are at least as many, and probably more, teachers who are still highly motivated, and not overstressed than there are overstressed, demotivated, or burned-out teachers (Pithers and Fogarty, 1995). Who are the teachers who suffer from stress and burnout and how do they differ from their colleagues without those problems? Research in "high-vitality teachers" (Sederberg and Clark, 1990) could help to identify the qualities of highly motivated, nonstressed teachers

The danger with the media hype around students' lack of motivation and teachers' stress and burnout is that it might cause the many teachers who are still highly motivated and who still love their jobs to feel outdated and awkward. Teachers' stress and students' demotivation (Lens and Decruyenaere (1991) seem to be contagious.

So, there are many teachers who are not strained and there are many nonteachers who suffer from stress that is related to their job. The problem of occupational stress is not new and it is certainly not specific to teachers (Kahn, Wolfe, Quinn, Snoeck, and Rosenthal, 1964).

Lens and Schops (1991) report that in a group of 718 junior high school and high school teachers in Flanders, only 5% said that their job was a more or less permanent source of stress; 42% said that they were regularly stressed in their job. However, 41% answered that this was very seldom the case and 12% were never stressed by their job. A large majority – 67% – were rather or very satisfied with their jobs and only 17% were rather or very dissatisfied.

When the researchers asked the teachers in their sample if they would choose to become a teacher again if they could restart their career, not more than 20% said "certainly," 31% said "probably," 20% said "it depends," 20% answered "probably not," and 9% said "certainly not." This is a very gloomy picture. But what are the numbers among other professionals such as nurses, bank tellers, insurance agents, and salespersons?

Complaining teachers very often compare themselves with employees with about the same level of educational training but holding a job in private companies. In general, teachers think that those people are much better off professionally. They think their neighbor – unlike teachers – has a lower workload, is less stressed, is paid or rewarded as a function of his or her merits, can be promoted, and so on: "The grass is always greener on the other side" (Jeurissen, 1992).

In a pilot study, Lens and Creten (1995) compared a group of 110 junior high school and high school teachers (from only two different schools) and fifty white-collar employees (from also fifty different companies) with a corresponding level of education. They found that 92% of the teachers and 88% of the employees were at least "rather satisfied" with their jobs. The mean score (on a 7-point scale: 1 = very satisfied; 7 = very dissatisfied) for teachers (M = 2.20) is not different ($F[1, 147]$ < 1.0) from the mean score for employees (M = 2.28). However, they also found that 95% of the teachers and only 76% of the employees reported feeling that what they contribute to their job (their input) is smaller or less important than what they get out of it (their output). More teachers than employees subjectively felt that they get more out of their job than they have to contribute (the input/output ratio being smaller than 1.00). The mean input/output ratio is significantly ($F[1, 142]$ = 6.82, p < .01) lower for teachers (M = 0.70) than for employees (M = 0.84). So, the grass is not really greener on the other side, or is it greener on both sides? The big majority of the teachers (89%) and of the employees (84%) considered their input/output ratio to be fair (see Adams' equity theory: Adams, 1965; Adams and Freedman, 1976). This difference is not significant.

Twenty-four percent of the teachers had the feeling that they are now more motivated for their job than they used to be, 30% said that they are now less motivated, and the other 46% do not experience any difference. For the employees, the picture is somewhat less positive: The corresponding percentages are 20%, 42%, and 38%. The chi-square (2) = 2.22, however, is not significant. Also, Pithers and Fogarty (1995) unexpectedly found almost no differences in occupational stress between vocational teachers and a professional/business reference group.

Diekstra, de Heus, and Schaufele (this volume) asked the research question, "Do teachers burn more easily?" (than other social professionals), and found a strongly affirmative answer. Several studies show that burnout is a more important problem in the teaching profession than in many other professions with similar academic and personal requirements (Kyriacou, 1987; Punch and Tuetteman, 1990).

Probably for the sake of simplicity, Woods distinguishes among only four types of accommodating teachers and nonaccommodating teachers. We prefer to consider stress as a continuous independent variable. People are more or less stressed. From a psychological point of view, stress or strain results from subjectively weighting on the one hand the demands that are made by the job and the circumstances in which the job has to be done, and on the other hand the available resources one is willing to put in the job (Beehr and Newman, 1978; French, 1973). This means that whether a job is stressful or the degree to which it is stressful is a highly individual determination. In Woods's case study, teachers became stressed mostly because the demands on them were increased, due to "the intensification" of their work. In our own studies, about 20% of teachers refer to their decreasing individual resources (due to age, health, and lack of on the job training in, for example, the psychology of today's adolescents) as an important cause of stress. Of course, there are many other factors that may lead to teacher burnout (Friedman, 1991; this volume). Farber (this volume) discusses a "hypothetical experiment" illustrating changes in the teaching profession that can contribute to the increase of teacher burnout.

The relationship between the level of experienced stress and psychological well-being is curvilinear or an inverted U-shape. Recall the old and often neglected Yerkes-Dodson Law indicating, in this case, that stress levels below or above an optimal point have negative consequences. The level of stress at which people function most optimally is very individual and depends on the kind of task to be done (e.g., complexity, difficulty, novelty). Some people would feel much better and perform more efficiently if they were more stimulated and stressed. The concept of stress refers almost always – and also in these chapters – to levels of stress beyond the optimal. It is then also referred to as "distress" (versus eu-stress or optimal stress). But we have limited this discussion to stress as distress and eventual burnout.

A Multilevel Approach: Stress as a Function of Person and Situation Interactions

As suggested by Lewin's paradigmatic behavioral formula $B = f(P, E)$, all behaviors and psychological processes result from the interaction between individual and situational variables. Woods (this volume) also refers to these two categories of causal variables to explain stress. What are the personal and the situational variables and circumstances that cause stress in nonaccommodating teachers and that can account for the four different types of accommodating teachers? In a somewhat different question, how do teachers explain that they are stressed (demotivated, burned out)? What type of causal attribution do they make? From a psychological point of view, this second question is at least as important as the first one. It is indeed the teachers' perception or interpretation of situational, social, or sociological factors (the potential stressors) that will affect their functioning. And it is well documented in research on social cognition and self-perception that causal attributions can be very biased (Fiske and Taylor, 1991). For example, when Lens and Schops (1991) asked teachers what motivates them for their job, 68% of the teachers made an internal attribution and referred to themselves; 34% made an external attribution by referring to the pupils and their parents. When asked what de-motivates them, only 33% of the teachers referred to variables within themselves and 43% refered to the pupils and their parents.

Initially, Woods (this volume) situates the teachers' experiences on "a field" that is constituted by the interaction between sociological factors at the micro level ("the teacher's biography and person"), the meso level ("institutional and middle-range factors"), and the macro level ("global trends and government policy"). In our own educational research on students' and teachers' motivation, we prefer the Lewinian formula and we distinguish between four types of factors: the teachers themselves or the P in the formula (their gender, age, and seniority, level of professional training, career expectations, marital status, physical and psychological health, etc.), and three levels of situational variables, the E in the formula: the class level (the teaching requirements and didactic instruments, the type and the level of the curriculum, the pupils and their parents), the school level (the principal or directorate, the board of management, the representatives of parents and of the local community, the colleagues, the local community, the school culture, etc.), and the national level (the government, the national church and their inspection or supervision, the labor market, socioeconomic variables, society in general, etc.). But these four categories largely correspond to the distinction made by Woods when he discusses nonaccommodation in the second part of his chapter.

Teachers and Their Careers

Woods (this volume) argues that teachers with strong feelings of vocation are more at risk of stress. Highly committed teachers derive their personal self-esteem to a large extent from their professional career and how they define it. They do not want to adjust to new demands that are contrary to their habitual style of teaching. All kinds of professional changes and renewals that are imposed on them are easily interpreted, not as a change for the better or as a challenge, but as a personal criticism. These hurt their self-esteem.

We cannot test this hypothesis in our data, but we did find that teachers, when asked to give the important reasons for their being positively motivated, refer most frequently to themselves. They say that for highly motivated teachers, teaching is not a job but a vocation. If that is true, it may be part of the teachers' motivational problems. At least in Belgium, for many teachers in elementary school and in junior high school, teaching was not their first choice. Before entering a teachers' training college (outside the university system), most of them enrolled first at a university to prepare for a nonteaching job (e.g., law school, medical school, engineering, psychology, or educational sciences) but failed their freshman exams. They left the university to enter lower-level teacher training colleges. This pattern, of course, does not totally preclude strong feelings of vocation. But we would argue that, in general, such teachers identify less with the job than men and women whose first and only choice was to become a teacher (as it used to be "in the old days"). In Portugal, only 31% of the preservice teachers for elementary and junior high school say that teaching is their first professional project and that they want to be a teacher (Jesus, 1993). Contrary to Woods, Jesus (1995a) found that beginning teachers who really wanted to become teachers and who went to a teacher training college to realize their professional goal are more motivated for their job and show more resistance against potential causes of burnout (Jesus, 1995a).

From a motivational point of view, it would indeed be regrettable if Woods's argument would hold. Good teachers should also stay lifelong students or continuing learners, as they expect their pupils to be (Maehr, 1984). Teaching is not so much an achievement as a continuous learning experience in which one must grow and become more proficient. Lens and Schops (1991) found that highly motivated teachers, unlike demotivated teachers, are strongly interested in inservice training and other types of professional development. They also found that only 13% of 718 teachers do indeed refer to their colleagues and 15% to their principal as a source of motivation. It seems that teachers do not learn very much from each other professionally. We strongly agree with Woods where he refers to D. Hargreaves (1994). Teachers do indeed need a "new professionalism," less individualism and more collaboration, less supervision and more mentoring, less resistance to change and more creativity, flexibility, and team spirit (Jesus, 1995b). It is easier to adapt in a constructive and efficient way to externally imposed changes in a group than as an individual. Teachers-in-training and teachers on the job should be given plenty of opportunities to acquire a more scholarly attitude, not so much for the content of the curricula that they are or will be teaching, as for the teaching itself and for the psychology of children and adolescents. It is amazing to see that in many schools, young and inexperienced teachers get the most difficult classes to teach. In private companies, however, the newly recruited professionals are given the time to grow into their new jobs; they are assisted and coached by experienced colleagues. Also at the university level "mentoring partnerships with senior faculty give young professors the help they need to thrive when launching a career in academe" (Murray, 1995).

Regarding the age variable, we also found that younger teachers (ages 23 to 35) are generally less stressed and more satisfied than are the teachers in the age groups of thirty-six to forty-five and forty-six to sixty-five. Most of the teachers who experience stress more or less continuously belong to the oldest age group. Those least satisfied with the job are in the middle group. We also found that female teachers are significantly less stressed and more satisfied than male teachers. In the Lens and Creten (1995) data, this difference was in the same direction but not significant. For the employees the difference was in the other direction: Males were more satisfied with their job than females. However, this difference was not significant (nor was the interaction between gender and profession). The mean input/output ratio is not different for male ($M = 0.69$) and female teachers ($M = 0.71$).

Teaching in higher, more difficult levels of secondary education (e.g., the humanities) seems to be less stressful and more rewarding than teaching in lower levels of technical or vocational schools. Especially teaching general courses such as math and languages at the lowest levels of vocational education is a very nerve-racking enterprise for many teachers. This has, of course, to do with the type of students at that "bottom end."

We also found, as Woods does, that teachers complain about their horizontal career. Most teachers cannot be promoted in their jobs. Only a very few can realistically aspire to become a principal, an inspector, or other administrator.

Many younger teachers have no job security and/or are forced to teach in different schools to have a full load. It is not easy to invest oneself in different institutions, each with its own climate and culture. This is even more difficult for older teachers who may have tenure but who are supernumerary in their school. Such teachers have – at least in Belgium – a priority when there is a vacancy and they are also a constant threat to younger colleagues without tenure in other schools.

Being a teacher implies, of course, much more than teaching. Many teachers in our elementary and secondary school samples complain that they have too many additional odd jobs (e.g., watching over the children in the playground, fund-raising, making house calls to recruit new pupils to the school, being involved with the sociocultural life of the local community).

Situational Variables

We distinguished three levels of situational factors: the class level, the school level, and the national level.

The Class Level

Lens and Schops (1991) found that for secondary school teachers, the pupils and their parents are the most important source of stress: 26.5% of all listed reasons for being stressed, expressed by 30% of the teachers. Many teachers have problems with children's negative attitude, their lack of motivation, their disruptive behavior in class. Students' lack of discipline is another important cause of teacher burnout (Jesus, 1995a). It seems to be stressful for teachers to cope with underachieving students; but teaching children who lack the necessary intellectual abilities and skills to be successful in the curriculum their parents selected for them is also stressful. Additionally, the psychological and emotional problems of children from broken families or with other problems at home are a burden for teachers.

Many teachers (about 20% in our data) admit they have disciplinary problems and feel handicapped by them because they know that in many cases, they will not be supported by their director and/or the parents. Indeed, teachers complain about two types of parents. Some parents are interested very little or not at all in the school career of their children. This attitude is more typical in lower-level technical and vocational education than in other types. Other parents are too much involved and obtrusive. They know everything better than the teachers. It is no longer true that the parents usually take the teacher's side when there is a problem at school. They would rather blame him or her and believe the child's point of view: "my child, beautiful child."

The School Level

Teaching is a very lonely activity, even in large schools. We found that only a very small percentage of the teachers refer to their colleagues (13%), their director or principal (13%), or the inspector/supervisor (1%) as a source of motivation, help, and support. We refer to Friedman's contribution to this volume for a discussion of how to prevent or mitigate teacher burnout by creating healthier work environments in schools.

The National Level

The second most important category of causes for teacher stress is from the national level. The Education Reform Act of 1988 and the resulting intensification in teachers' jobs are a very good example (Woods, this volume). We see at least two important problems with nationwide educational reforms. First, they are too frequent; second, they are dictated or imposed on the schools and the teachers without much educational justification. The combination of both is, of course, the best way to demotivate people in whatever job or career.

First, each reform in educational programs or didactic approach is seen by teachers as an accusation of failure of the old system. You can imagine the motivational and emotional reactions of teachers who believed in and worked hard for the old program. They feel like many of the dogs in Seligman's experiments on learned helplessness. They experience not just helplessness but also hopelessness. They worked hard to make the program successful; nevertheless, someone "way up there" has decided to change things. Many of the things they worked hard for now seem to be superfluous. If they had not put in so much effort, the outcome would have been the same: failure. Experiencing no connection between action (input, effort, caring, etc.) and outcome is the best soil for cultivating helplessness, hopelessness, demotivation, stress, and depression. No wonder teachers who experience this a few times get burned out. They give up. They are no longer able to summon the energy, the enthusiasm, and the hard work to make the next new program succeed. Experience tells them that it does not matter at all, that things will be changed after a while, anyway. For example, the Flemish ministry of education decided recently that school directors or principals should no longer be educationally trained people or former teachers but management people. The present directors will have to limit their responsibilities to education as such. Finances, personnel management, human resource management, buildings, and so on will be handed over to business school graduates. What do you think the reaction will be among the present school directors who identify themselves to a large extent with their job and their school?

Second, most of the changes are imposed on the schools and the teachers from the top down. The teachers have no voice. "Teachers have little or no choice but to carry out the dictates of others" (Woods, this volume). Nobody asks for their opinion – even though we have known for a long time how important this is. Many teachers feel like pawns in the present school system, moved around by external forces (the government, the principal, the inspector, the parents). They live there with an external locus of causality, with no feelings of self-determination, and this totally undermines their intrinsic motivation (DeCharms, 1984; Deci and Ryan, 1985). Usually little or no justification is given for the new program (why is it better from

an educational point of view) and why teachers should be highly motivated to do more things if they do not see their educational benefits
(Woods, this volume). We guess that the negative effects of the intensification program in England and Wales are due mostly to these two aspects.
The right kind of job intensification program could also be a job enrichment program. And we do know from research in organizational psychology that the motivational, behavioral effects of job enrichment are the opposite of stress, demotivation, and burnout.

Conclusion

Teaching should be a *we* thing, not a *me* thing. Although teachers are finally
alone with their children in the classroom, teachers should see themselves
as team players who can learn a lot from professional exchange with colleagues. They should be given more opportunities for continuous learning
and professional development, as is the case in many other jobs held by educated people. Teaching young children is certainly much more difficult in
this extremely permissive, anti-authoritarian, open society than it was in
the "old" days, when most of the children would immediately obey their
parents and teachers, and when discipline was not a problem.

Some teachers overestimate their stressors and strains and should be
more realistic when comparing themselves with other professionals. They
probably underestimate the impact they still have on the learning process
and the personal development of the children in their class. It is true that
the status of their job has decreased in the society, but that did not start recently and it is true for many other jobs too – such as medicine and law.

"Teachers are made for teaching, and teaching shall they do." That means,
however, that as a group, they should also be much more involved in developing and evaluating educational programs and reforms. They should
feel like "origins," not like pawns, not only in their class but in the school
system at large.

11. Burnout Among Teachers as a Crisis in Psychological Contracts

MICHAEL P. LEITER

Burnout was first investigated in the 1970s as a crisis of overextended and disillusioned human service workers. Cherniss (1980b) described burnout among human service workers as resulting from the collapse of the professional mystique, in that people entering public human service careers had developed unrealistic expectations about their professions on the basis of their training and general cultural background. They found that their professions did not provide the degree of autonomy and collegiality necessary for fulfilling a professional role. Further, they found much of the work to be tedious, providing routine services to reluctant and ungrateful recipients. The collapse of the professional mystique produced in many new professionals serious doubts about their effectiveness. At the core of the burnout syndrome are conflicts of caregivers' values for enhancing the lives of their recipients with limitations in the structure and process of human service organizations.

In the ensuing two decades, training programs have taken a more proactive approach to preparing students for the real demands and limitations of human service work, and cultural depictions of service providers have become more realistic as well. Service providers continue to experience burnout when resources are inadequate to meet the demands of their work. However, the nature of the syndrome changed as human service occupations evolved as professions.

Currently, the experience of burnout occurs within a decidedly different social context, with human service workers struggling for social credibility and fearing job insecurity. Their relationships with their careers and their employing organizations are changing in a manner that is highly relevant to burnout. Retrenchment, downsizing, mergers, and changes in mandates throughout the human service sector in the postindustrialized world are redefining the relationships of service professionals with their employers. Often these changes are initiated by other parties, such as external

202

funding agencies. The changes are more profound than a realignment of job responsibilities or an increase in day-to-day demands. They alter the meaning of work.

These changes are felt through a large-scale redefinition of psychological contracts, which are a set of assumptions and expectations between individuals and the organizations within which they work. Rousseau (1995) defined psychological contracts as "individual beliefs, shaped by the organization, regarding terms of an exchange agreement between individuals and their organization" (p. 9). She emphasized that contracts are voluntary for both individuals and organizations and that they are self-organizing in response to emerging demands. Rousseau considered the duration and the specificity of performance requirements to be the primary dimensions of psychological contracts. In terms of duration, she differentiated relational contracts, that exchage loyalty for long-term job security, from transactional contracts, that emphasize short-term provision of expertise. In terms of performance requirements, relational contracts give employees discretion in determining the nature and scope of their contribution and give the organization discretion in determining how to provide recognition and reward. In contrast, transactional contracts clearly specify expectations about the nature and quality of employees' contributions and the compensation the organization must provide for acceptable performance.

Tenured faculty members of a university or clergy in an established church are examples of those with relational contracts. They have long-term job security and a wide range of discretion in determining the nature and extent of their performance. The organization in turn expects considerable loyalty and diverse contributions from such individuals, while maintaining discretion in the manner and extent of rewards. Extra sales clerks hired for the Christmas shopping season, students on summer jobs, and university instructors hired to teach a single course exemplify those with transactional contracts. They are engaged with the organization for a brief, prescribed period during which they are expected to provide specific services. They expect the organization to provide clearly defined compensation, while making few demands for additional services.

The duration and performance specificity of contracts shape aspects of a job. Relational contracts are consistent with broadly based, employer-supported skill development in that employers have a reasonable expectation that employees will repay their educational investment through a variety of ways over the long term. Transactional contracts are consistent with a highly focused approach to education in that the employee is primarily responsible for providing expertise to the employer. Brief, job-specific training sessions necessary for the individual to adapt skills to the specific setting are usually provided, and intrinsic learning occurs on the job. In fact, part of the compensation employees receive from a transactional contract is the opportunity to build their skills and experience, thereby increasing their capacity to find subsequent employment.

The education that is provided to transactional employees is specific, permitting the employer to recover the investment in training within the short duration and the specified performance standards of the contract. A classic example of training for transactional employees is provided by Garson's (1988) description of the training of food service employees at a fast-food restaurant. The manager taught employees the basic skills of the highly structured, machine-paced job in thirty minutes prior to the beginning of their workday, so no salary was paid for training time. Garson noted that the employer could recover the training investment of the trainer's time in a single day's work.

Rousseau's view of psychological contracts provides a useful starting point for considering current changes in the teaching profession in North America and Europe. However, the perspective, developed primarily on the basis of studies of MBA graduates, misses important dimensions of teaching. For teachers, issues of job security and performance specificity are secondary to values. The most important aspect of a teaching position is its potential for influencing other people through teaching using one's particular strengths. Job security is important in that developing as an effective teacher requires a relatively long time frame with opportunities to learn from experience and to recover from errors without the risk of immediate retribution. Specific performance requirements are a problem, as centrally dictated performance indicators invariably miss the mark. Teachers are most concerned with the affective outcomes of teaching that are overlooked by systems designed to amass quantitative data on school or system performance. Quantitative data looks at performance on standardized tests whereas most teachers are committed to instilling a desire and a capacity for lifelong learning. Although issues of job security and accountability are relevant to teachers, they pertain overwhelmingly to the explicit, legal employment contract. Conflicts in values between teachers and their employers disrupt relational contracts, creating crises that lead to burnout.

In human services, the change is away from relational contracts. This change is especially evident in North America, consistent with a culture that values individual responsibility for being employed. "In the American system, the employee is disposable – a cog in the industrial machine to be discarded when management decrees and left to fend for himself [sic] in the marketplace" (Smith, 1995, p. 197). Retrenchment within the public sector, rationalized by considerable government debt, is following the process of downsizing seen in the private service and industrial sector, despite considerable evidence of the strategy's ineffectiveness (Burke and Leiter, in press; Cascio, 1993).

What is replacing relational contracts remains unclear. Rousseau (1995) stated that major organizational change, such as downsizing or mergers, is characterized by transitional contracts. The uncertainty of turbulent times focuses management on short-term employment contracts without specific performance terms. Neither employees nor employers have a clear idea during the change of the length of employment or what constitutes excellent performance. However, this characterization runs contrary to what Rousseau defined as the basic features of a psychological contract: voluntariness. Employees do not enter into what Rousseau describes as a transitional contract willingly. These are better described as an employment relationship without a contract in which employees are present and compensation is delivered, but there is no agreement on the nature of the exchange.

Rousseau presents the balanced contract as a positive alternative, and one that may result after a transitional phase. Balanced contracts are characterized by long-term commitment and clear performance standards. Considerable activity in the public and private sectors of postindustrialized societies toward defining performance indicators is consistent with developing balanced contracts, especially when employees are actively involved in defining the indicators. Currently, the identification of performance indicators is accompanied by attempts to increase productivity, such that the new contract changes the nature and quantity of employees' contributions while clarifying performance standards. Redefining contracts to this extent can be a demanding process. However, it is not clear that the result is a qualitatively different type of contract. That is, what Rousseau describes as a balanced contract may be more accurately described as a renegotiated relational contract, one in which organizations and individuals, often prompted by external pressures, clarify performance indicators more specifically.

Whereas the length of the contract and its performance specifications are the measurable signs of a contract change, for teachers the central issue remains acting on their values within their profession. Loss of job security undermines their capacity to pursue what they value in the learning–teaching situation. New performance indicators often miss the essence of teachers' affective objectives for student learning. Teachers experience the impact of changes in formal contracts through the effect of these changes on teachers' values. In a manner similar to the initial career crises Cherniss (1980b) identified as a source of burnout, human service providers in health care, social services, and education are experiencing burnout in reaction to breakdowns in psychological contracts.

Woods in this volume describes changes to the teaching profession in the United Kingdom as part of a widespread move toward deprofessionalization resulting from intensification of teaching. He also acknowledges contrary trends enhancing professionalism, including action research and administrative restructuring that empowers teachers. The four types of accommodation that Woods outlines fit within the context of renegotiating the psychological contract. Contestation is the active process of assertive negotiation in which teachers reject aspects of educational reforms that clash with their values. In appropriation, teachers achieve a new psychological contract with their work by adapting reforms that are consistent with their core values and challenging those that are not. Realignment is accepting the new psychological contract without an apparent struggle. Teachers adjust by altering their ideals and values to fit the reform dictates. What Woods terms strategic action encompasses largely avoidance actions that work around unwanted changes without addressing the fundamental problem. Strategic action shares various features of nonaccommodation in that teachers are working without a negotiated understanding with their employer. Woods presents examples of nonaccommodation leading to burnout and eventually to exit from the profession. The central point is that working outside of a mutual understanding with one's employer is stressful, with consequences for both physical and psychological well-being.

In contrast with Rousseau's (1995) emphasis on the job security and accountability inherent in psychological contracts, Woods emphasizes values. He sees the primary issue confronting teachers as intensification: time-consuming work that the teachers consider to be of little educational value. For teachers, the stress arising from working outside a psychological contract takes the form of burnout. Emotional exhaustion comes from striving to maintain personal relationships with an expanding number of students while engaging in tasks that teachers see as inconsistent with productive learning. Exhaustion leads to depersonalization, as the emotional distance between teachers and students increases with excessive demands. Ironically, depersonalization is consistent with intensification. Increasing involvement in prescribed work activity of dubious value diminishes teachers' sense of personal accomplishment. Researchers in a variety of professions have found that these qualities of burnout are associated with health problems (Leiter, Clark, and Durup, 1994), psychological distress (Leiter and Durup, in press), and personal psychological crises (Leiter and Durup, 1994). Further, analyses of burnout models have consistently confirmed paths from diminished personal accomplishment to lower organizational commitment (Leiter, 1991b; Leiter, 1993; Leiter, Clark, and Durup, 1994). This direct relationship with commitment underscores the sensitivity of personal accomplishment to breakdowns in psychological contracts. Consistent with Woods's emphasis on values, teachers consider opportunities to make meaningful contributions to their students as a central aspect of their contract with their school. When those opportunities are constrained or impoverished, the relationship of teachers with their schools deteriorates.

My recent research has found considerable evidence of mid-career burnout in response to breakdowns in psychological contracts. A survey of 3,312 Canadian hospital employees (Leiter, 1995) that used a new measure of burnout, the Maslach Burnout Inventory – General Survey (Schaufeli, Leiter, Maslach, and Jackson, 1996), found both exhaustion and cynicism (a revised measure of depersonalization) to be significantly greater for staff members with three to fifteen years' experience than for their colleagues with fewer than three years or more than twenty years of experience (see Figure 11.1). Professional efficacy (a revised measure of personal accomplishment) was lower for this group as well. A breakdown in psychological contracts was reflected by this group's giving less positive ratings of their immediate supervisor, senior management, and their commitment to the hospital's corporate goals (see Figure 11.2). A pervasive problem for the hospital under consideration was a negative view of change. Hospital staff members reported that they saw job security and morale decreasing sharply along with the quality of patient care as a function of cost constraints and changes in the hospital's mandate. The concern with job security is consistent with Rousseau's emphasis on the duration of contracts whereas the concern with quality of care is consistent with Woods's emphasis on the central role of values. These concerns were most evident for the mid-career group who had worked at the hospital long enough to have developed clear expectations and values about their involvement, and who were sufficiently young that early retirement was not an attractive option.

Byrne's analysis of the nomological network of burnout among teachers acknowledges organizational and personality factors that influence the experience of emotional exhaustion, depersonalization, and diminished personal accomplishment. The organizational factors identified in her analysis are highly sensitive to major organizational restructuring. Workload

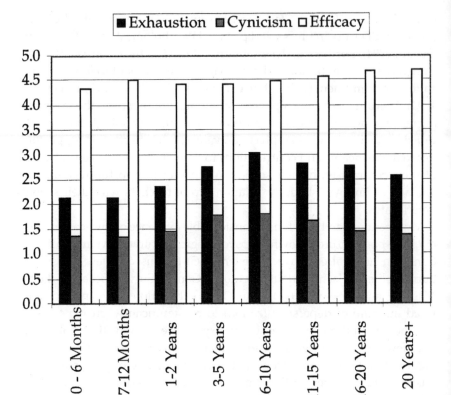

Figure 11.1. Burnout as a function of years of employment.

and role conflict increase directly during downsizing, as there are fewer people to manage the volume of work and the continuing employees must expand their roles to perform a wider range of tasks. If downsizing is accompanied by significant changes in the organization's work, the change may produce entirely new roles. Involvement in decision making decreases as management tends to centralize control during turbulent times. Even when management makes sincere attempts to maintain or enhance the involvement of employees in decision making, they cannot change the reality that the most far-reaching decision in the organization – the decision on how to reduce expenditures – did not arise from a participative process but was imposed by others. Both downsizing and the process of deprofessionalization discussed in Woods's chapter have an impact on the personality variable of greatest importance in Byrne's analysis – self-esteem. Constraints on professional prerogatives throughout society and growing criticism of professionals in popular media exacerbate the impact of orga-

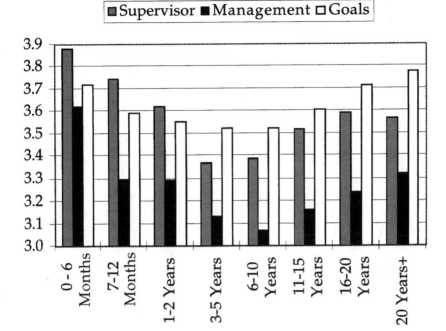

Figure 11.2. Organizational perceptions as a function of years of employment.

nizational downsizing and retrenchment on staff members' sense of themselves. The idea of their work as a way in which to make a meaningful contribution is overwhelmed by mundane tasks and perceptions of diminishing service quality. As Smylie pointed out in Chapter 3, inconsistencies between expectations for centralized accountability on the one hand and greater professional initiative on the other produce demands beyond those arising from either change by itself. Together, they compromise the individual teacher's capacity to fulfill what Smylie identified as three interrelated psychological needs associated with work: meaningfulness, self-determination, and accomplishment of valued goals.

Miller's chapter presents an optimistic view that a reorientation of values within the context of a redefined sense of professionalism can produce schools characterized by vibrant learning environments that meet the needs of children, teachers, and the broader community. She contrasts discouragement arising from professional development activities that do not enhance the teachers' affective learning objectives with efficacy arising from a firm base of community-centered professional activity. Her example of successful appropriation underscores the dynamic quality of values: They are not static. The ideal form, content, and objectives of education change with developments in the larger community. A successful resolution requires flexibility as well as a commitment to principles.

Management-initiated changes in educational systems increase teachers' vulnerability to burnout because they disrupt hard-won balances in the pursuit of individual and organizational goals. For teachers, absolute resistance to change is both unlikely and undesirable in that alterations of organizational mandates often reflect meaningful developments in the larger social context. A new resolution is necessary. Until a new resolution is achieved, teachers, working without a psychological contract regarding the most important aspect of their work, experience exhaustion, cynicism, and doubts about their professional effectiveness. It serves the interest of all stakeholders in the educational system – management, teachers, parents, students, employers, government – for changes to evolve in the context of open, honest communication, facilitating the establishment of a new understanding.

12. Progress in Understanding Teacher Burnout

CHRISTINA MASLACH

Burnout is a type of prolonged response to chronic emotional and inter-personal stressors on the job (Kleiber and Enzmann, 1990; Schaufeli, Maslach, and Marek, 1993). As such, it has been an issue of particular concern for people-oriented occupations in which (a) the relationship between providers and recipients is central to the work and (b) the provision of education, service, or treatment can be a highly emotional experience. The first articles about burnout, which appeared in the mid-1970s in the United States (Freudenberger, 1974, 1975; Maslach, 1976), provided an initial description of the burnout phenomenon, gave it the identifying name of "burnout," and showed that it was not an aberrant response by a few deviant people but was actually quite common. My own article focused on the experiences of 200 workers in such occupations as health care, poverty law, social welfare, and mental health care. Interestingly, one of the occupational groups I did *not* study in this pioneering research was teachers, and among the most frequent comments I received about my article was "teachers have the most experience with the phenomenon you are describing, so why didn't you study them?" Since that time, many researchers and writers have risen to that challenge, so that we now have a substantial literature on burnout within the teaching profession and the opportunity, within this volume, to assess its implications.

Historical Overview of the Burnout Construct

Before commenting on some of the papers that were prepared for the Johann Jacobs Foundation Conference and appear as chapters in this volume, I thought it would be useful to give an overview of the larger field of job burnout, as it occurs across a range of occupations (see Maslach and Schaufeli, 1993, for a more detailed presentation). A better understanding of how the concept has developed and how it has been studied could

211

provide some insights for the current discussion and evaluation of burnout as it exists for teachers. It is important to recognize that burnout emerged as a social problem, rather than a scholarly construct, and thus its initial development was shaped by pragmatic rather than academic concerns.

The Pioneer Phase

In response to the first articles on burnout, there was a virtual flood of writing about this phenomenon during the late 1970s, much of which appeared in magazines or journals directed to various professional audiences. Most early articles on burnout followed a typical pattern. The stressful nature of the particular profession was described, and then this job stress was related to burnout, with one or more case studies or vignettes being used to illustrate the issue. Usually, some preventive strategies were recommended. Although much was being said about burnout, and there were many ideas about its causes and consequences, little empirical evidence was presented either to support or refute these statements (see Maslach, 1982a, and Perlman and Hartman, 1982, for reviews of this early literature).

In addition to its more clinical, nonempirical quality, this early burnout literature was characterized by definitional fuzziness. What was meant by "burnout" varied widely from one writer to the next, so that often they were discussing different concepts rather than the same one. Moreover, the concept of burnout was stretched and expanded to encompass far more than it did originally. Almost every personal problem imaginable has been described as "burnout" at some point. However, a concept that has been expanded to mean everything ends up meaning nothing at all, an issue that has been discussed elsewhere (Maslach, 1982b; Maslach and Jackson, 1984).

One reason for the initial sparseness of empirical research on burnout is that practitioners were far more interested in burnout than were academic scholars. This is not surprising, given that practitioners are more likely to be dealing directly with the problem of burnout on a daily basis, but this meant that the primary concern was with *intervention* rather than with theory and scholarly research. In addition, many researchers were not interested in burnout at first, partly because the term seemed to evoke an image of "pop psychology" rather than a legitimate scientific concept.

Because there was not an early emphasis on developing theories of burnout, there was not a conceptual framework for integrating and evaluating the various findings and proposed solutions. To some extent, the lack of theory reflected the newness of the phenomenon – much had to be discovered about its parameters before a model could be developed. Also, a different process occurs when one starts with a real-world problem and works back toward a theoretical model rather than the other way around. Moreover, different people will work back toward different theoretical models for the same problem, depending on their particular perspective. For example, someone with a clinical perspective may conceptualize burnout in terms of depression, but someone with an organizational perspective may approach it as an issue of job satisfaction. Initially, it can be hard to compare and integrate these different perspectives (especially if there is definitional variation as well), and this may be one reason the earlier burnout literature lacked theoretical coherence. However, as has been pointed out elsewhere, this rich diversity of theoretical perspectives, as well as of related methodological techniques, is one of the special virtues of the eclectic, problem-oriented approach that has typified the burnout field (Maslach and Jackson, 1984).

The Empirical Phase

During the next phase of the 1980s, the work on burnout entered a more focused, constructive, and empirical period. Many books and articles were written about burnout, in which the authors outlined their working models of the phenomenon, proposed various ideas and interventions, and presented various forms of corroborative evidence (survey and questionnaire data, interview responses, clinical case studies). Standardized measures of burnout were developed, thus providing researchers with more precise definitions and methodological tools for studying the phenomenon. In particular, the development and widespread acceptance of the Maslach Burnout Inventory (MBI; Maslach and Jackson, 1981, 1986; Maslach, Jackson, and Leiter, 1996) fostered systematic research on burnout, resulting in an increased number of articles published in scholarly journals (including several issues devoted entirely to burnout). In the case of teacher burnout, the extensive interest in this phenomenon led to the development of a special form of the MBI designed especially for teachers (MBI - Educators Survey; Maslach, Jackson, and Schwab, 1986).

Until the early 1980s, burnout was studied exclusively in the United States. Gradually, the phenomenon drew attention in other countries as well, beginning with such English-speaking countries as Canada and Great Britain. Soon articles, books, and research measures were being translated into many languages, and the first cross-national studies on burnout were carried out. Because international burnout research started after the concept had been established in the United States and after measurement instruments had been developed, there was not the same "pioneer phase" of conceptual debate within these other countries. Only recently have theoretical contributions been made by non-Anglo-Saxon scholars (see Schaufeli, Maslach, and Marek, 1993).

A general review of the more recent burnout literature indicates several trends. First, much of the work has continued to be done within people-oriented, human service occupations, although the variety of these occupations has expanded. Second, the burnout concept has been extended to other types of occupations (see Maslach, Jackson, and Leiter, 1996) as well as to nonoccupational areas of life (such as burnout in the business world, in athletic sports, in political activism, and within the family). Third, the research has tended to focus more on job factors than on other types of variables. This is quite consistent with most of the conceptual models that have been proposed. Thus, researchers have studied such work variables as job satisfaction, job stress (workload, role conflict, and role ambiguity), job withdrawal (turnover, absenteeism), job expectations, relations with co-workers and supervisors (social support on the job), relations with clients, caseload, type of position and time in that job, agency policy, and so forth. The personal factors that have been studied are most often demographic variables (sex, age, marital status, etc.). In addition, some attention has been given to personality variables (locus of control, hardiness), personal health, relations with family and friends (social support at home), and personal values and commitment. In general, job factors are more strongly related to burnout than are biographical or personal factors.

Most of the empirical work on burnout consists of correlational studies that collect subjective, self-report data at one point in time from a nonrepresentative sample. Although some interesting findings have come from this research, its limitations must be recognized. First, some of the correlations may be an artifact of reliance on a single method or use of a specialized group. Second, response rates tend to be rather low. Third, such studies do not permit a test of causal hypotheses, even though causal links are usually presumed and discussed. Fourth, the subjective assessments of certain variables may not accord with their "objective" status.

Recently, several longitudinal studies of burnout have been conducted, and their findings suggest three conclusions. First, the level of burnout seems fairly stable over time. Obviously, its nature is more chronic than acute. Second, burnout predicts some physical symptoms, job withdrawal behaviors, and job dissatisfaction. Third, role conflict and lack of social support from colleagues and supervisors appear to be important antecedents of burnout.

Conceptual and Measurement Issues

Unfortunately, many of the early studies were not grounded in a theoretical framework. That is, they did not utilize a conceptual model of burnout from which hypotheses could be derived and tested. In many cases, there was not even a clear rationale for the choice of variables. Needless to say, this atheoretical stance can cause problems in interpretation of the results.

However, in recent years, much progress has been made on the theoretical front. One factor that has helped facilitate this progress is the greater consensual agreement on an operational definition of burnout, largely because of the development of validated research measures. Consequently, researchers now have a common language for studying burnout and can make direct comparisons between their own findings and those of others – thus allowing new studies to build on the contributions of previous ones. Good opportunities now exist for integrating empirical results within a particular conceptual framework and for carrying out theory-driven research.

A Multidimensional Model of Burnout

The operational definition, and the corresponding measure, most widely used in burnout research is the multidimensional model developed by Susan Jackson and myself (Maslach, 1993; Maslach and Jackson, 1981, 1986; Maslach, Jackson, and Leiter, 1996). We have conceptualized burnout as an individual stress experience that is embedded in a context of social relationships, and thus involves the person's conception of both self and others. Our model includes the three components of experienced stress, evaluation of others, and evaluation of self. More specifically, we have defined burnout as a psychological syndrome of *emotional exhaustion* (stress component), *depersonalization* (other-evaluation component), and *reduced personal accomplishment* (self-evaluation component). This syndrome can occur among individuals who work with other people in some capacity. Emotional exhaustion refers to feelings of being emotionally overextended and depleted of one's emotional resources (it has also been described as wearing out, loss of energy, depletion, debilitation, and fatigue). Depersonalization refers to a negative, callous, or excessively detached response to other people, who are usually the recipients of one's service or care (depersonalization has also been described as negative or inappropriate attitudes toward recipients, loss of idealism, and irritability). Reduced personal accomplishment refers to a decline in one's feelings of competence and successful achievement in one's work (it has also been described as reduced productivity or capability, low morale, withdrawal, and an inability to cope).

This multidimensional model includes the single stress component that is found in simpler, unidimensional models of burnout, but it goes beyond those models in considering how that stress experience is related to one's response to others (especially critical for people-oriented professions) and one's sense of self. What is needed now is the generation of better hypotheses about both the social and personal causes and consequences of each of the three burnout components. The nomological network approach of Byrne (this volume) is certainly an important step in that direction.

A related issue, which is evident in Byrne's work and other contributions to this volume, is whether the predictors of the three components are similar across occupations, or whether they differ in response to the unique job requirements of various occupations. For example, Byrne's research does not find evidence that supervisory support is an important predictor of teacher burnout, although this same factor has played a significant role in burnout among nurses (e.g., Leiter and Maslach, 1988). The difference in these findings may be best explained by occupational differences in the definition of the job roles (e.g., teachers are more likely than nurses to work alone and independently, with less direct supervision). Thus, factors that have been identified as critical for burnout may not be as generic as assumed by prior theorizing but may be more limited by the relevant job context. The significance of job definition is also demonstrated by differences between occupations in overall patterns of burnout. For example, in comparison to Dutch human services professionals, Dutch secondary teachers experienced more emotional exhaustion and somatic complaints but less depersonalization and more personal accomplishment (Schaufeli, Daamen, and Van Mierlo, 1994). All this underscores the importance of the particular *social environment* in which work takes place – a point that is raised in other chapters in this volume (e.g., Miller, Rudow) and is supported by Byrne's findings with respect to context variables (classroom climate, role conflict, work overload).

In addition to identifying the various antecedents of the three burnout dimensions, there needs to be a better articulation of the interrelationships among these three components. The most promising model in this regard is that of Leiter (1993), who proposes that emotional exhaustion occurs first and is linked sequentially to the rise of depersonalization, and that personal accomplishment develops separately from these two components. In other words, some burnout components may develop in parallel, rather than in sequence, because they are reactions to different factors in the work environment. Interestingly, Byrne's findings provide additional support for Leiter's theorizing.

Burnout as a Distinctive Construct

As mentioned earlier, burnout emerged first as a pragmatic issue, and so the research literature has developed within a framework of various theoretical perspectives rather than in a single one. This diversity of perspectives has made issues of definition, construct specificity, and discriminant validity especially challenging. From the beginning, questions have been raised about how burnout is distinguished from other psychological constructs: Is it truly a distinct concept or simply an "old" phenomenon with a new label? In particular, the issue has been whether burnout is "just the same thing as" a host of other theoretical concepts, although most of the emphasis has been on burnout's distinctiveness from stress or depression. Note that these latter concepts are plagued with the same sort of definitional ambiguity as burnout, so the problem of specifying burnout is by no means an exception.

The upshot of various theoretical discussions and empirical tests is that burnout can indeed be distinguished in a relative way from these other concepts, with respect to both *time* and *domain* (Maslach and Schaufeli, 1993; also see Cox, Kuk, and Leiter, 1993, and Leiter and Durup, 1994). Unlike acute forms of stress, burnout is considered by most researchers to be a long-term process, in which prolonged exposure to chronic job stressors results in increased emotional exhaustion and depersonalization as well as reduced personal accomplishment. Thus, it seems to parallel the final exhaustion phase of the general adaptation syndrome (Selye, 1967) rather than the earlier alarm or resistance phases. This distinction with respect to time between (job) stress and burnout implies that both concepts can only be discriminated retrospectively when the adaptation has been successfully performed (job stress) or when a breakdown in adaptation has occurred (burnout). With respect to domain, burnout is generally distinguished from the global, context-free nature of depression by its specificity to the social and organizational context of the job setting. Thus, even though burnout is characterized by some dysphoric symptoms that are similar to those of depression (e.g., feelings of failure, sadness), their etiology lies specifically in the job setting of people-oriented professions. In contrast, depression can arise from problems in any domain of life and not just the workplace.

Although the conceptual boundaries of the burnout concept are now being distinguished, there are still a number of assumptions about burnout that, while widely believed, have still not received empirical validation. Rudow mentions several of these assumptions in his chapter. For example, his assertion that burnout takes time is in accord with the longer time perspective for burnout (which was mentioned earlier), but there is no empirical support for the statement that burnout does not show until after fifteen or twenty years on the job. Similarly, with regard to which teachers are more prone to burnout, the notion that it is those who are "on fire" or "burning" has not led to the development of any clear hypotheses about just what the relevant individual variables are, nor to tests of those hypotheses.

Rudow also raises the basic theoretical issue of causality, in terms of what variable leads to, or "brings on," what. Although theories about the development of burnout contain many assumptions about causal relationships, the methodological constraints of most of the empirical research have left these assumptions largely untested. For example, Byrne presents evidence about the relation of self-esteem to the personal accomplishment dimension of burnout but the nature of the causal (and perhaps reciprocal) relationship is still unclear. Higher self-esteem may protect people from declining on this dimension, or the experience of burnout may lead to decrements in self-esteem, or there may be a third factor responsible for the observed correlation. The resolution of this question would not only improve our theoretical formulations about burnout but could have some interesting implications for interventions.

Intervention Issues

Given the state of current research and theorizing about teacher burnout, do we now know enough to recommend changes that would either reduce its incidence or help teachers cope with it? The answer to that question is still equivocal – both yes and no.

Limits on Our Knowledge About Burnout

To begin with the "no" part first, there is clearly much that we need to learn to be able to predict when burnout will occur and why. The inevitable call for "more research" is still an important truism. The significance of the Byrne model is that it can provide a much-needed guiding framework for future research, so that new studies will build more clearly on prior work. However, as a better articulated model of teacher burnout is developed, it will be important to integrate it within a larger theoretical context so as to bring conceptual coherence to the knowledge base. Recent theoretical advances, which go beyond the early stress literature reviewed in Smylie's chapter, seem particularly promising in this regard – for example, the transactional model of work stress and health (Cox, 1990; Cox, Kuk, and Leiter, 1993) or social comparison theory (Buunk and Schaufeli, 1993). Especially noteworthy is the research model developed at the Johann Jacobs Foundation Conference (and presented in this volume by Maslach and Leiter in Chapter 19), which provides a good framework for future work on teacher burnout.

In addition to more theory-driven research, there are several important needs to be addressed in future work on burnout. Primary among these is a focus on the *process* of burnout rather than on just the end state. Such a focus requires process models and hypotheses about sequential relationships of key variables and/or developmental stages as well as *longitudinal* studies (a need that has also been noted by Rudow). Second, it is critically important that researchers expand the methodologies they use and include measures other than just self-report – for example, evaluations by relevant others (e.g., colleagues, students, administrators, family), behavioral indices of job performance, physiological assessments of health, and so forth. Third, there is a clear need for basic statistics, by occupation, on base rates and criterion levels for burnout. Thus, base rate data would inform us about the rate, frequency, and ubiquity of burnout, both for teachers overall and for teachers at different educational levels or school settings (for example, Farber, 1991a, estimates that between 5% and 20% of American teachers are burned out at any given time). The establishment of criterion levels would address the question of when burnout becomes a serious enough problem to warrant serious attention, either by the individual or by the organization. In other words, at what point or level of experience does burnout cause a deterioration in job performance, job withdrawal behaviors, or a significant decline in physical and mental health? This issue of base rate and criterion levels is related to Smylie's point about whether reported levels of burnout are "high" or "low."

Finally, if we are going to make any serious headway on the question of effective interventions within the teaching profession, then it is essential that we conduct good evaluation studies of planned changes or demonstration projects of reform. Although there have been many proposals about how to deal with burnout (some of which have been put into operation), there is a dearth of empirical evidence about whether such interventions will actually achieve the expected outcomes. Too often, researchers are not included in the planning or implemention of reforms, with the unfortunate consequence that they are not in a position to define the critical variables (e.g., what behaviors or experiences are expected to change) or to collect the necessary information for evaluation (e.g., baseline measures prior to the intervention; multiple follow-up assessments). Although often complex and costly (in terms of time and effort as well as resources), evaluation research is a crucial element for future progress in dealing with burnout.

Opportunities Within Our Knowledge of Burnout

Despite these limitations, both on how much we know about burnout and what inferences we can make from what we know, there is a basis for some recommendations about change. That is, there are some things about burnout that we know fairly well – "key factors" that appear fairly strongly and consistently in the research literature – and thus we can have some confidence in considering these factors within efforts at reform. In assessing the literature on teacher burnout, as summarized by the framework of the Byrne model, we can identify some points where there is likely to be a greater payoff from any investments in intervention. These points include the key factors of classroom climate, role conflict (especially for elementary and intermediate teachers), and work overload (especially for secondary teachers). As noted earlier, the location of these factors within the social context of the job underscores the crucial role of the social environment in teacher burnout and also supports Smylie's and Miller's arguments for social and organizational solutions to burnout, not just individual ones.

From Research Knowledge to Actual Intervention

In some ways, it is easier to identify key factors for burnout than to figure out how to translate those broad, abstract, conceptual variables into specific, concrete, practical applications. This is especially true when these variables have been assessed in terms of general self-reports (e.g., teachers' ratings of their experienced role conflict), rather than measures of the actual job elements that produce that variable (e.g., the specific job requirements or policies that cause conflict). The challenge in designing any reform is to ensure that the planned changes both (a) capture the generic elements of the key factor in question, but (b) embody these elements within the unique terms of the local context. By the latter, I mean that the changes have to fit and make sense within the particular social environment in which the intervention is being implemented. Thus, the same change may work effectively within one school setting but be completely inappropriate within another.

To meet this challenge successfully, the planners of reform need to be able to *specify* the changes or outcomes that are desired and to articulate clearly both the presumed causal factors and their presumed linkages to the outcomes. Specific outcomes can be identified and evaluated more clearly than ones that are vague and hard to define (such as "improve morale"). The same holds true for causal factors; for example, within a particular school and grade level, what specific changes are hypothesized to "improve classroom climate"?

In this regard, a multidimensional model of teacher burnout has some important implications for interventions. First, it underscores the variety of psychological reactions to the job that different teachers can experience. Such differential responses may not be simply a function of individual factors (such as personality) but may reflect the differential impact of situational factors on the three burnout dimensions. For example, certain job characteristics may influence the sources of emotional stress (and thus emotional exhaustion), or the resources available to handle the job successfully (and thus personal accomplishment). This multidimensional approach also implies that interventions to reduce burnout should be planned and designed in terms of the particular component of burnout that needs to be addressed. That is, it may be more effective to consider how to reduce the likelihood of emotional exhaustion, or to prevent the tendency to depersonalize, or to enhance one's sense of accomplishment rather than to use a more general approach to "reduce burnout."

The Stress and Challenge of Social Change

As noted by many observers, the path of social change does not always run smoothly. In some cases, the reform has unanticipated consequences – that is, in addition to the desired outcome, it produces others that are not necessarily desired and may even be detrimental. Both Miller and Smylie provide a relevant example in which a reform designed to give teachers a greater sense of control over their work (i.e., a greater role in decision making) has the unintended outcome of greater work overload. To some extent, this result demonstrates that any policy or procedure is a double-edged sword. Benefits do not usually come without some costs (or, as Smylie puts it, solutions can contain seeds of stress), and thus any proposal for change needs to anticipate and take all these into account prior to implementation.

Sometimes the process of change itself is a source of stress, for the various reasons reviewed by Smylie; I wonder, however, if there is not more that could be added to the analysis to explain those instances when change is not so stressful or when people are willing to endure any initial difficulties or uncertainties to achieve a desired outcome. What can make reform stressful is having unrealistic expectations about the change process – for example, expectations that the proposed solutions will be easy to implement or that they will generate immediate results, or that the results will always be big ones. When expectations are not met, especially when considerable effort has been expended, the resulting frustration and disappointment may preclude the recognition of any progress or accomplishments that were actually achieved.

Conclusion

The contributions in this volume show clearly how far we have come in our understanding of the phenomenon of teacher burnout, but they also point out the areas where there is still inadequate theorizing or insufficient empirical tests. In terms of interventions for burnout, one message seems to be that the solutions for such a complex social issue are themselves complex, rather than the simple strategies that might be desired. A second message is that the nature of the social environment is at the heart of both understanding the teacher burnout phenomenon and ameliorating it.

13. Teachers' Moral Purposes: Stress, Vulnerability, and Strength

JENNIFER NIAS

In this chapter, I focus on values as a central component in teacher burnout. The ideas I explore were triggered in the first instance by Woods's chapter and in particular by his distinction between micro, meso, and macro levels of stress. Whereas Leithwood, Miller, and Smylie explore organizational factors (the meso level), Woods emphasizes changes in government policy and resourcing at the macro level and their impact on individuals (the micro level). I take this idea further, with particular reference to a small but highly significant aspect of teachers' lives. Woods suggests that teachers are likely to suffer stress when their "personal interests, commitment, and resources" get out of line with or pull against key aspects of their social, economic, or institutional environments. Later, he identifies a conflict in values as one of the factors leading to nonaccommodation ("the seedbed of stress and burnout"). By implication, therefore, Woods sees values as part of the "personal interests, commitment, and resources" that teachers need to protect from disharmony if they are to avoid damaging exposure to stress.

To justify this implication, in the first part of the chapter I trace the connection among the notions of commitment, values, identity, and interests. I then focus on two moral values that are a key part of many teachers' commitment and interests. Such teachers value (i.e., they attach worth and importance to [Oxford English Dictionary]) the idea that they are morally rather than legally accountable to their pupils, and therefore, that the job of a teacher involves "caring" for them. I then consider reasons why, by contrast, teachers often care so little for themselves that they fail to see and respond to the early physical and emotional symptoms of stress. Finally, I suggest that appropriate collegial relations provide teachers with a moral reference group and with a social environment that may protect them from

I am grateful to Penny Henderson for discussions that helped to form the ideas in this chapter.

burnout, or at the least, alleviate the ethical conditions that make it likely. Throughout, like Woods, I have had in the forefront of my mind the impact of recent educational changes in England and Wales, especially, though not exclusively, on primary school teachers. My reflections have also been informed by twenty years of my own ethnographic research into primary, and to a lesser extent, secondary teachers and schools.

Commitment, Values, Identity, Interests

Like Woods, I find it unhelpful to think of "commitment" as an all-embracing term (Nias, 1981). Of course, types of commitment, as categories, are neither clear-cut nor mutually exclusive, nor can one allocate individuals tidily to one or another for all of their professional lives. Nevertheless, the categories are useful analytic tools. Accordingly, in this chapter I refer to teachers' vocational and professional commitment, taking commitment to mean, in Lortie's terms (1975, p. 189), a willingness to allocate scarce personal resources (e.g., time, energy, money) to the day-to-day performance of one's job.

There is ample evidence that what teachers feel to be worthwhile or important is central to both vocational and professional commitment. Behind the idealism and, for some, the missionary zeal of those who see teaching as a vocation lies a desire to promote particular beliefs or perspectives, be they educational, religious, sociopolitical, or moral. Professional commitment is different in that it gives priority to teaching as a craft or, more generally, to the concept of education. Teachers with this kind of commitment may have varying educational aims but they share a common desire to achieve high professional standards. The resulting values to which they are committed often reflect the work ethic in which they were themselves reared (Nias, 1989).

Judgments of worth are, by definition, personal even though they are socially mediated. They may also be unconscious, especially when acquired in childhood or adolescence through the influence of significant others (Nias, 1993a). All teachers bring such judgments to their work. Their working "selves" therefore contain a strong personal component that is particularly pronounced when they are vocationally or professionally committed.

Indeed, for such teachers, the personal and occupational self may be so closely related that, in their own terms, they "become" teachers: The persons they perceive themselves to be go to work and the teachers they feel they are come home, often to occupy their sleeping as well as their waking hours. There are many sociological and historical reasons that the self is so deeply involved in teaching (Nias, 1989). Here, I simply accept the claim that many teachers, for part or all of their working lives, invest their personal sense of identity in their work. It represents for them an arena in which they can act out or propagate their values. Through their teaching and their lives as teachers they can translate into action their sense of what is important and worthwhile.

It is also clear that teachers go to considerable lengths to protect their sense of individual identity (Nias, 1989; Pollard, 1985; Woods, 1981). The preservation of self-image is one of teachers' most powerful "interests-at-hand" (Pollard, 1985, p. 160). Any perceived attack on it is experienced as threatening and painful. When vocationally and professionally committed teachers are put under pressure from meso or macro forces to act in ways that appear contrary to their values and so to their sense of identity, they feel stressed, as Smylie also argues. Woods's case examples make this abundantly clear. My evidence (Nias, 1993b) supports Woods's contention that for such teachers, the costs of "accommodation" to imposed changes may be almost as high as those of "nonaccommodation." Guilt and loss of self-esteem through the betrayal of deeply held values can be as emotionally damaging as appropriation or resistance.

Moral Values

It is therefore important to our understanding of burnout to examine in greater detail the nature of the values that teachers treasure. Many of these are educational, as teachers' response to changes in government policy since 1988 have made clear. Woods touches on them; they are examined in greater detail in Bernstein and Brannen (1996), Campbell and Neill (1994b), Croll (1996), Drummond (1993), Evans, Packwood, Neill, and Campbell (1994), Hughes (1995), Osborn and Black (1994), Osborn and Broadfoot (1992), Pollard, Broadfoot, Croll, Osborn, and Abbott (1994), and Webb (1993, 1994). Teachers' own voices are also vividly recorded in letters to and articles in the educational press. The tacit or explicit beliefs that many primary teachers have about the nature of knowledge, learning, and teaching has led them to hold a broad and loosely connected set of values relating to children, pedagogy, and the curriculum (see, e.g., Nias, 1988a). The extent to which individuals have found these values to be compatible with the National Curriculum and national assessment varies from one teacher and school to another and probably accounts a good deal for the types of accommodation and nonaccommodation that Woods identifies. I do not propose to carry further the recent and extensive analyses of educational issues that he and other researchers have undertaken. However, I do wish to assert, on the basis of my research into, experience of, and work with the teaching profession during the past decade, that the perceived threat to their educational values and so to their sense of occupational identity has caused many teachers to opt out to burnout or at the least, as Kelchtermans (1996) suggests, to suffer profound emotional disturbance.

They have also experienced a devastating attack on their moral values. Of course, this is a difficult area to explore. Beliefs and values are individual, perhaps unique; they are difficult to elicit or verify; their relationship to behavior is complex and sometimes contradictory; the influence of social context is uncertain; no analysis can be exhaustive, or even accurate, for more than a brief period. A good deal of life history and in-depth ethnographic research is required before one can make any firm claims about the kinds of attitudes, relationships, family and societal structures, moral codes, and so on that particular individuals or groups of teachers espouse or wish to promote. Nevertheless, I shall risk three generalizations. First, most teachers regard their relationship with their pupils as a personal rather than an impersonal, bureaucratic one. Second, they derive from the interpersonal nature of this relationship a moral, as distinct from legal, sense of responsibility for and accountability to pupils and often to their parents. Indeed, Elliott, Bridges, Ebbutt, Gibson, and Nias (1981, p. 17) describe this awareness as "answerability" to stress its interpersonal nature. In other words they are conscious that their work has an ethical dimension that stems from personal knowledge and interaction. (I first became aware of this view of morality during case study research into secondary school accountability [Elliott et al., 1981]). Only later did I encounter the work of Gilligan [1982] and realize that she was making very similar claims for women's moral preferences and judgments. The question of whether the similarity between the ethical basis of teachers' work and the ethical decision making of women is causal, correlational, or coincidental deserves further investigation.) Third, most teachers feel that their moral "answerability" to pupils puts on them an obligation, often experienced as a desire, to "care" for them, even though this is itself an ambiguous term, open to different interpretations (Acker, 1995; Nias, 1997).

Teachers' interpersonal relationships, especially with pupils, are therefore of fundamental importance to them. There is overwhelming evidence that they prize these relationships and that their main job satisfactions come from helping children to learn and develop. It is also clear that teachers set great store by their sense of moral responsibility for the work they do. Many would see it as one of the defining characteristics of what it is to "feel like a teacher" (Nias, 1988b). Yet recent government policies take little account of teachers' views. Instead, they emphasize their formal relationships and legal accountability. Teachers' sense that they have a personal relationship with and moral obligation to children and their parents is constantly overridden by an official spirit of contractualism that they do not endorse and over which they have little control. In simplistic terms, they feel that the traditional service ethic of education has been replaced by one of consumerism. Many react with moral outrage to the assertion of the New Right that education is not a right but a commodity that can be bought and sold like any other. A recent incident (Drummond, 1994) makes this point: As tutor to an inservice course, Drummond had been reviewing with a group of teachers and headteachers the research findings on the most appropriate education and facilities for four-year-olds. Funding in English schools is now on a per capita basis, so it is expedient for schools to attract as many pupils as possible. Hence, many primary schools have begun to admit four-year-olds without additional resources in the hope that they will stay on to become fully funded pupils at five. The children do not always benefit. One teacher who was resisting pressure from her male headteacher to take four-year-olds into her class reported that he had said to her: "It's all right for you. When you look at a four-year-old, you see a child. When I look at a four-year-old, I see bank notes." The words by themselves do not do justice to her sense of "emotional exhaustion" nor to the "depersonalization" revealed in his comment, reactions that Byrne identifies as key components of burnout. In other words, an underlying cause of burnout among English teachers, as among many ex-public sector workers in the United Kindgom, is a deep-seated, passionately felt sense that the moral person-related basis of their work is being eroded, to be replaced by formal accountability and the accountancy of cost effectiveness.

The interconnected nature of teachers' relationships with their pupils also leads teachers to "care" for them. Because they feel responsible for the children, teachers believe that they must act in the children's best interests. This does not always mean that teachers like them. To "care," as it is used by teachers themselves, may be affective (e.g., to feel affection, even love, for; to feel empathy with; to try to establish or maintain a personal relationship with). But it may also refer to thoughts or actions rather than feelings (e.g., to be concerned or anxious about; to act supportively toward; to act in the interests of, even when such action is costly or runs counter to one's own interests). In addition, teachers' felt obligation to "care" for pupils may be directed toward their physical, social, emotional, or moral welfare, to their learning, or to both. It is a term that deserves to be approached cautiously in discussions of teachers' responsibilities or of occupational burnout (Nias, 1997).

Whatever its precise meaning and however superficially the individual's emotions are engaged in a particular context, "caring" is part of most teachers' self-image. During the past decade they have come to feel that this too is under attack. The rhetoric of official statements continues to give it importance, but the reality of under-resourcing, repeated emphasis on competition within and between schools, and the narrowing base of the National Curriculum and of pupil assessment tell teachers a different story. To many, it appears as if politicians consider some children more deserving of care than others and are encouraging parents in this view. For example, research published in 1995 (Power, Whitty, and Youdell, 1995) indicates that the pressures of competition, operating through published test results and league tables, may make schools reluctant to accept homeless pupils because they take an undue proportion of headteachers' and teachers' time and because they are likely to depress test scores.

In addition, researchers (already cited) who have documented the effects of educational changes in England and Wales suggest that the pressure on teachers' "caring" selves has increased both in the classroom and outside it, especially when "caring" relates to the whole child rather than simply to cognitive development. Teachers say that inside the classroom there is less time for them to respond to individual interests and concerns, to listen and talk to children about extracurricular matters, to abandon their planning and follow matters raised by the children that are extraneous to the National Curriculum. "Spontaneity" has, in this context, more than a pedagogic or curricular meaning; it also signals to teachers and, they believe, to their pupils that teachers know about, are interested in, and are concerned about their students as individuals. "Caring" is also threatened outside the classroom (e.g., by budgetary cuts, pressures on teachers' time, and the increase in their curricular and administrative responsibilities). Teachers claim that they have less time, incentive, and school resources to socialize with children (e.g., in meal breaks), to engage with them in clubs and other extracurricular activities, to go with them on school journeys or camps, to help them and often their parents overcome social difficulties. Yet many teachers would subscribe to Best's (1995, p. 2) claim that "to be an uncaring educator might be seen as a contradiction in terms." Such teachers daily face the strains of living with or accommodating to this contradiction. It increases their moral distress and their resulting sense of professional bereavement (Nias, 1993b).

It would be easier for teachers to resolve contradictions such as these if they were not also caught in the "trap of conscientiousness" (Campbell and Neill, 1994b). This too grows from the interpersonal basis of their work. The notion that teaching and learning are built on personal relationships has a long history in the United Kingdom. It owes much to the influence of Rousseau, though it has been present, through the tradition of discipleship, for much longer than that. The Christian influence on state education for the masses in the nineteenth century also encouraged teachers to think in these terms (Rich, 1972; Tropp, 1957). "Caring" for individuals has similar origins and a similarly long history. Yet, as Alexander (1984) has pointed out, the impossibility of teaching and caring for every individual in a large group has never been properly faced. Instead, the teaching profession has implicitly continued to fulfill the expectation of James Kay Shuttleworth (an influential teacher educator in the early nineteenth century) that teachers should show "religious devotion to their work" (quoted in Rich, 1972). The result, as Campbell and Neill (1994b) and Evans et al. (1994) make clear, is that most teachers are socialized into a "sense of obligation to meet all work demands to the best of their ability" (Campbell and Neill, 1994b, p. 223).

"Conscientiousness" then contributes to the pressure on teachers, both because it increases their chronic sense of guilt (A. Hargreaves, 1994; Nias, 1989) and because it encourages them to neglect the early signs of stress in themselves and others. It is not clear, however, why teachers should have allowed themselves to become trapped in this way, though in Nias (1997) I have explored three possible historical reasons: the influence of the Protestant work ethic on teacher education and the teaching profession in the United Kingdom; the socialization of women into a view of teaching as motherhood with the expectation that it will involve "altruism, self-abnegation and repetitive labour" (Grumet, 1988, p. 87); the pervasive "authority-dependence" of the teaching profession (Abercrombie, 1984).

Stages of Stress

One of the practical consequences for teachers of this combination of personal responsibility is caring and conscientiousness. My consistent experience for forty years has been that most teachers ignore the early signs of stress, failing to see physical and emotional symptoms as signals of a deeper disequilibrium and distress. Yet the neglect of these symptoms and of their place in the "stages of stress" (Veninga and Spradley, 1981) can result in breakdown or burnout. Veninga and Spradley posit a five-stage model:

1. *Eustress,* characterized by a "healthy sense of being stretched and challenged and sufficiently well-supported to meet the challenge"
2. *Fuel shortage,* marked by job dissatisfaction, inefficiency at work, fatigue, sleep disturbance, and escape activities such as excessive eating or drinking, leisure taken in "overdrive"
3. *Development of symptoms* (e.g., headache, back pain, fatigue, digestive disorders, anxiety, anger) that become more frequent and intense
4. *Crisis,* marked by acute symptoms, pessimism, self-doubt, a sense of being trapped, and an obsessional concern with all of these
5. *"Hitting the wall,"* at which point external help is usually needed to effect recovery.

With hindsight, I think many of the teachers I interviewed between 1975 and 1985 (Nias, 1989) were at stages 1 and 2, with some at stage 3. I met only three who could be described as being at stage 4, none at stage 5. By contrast, Woods's paper suggests the existence in England and Wales of large numbers of teachers at stages 4 and 5, and his case examples fit into these categories. My own recent experience confirms his evidence.

Accepting the many reasons advanced by Woods, Miller, and Smylie (this volume) for the increased pressure on teachers, we lack the evidence to answer the question: Why have so many teachers in the past decade neglected their early signs of stress and ended up in crisis or hitting the wall? Guilt and conscientiousness obviously play a part, and there are other plausible answers: excessive pressure on, or the dissolution through policy changes of structures (e.g., local authority advisory and counseling services) that in earlier years diagnosed incipient crises and intervened to help alleviate them; a recession, making it hard for individuals to leave teaching for other jobs, especially when taken in conjunction with an increase in teaching, as in other occupations, in single parenthood and so of the single-income family; and the incremental nature of change, which encourages individuals to behave like frogs that, put into a pot of cool water whose temperature is then raised by small degrees, fail to jump out and are boiled alive (Henderson, 1995).

I wish to offer three other reasons. These are speculative in the sense that I do not have research evidence to confirm them, but they all grow out of my recent experience and of discussions with colleagues who work in and with the teaching profession.

First, in common with many other members of the care-based professions (e.g., medicine, social work, nursing), teachers are socialized into a service ethic that encourages them to ignore their own needs. It is also possible that some of the satisfactions of teaching depend, paradoxically, on taking more care of others than of oneself (Nias, 1989). Since 1981, I have undertaken four case studies of schools, all of them requiring intensive data collection during a full academic year. I have repeatedly been struck by teachers' neglect of their own physical and emotional health and their willingness to sacrifice these to the perceived needs of their pupils. The traditional individualism of teaching may well contribute to these habits. So, perhaps, the recent increase in burnout reflects in part teachers' lack of practice in attending to themselves. This topic too deserves further inquiry.

The second answer is related to the first. Teachers who respond to the early signs of stress by taking care of their symptoms usually take time off work. This disadvantages their colleagues as well as their pupils. Moreover, paradoxically, the greater teachers' sense of responsibility to their colleagues and the more they care for them, the less likely they are to heed their own early-warning signals. Clearly, the increased peer awareness that has been encouraged both by the growth of "collegiality" in schools (D. Hargreaves, 1994) and by cuts in resources is two-edged.

Third, most teachers, especially in primary schools, are women. Many women, in all forms of occupation, now work double shifts – that is, they carry a heavy load of domestic responsibilities in addition to their jobs. Sometimes, they work triple shifts, juggling work, home, and child care responsibilities (Acker, 1994, p. 118). There are obvious reasons that they should become physically and emotionally exhausted. However, women are less likely than men to look after themselves as long as they feel that there are others who need to be cared for, especially when there are social expectations that "women's caring work should blur the distinction between labour and love" (Acker, 1995, p. 24). Eichenbaum and Orbach (1983), writing from a psychoanalytic perspective, present a slightly different argument. There is, they suggest, a cycle perpetuated through child-rearing practices, which results in gender-related differences in the extent to which men and women express their needs and have them satisfied. Simply put, girls are brought up by mothers in ways that make them aware of their needs but lead them to expect that these will not be met. Boys, by contrast, learn that "needs" belong to women; they therefore do not learn to identify or recognize their own. However, with the tacit collusion of their mothers, sisters, and later wives, they grow expecting that their needs will be satisfied, usually by women. Both sets of propositions have an obvious bearing on gender-related differences in the extent and rate of burnout in the profession. Yet these differences are seldom mentioned in the literature on burnout and are not addressed by other authors in this volume. Further research in this area might well be productive.

Supporting Moral Values Through Collegial Relations

Many of the conditions for acute stress have existed in all the schools in which I and my colleagues have undertaken research since 1987. The schools were all subject to the constraints and changes that Woods describes. Most of their staff were, for most of the time, very tired, often to the point of exhaustion. They were frequently ill, yet they took little time off from school, instead spending their holidays receiving medical treatment or resting. Many also suffered additional tension from conflict between their professional and domestic commitments. Indeed, all the half-dozen or so heads or teachers who burned out during or after our research were the victims of great personal stress from bereavement or marital breakdown, events that coincided with particular periods of pressure at school. For the most part, however, notwithstanding all the strains of intensification and change, the staffs of these schools appeared to enjoy their work and the schools themselves were usually busy, vibrant, exciting, and frequently joyous places. Individual and collective morale were often low but never irretrievably; recovery always followed. Above all – and this should be set alongside the conscientiousness that characterized almost all the teachers and all the heads and contributed greatly to their fatigue and ill-health – the schools were full of laughter, there was a great deal of incidental or deliberate fun in classrooms and staffrooms, and a celebration or party took place on the slightest pretext.

It would require a separate paper to analyze fully the ways in that particular schools contain or reduce the pressure that adverse personal circumstances or classroom conditions place on individuals and which macro forces exert on whole staffs or groups. In any case, Leithwood, Miller, Smylie, and Woods all consider organizational factors that affect the job satisfaction of or pressure on teachers and their leaders. In my case, I found as I worked on this chapter that much of the relevant evidence already existed, albeit in scattered form. Specifically, it was when I was doing the longitudinal research for *Primary Teachers Talking* (Nias, 1989) that I first became aware of the profound effects on teachers of the adult relationships within their schools. Later, I analyzed in detail in Nias, Southworth, and Yeomans (1989) a supportive form of organizational culture ("a culture of collaboration") that seems to make all its members more resistant to burnout than does the traditional individualism of teaching. In Nias, Southworth, and Campbell (1992), we examined the ways that the development of shared curricular goals and a climate of continuous professional learning contribute to high self-esteem and job satisfaction among teachers and support staff. Later still, I looked, at the staff's request, into the main-streaming of children with learning difficulties in an urban school for four-to eight-year-olds (Nias, 1994). Although my focus there was quite different from that of previous studies, I recognized among the teachers and support staff much of the positive leadership, collaboration, and professional development I had come to associate with organizational resilience and individual growth. Further, the "effective schools" literature (e.g., Mortimore, Sammons, Lewis, and Ecob, 1988; Rosenholtz, 1989; Rutter, Maugham, Mortimore, and Ouston, 1979; Sammons et al., 1995) makes many of the same points that I and my colleagues have about the characteristics of supportive and developing schools. The problem appears to be not one of agreeing on the workplace conditions that give teachers a high level of job satisfaction but of implementing them in what is described in this volume as high performance–low burnout schools.

Instead of reiterating points made elsewhere, I wish here to suggest five ways that particular aspects of collegial relations in the schools where I have undertaken research appear to strengthen the moral perspectives and values of their staff and, in so doing, reduce the likelihood of burnout. A word of caution is in order. As I have a great deal of accumulated data, the generalizations I make obviously do not hold for every school or teacher or for all the time.

First, in the eleven case study schools, interpersonal relationships were at the center of every aspect of school life. Heads and other leaders used, and staff responded to, personal rather than positional authority; communication took place, conflict was resolved, and differences were turned to constructive uses through face-to-face contact; heads, teachers, and support staff interacted constantly, often for brief periods but in every area of the school from corridors to classrooms; people talked a great deal wherever they met, and they sought opportunities to meet, both formally and informally; volunteers, parents, and new staff members learned about and were socialized into the values of the school through personal encounters with children and with existing staff. Individuals learned from one another, sometimes in pairs and at others to ones in groups; indeed, most professional learning took place as a result of some kind of formal or informal interaction, in or out of school. Interpersonal contact was, to mix a metaphor, simultaneously the oil that helped the schools run smoothly and effectively and the glue that held them together. It is not surprising that the stated educational aims of each school gave priority not only to the all-round development of individual pupils but also to their ability to work and live productively together.

Second, these institutions were run by and for people rather than by rules or pieces of paper, and this approach helped to promote a shared sense of responsibility for persons that was the basis of many individuals' "moral purpose" (Fullan, 1993, p. 11) in entering and remaining within the teaching profession. As a result, their staffs were well placed to offer one another an alternative to legal accountability and contractualism. They formed, in effect, schoolwide reference groups that strengthened individuals' views of the rightness of their own beliefs, motivations, and actions. In their research into primary teachers' responses to the National Curriculum and assessment, Pollard et al. (1994) used a typology of responses that is similar to that of Woods: compliance, incorporation, mediation, retreatism, resistance. They claim that the majority response is incorporation, summed up in one teacher's words as, "I'll accept the changes, but I won't allow anything I consider to be really important to be lost." The nature of the "really important" was expressed by another "incorporating" teacher as, "I'll never sacrifice the children. I'll go on doing what I think best for them, regardless" (Pollard et al., 1994, p. 100). Teachers clearly still value their moral commitment to children's interests; the loneliness of that position is alleviated when it is shared by colleagues and headteachers.

However, the same study documents a shift among headteachers during the period up to 1992 – from mediation and incorporation toward compliance – coupled with an increased tendency to effect change through top-down approaches. Hayes (1995) has shown the damaging effect on a newly appointed headteacher who felt driven by her legal responsibilities and so drifted into conflict with her staff; the staff did not wish to oppose her but were alienated by the rapid and apparently ill-thought-out changes of policy that her stance forced on them. It may be that as we try to understand the course and causes of burnout, we need to consider school managers and teachers separately. For example, all the final case examples in Woods's paper are headteachers. Does similar evidence exist for teachers, and if so, would it support similar conclusions? The same question causes me to look critically at the claims Leithwood makes for transformational leadership, wondering whether it looks or feels the same from different organizational perspectives.

My third point is that our case study schools had, for most of the time, cultures in which individuals felt a sense of community with and obligation to one another. They had also developed structures (e.g., pairing, teams, meetings) that made such caring easier to effect in action. In other words, their ability to act in their pupils' interests was strengthened by knowledge that others tried to act in theirs. The resulting atmosphere of mutual concern and practical assistance often prevented intermittent stress from becoming chronic or acute. Collaborative cultures are built on a belief in the value of both the individual and the group to which he or she belongs. In schools with such cultures, people habitually praise, thank, appreciate, help, support, encourage one another, and welcome the differences between them as a source of mutual learning and enrichment. Staff know about and accept one another as people and are sensitive to one another's personal and professional needs, often acting with great kindness, and supportiveness, even toward people whom they do not particularly like. The group is important, too, and the sense of interdependence that comes from membership in it. After a particularly stressful term, the deputy headteacher in one "collaborative" school reflected: "I think we've made up our minds not to get riled by one another. . . . we have a commitment to one another as a team, we value what we've got and we want to keep it" (Nias et al., 1989, p. 162). Acker (1995) describes the ways in which the staff of an inner-city school cared for one another and fostered their sense of "togetherness," developed in part because of their need to find collective strategies to compensate for the frustrations of their teaching. She concludes, "Perhaps paradoxically, the attempt to do the impossible (in the classrooms) gave strong impetus to the development of a caring, supportive workplace culture" (Acker, 1995, p. 33).

Such a culture should not be mistakenly viewed as conflict free or cozy. Collaborative cultures are also built on a belief in the value of openness, tempered by a respect for individual and collective security. Another aspect of mutual support and of "care" within such institutions is that individuals feel able to express their emotions, negative and positive, to admit to failure and weakness, to voice resentment and frustration, to demonstrate affection. By contrast, a culture of individualism tends to increase emotional stress for its members by fostering an illusion that others are coping and that one's own fears are born of a unique incompetence; by requiring individuals to pretend to feelings they do not own; by failing to promote the habit of day-to-day communication so that small interpersonal or professional differences build up into major problems.

Finally, our case study schools tended also to be "caring" institutions in the sense that they offered their staff members opportunities for professional learning and extension, thus contributing to high self-esteem and encouraging a sense that individuals were in control of their own development. In the collaborative schools (Nias et al., 1989), professional development was a corollary of role blurring and of a noncompetitive environment in which individuals often undertook any job that needed doing, whether or

236   Jennifer Nias

not they were formally qualified for it. They were ready to take these risks because they knew that they would be supported by their colleagues if the need arose. In the schools that were focusing on curriculum development (Nias et al. 1992; Nias, 1994), professional growth was a concomitant of the schoolwide emphasis on continuous teacher learning. Individuals habitually took on new responsibilities; acquired fresh knowledge and skills, often as a result of a role change; and continued to strengthen their sense of professional efficacy. Moreover, in all these schools, the existence of shared social or curricular goals (Woods's "relational idea" and Leithwood's "vision") helped to promote individual self-esteem. Teaching and support staff shared a sense of common institutional purpose and knew how they were contributing to its fulfilment.

Conclusion

Other chapters in this volume paint on large canvases. I have attempted a miniature, informed to a large extent by my own research. Like all miniatures, it may be more or less successful in reflecting a particular reality but at the cost of discounting the contribution of other realities and neglecting the background.

In this miniature, I have focused on the moral purposes, felt responsibilities, and interests of teachers. I have argued that values, and a sense of acting in accordance with these values, play a central part in the decision of many teachers to continue their commitment to their work. Moreover, this commitment is so deep that it is incorporated in the self that is invested in the job. Attacks on these values, in this case from government policies, are therefore experienced as stress-inducing threats to the individual's sense of identity. Because few teachers are skilled in identifying or combating the early stages of stress, "eustress" or "fuel shortage" easily escalate into "hitting the wall." There is, however, evidence that the ways in which teachers conceptualize and act out their shared purposes and their relationships with one another may contain stress at its early stages or help to alleviate its "chronic symptoms."

However, there are dangers in placing too much emphasis on the help that teachers can give one another. There is less and less "slack" within the educational system in England and Wales. Many teachers are overburdened in the classroom and overwhelmed by administrative duties outside it. We cannot assume that they will have the time, energy, skill, or desire to commit their own scarce personal resources to co-counseling or mutual support. To make this assumption would be to increase rather than decrease their burdens of care. "Collegiality" and "collaboration," simplistically construed, are no answer to long-term social, demographic, and economic problems. Instead, we need to consider teachers' own understanding of their moral commitment to their work and to understand the kind of organizational cultures, structures, resources, and support that are compatible with it. Appropriate staff relationships can help individuals understand stress and avoid or resist burnout. In the long run, however, they will be little more than a palliative unless the public discourse and the macro forces that frame it also change.

14. Teacher Burnout From a Social-Cognitive Perspective: A Theoretical Position Paper

RALF SCHWARZER AND ESTHER GREENGLASS

The chapters in this volume by Miller, Smylie, and Woods reflect a socio-logical approach to understanding the burnout phenomenon. This view implies that the objective situation has changed for the worse for teachers who increasingly experience constraints on the job – for example, intensi-fication of teaching, compliance with administrative regulations, conflicts with parents and supervisors, and unmotivated students. To balance this sociological view, we have decided to compose a psychological position paper that focuses on the responses of the individual teacher to this situa-tion. Thus, we have chosen the opposite extreme to shed some light on the issue. This does not necessarily mean that the blame is put on the teacher when he or she suffers from burnout. Rather, our theory tries to explain why there are individual differences and why not all teachers become vic-tims of a school-system-induced burnout syndrome.

There is ample evidence that teachers, in the course of their careers, ex-perience a great deal of stress that may result in depressed mood, exhaus-tion, poor performance, and attitude and personality changes, which, in turn, may lead to illness and premature retirement. In some societies or school systems, this might occur nowadays more often than in the past (see chapters by Miller, Smylie, and Woods, this volume).

The label "burnout" has been suggested for this phenomenon, and clin-ical observations have been made and empirical research has been con-ducted for more than two decades (for an overview, see Byrne, this volume). In this chapter, we comment in a general manner on the work done so far. As there is already so much good research on this topic, we have chosen not to add another piece of evidence but rather to suggest a new theoretical perspective that might help to direct further research to gain more specific knowledge about the actual genesis of burnout in the individual teacher. Thus, individual differences in the degree to which teachers develop this syndrome might be better explained by the model that is put down here.

238

We first comment on the construct of burnout and then deal with a stress and coping approach, followed by a new action-oriented motivational perspective. Special emphasis is given on resource factors and vulnerability factors that can moderate the burnout process.

The Theoretical Construct of Burnout

Burnout is sometimes defined in a very broad sense and is equated with stress, depression, and adverse health; however, other, narrower definitions have become more popular. These relate burnout to long-term interpersonal stress within human service professions; that is, burnout pertains to feelings experienced by people whose jobs require repeated exposure to emotionally charged social situations. Thus, burnout can be defined as a syndrome of emotional exhaustion, depersonalization, and reduced accomplishment that may occur among individuals who do "people work" (Maslach and Jackson, 1986). Burnout can be conceived of as a product or as a process. The way it is normally measured suggests that it should be understood as a product. The widely used Maslach Burnout Inventory (MBI; Maslach and Jackson, 1986) refers to a "syndrome," which may be understood as the product of a long-term stressful encounter. Moreover, it is not a state but a trait because it has become a stable phenomenon during one's career. Because the MBI has been around for a while already and has stimulated a great deal of good research, we could resort to a narrow operational definition of burnout as a "tripartite trait construct (emotional exhaustion, depersonalization, poor accomplishments) as measured by the MBI." Nevertheless, our suggestion is to add a broader process perspective that does not conflict with that definition. Rather, it comprises the developmental conditions that create trait burnout as a product.

There have been some process definitions before. Cherniss (1980b) defined burnout as negative personal changes that occur over time in helping professionals working in demanding or frustrating jobs. He proposed a process model that focused on stress and coping experiences resulting in negative attitude change (Cherniss, 1980b, 1989, 1990). According to this model, particular work settings interact with individual differences. Factors such as particular career orientations and extra-work demands and supports represent sources of stress that are experienced to varying degrees by job incumbents. Individuals cope with these stresses in different ways. Some employ strategies that might be active problem solving; others respond by exhibiting negative attitude changes – that is, burnout. This is a kind of avoidant, resigned, coping process that leads to reduced well-being (see Burke and Greenglass, 1989c, 1995).

Golombiewski, Munzenrider, and Stevenson (1986) have proposed eight stages of burnout by dichotomizing the three components of the MBI into low and high ($2^3 = 8$) and giving them different weights in the developmental process of burnout. Emotional exhaustion is seen as the most important component, and it shows up only during the second half of the process. Initially, all three components are low; eventually, they are high. Some research has provided empirical evidence for such a stage model (see for example, Wolpin, Burke, and Greenglass, 1990, 1994).

One weakness of these models lies in their descriptive nature. They do not explain what is really going on in the individual. What is missing in this entire research tradition is a microlevel theory that identifies the major psychological constructs and developmental stages that cause burnout. A closer look at the transactional-cognitive stress and coping perspective may serve as an introduction to microlevel causal modeling.

The Stress and Coping Perspective

Burnout develops after an extended period of job stress and thus can be understood as one manifestation of stress consequences. Within the transactional, cognitive framework of stress and emotions (Lazarus, 1991, 1993, 1995), these consequences depend on a number of factors. First, objective antecedents of stress, such as overwhelming job demands combined with a lack of coping resources, are of importance (Hobfoll, 1988, 1989). Second, the cognitive appraisals need to reflect this imbalance – that is, the demands must be seen as taxing or exceeding one's resources, which in turn would result in either challenge, threat, or harm/loss. In the case of teacher stress, individuals frequently come up with appraisals of threat and loss of control. Third, subsequent coping with stress must be maladaptive in the long run; that is, teachers might find ways of emotional coping that help them to overcome temporary crisis situations, but their problem-focused coping strategies appear to be insufficient to deal effectively with the constantly changing job demands.

One way to gain more detailed knowledge within this framework is to identify specific demands that are appraised as threatening. These can be external demands, such as high workload, time pressure, high expectations from headmasters or parents, or ambiguity of goals, or they can be internal demands, such as high aspirations, overcommitment, or role conflict. Another way to examine stress and coping is to focus on resources of the individual. These resources can be external, such as social support, or internal, such as job experience, classroom management skills, or perceived professional self-efficacy. The lack of these resources predisposes teachers to make unfavorable stress appraisals and to cope poorly with stress. This social-cognitive, resource-oriented approach to understanding stress and coping processes represents the state of the art and has been applied to various settings (Bandura, 1995, 1997; Jerusalem, 1990; Lazarus, 1993, 1995; Schwarzer and Jerusalem, 1992). A more detailed discussion of the resource issue appears later in this chapter.

Goals, Actions, and Demotivation

The present perspective goes beyond the general stress and coping paradigm by aiming at the individual teachers' motivation and action process. This does not mean that the individual is to blame for his or her burnout syndrome. Rather, it is necessary to understand how the individual typically responds to situational constraints on the job. Not every teacher suffers from burnout. Therefore, individual differences need to be explained.

Burnout is commonly seen as resulting from a sequence of inappropriate goal setting, poor planning, action failure, and unfavorable causal attributions. These are mainly instigated by job-specific self-inefficacy and lack of social support.

The theory of reasoned action (Fishbein and Ajzen, 1975) claims that behavior is dependent on intentions that, in turn, are caused by attitudes and social norms. The theory of planned behavior (Ajzen, 1991) includes perceived control as an additional determinant of intentions and behaviors. These and other well-confirmed theories (for an overview see Schwarzer, 1992) reflect a motivation or decision-making process that emphasizes goals or intentions as necessary antecedents of actions. Goals are underrepresented in stress and coping theories. Moreover, action theories postulate a sequence of processes or stages beyond the decision point. Postdecisional processes include planning, acting, and evaluating action outcomes. This has been referred to as a volition process (Heckhausen, 1991; Kuhl and Beckmann, 1994; Schwarzer, 1992), in contrast to its preceding motivation process (see also Prochaska, 1994).

A well-functioning teacher can be defined as someone who passes successfully through self-regulatory goal attainment processes. Professional goals can be of different scope; for example, "Tomorrow I intend to manage to keep the class quiet and attentive," or "By next year, I will have moved my class to a top level of reading skills." Compared to wishful thinking, goals are realistic and specific. Wishful thinking ("I wish I were a better teacher") is considered a maladaptive, emotional way of coping whereas goal setting represents an instrumental, problem-focused coping strategy. Goals have to be translated into action, and this requires optimistic self-beliefs. Self-efficacious teachers develop success scenarios in which they see themselves as effective copers with job-related demands. One has to make plans about the where and when of an action attempt. This postdecisional and preactional stage is crucial for turning an intention into an action.

If goals are specific and realistic and if the planning is well done, the chance of meeting the challenges successfully is high. However, actions are multiply determined, and there are plenty of reasons a teacher may fail, for example, to implement the curriculum, to raise class participation, or to master the teaching objectives. At this point, when actions fail, a well-functioning teacher would make causal attributions that help to avoid a pessimistic interpretation. Instead of catastrophizing, the teacher makes an optimistic attribution, typically by either externalizing the cause of the failure (demands too high, class too difficult) or by making unstable factors responsible (lack of effort, a bad day, poor timing). Failure can be seen as an opportunity to redefine goals, to create alternative strategies, and to mobilize social support.

In hard times, the well-functioning teacher does experience job stress, but he or she perceives more challenge than threat or loss of control. Such teachers have ups and downs in mood and performance; they also have temporary exhaustion and worry, but these are present only at the state level and do not stabilize into the trait level, exhibiting the burnout syndrome. When teachers experience the same level of external demands, the individual differences in their responses are due to their stress resource factors. The next section, therefore, gives a more detailed account of internal and external resources.

Coping Resources

Among the many coping resources, two have received most of the attention: Self-efficacy is regarded as the most influential internal resource, whereas social support is the most conspicuous external resource.

Self-Efficacy

In a self-regulatory goal attainment process, one needs to believe in one's competence to meet novel challenges, to overcome barriers, or to recover from setbacks. Such optimistic self-beliefs have been labeled "perceived self-efficacy" (Bandura, 1995, 1997). Perceived self-efficacy represents the belief that one can change behaviors by personal action. Behavior change is seen as dependent on one's perceived capability to cope with stress and boredom and to mobilize one's resources and courses of action required to meet the situational demands. Efficacy beliefs affect the intention to change behavior, the amount of effort expended to attain this goal, and the persistence to continue striving in spite of barriers and setbacks that may undermine motivation.

Self-efficacious teachers set realistically high goals for themselves; they develop strategies and maintain a course of action even when obstacles occur or when failures mount. Self-efficacy is not identical to self-esteem. Rather, it is a belief in one's capability to overcome a specific barrier by investing effort and strategies. Thus, a self-regulatory goal attainment process needs to be at stake, not simply a feeling about oneself.

A lack of self-efficacy is associated with anxiety – in particular, worry. Worry is a vulnerability factor that exerts a negative influence on motivation and volition. A subset of worry cognitions pertains to negative thoughts about oneself, one's competence, or one's ability to cope with challenging or threatening demands (see Schwarzer, 1996; Schwarzer and Wicklund, 1991). These are labeled here as self-doubts. Self-doubts are unfavorable thoughts that refer to personal deficits in the self-regulation process and therefore represent one example of cognitive interference. Self-doubts are specific pessimistic beliefs experienced while facing a stressful encounter. Thus, self-doubts reflect perceived self-inefficacy at the state level of functioning. Here are some examples: "I doubt whether I can solve this problem." "It is difficult for me to make friends." "I am not confident that I can stick to this diet." "I feel unable to adopt a strenuous exercise regimen." All these thoughts are self-related and pertain to one's competence or to similar personal coping resources. In contrast, a homemaker who waits nervously for her husband to return from work may worry about his safety, health, or life, but those are not self-doubts. Self-doubts represent a specific class of worries that are maladaptive in attaining goals because they interfere with an intended self-regulation process. In contrast to rumination or worry, self-doubts are always tied to personal goals. Self-doubts are worries about specific coping capabilities in a self-regulatory process. They have a detrimental motivational effect that adds to the reduced information processing efficiency that is characteristic for anxious individuals.

Social Support

Burnout has been linked to deficits in personal relationships (Burke and Greenglass, 1993, 1995; Greenglass, Fiksenbaum, and Burke, 1994). A few conceptual remarks about social integration and social support are needed at this point. Whereas social integration refers to the size and density of a social network and to the frequency of contact, social support pertains to the functional value of social relationships, in particular to their supportive quality in times of need. Both social integration and social support can be coping resources, and their absence represents a stress vulnerability factor.

Social support can be further subdivided into the perceived availability of support as opposed to actually received support (see Schwarzer and Leppin, 1991). The former has been found to be a stable characteristic that resembles a personality trait acquired by secure attachment experiences. The latter is a situation-dependent social resource in stressful encounters. Moreover, various sources of support have to be taken into account (Schwarzer, Dunkel-Schetter, and Kemeny, 1994). Obviously, job stress can be ameliorated by supervisor and peer support at the workplace. But support from family and friends appears to be important as well because it can compensate for the lack of social support at work and may help to rebuild coping competence and motivation.

Teachers with high burnout levels report lower levels of social support (Burke and Greenglass, 1993; Greenglass et al., 1994). There might be a predominant causal pathway from lack of support to burnout, but the opposite causal direction should not be excluded prematurely: Exhausted, depersonalized teachers with poor job performance are less likely to make friends and to maintain satisfactory close interpersonal relationships at the workplace. To understand the causal role of social support and other potential coping resources, one needs to consider a more comprehensive theoretical framework with reciprocal relationships over time.

The Social-Cognitive Process Model of Teacher Burnout

An attempt has been made to condense this theoretical framework into one illustrative figure (see Figure 14.1). The basic idea is that teacher burnout develops within a demanding job stress context that is characterized by the pursuit of professional goals and actions that do not yield personally satisfactory results. Teachers are constantly involved in self-regulatory goal attainment processes that require a great deal of resources to meet the taxing demands. Setting goals can be seen as the motivation phase. This is influenced by distal antecedent factors such as high job demands, ambiguous professional values, or lack of objective resources. Examples of proximal factors are negative outcome expectancies (inappropriate behavioral beliefs), lack of encouragement by others, and self-doubts. These determinants

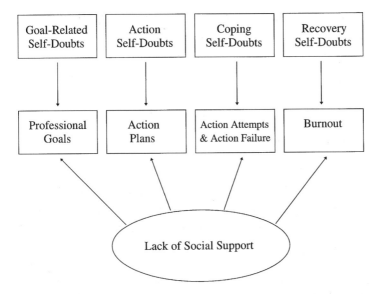

Figure 14.1. The social-cognitive process model of teacher burnout.

might lead to goals that are unrealistic or too low. When teachers do not dare to impose difficult demands on themselves and to adopt a behavioral change regimen, they cannot expect to solve their job problems. Facing the job demands in a more problem-oriented manner would include searching for better teaching strategies, observing behavioral models, asking for help, taking inservice training courses, investing more effort, being more persistent, organizing resistance against pressures at work, filing complaints, and other strategies. If such specific goals are set, there is no guarantee that they would be translated into corresponding actions. In the volition phase, teachers often fail to develop creative action plans because they harbor action self-doubts or do not receive sufficient support. When action attempts are being initiated, teachers often fail to maintain the desired action because they lack support or harbor coping self-doubts – that is, they believe they cannot cope with upcoming crises or barriers. For example, teachers may have the good behavioral intention to ignore systematically those students who provoke others, but they appear to get out of control, lose their patience, and sanction critical student behavior. When teachers realize after years of stress and unsuccessful coping that they feel burned out, they experience helplessness and resignation, harbor recovery self-doubts, and believe they are incapable of taking instrumental action or mobilizing efficient social support. Burnout, then, becomes itself a determinant of subsequent goal setting and action processes. The vicious cycle continues – unless self-doubts are overcome or social support is provided.

Conclusions

The present individualistic view of teacher burnout does not necessarily imply that teachers require therapy to prevent or alleviate burnout. It merely may explain which social-cognitive factors are involved in the development process of burnout. In contrast to previous models, emphasis is given to lack of self-efficacy at different stages of a self-regulatory goal attainment process. To prevent or alleviate burnout, therefore, all measures taken at the collective or individual level to influence this mechanism can be seen as appropriate. Lowering the external demands, structuring clearly the priorities on the job, removing ambiguity, removing role conflict, providing social support, among others, can be effective means. However, the key issue remains the degree to which job specific self-efficacy can be built up. As Bandura (1995, 1997) has suggested, there are three major pathways that help to improve self-efficacy: verbal persuasion, vicarious experience (modeling), and personal mastery experience. How these have to be implemented is beyond the scope of this chapter, but these learning principles can be integrated into preservice and inservice teacher training as a way to combat future burnout.

15. Professional Identity, School Reform, and Burnout: Some Reflections on Teacher Burnout

PETER SLEEGERS

The reflections on teacher burnout in this chapter are inspired mainly by the contributions of Byrne and Miller. Taking these two as a starting point, I offer comments related to three different perspectives on teacher burnout: the sociological, psychological, and organizational perspectives. The first comment concerns the absence of a sociological perspective. My argument is that factors at the macro level of society are important to the analysis and explanation of teacher burnout. My second comment concerns the psychological perspective and the personality factors included in the model of burnout tested in Byrne's study. I argue that specific teacher-related personality factors must be taken into account to explain teacher burnout. My third comment concerns the organizational perspective on teacher burnout and the impact of working conditions on teacher stress, dissatisfaction, and workload. I argue that burnout can often be traced to a particular combination of school organization and teachers' professional orientation. In closing, I reflect on Miller's idea that some new forms of learning can provide a buffer against burnout and report on the results of research into the innovative capacity of schools. These findings confirm Miller's claim that teacher learning and development are contextually determined.

The Sociological Perspective

In Byrne's as well as in Miller's contributions, teacher burnout is analyzed from an organizational and/or social-psychological perspective. The impact of social developments on the well-being and life of teachers is neglected. Although Byrne distinguishes the historical-social perspective as one of three possible perspectives on the concept of burnout, it does not occupy a central position in her review. Miller starts with a brief historical description of current school reform in the United States. In her reflection on the implications of these changes for the concept of teacher burnout, however, she focuses on the reframing of organizational variables alone, which makes Miller's perspective on teacher burnout also largely organizational in nature.

With Woods (1995), I agree that a (macro) sociological perspective can contribute to a greater understanding of the issue of burnout. The objective characteristics of the social context have consequences for the identity development of teachers as acting individuals. In every interaction, the teacher must balance his social and personal identities. This is a dynamic process, and both changes in social expectations and the accumulation of biographical experiences result in a continuous modification of one's ego identity (Jansen and Klaassen, 1994). The learning and development of teachers occurs in constant interaction with the individual and the environment. From this perspective, teacher burnout can be understood to occur when learning and development no longer take place.

In the Netherlands, as in other countries, an erosion of the professional image of teachers has occurred over the past few years as a result of various social developments (Sleegers and Wesselingh, 1995). The image of the autonomous person practicing the profession of teaching, the authority in the classroom who is responsible for not only the content but also the course of the educational process, has disappeared. Underlying this damaged self-image are the bureaucratization of the profession, the experience of stronger control, and stagnating salaries. At the same time, all sorts of educational developments are being strongly directed at improvement of the educational process and the monitoring of this process by splitting teaching practice into clearly measurable competencies. This shift has clearly influenced the self-concepts of those within the teaching profession. In the framework of the professionalization of teachers, the teacher as the expert with regard to the educational process has in some sense been forced aside in the last decade by other educational experts concerned with the content and structure of education as both a process and a system. Under the influence of these external experts, the expertise and independent decision space of teachers as autonomous professionals has been largely reduced. No wonder the meddling of these well-paid, so-called educational experts is not always valued by the teachers on the work floor. In fact, the clear de-professionalization of the occupation of teaching or what some have referred to as the de-skilling of teachers (Apple, 1982; King, 1993) appears to be the case. As a result of such de-professionalization, the social status of the teaching profession no longer compares to that of the medical or law professions. According to Woods (1995), moreover, this intensification of teachers' work may cause stress and burnout. For the Dutch situation, there is some empirical evidence for this assumption. In a recent study among 2,400 primary and secondary school teachers, external factors such as social status and salaries were found to influence work satisfaction negatively (Van Gennip and Pouwels, 1993; Van Gennip and Sleegers, 1994).

The possibilities for making the profession more attractive have recently been examined in the Netherlands. Increasing the autonomy of schools is considered an appropriate strategy for the revitalization of the teaching profession. The idea behind this strategy is that increased school autonomy will make the teaching profession more diverse and thus more attractive. To the degree that schools have greater responsibility, teachers will have more authority and, as a possible consequence, experience the profession as more attractive. The English language literature speaks of "teacher empowerment" or the involvement of teachers in their own professional existence by giving them the power to participate in decision making (Brandt, 1989). This gives teachers not only the opportunity to view themselves and others with respect and dignity but also to practice their profession with greater self-confidence (Kirby and Colbert, 1992). At the moment, the consequences of decentralization and increased school autonomy are simply unknown in the Netherlands. This means that the pronouncements of committees and ministers on this issue are, without additional empirical evidence, little more than plausible speculations.

The Psychological Perspective

My second critical comment pertains to the personality variables included in the study of teacher burnout. In her study, Byrne selected two personality factors considered important to an individual's ability to withstand job stress: locus of control and self-esteem. The results show self-esteem generally to affect personal accomplishment. An effect of an external locus of control on personal accomplishment was found only with secondary school teachers. Dutch research has also shown that personality characteristics such as locus of control, self-efficacy, and attribution styles influence to the experience of helplessness, stress, and work satisfaction (den Hertog, 1990; Van Opdorp, 1991). Especially those teachers tending to attribute problems to external, stable, global, and uncontrollable causes are at risk of experiencing the symptoms of helplessness and stress. They report more frequent thoughts of helplessness, demotivation, depression, lower self-esteem, and less job satisfaction than teachers with other causal attribution patterns.

These results underline the influence of teachers' beliefs and experiences on their professional practice. The relevance of such general variables for the explanation of teacher burnout is open to question, however. The consequence of using such general psychological concepts is that the distinctive qualities of teachers and the specific characteristics of teaching are largely overlooked or ignored. General psychological concepts are quite acceptable for comparison to the providers of other human services (e.g., nurses, doctors, social workers). Greater insight into the work and specific experiences of teachers requires a change of perspective, and questions concerning the orientations, value systems, beliefs, and knowledge of teachers become important (see, for example, Nias, this volume). I therefore propose that the specific character of the work of teachers be explicitly taken into account in studying the issues of stress and burnout.

Such teaching-related personality factors are not included in the model of burnout tested by Byrne. Another presupposition is that all teachers share a common orientation toward the professional, pedagogical, and organizational aspects of their tasks, although this idea is not realistic. Teachers do not constitute a monolithic block with the same attitudes, same educational philosophy, same values, or same subjective educational theory (Kelchtermans, 1993c). In this context, Hoyle's (1975, 1989) distinction between "restricted" and "extended professionality" is interesting.

The term "restricted professionality" refers to the type of teacher who adopts an autonomous attitude and locates good education in sound instruction. Additional characteristics are the isolated perception of classroom events, restricted participation in activities other than teaching, and an exclusively instructional view of teaching methods. The term "extended professionality" refers to the type of teacher who is involved in not only sound instruction but also decision making that goes beyond his or her own autonomy. This type of teacher emphasizes professional cooperation and also relates classroom events to the more general policy and goals of the school. The restricted professional is mainly subject-minded and therefore strongly focused on daily classroom practice. The extended professional is less subject-minded and clearly defines himself or herself as a member of the school organization. Both professional attitudes (and amalgams thereof) are found among teachers.

Nias (1989) introduced a third type of professionality to describe teachers who have a broader school perspective and an interest in collaboration and collegiality but are largely a theoretical and school-bound in their approach to other educational issues. Like extended professionals, such "bounded professionals" derive satisfaction from problem-solving activities and from greater control over their work situation; like restricted professionals, they find significant reward in successful classroom practice.

Van Gennip and Sleegers (1994) found four orientations that teachers share toward the professional and pedagogical aspects of their tasks: teachers who are primarily subject centered, teachers who strongly emphasize pedagogical matters, teachers who stress instructional concerns, and teachers who are primarily focused on the organization of the daily classroom practice. Teachers also differ with respect to their orientations toward the organizational aspects of their jobs as well. In a recent Dutch study among 1,002 secondary school teachers, four types of organizational orientations could be identified. That is, the extent to which teachers possess a development-directed orientation toward the organizational structure of their school was found to vary widely (Schuit, 1993).

These results show teachers to have their own orientations toward teaching and the organization in which they work. The personal beliefs, attitudes, and value systems of teachers constitute their subjective educational theory, which is defined as the personal system of knowledge and beliefs from which a teacher shapes, legitimizes, and evaluates his or her professional activities (Kelchtermans, 1993b, 1993c). For a good understanding of the way teachers behave, react, feel, and give meaning to their professional lives, the concepts of professionality and subjective educational theory certainly seem to be relevant (Kelchtermans, 1993a, 1993c). This also means that personality factors related to the specific nature of the work that teachers do may be relevant for explaining teacher burnout. The results of two recent Dutch studies of the career development and career wishes of teachers can help illustrate this point. In both studies, the work satisfaction of teachers was found to be influenced by two different factors: the attractiveness of teaching, on the one hand, and working conditions, on the other. Teachers can be more satisfied with their jobs when they experience greater variation and challenge and less satisfied when they experience career obstructions (Van Gennip and Pouwels, 1993; Van Gennip and Sleegers, 1994). These results suggest that teachers differ on those aspects of their work from which they derive satisfaction. Such differences may also reflect differences in the professional orientations of teachers.

The Organizational Perspective

As described above, the development of the professional identity of teachers is a continuous and dynamic process in which both the developing person and the social environment play a role. Inspired by Dutch and Flemish research on the impact of both the structural and cultural components of the school organization, the implementation of innovations, the educational improvement process, and the professional development of teachers, I propose a definition of teacher burnout in terms of an interactional paradigm (Clement and Staessens, 1993; Imants and Bakkenes, 1993; Imants, Tillema, and De Brabander, 1993; Staessens, 1993; Van Gennip and Sleegers, 1994). In an interactional approach, teacher burnout is considered to be the outcome of the interactions between the intentions and actions of the individual teacher and the organizational characteristics of the professional environment. The interactions between teachers and their working conditions shape the professional identities of teachers, which in turn influence the manner in which teachers perceive and respond to their work. For this reason, organizational variables as well as personality factors should be included in any model of teacher burnout.

Next, I discuss the relevance of the organizational variables selected by Byrne in light of the need to consider more specific personality factors. If, as I have argued, it is important to include teaching-related personality factors in a model of teacher burnout, the question is which organizational characteristics of schools may be of interest. Hoyle (1975) argues that the professionality of teachers and the school organization are related. The "restricted professional" and a relatively closed school organization are a well-matched couple, for example. In this type of school, teaching is restricted to classroom-related activities. The "extended professional" is suited to a more complex, open school organization. In this type of school, teachers are involved in decision-making processes at the school level and in different forms of collaboration in addition to teaching.

The results of Dutch school-organization research demonstrate the validity of Hoyle's assumption (see Giesbers and Sleegers, 1994). One of the things emerging from these studies is that teachers are more involved in consultations in collegial schools than in so-called segmental schools. In segmental schools, teachers are considered autonomous specialists. In collegial schools, the teachers are involved in not only their capacity as teachers, but also as members of departments or other representative bodies. The teachers are involved in consultations expressly to elicit different points of view.

Sleegers (1991) investigated the relation between the policy-making capacity of schools and their utilization of the available scope for policy making. On the basis of empirical data, three types of schools could be distinguished: schools with a policy-making capacity that is hierarchically oriented and where school management predominates; schools with a policy-making capacity that is collegial and where teachers predominate; and schools with a policy-making capacity that is collegial but nevertheless restricted in certain ways. The last type represents an intermediate form of conduct with the collegial aspect nevertheless predominating (see Sleegers and Wesselingh 1993; Sleegers, Bergen, and Giesbers, 1994). Note that the policy-making capacity of a school appeared to be determined largely by the degree to which the teachers in these schools participated in the decision-making process. That is, the teachers in schools with a collegial policy-making capacity were found to be more involved in decisions regarding administrative and educational tasks than were the teachers in schools with a more hierarchically oriented capacity.

The results of this Dutch research suggest that teachers in a collegial and more complex school operate as "extended professionals." Such teachers appear to have an eye for not only their own subject but also for the policy and identity of the school as a whole, as demonstrated by their involvement in tasks other than teaching. In more segmental and simply organized schools, in contrast, the teachers can be characterized as "restricted professionals."

The results of other Dutch research also show a more marked contrast between the organizational structure of the school and the professional orientations of the teachers in the school to produce increased tensions, stress, job dissatisfaction, and perceived problems among the teachers (Pelkmans and Vrieze, 1987; Schuit, 1993). These findings suggest that stress and burnout can be traced to specific combinations of school organizations and professional orientations.

Dutch research into teacher workload has demonstrated the plausibility of this assumption. No specific organizational characteristic has been found to increase or decrease directly the general workload of teachers. However, particular types of schools can be distinguished on the basis of the presence of certain factors that may increase or decrease the tolerance of teachers with respect to workload (Fruytier, 1988; Gooren, 1989). In "strong" schools, a relatively heavy workload is considered acceptable. This is because strong schools have more means at their disposal for coping with the factors contributing to such a heavy workload: a collegial organizational structure with straightforward decision-making processes and a clear allocation of tasks and powers or a transparent structure with strong management. "Vulnerable" schools, in contrast, have a low tolerance with respect to workload and few means for the regulation of the workload at their disposal. Vulnerable schools may be segmental schools, those lacking a well-structured organization, or schools where teachers work in the isolation of their classrooms.

Considering these factors, including only isolated characteristics of the school organization in a model of teacher burnout is probably fruitless. The absence of attention to the interaction between personality and organizational factors may explain the relatively low impact of the organizational variables considered in Byrne's study. A more meaningful strategy would be to distinguish types of schools by the presence or absence of certain organizational factors that may in turn affect teacher burnout. Questions about management, the allocation of tasks, the structure of consultations, the forms of collaboration between teachers, and the role of departments then take on importance.

Learning as a Buffer Against Teacher Burnout

This and the closing section are a reflection on Miller's idea that learning and the professional development of teachers can provide a buffer against teacher burnout. In her contribution, Miller presents a case study and shows teacher learning and development to be contextually determined in the sense that school development and professional learning are related. What remains unclarified, however, is specification of the structural and cultural characteristics of schools that enhance the learning and professional development of teachers. Research into the innovative capacity of schools can provide more insight into this matter. Van den Berg and Sleegers (1996a) define the innovative capacity of schools as their competence to implement innovations initiated by either the government or the school itself and their competence to coordinate or align the different types of innovation when necessary. To explore this trait, researchers selected schools with a high innovative capacity and schools with a low innovative capacity. The results of two qualitative studies showed that the intensity of the collaboration between the teachers differed between the two groups of schools; as might be expected, much more collaboration was observed among the teachers in high-innovation schools than among those in low-innovation schools (Geijsel, Van den Berg, and Sleegers, in press; Van den Berg and Sleegers, 1996a). Large differences were also found between the leaders of high- versus low-innovation schools, with these differences reflecting the major dimensions of a transformational leadership (Leithwood, 1994). In high-innovation schools, the principal was focused on the enhancement of both individual and collective problem-solving capacities, paying particular attention to developing vision, stimulating collaboration, and providing individual support. The teachers in high-innovation schools were also found to have a particular need for personal growth and continued schooling/training. In schools with a high innovative capacity, moreover, the professional development of the teachers was carefully attuned to the development of the school as a whole. This alignment maximizes the potential power of the school to develop itself, and the school thereby becomes a self-developing force.

The research findings indicate that in high-innovation schools, the opportunities for participation, learning, and development are maximized. This conclusion corresponds to Miller's description and analysis of the lessons learned at Central High School. Within the context of educational restructuring, these results also have clear implications. School restructuring calls for greater emphasis on collective problem solving, teacher empowerment, experimentation, and teacher reflection. As studies of the innovative capacities of schools have shown, moreover, the principal's role becomes crucial in restructuring. Transformational leadership can create educationally inviting settings that also drive teachers to a higher level of concern, increased motivation, and reduced stress (Van den Berg and Sleegers, 1996b). In other words, expanding the innovative capacity of a school can provide a buffer against teacher burnout.

Conclusion

In this chapter, I have reflected on the issue of teacher burnout in light of the results of Dutch and Flemish educational research. I argued that teacher burnout needs to be analyzed from a sociological, psychological, and organizational perspective. This means that social, personality, and organizational factors should be taken into account in the study of teacher burnout. Teacher burnout can be conceptually defined within an interactional approach and considered to be the outcome of the interaction between the intentions and actions of the individual teacher and working conditions. Therefore, the specific character of the work of teachers and the specific character of schools should be explicitly taken into consideration in any study of teacher burnout. This means that *differences between teachers* and *differences between schools* should both be included in any model of teacher burnout. As Smylie (this volume) has observed, more careful study at the level of the individual school can yield greater insight into the influence of teachers and schools on the process of teacher burnout.

16. Conflicting Mindscapes and the Inevitability of Stress in Teaching

THOMAS J. SERGIOVANNI

In Chapter 5 of this volume, "Intensification and Stress in Teaching," Peter Woods argues that stress (caused by the misalignment of factors that are expected to be in harmony) is a social issue that can be examined at the micro, meso, and macro levels. The common seam for all three can be found at the meta level – the level of theory. Stress in teaching, I suggest, is an artifact of competing mindscapes that exist at the meta level. These competing mindscapes create different epistemological and axiological realities at micro, meso, and macro levels. Different realities provide the seedbed for stress for those whose realities are less powerful. In this chapter, the emphasis is on sorting out the conflicting meta-level mindscapes that contribute to stress.

Mindscapes are the reasons that people line up on different sides of the same issue even when exposed to the same facts and circumstances (Sergiovanni, 1985). Mindscapes function as personal theories and mental frames that help us shape reality. They are intellectual security blankets that affirm what we believe, say, and do. And they are road maps that provide assumptions, rules, images, and practice exemplars we need to navigate an uncertain and complex world. Teachers, school administrators, policy makers, educational researchers, corporate executives, and other groups often disagree on what constitutes good teaching, what school purposes should be, and what organizational arrangements are needed in schools because these issues are framed and understood by different mindscapes.

Not all mindscapes carry equal weight. The potential for stress arises when the mindscapes of teachers are at odds with the more powerful ones held by educational or outside elites and the more powerful ones sanctioned by officially established school arrangements.[1] Yielding to more

1. Not all educators share the same mindscapes. Nonetheless, an image of good teaching emerges from research, philosophical discourse, and ordinary thoughtful commentary that comes to represent the profession's perspective. Teachers in practice, however, may

powerful mindscapes forces teachers to think, speak, and behave in ways that may be at odds with what they believe or what they might prefer to do. Not yielding to more powerful mindscapes brings with it various organizational and psychological penalties that can be personally and professionally distressful. Problems are compounded when powerful mindscapes differ from each other. Teachers receive conflicting behavioral expectations and are confronted with conflicting role demands. Mindscapes are translated into educational practice through theories. Competing mindscapes provide us with dominant and subordinate theories for the school, of people, of teaching, of action, and of leadership. Unless dominant theories are sufficiently aligned with those of teachers, stress in teaching is inevitable. The cumulative effect of misalignment can contribute to role conflict, deteriorating classroom climate, and feelings of nonparticipation in decision making as organizational variables, and to lower self-esteem as a personal variable – all identified by Byrne (this volume) as being key determinants of teacher stress.

School as Formal Organization or Moral Community

The dominant theory for the school is that of formal organization. This is the view established in the traditional literature of educational administration and the perspective most often chosen as the frame for understanding and reforming schools by policy makers, corporate executives, and other elites outside the educational establishment. Educational elites, by contrast, are inclined to view schools as moral learning communities. The organization and community dichotomy follows Tonnies's (1957) representation of *Gesellschaft* and *Gemeinschaft* ideal types.[2]

    not subscribe fully to this official view – identifying instead with an unofficial but more
    pervasive one. Not all outside elites share the same mindscapes, either. Still, within most
    groups an "official view" (i.e., the corporate view; the conservative view) emerges over
    time.
2. Though neither *gesellschaft* nor *gemeinschaft* exists in pure form in the real world, they represent two different ways of thinking and living, two different types of cultures, two alternative visions of life. In *gesellschaft* organizations, for example, there is an assumption that hierarchy equals expertise. Those higher in the hierarchy are presumed to know more about teaching, learning, and other matters of schooling than those lower, and thus each person in the school is evaluated by the next higher level. Further, organizational thinking assumes that hierarchy equals moral superiority. As teachers move up the ranks into supervisory positions, not only is it presumed that they know more about teaching and learning and other matters of schooling but that they care more as well. That's why those higher in the hierarchy are trusted with more responsibility, more authority, and less supervision. Organizations are creatures of people, but over time they become separated from people by functioning independently in pursuit of their own goals and purposes. This separation has to be bridged somehow. Ties have to be developed that connect people to

Educational elites are those who shape images of best teaching practice within educational circles. They do this by conducting research, and engaging in thoughtful commentary that provides an official (at least within the profession) image of good teaching and by controlling key access routes to professional certification and advancement. Controlling access allows educational elites to reproduce themselves by training others in the "correct" knowledge perspectives and socializing them with the correct values. The views of educational elites are forged in part by the findings of educational research and in part by commitment to progressive values, with the latter playing a key role in shaping the former.[3] The official image of teaching now being embraced by the profession includes such ideas as teaching for understanding, active construction of knowledge, the integration of procedural and declarative knowledge, the importance of personal meanings, and the acknowledgment that learning is a social as well as individual process. All these ideas are best embodied in teaching practice in classrooms and schools that resemble communities. Educational elites propose that characteristics of community should shape our present policies with respect to how schools are organized, how students are evaluated, how supervision is practiced, how teachers and students are motivated and rewarded, what leadership is and how it works, and most important, how teaching and learning take place.

their work, and ties have to be developed that connect people to others with whom they work. In schools as organizations, these ties are contractual. Each person acts separately in negotiating a settlement with others and in negotiating a settlement with the school itself that best meets his or her needs. Everyone becomes connected to his or her work for calculated reasons. Students behave as long as they get the rewards they desire. Teachers respond for the same reasons. When rewards are no longer available or valued, less effort is given in return. Communities differ from organizations by being organized around relationships and ideas. They create social structures that bond people together in a oneness, and that bind them to a set of shared values and ideas. Communities are defined by their centers of values, sentiments, and beliefs that provide the needed conditions for creating a sense of "we." Within communities, members create their lives with others who have similar intentions. Instead of relying on external controls, communities rely on norms, purposes, values, professional socialization, collegiality, and natural interdependence. As community connections become established, they become substitutes for formal systems of student and teacher control. Relationships in communities are both close and informal. Individual circumstances count. Acceptance is unconditional. Subjectivity is okay. Emotions are legitimate. Sacrificing one's self-interests for the sake of other community members is common. Members associate with each other because doing so is valuable as an end in itself. Knowledge is valued and learned for its own sake, not just as a means to get something or to go somewhere (Sergiovanni, 1995).

3. Gooding (1990), for example, provides a compelling argument for the role of human agency in the shaping of scientific reality. Even in laboratory experiments where absolute objectivity is presumed, not all protocols are equal. A researcher deciding to proceed one way as opposed to another and a researcher making one set of assumptions instead of another at any stage of the research can produce quite different scientific results.

Images of best practice espoused by both educational and outside elites are often at odds with the ordinary practice of teachers (Elmore, 1995). Teachers, for example, face obstacles imbedded in the present *Gesellschaft* design, structure, and operation of schools that keep them from teaching in desired ways. And they are forced by *Gemeinschaft* values into "professional community" and other collaborative arrangements that can challenge their implicit understandings of teaching. *Gesellschaft* images of teaching emphasize the establishment of instructional delivery systems made up of tightly aligned objectives, curriculum, teaching protocols, supervision, and assessment. *Gemeinschaft* images of teaching emphasize the development among teachers of disciplined norms, tight connections, and shared conceptions of work. Both elite images differ from that of the independent artisan view of teaching – the view that seems to characterize teachers engaged in ordinary practice (Huberman, 1990).

To the independent artisan, teaching is characterized by uncertainty, instability, complexity, and variety that requires reflection in action and the creation of one's practice in use (Schön, 1983). Key to success is the development of augmented professional intelligence – a body of formal and informal knowledge, understandings, and models of practice that does not specify what to do but informs the decisions that teachers make (Sergiovanni, 1985). Much of this intelligence is tacitly held, and the rationale for its articulation into practice remains implicit. The implicit nature of artisan practice can make teachers feel uncomfortable and even threatened when they are forced into "professional community" settings that require formal sharings of what they know. This may be why a distinct preference for privacy in practice seems to categorize teaching. Further, the tempo and uncertainty of artisan practice makes it important that teachers have a great deal of discretion – discretion that allows for the creation of one's practice in use. Teachers as independent artisans, it appears, may share some of the educational elite's image of learning community for defining the context of teaching and learning but little of the educational elite's image of professional community for defining their relationships with colleagues. Their image of teaching may be more like that of a guild of artisans who share a common cause, who tell stories about their experiences, who share proven tools of the trade, who are committed to similar values such as the importance of caring, who work together to advance the guild, but who nevertheless practice their teaching privately (Huberman, 1990). To them, the school is a work context defined by the accumulation of individual teaching practices rather than by a single shared practice of teaching in a given school as proposed by advocates of building professional community in schools

(Sergiovanni, 1994b). Whatever their views, teachers are forced by more dominant views of outside and educational elites to think and act differently. And because these dominant views often conflict, pleasing one group of elites displeases the other, creating still more potential for stress.

Constrained and Unconstrained Views of Human Nature

Within the formal organization mindscape, three theories compete for attention: pyramid, railroad, and high performance (Sergiovanni, 1994a, 1996). All three share a pessimistic view of human nature, and all three prescribe constraints aimed at controlling what teachers do. Pyramid theory relies on direct supervision, rules, and other top-down arrangements to get control. Railroad theory controls the work of teachers in more impersonal ways by standardizing the work processes that teachers engage in through tightly aligned and scripted goals, curriculum, teaching protocols, and assessment strategies. Both theories are institutionalized in present school structures and account for many of today's regularities in teaching. Both theories were proposed by yesterday's outside elites who imported factory models to the school. Today's outside elites, who are spearheading present school reform efforts, offer the more progressive high-performance theory as an alternative. This theory allows for the setting and measuring of standard outcomes for the school. It then allows for "empowering" teachers, and "empowering" schools through site-based management and other means. These empowered groups are then responsible for figuring out how the standardized outcomes will be achieved. Incentives and disincentives are then provided to be sure that "empowered" groups will be properly motivated.

High-performance theory controls teachers by connecting them to outcomes rather than hierarchies or scripts. Borrowing from the lessons that Peters and Waterman (1982) and their numerous successors have learned from successful corporations, high-performance theory assumes that effectiveness is achieved by loosely connecting teachers to means, but tightly connecting them to ends. In pyramid and railroad theories, planning *how* teaching will be done is separated from doing it. The elites decide and the teachers do. In high-performance theory, teachers get to decide how and get to do, but the planning of *what* to do is separated from planning how to do it. Elites are responsible for the former, and teachers are responsible for the latter. All three formal organization theories, it appears, share the same assumptions. External controls may differ, but they must always be provided. If you don't provide external controls, teachers will take advantage. If you trust teachers in schools too much, they will do the wrong things.

If you don't provide incentives and disincentives, nothing will happen. As a side effect, dominant mindscapes have a way of creeping into the psychology and then the behavior of teachers. This contagiousness may account for why pyramid, railroad, and high-performance theories seem so evident in today's classrooms as teachers seek to manage and motivate students.

The school as moral learning community envisioned by the education elites is based on more optimistic assumptions. Educational elites believe that given the opportunity and the right conditions (the right leadership, training, discretion, and support), teachers will make the right decisions. They will be morally responsive. Control need not be externally provided but will come from within. And further, educational elites believe that only when we provide the opportunity, give teachers the needed training and support, connect teachers to colleagues in a shared practice, and call teachers morally will they be able to make the kinds of decisions about teaching and learning that will improve schools. This is the position argued in the chapters by Kenneth Leithwood and his colleagues and by Lynne Miller. They propose versions of transformative leadership and the building of school learning communities as the way to create more effective teaching and learning environments while at the same time reducing teacher burnout.

It appears that both outside and educational elites want to improve schools but have two different visions of how to accomplish this goal. These visions are based on competing mindscapes of human nature. The mindscape that dominates affects the practice of teachers whether they initially agree with it or not. When both mindscapes are pushed at the same time, teachers are caught in the middle.

In Texas, for example, new standards in the form of proficiencies themed to teaching and learning communities have been created for teachers. Teacher education programs are expected to prepare teachers to be competent in these proficiencies and teacher evaluation systems are expected to evaluate for these proficiencies once teachers are in service. Other school reforms are also based on the school-as-learning community theme.

This community emphasis reflects the visions of Texas's educational elites. At the same time, Texas holds teachers accountable for the scores of its students on state tests that require teaching to the state's essential elements of the official curriculum. Schools are sorted into one of four categories – exemplary, recognized, needs improvement, low performing – depending on how well their students do on the tests. High-performing schools are rewarded with cash bonuses provided by the state. Low-performing schools must develop and submit to the state school improvement plans. This accountability emphasis reflects the vision of Texas outside elites.

Pleasing both masters (the state tests on the one hand and the new com-
munity-oriented competency standards on the other) at the same time is
not easy and creates conditions for stress. Choosing one master over the
other leads to different problems but the same kinds of stress conditions.
The teacher burnout problem is complicated by this possibility: that the
theories of human nature that govern the reform proposals of outside elites
and educational elites are different, and that both theories appear to be out
of alignment with those held by teachers.

Plato, Hobbes, and other classical political theorists believed that human
nature had both a reasonable side rooted in moral conceptions of goodness
and a passionate side rooted in psychological egoism. The reasonable side
includes propensities toward embodying such virtues as altruism, self-
sacrifice, and cooperation aimed at the enhancement of the common good.
The passionate side includes need-satisfying propensities such as physical
and psychological gratification, competing to win, and accumulation of
wealth aimed at the enhancement of the individual good. For most people,
these two sides of human nature coexist in reasonable balance. Pursuit of
self-interest helps to navigate through our *gesellschaft* world where "Let's
make a deal" is the norm. Moral bearing helps navigate through our more
personal *gemeinschaft* world where connections to others are based on obligations and commitments. Allocating resources among employees based
on merit is an example of the first. Allocating resources among one's children based on need is an example of the second. The first is based on egocentric love, and the second is based on altruistic love (Rousseau, 1991).[4]

Though most people acknowledge this complexity verbally, they tend to
operate from more simple theories of human nature. They tend to believe
that people are either largely inclined toward good, or they are largely inclined toward evil. The first inclination represents the unconstrained view
of human nature and the second inclination represents the constrained
view (Sowell, 1987).[5] Those holding the unconstrained view believe that
teachers can be trusted to act morally and therefore must be provided with
the freedom to optimize their moral propensities to do what is right. They

4. Egocentric love is emotionally and psychologically self-gratifying. When egocentric love
    is the motive, parties to a relationship enter into an implicit contract for the exchange of
    needs and satisfactions that benefit both. Altruistic love is an expression of selfless con-
    cern for others that stems from devotion or obligation. The first is psychologically based;
    the second is culturally based.
5. Constrained and unconstrained views of human nature are not discrete categories but
    ends of a continuum. Few people are likely to be positioned in the same place on this con-
    tinuum. Nonetheless, it is useful to think about two constellations comprising people
    with views similar enough for each group to be considered either largely constrained or
    largely unconstrained.

have both the capacity and the need to sacrifice their self-interests for valued causes and for conceptions of the common good they value. As professionals, they willingly accept responsibility for their own practice, and they commit themselves to the learning needs of their students above other concerns. When they fail, it is not because of their human nature but because of factors that they do not control. Organizational arrangements and practices based on the *gesellschaft* values that now dominate schooling are the favored reason given for failing by those who hold the unconstrained view. Those embracing the constrained view, by contrast, believe that teachers will act selfishly if given the chance. Their primary concern is to maximize their own self-interests. Thus constraints must be provided to force them to do the right thing. Advocates of this view believe that the moral limitations of human nature must be accepted, but these can be manipulated to serve the common good by the proper use of constraints such as rewards and punishments (Smith, 1937).

Teachers tend to share some of the pessimism about human nature found in the constrained view when they think about students. Whereas all students can learn, some just will not. Students will make good choices about their learning if extrinsic and intrinsic incentives are provided, but not otherwise. Students want to behave properly in theory, but in reality (as a result of group norms to the contrary and other factors), they do not. This pessimism may in part be an artifact of having to teach in *gesellschaft* schools that are large and impersonal, that are characterized by urgent coverage of subject matter, and that have student subcultures that are typically stronger than and at odds with the school culture teachers seek to establish. Pessimism may also stem from teachers' having internalized practical theories of child development that consider the constrained view to be correct but not immutable. In time, and with proper teaching, students will learn to behave in more unconstrained ways. For these reasons, teaching in ways described by the educational elites may work in theory, but given the conditions they face, many teachers feel it is more prudent to stick to more teacher-centered approaches that give them the flexibility to make on-the-spot decisions about how tight or loose their control should be. On the other hand, teachers are inclined to want the more optimistic unconstrained view of human nature applied to them without question. This optimistic view can provide the autonomy teachers need to function as independent artisans. With this autonomy, they can build as much learning community with students as they dare while still being able to avoid too much professional community. This balancing of both dimensions of human nature allows teachers to meet commitments to students while ensuring them enough privacy to practice comfortably as independent artisans.

The complex view of human nature held by teachers remains subordinate to the views of both outside and educational elites. As a result, pyramid, railroad, and high-performance theories prevail, providing structural-functional parameters for schooling that box teachers in. At the same time, moral learning community theory prevails, providing normative parameters for schooling that also box teachers in. When teachers try to accommodate both elite views – at the same time or by alternating from one view to the other – they wind up with less control over their practice. Loss of control, as Byrne, Leiter, and other contributors to this volume point out, is a key factor in the teacher burnout equation.

Is the situation better when a single mindscape of human nature emerges as the powerful one that teachers must contend with? Probably not. The two sides of human nature, for example, function as "muscles." When both sides are acknowledged, the muscles get equal training, and their capacity for use in helping teachers make decisions is preserved. But when a single view of human nature emerges as dominant, it shapes the development of school policies and the making of teaching and learning decisions in only one direction, upsetting the balance.

The constrained view now dominates the educational scene. This is the view informing the school policies that outside elites push, and the one embodied in present school structures that account for existing regularities of teaching. The overuse of action strategies from this view trains our reasonable and passionate muscles to respond disproportionately. Over time, our reasonable muscle can weaken from lack of stimulation, and our passionate muscle can be exercised to function much like a stimulus-response reflex. At one level, teachers may want to behave one way, but exposure to practices that train the wrong muscle conditions them to behave another way. This strengthening and weakening has consequences for evaluating the theories of action that are used to motivate teachers (and students, too) and the theories of action that are used to bring about change.

Market and Virtue as Theories of Action

Both constrained and unconstrained views of human nature are probably true, but for different spheres of our lives. Normally, the more *gesellschaft* is the setting, the more likely we are to respond in constrained ways; and the more *gemeinschaft* is the setting, the more likely we are to respond in unconstrained ways. How does one motivate action under these different conditions? Market values are dominant in the former, and the values of virtue are dominant in the latter. Relationship in *gesellschaft* settings, for example, are predicated on contracts. Relationships in *gemeinschaft* settings, by contrast, are based on commitments.[6] This arrangement works well as long as the right match between action strategy and setting is maintained.

Problems arise when market values become the basis for action in community settings where virtue should be the governing variable. If schools should be communities, for example, then theories of action based on virtue are appropriate. When market values invade community settings, however, they drive virtue away. Consider the following example. A group of high school teachers of advanced placement (AP)[7] courses were attending a conference at Trinity University recently. One speaker, representing a foundation interested in promoting advanced placement courses in America's high schools, announced a new incentive program designed to motivate AP teachers to do better. Teachers would receive cash bonuses of several thousand dollars depending on the scores their students made on the AP exam. Participating teachers typically have two AP courses and two or three regular courses to teach each day. The reasonable side of human nature and the professional values of teaching call them to give each of the courses taught full attention. The passionate side that favors self-interest, however, encourages teachers to spend more time with the two advanced placement courses in pursuit of cash bonuses and less time with the other courses. Most teachers will be able to resist the force of market values in an isolated incident or two, but when reformers constantly seek to motivate teachers by using rewards and punishments, market forces strengthen. Over time, the reasonable side of our nature weakens and the passionate side strengthens. Market values begin to drive out virtue. Teachers become more inclined to go for the cash. In the beginning, teachers may not notice what is happening to them. But soon, they will; and this awareness can

---

6. Market values have their origin in the disciplines of economics, evolutionary biology, and behavioral psychology (Schwartz, 1994). Seminal works include Smith (1937), Samuelson (1947), Darwin (1985), and Skinner (1953). The basic principles derived from the three disciplines are the economic nature of humankind motivated by self-interest, the competitive nature of humankind motivated by natural selection, and the conditioned nature of humankind motivated by rewards and punishments. The values of virtue, by contrast, are based in part on conceptions of human beings as moral agents who not only know what is good but who can also choose to be good. Humans are not preconditioned to respond to the market. The values of virtue are also based on an expansive view of professionalism that calls teachers to serve the common good by transforming their roles from that of job to that of vocation.
7. Advanced placement courses are those offered for university level credit. Students qualify for this credit by taking special advanced placement examinations.

cause problems of dissonance that can lead to lower self-esteem, guilt, and perhaps cynicism.

By no means have all the combinations of competing mindscapes that contribute to stress in teaching been exhausted. Teachers, for example, are caught in the middle of two competing theories of leadership – a dominant view that places process over substance, and a subordinate view that places substance over process. The dominant view, borrowed from corporate conceptions of leadership and espoused by outside elites, has been embraced by the educational administration establishment; it is institutionalized in a rigid credentialing system that one must endure to qualify for an administrative position. The leader's authority, in this view, comes from bureaucratic rules and roles on the one hand (bureaucratic authority) and from her or his ability to influence the feelings and motivations of people on the other (personal authority). The subordinate view of leadership, by contrast, relies on professional and moral authority for its legitimacy – the authority of ideas that represent good educational practice and the authority of ideas that represent shared commitments (Sergiovanni, 1992). When bureaucratic and personal authority dominate in schools, they become substitutes for the authority embedded in good ideas and shared commitments (Zaleznik, 1989). Leadership then becomes vacuous and teachers lose confidence in their leaders. Vacuous leadership spills over into organizational structures and other arrangements that place form over function, frustrating the work of teachers further and alienating them from the decision-making process.

Leadership based on moral authority is described in the chapter by Leithwood and his colleagues as being transformational. It is also at the heart of the reform proposals discussed by Miller in Chapter 6. Both transformational leadership and the reform proposals are offered as antidotes to teacher burnout. But both can actually contribute to teacher burnout if they run against the grain of the existing culture of teaching, craft conceptions of teaching practice, or the existing regularities of schooling that have institutionalized bureaucratic and personal leadership.

The Inevitability of Stress

As long as different people inhabit the earth, different mindscapes will contend with one another to account for life's dimensions. But the existence of different mindscapes is not in itself a condition for stress in teaching. Stress is an artifact of the interplay of dominant and subordinate theories for the school, of human nature, of action, of leadership, and of other aspects of schooling. Its inevitability is caused by the fact that the views of teachers are subordinate to those of various elites. The views of teachers are also subordinate to the views that are institutionalized in the present regularities of teaching. Changing this equation requires making the views of teachers more dominant.

The views of teachers can be strengthened in an absolute sense. They can also be strengthened by diluting the dominance of educational and outside elites. Diluting the dominance of elites can be done by teachers forging new connections with parents (Sarason, 1995). New connections with parents makes possible the deinstitutionalization of schooling by allowing for the creation of small, autonomous schools and small, autonomous schools within schools whose educational program concerns are governed by local committees of parents and teachers. Shifting responsibility for the school's teaching and learning policy structure to parents and teachers places the views of educational elites and outside elites in a subordinate position. Parents and teachers can then choose from among the proposals offered by the elites those ideas that they feel make sense.

The enhancement of teacher professionalism and the subsequent strengthening of professional authority as the basis for making decisions about educational matters are the long-term means to diluting the views of today's educational elites. The sources for professional authority are an expanding knowledge base of teaching, the use of this knowledge base to inform the decisions that teachers make, and an expanding commitment by teachers to professional virtue (Sergiovanni, 1992). The knowledge base for teaching comprises research, sound theory, and the wisdom of practice as they relate to how students learn, effective teaching strategies, curriculum development and use, and other pedagogical issues. The dimensions of professional virtue include these:

- A commitment to practice to the best of one's ability and at the edge of one's field, to accept responsibility for one's own professional development, to stay alive intellectually, to become a lifelong learner
- A commitment to a sense of collective practice, to being part of a shared practice that broadens responsibility beyond one's own individual practice
- A commitment to a sense of collegiality and caring, to being connected with colleagues with whom one works because of common purposes, common traditions, and moral commitments that are shared (Sergiovanni, 1995, p. 29)

As both competence and virtue develop, the professional authority of teachers will be recognized, enabling them to move to the center of the decision-making process as it affects both pedagogical policy and practice.

Changing the equation by making the views of teachers and parents more dominant does not eliminate the need for traditional governance arrangements. They would still be needed to provide for the more general management needs of schools. Changing the equation does not alter government's responsibility to hold schools accountable, either. The ways in which schools are held accountable, however, would change. Increasingly, each individual school site would be responsible for setting its own standards. Government's responsibility would then be twofold. It would ensure that the standards set are good ones, and it would ensure that each school keeps the promises it makes.

One could argue that giving new weights to various mindscapes would not result in a reduction of stress in teaching. Instead, only the kind and character of stress teachers experience would change as new configurations of dominant and subordinate mindscapes emerge. As Smylie points out in Chapter 3, developing new leadership roles and responsibilities for teachers may reduce stress on the one hand but increase stress on the other. Stress in teaching may be inevitable after all; but for it to be adequately understood and controlled, emphasis must shift from focusing only at the micro and meso levels to the macro and meta levels as well.

17. Do Teachers Burn Out More Easily?
A Comparison of Teachers with Other Social Professions on Work Stress and Burnout Symptoms

PETER DE HEUS AND RENÉ F. W. DIEKSTRA

It is well known that teachers have a demanding and in many cases stressful job. Work overload (Van Ginkel, 1987), lack of autonomy (Jackson, Schwab, and Schuler, 1986), disrespect, inattentiveness and low sociability with pupils (Friedman, 1995d), lack of support from colleagues and management (Brissie, Hoover-Dempsey, and Bassler, 1988), and loss of status of the teaching profession (Friesen and Sarros, 1989) are only a few examples of the stressors that teachers have to cope with.

These and other work-stressors appear to manifest themselves in teachers as physical and psychological problems. Premature retirement is the fate of the greater number of Dutch teachers; teachers still active in their job show high rates of sick leave in comparison to workers in many other professions, especially teachers older than fifty (Van Ginkel, 1987). Because of the thoroughly interpersonal character of the teaching job (which demands from the teacher the ability to manage extensive and often intensive contacts with pupils), teachers are also vulnerable to the common burden of the so-called social professions (i.e., jobs characterized by many interactions with other people that place high demands on the social skills of their professionals): *burnout* (e.g., Maslach, 1982a).

Burnout among teachers was the focal topic of the study reported here, in which a sample of about one thousand teachers is compared with members of other social professions on burnout symptoms and, in an attempt to explain the obtained differences in burnout, on work stressors and social support.

Burnout and the Teaching Profession

Burnout can be depicted as a professional disease; in its causes as well as in its symptoms it is specific to the social professions. There is no consensus about the precise mechanisms and stages of the process leading to burnout (e.g., Cherniss, 1980a; Edelwich and Brodsky, 1980; Golembiewsky, Munzenrider, and Carter, 1983; Leiter, 1993), but a general picture has emerged: Although professionals doing "people work" often are initially enthusiastic, hopeful, and concerned with their clients or pupils, sooner or later they may have to cope with one or more of the following realizations (for a more exhaustive list, see Schaufeli, 1990):

- The job does not live up to one's expectations (e.g., pupils are less interested or teaching is less effective than one had expected).
- Too much time must be spent on peripheral activities, especially paperwork (e.g., preparation and correction of tests).
- Working conditions are unfavorable (e.g., chronic time pressure, classes that are too large).
- There is inequity in relationships with pupils, in which much more is perceived to be given than received (e.g., emotional involvement in lessons or pupils' well-being meeting little appreciation by pupils).
- The relationship with management is perceived as unfair (e.g., not getting the salary, career options, or acknowledgment that one thinks is deserved for one's efforts).

Different authors emphasize different factors. Freudenberger and Richelson (1980) see unrealistically high expectations as the decisive factor in burnout; others (e.g., Cherniss, 1980a) put more emphasis on social and organizational factors such as those mentioned earlier in the chapter. Although there is no consensus over the decisive factors causing burnout, prolonged exposure to the factors listed earlier is generally acknowledged as possibly having very serious (and sometimes irreversible) consequences. Taken together, these consequences are called the burnout syndrome.

Many physical, psychological, behavioral, and social reactions have been mentioned as characteristic symptoms (for a review, see Schaufeli, 1990), but the three commonly acknowledged "core" symptoms are emotional exhaustion, depersonalization, and reduced personal accomplishment (Maslach and Jackson, 1986). *Emotional exhaustion* refers to feelings of being "empty," being depleted of all energy by interactions with pupils, feeling too exhausted to go on. *Depersonalization* refers to a negative, cold, or cynical attitude toward pupils, which may manifest itself in diverse behaviors (e.g., showing disinterest or dislike). *Reduced personal accomplishment* refers to a decline in (perceived) successful achievement, which is usually accompanied by reduced feelings of competence and self-esteem. Because feelings of exhaustion, hostility, and incompetence do not make working with pupils or clients any easier, a negative spiral may arise (problems in professional functioning leading to burnout, leading to even more problems in functioning, and so on), which may explain why burnout often becomes a chronic condition. Emotional exhaustion, depersonalization, and reduced personal accomplishment are usually measured with the Maslach Burnout Inventory (MBI, Maslach and Jackson, 1986), which (in an abridged version) was also used in the study reported here.

Empirical studies have shown that burnout is rather common among teachers, especially among secondary school teachers (Burke and Greenglass, 1989b), but how do teachers compare to members of other social professions? This question is important, because for identifying burnout-inducing job-stressors, the usual procedure of comparing teachers with and without burnout is not sufficient; it may not reveal the sources of stress that are an integral part of the teaching job and therefore may be shared by all teachers. Comparing different social professions on burnout symptoms not only reveals which professions are especially at risk but in combination with comparisons on measures of work stress and social support, the results can also suggest which stressors may be particular risk factors.

Earlier studies have produced somewhat inconsistent findings, of which only a few examples are given. Tang and Lau (1996) found no differences among teachers, police officers, and nurses in Hong Kong on emotional exhaustion and depersonalization, but teachers and police officers (who were not significantly different from each other) showed less reduced accomplishment than nurses. In a comparison of Slovakian teachers, social workers, and surgeons and nurses, Daniel and Szabo (1993) found the highest levels of emotional exhaustion and depersonalization for the social workers whereas reduced personal accomplishment was most common among surgeons and nurses. These studies suggest that teachers are relatively well-off as far as burnout is concerned, but a study of Dutch teachers by Schaufeli, Daamen, and Van Mierlo (1994) revealed a more mixed picture. Teachers showed less depersonalization and less reduced personal accomplishment but more emotional exhaustion than a large reference group of various social professionals (e.g., nurses, physicians, correctional officers, and social workers). This finding is important because some have argued (Shirom, 1989) that emotional exhaustion is the defining feature of burnout.

In the study reported here, a large ($N = 1,018$) sample of Dutch teachers was studied and compared with a large and heterogeneous ($N = 2,740$) sample of other social professionals on burnout and other symptoms, work-stressors, and social support. The following questions were addressed.

1. Do teachers burn out more easily? Do they show more burnout symptoms (and other symptoms of strain) than workers in other social professions?
2. Do teachers have more reasons to burn out? Do they experience more work-stressors and less social support in their jobs than workers in other social professions?

3. Which teachers are at risk? Are burnout symptoms among teachers correlated with work-stressors, social support, and demographic characteristics?

Method

Subjects

Our original sample consisted of 13,555 individuals who were gainfully employed, were between the ages of 18 and 64 years, and had filled out a one-page questionnaire (called "How's Work in the Netherlands?") that was printed in 14 Dutch newspapers in the 1993 Whitsuntide weekend (the weekend of Pentecost, the seventh Sunday after Easter).

One of our primary goals was to compare teachers with workers in other professions on burnout symptoms, a condition that presupposes contacts with customers, clients, or patients; therefore, only people in the so-called social professions were selected for analysis. In the absence of a universally accepted definition, the social professions were operationally defined as those in which at least half the respondents gave an affirmative answer when asked whether they were working professionally with other people. This led to identification of six types of social professions; the percentages show the number of respondents who indicated that they work with people: mental health professions (99.9%), physical health professions (99.9%), nursing professions (99.5%), domestic and personal care professions (99.7%), teachers (99.7%), and managers (57.1%). To define social professionals as unambiguously as possible, only respondents in these professions who answered "yes" to the "working-with-people" question were selected ($N = 3,758$); of these categories, teachers were one of the larger groups ($N = 1,018$).

Although a sample as large as ours has the clear advantage of allowing detailed comparisons with statistical power among many groups, our method of data collection has the disadvantage of *self-selection:* Subjects were not personally asked to participate; rather, at their own initiative and for their own reasons they decided to fill in and mail a somewhat time-consuming questionnaire. As a consequence, our sample is not in all respects representative of the population of Dutch working social professionals. Comparisons of the original sample (including the nonsocial professions) with normative data revealed that our sample mirrors the distribution of sex and number of working hours very well but shows clear underrepresentation of young workers (4% versus 16% under age 25) and the less educated (11% versus 27%). A related problem is that people experiencing work stress and burnout may either be especially attracted to or, on the contrary, be especially repulsed by a questionnaire with many questions about the darker sides of work. A comparison of our results with available normative data suggested that respondents in our original sample did not suffer more from work stress than other Dutch working people, but they did suffer more from physical complaints than a representative sample of Dutch working people. (Physical complaints were measured with the VOEG (Vragenlijst voor Onderzoek naar Ervaren Gezondheid, i.e., Questionnaire for Research into Experienced Health; Dirken, 1969). For a more detailed discussion, see Diekstra, De Heus, Schouten, and Diekstra (1994).

Measures

The following measures of strain, work stress, and social support were used.

Burnout. A shortened version of the Maslach Burnout Inventory (MBI: Maslach and Jackson, 1986) was used to measure emotional exhaustion, depersonalization, and reduced personal accomplishment. For each subscale, the three items with the highest item-subscale correlations in a Dutch sample of nurses (Schaufeli and Van Dierendonck, 1993) were selected, reducing the total number of items from twenty-two to nine. Answering possibilities were also reduced, from seven-point scales to three-point scales (never/sometimes/often). Exploratory and confirmatory factor analyses demonstrated a satisfactory factor structure, but somewhat disappointing Cronbach's alphas (for a more extensive discussion, see De Heus, Schaufeli, and Diekstra, 1996).

Psychological Symptoms. The Dutch version (SCL-90; Arrindell and Ettema, 1986) of the Symptom Check List (Derogatis, Lipman, and Covi, 1973) was used to measure depression (16 items, e.g., "Feeling desperate about the future"), anxiety (10 items, e.g., "Feeling afraid"), and hostility (6 items, e.g., "Often becoming involved in quarrels"). The SCL-90 has been proven a reliable and valid instrument for measuring depression, anxiety, and hostility (Arrindell and Ettema, 1986).

Physical Symptoms. Perceived health problems were assessed by the 13-item version of the VOEG. Subjects are asked to indicate in a yes/no format the presence or absence of thirteen physical symptoms (e.g., stomach troubles, fatigue). The VOEG has been shown to be a reliable and valid indicator of general well-being (Joosten and Drop, 1987).

Job Dissatisfaction, Work-Stressors, and Social Support. To cover a very broad range of work stress and social support characteristics, 135 items were selected from various work stress questionnaires (e.g., the Job Content Questionnaire; Karasek, 1985). Factor analyses on these items (Diekstra

et al., 1994; De Heus et al., 1994) led to the construction of eighteen work
stress and social support scales, of which nine scales were selected for the
study: job dissatisfaction, two indicators of high task demands (work overload and job ambiguity), three indicators of decision latitude (time control,
responsibility and task control, and participation in decision making),
monetary satisfaction, and two measures of social support (supervisor
support and colleague support). These nine scales can be described as
follows:

- *Job dissatisfaction:* fifteen items measuring the perceived quality of the job (e.g., "I
  would advise my friends to accept this job")
- *Work overload:* five items measuring time pressures and necessary effort for the
  job (e.g., "I have to work fast")
- *Job ambiguity:* six items on the (absence of) clarity of one's tasks and responsibilities (e.g., "I know exactly what others on the job expect from me")
- *Time control:* eight items measuring (the absence of) freedom to make one's own
  time planning for different tasks and breaks (e.g., "I can decide the order of doing different tasks")
- *Responsibility and task control:* eight items measuring the (absence of) responsibility for others and the possibilities to choose one's own tasks (e.g., "I have to follow orders from others continually")
- *Participation in decision making:* three items measuring the presence and perceived
  quality of team discussions aimed at monitoring and improving working conditions (e.g., "I think that our team discussions are useless")
- *Monetary satisfaction:* three items measuring dissatisfaction with payment for the
  job (e.g., "I am satisfied with my salary")
- *Supervisor support:* six items on the quality of the relationship with the supervisor (e.g., "My supervisor cares for his people")
- *Colleague support:* nine items measuring the quality of relationships with colleagues (e.g., "My co-workers are personally interested in me")

Do Teachers Burn Out More Easily?

Although teachers are certainly at risk of developing burnout symptoms,
teaching is not the only profession in which high and enduring social demands may finally deplete the resources of many of its members. How do
teachers compare to the other social professions when it comes to burnout
symptoms? Do they burn out more often or more easily? To address this
question, a multivariate analysis of variance (MANOVA) was performed,
with sex and profession as the independent variables and the three burnout scales as the dependent variables.

The multivariate tests for the sex and profession main effects and for the
sex by profession interaction were highly significant ($p < .001$). The univariate main effects for profession were highly significant ($p < .001$) for all
three burnout measures. Inspection of group means (Table 17.1) reveals

Table 17.1. *Group Means of Burnout Symptoms by Sex and Profession*

Profession	Emotional Exhaustion		Deperson-alization		Reduced personal accomplishment	
	M	F	M	F	M	F
Teacher (N = 1018)	2.90	2.80	1.90	1.15	1.22	1.06
Manager (N = 944)	2.35	2.60	1.31	1.20	.75	.57
Psychotherapist, social worker (N = 227)	2.65	2.77	1.51	1.23	.93	.76
Physician, dentist (N = 196)	2.30	2.44	1.43	1.04	.63	.70
Nursing professions (N = 825)	2.42	2.57	1.41	1.13	.73	.75
Household and caring (N = 343)	2.73	2.43	1.16	1.21	.92	.93

that teaching had higher burnout scores than any other profession: Both male and female teachers showed more emotional exhaustion and more reduced personal accomplishment than their counterparts in all other social professions, whereas male (but not female) teachers showed more depersonalization than any other group. Of the other F-tests, only the main effect of sex and the sex by profession interaction for depersonalization were significant (in both cases $p < .001$): Males showed more depersonalization than females, but this difference was especially pronounced for teachers. Our general conclusion is that teachers, especially male teachers, are seriously at risk for burnout, more than members of any other social profession.

Are the problems of teachers limited to burnout symptoms, or do they generalize to other measures of strain? To answer this question and to allow a straightforward visual presentation of the results, all measures of burnout – depression, anxiety, hostility, physical symptoms, and job dissatisfaction – were transformed to z-scores, referring to the number of standard deviations above (positive z-score) or below (negative z-score) the general mean of each measure of strain. This transformation to z-scores not only shows immediately whether a certain group mean is above or below average but also allows us to compare the magnitude of group differences on different measures of strain. A MANOVA with sex and profession (teachers versus all other social professions taken together) as independent variables and all symptom measures as dependent variables demonstrated sig-

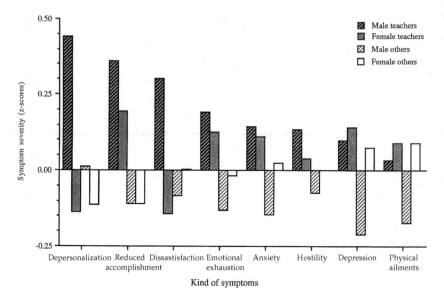

Figure 17.1. Group means of burnout symptoms and other symptoms by sex and profession.

nificant differences between teachers and others on all symptom measures. Group means for male and female teachers and their counterparts in other social professions are presented in Figure 17.1. From left to right, measures are presented in descending order according to teachers' average z-scores.

Figure 17.1 reveals that male teachers very consistently show above-average levels on all symptoms. The results for female teachers are less pronounced and even below average symptom level on depersonalization and job dissatisfaction; overall, however, female teachers show more strain than men and women in other social professions. Differences with other social professions are most pronounced for depersonalization (male teachers only), reduced accomplishment, job dissatisfaction (male teachers only), and to a lesser extent, emotional exhaustion.

Taken together, our results for burnout and other measures of strain support the idea that the teaching job carries more psychological and, to a lesser extent, more physical symptoms than other social professions. The main question receives an affirmative answer: Teachers *do* burn out more easily than members of other social professions.

Do Teachers Have More Reason to Burn Out?

Knowing that teachers show more burnout and other symptoms than members of other social professions has little practical value if we are unable to

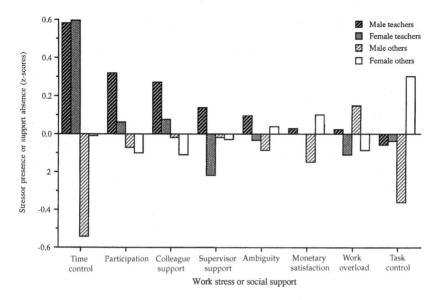

Figure 17.2. Group means of work-stressors and social support by sex and profession.

point out which factors in the teaching job are responsible for those symptoms. What makes teachers disproportionately vulnerable to burnout? To answer this question, we compared group means of teachers on all work stress and social support measures to the means of all other social professionals taken together. For ease of interpretation, some indicators of work stress and both measures of social support were recoded so that in all cases higher scores indicated more work stress (i.e., *low* task control, *low* time control, *low* participation in decision making, and *low* monetary satisfaction), or *low* social support. All scores were then transformed to z-scores, and the same statistical and graphic procedures were done as for symptom measures in the last section (Figure 17.2).

In general, differences between teachers and other social professionals proved to be less pronounced than in the analysis of symptoms. Only three of eight F-tests for the main effect of profession were significant (in all cases $p < .001$). Teachers reported less time control, lower participation in decision making, and less colleague support than other social professionals. These results suggest that teachers are not especially plagued by task demands that are too high or ambiguous. Low decision latitude appears to be a more serious problem, but according to only some indicators of decision latitude and not to others. Teachers are not without task control (after all, one can make his or her own decisions about how to prepare lessons and teach classes), but time control appears to be very low for teachers (perhaps because of fixed lesson hours and fixed goals that have to be reached in well-defined time periods). Teachers (especially males) are also dissatisfied about their participation in (more general) decision making.

Social support from colleagues is relatively low for teachers (especially for males), as is supervisor support for males, but not for females (female teachers report more supervisor support than any of the other groups). These results perhaps suggest that teachers are not used to discussing their problems in class with their colleagues or supervisors. Despite the thoroughly social nature of contacts with pupils and colleagues, teaching may be a rather lonely job.

Although these results are informative, they are not sufficient to explain the high amount of symptoms among teachers. Repeating the ANOVAs of the preceding section – with statistical correction for the effects of job-stressors and social support (by treating them as covariates) – did not greatly change the relationships between profession and burnout symptoms. The main effects of profession on emotional exhaustion and reduced personal accomplishment became somewhat weaker but remained significant. The main effect of profession on depersonalization disappeared, but the profession by sex interaction, indicating that male, but not female, teachers were more plagued by depersonalization than other social professionals, remained as strong as in the analysis without covariates.

All in all, these results imply that teachers indeed have more reason to burn out. Some of these reasons may be a low level of time control, little participation in decisions, and low colleague support. However, these factors can definitely not be the whole story, as follows from the continued existence of the relationships between profession and burnout symptoms after statistical correction. Other measures of job stress, perhaps more specifically aimed at the social professions in general and/or the teaching profession in particular (e.g., keeping order in the classroom), are necessary for a full explanation of why teachers burn out more easily than workers in other professions.

Which Teachers Are at Risk?

Because teachers as a group can be declared to be at risk for burnout does not, of course, preclude tremendous variation in burnout *within* the group of teachers. Clearly, many teachers do not and perhaps never will develop any sign of burnout whereas others are heavily plagued by burnout symptoms. Is there any system in this variation? Which characteristics of the teacher and his or her work can make a teacher vulnerable for developing burnout?

Table 17.2. *Correlations of Work-Stressors and Social Support with Burnout Symptoms (Teachers Only)*

	Emotional exhaustion	Depersonalization	Reduced personal accomplishment
Work stress:			
Work overload	.48	.14	.11
Job ambiguity	.19	.28	.26
Low time control	.26	.17	.19
Low responsibility and task control	.04	.21	.19
Low participation in decision making	.22	.31	.25
Monetary dissatisfaction	.12	.10	.04
Social support:			
Low supervisor support	.26	.27	.25
Low colleague support	.25	.33	.32

if . | r | > .07, p < .01; if | ρ | > .11, p < .001;

This question is addressed by analysis of the relationships of burnout symptoms with work-stressors, social support, other work characteristics (leadership and weekly working hours), and demographic variables (sex, age, marital status, and children). As a first step, Pearson product correlations were computed for emotional exhaustion, depersonalization, and reduced personal accomplishment with work-stressors and social support (Table 17.2). Almost all correlations are positive and highly significant (mostly p < .001), indicating that higher levels of work stress and lower levels of social support are usually accompanied by higher levels of all burnout symptoms.

Low supervisor and colleague support appear to be strongly related to all burnout symptoms (correlations between .25 and .33). However, work-stressors show a different pattern of relationships with emotional exhaustion on the one hand and depersonalization and reduced personal accomplishment on the other hand. Emotional exhaustion shows the highest correlations with work overload (r = .48) and low time control (r = .26), both factors indicating too high an *amount* of work (at least sometimes). Depersonalization and reduced accomplishment are more strongly related to job ambiguity (correlations of .28 and .26), low participation in decision making (.32 and .25), and to a lesser extent, low task control (.21 and .19), factors indicating a lack of *control* over work. These differential effects of quantitative overload and more qualitative control problems make intuitive sense: The primary effect of too much work is that the teacher becomes exhausted, whereas lack of control over work may lead to frustration (depersonalization) and insecurity (reduced accomplishment).

Apart from differences in work stress and social support, different *demographic and work characteristics* of teachers may involve more or less vulnerability for burnout symptoms. A multivariate analysis of variance (MANOVA) was done with the three kinds of burnout symptoms as the dependent variables, and sex, age (three groups: 18–35, 36–50, and 51–64 years of age), marital status (married or living together versus alone, widowed, or divorced), children under twelve (one or more versus no children below twelve years of age), number of weekly working hours (below 36 hours versus 36 hours or more), and leadership (being a leader or supervisor to at least one person versus to nobody). To avoid interpretation problems and loss of statistical power caused by too many interactions in a six-way analysis, all three-way and higher-order interactions were suppressed. A consequence of this choice of analysis is that all main effects and interactions reported are unique effects that have already been corrected statistically for possible overlap with all other independent variables or interactions.

Multivariate test results were significant for five of six main effects (children being the only exception) but for only one of fifteen two-way interactions (sex × marital status); therefore, univariate F-tests were conducted for only these six effects. The only significant *sex* difference ($p < .001$) was that men ($M = 1.87$) showed more depersonalization than women ($M = 1.16$). Significant *age* effects for depersonalization ($p < .001$) and reduced accomplishment ($p < .01$) indicated much lower levels of depersonalization in the youngest group ($M = 1.07$) than in the middle ($M = 1.67$) and oldest ($M = 1.57$) age groups, and also much lower levels of reduced accomplishment in the youngest ($M = .89$) than in the middle ($M = 1.19$) and oldest ($M = 1.25$) groups. As far as burnout symptoms are concerned, teaching appears to become much harder when one gets older.

Main effects of *marital status* were significant for emotional exhaustion ($p < .01$) and depersonalization ($p < .05$) whereas reduced accomplishment showed a significant sex × marital status interaction ($p < .01$). Inspection of group means revealed that married or cohabiting persons were less emotionally exhausted ($M = 2.76$ vs. 3.16) and showed less depersonalization ($M = 1.48$ vs. 1.60) than single persons. Married men ($M = 1.15$) also suffered less from reduced accomplishment than unmarried men ($M = 1.48$), but this difference did not apply to women, where the difference was even slightly reversed (means of 1.09 and 0.98 for married and single women, respectively).

Univariate F-tests for weekly *working hours* were significant for emotional exhaustion ($p < .001$), depersonalization ($p < .05$), and reduced accomplishment ($p < .05$). Longer working weeks appear to be a risk factor for all three kinds of burnout symptoms. Teachers working more than thirty-five hours a week suffered much more from emotional exhaustion than teachers with a shorter working week ($M = 3.31$ vs. 2.71), and somewhat more from depersonalization ($M = 1.81$ vs. 1.42) and reduced accomplishment ($M = 1.26$ vs. 1.09) than teachers with shorter working hours. *Leadership* made a significant difference ($p < .01$) only for reduced personal accomplishment, a predicament from which nonleaders ($M = 1.21$) suffered somewhat more than leaders ($M = 1.04$).

Summarizing, some teachers seem to be much more at risk for burnout than other teachers. Although the precise pattern of results varies across different burnout measures, experiencing work stressors and having little social support at work seem to be risk factors for developing teacher burnout. Additional indicators apparently are being male, older, or single; working long hours; and not being a leader.

Discussion

Limitations of the Present Study

The most important limitation of the study discussed in this chapter lies in the lack of representativeness of the sample for the Dutch working population with its underrepresentation of younger, poorly educated, and blue-collar workers. We can argue, however, that selection effects may not be too deleterious to the study, which was not aimed at estimating absolute burnout levels and other variables but instead focused on relative levels by emphasizing comparisons between different groups. As a consequence, self-selection is a problem only if it operates differently in different groups (e.g., overestimation of burnout symptoms in teachers and underestimation in other social professions). The good news is that such a "selective self-selection" is not a plausible option; the bad news, of course, is that even implausible things sometimes happen, and nothing in our design would warn us if this were the case.

A second limitation, the general purpose character of the questionnaire with its aim of asking only questions that are relevant to *all* professions, is actually a mixed blessing. On the positive side, it allows comparisons between completely different professions; the price for this generality is lack of specificity. Many important stressors of the teaching profession, especially problems in classroom interactions, are outside the scope of the study.

A third limitation, also following from the general purpose character of the questionnaire, lies in the undifferentiated character of the category "teacher" in this study. As used here, the category included teachers of all levels and types of schools, without any possibility of distinguishing among them. Consequences of this lack of differentiation are that we do not know exactly to which population our results can be generalized, that we are unable to say anything about differences between teachers from different types of schools, and most seriously, that our estimates of relationships between burnout and other variables may be disturbed by relationships of these other variables with school type. For example, if secondary school teachers are more at risk for burnout than primary school teachers (Burke and Greenglass, 1989b), and if primary school teachers are more often females, then (the absence of) some sex differences in burnout may actually be caused or suppressed by differences in school type.

A last limitation is that the strictly correlational design of our research forms an insufficient basis for causal inferences. All in all, these limitations imply that our conclusions have a somewhat tentative character.

Dutch Teachers (in General) Burn Out More Easily

The most important conclusion of the study is that teachers are especially vulnerable for burnout, more than workers in any other social profession. This rather unexpected result leads to the question of why this special vulnerability has not emerged from earlier studies.

It can be answered in at least two different ways – one methodological, one substantial. The methodological answer is that in earlier studies, usually *ad hoc samples* have been compared with each other – for example, teachers from institution X with police officers in three offices in district Y, instead of more general, national samples as in the study reported here. As a consequence, in earlier comparisons between teachers and other professional groups, profession effects may have been entangled with institution effects. Because "organizational healthiness" is an important factor in the development or prevention of burnout in its members (Cox, Kuk, and Leiter, 1993), and some schools (or other organizations) appear to be much healthier for their members than others, general conclusions about differences between different professions can be drawn only from general samples in which professionals from many different institutions are represented.

This brings us to a more substantial answer to the question of why the special vulnerability of teachers has not systematically emerged from earlier studies. It may be a *local phenomenon*, reflecting the specific historical and local circumstances of teaching and other social professions in the Netherlands.[1] The point is that burnout levels of different professions are not exclusively determined by job-intrinsic aspects (factors that may or may not be constant across different nations or institutions) but are to a large extent codetermined by the ways work is organized, how schools treat their teachers, and how teachers are perceived and treated by the larger public (factors most certainly *not* constant across different nations or organizations). An implication of this reasoning is that studies comparing different professions in general (like the study presented here) may have some heuristic value in explaining burnout but should be followed by more detailed studies, focused on working conditions and other organizational factors discriminating between organizations with high and low levels of burnout.

Why are teachers more vulnerable than other social professionals in the Netherlands? Our data do not permit a definitive answer to this question because, as we concluded from our statistical correction analyses, important variables were not measured in our study. However, by considering together the between-professions and within-teaching-profession results, we can make some suggestions. Teachers were not significantly different from other social professions on work overload, but work overload is a burden of all social professions (in comparison to most other professions; see also De Heus et al., 1994, p. 32). Furthermore, work overload may have especially deleterious consequences in combination with the most distinguishing job-stressor among teachers: low time control. This possible interaction of general work overload and teacher-specific low time control may be an important (although not the only) cause of high emotional exhaustion among teachers.

The other work factors distinguishing teachers from other social professionals – low participation in decision making and low colleague support – appear to reflect a somewhat unpleasant social climate at school. Teachers have a lot of discretion in deciding *how* to do thing in their own classroom

---

1. This conclusion appears to go against the results of two earlier studies of Dutch teachers. Van Ginkel (1987) reported that teacher burnout was relatively low in the Netherlands, but this conclusion was based on comparisons with *American* teachers and social professionals. Schaufeli, Daamen, and Van Mierlo (1994) reported more emotional exhaustion, but in direct contradiction to the present study, less depersonalization and less reduced accomplishment among Dutch teachers than among other Dutch social professionals. These divergent results may be caused by the use of ad hoc groups in the Schaufeli et al. study; but for a more decisive answer, more research is needed.

284 Peter de Heus and René F. W. Diekstra

(so there are not many complaints about task control), but they have little to say about *what* to do (fixed study programs and little voice in management affairs). As a consequence, there may be little shared responsibility and even less mutual feedback and advice among teachers (each teacher is on his own in the classroom), which may be the reason for the low levels of colleague support among teachers. The admittedly speculative picture emerging from our results is one of skilled, autonomous, but busy professionals, having to cope on their own with circumstances they did not and perhaps would not choose. The classroom may be crowded, but school can be a lonely place.

18. Teacher Burnout

PATRICIA ALBJERG GRAHAM

For the teacher who suffers it, burnout is a tragedy, accompanied by intense personal pain and causing the need for immediate and often dislocating professional change. Individually, burnout is a terrible ordeal.

For the schools whose teachers and administrators suffer burnout, however, the pressing issue is this: "What is its significance for the educational enterprise?" What does burnout as a phenomenon tell us about schooling? Most important, what are its effects on the students, whom presumably the school is supposed to serve? Do good teachers and bad ones suffer from it equally, or do we know? If burnout disproportionately affects good teachers, then its impact on the school is grievous. If, on the other hand, burnout primarily characterizes teachers who are failing to help their students learn, then their departure from teaching is less to be lamented.

Is burnout new? One of our colleagues represented in this volume implied that it was when noting that it was first named and identified in 1973 and applied to health workers. If it is new, does it replace some earlier dysfunctional state? Could burnout be the late twentieth-century manifestation of the neurasthenia reportedly prevalent among middle- and upper-class American women of the late nineteenth century? What are the characteristics of the late twentieth century that seem to make this malady widespread? In short, what in our current circumstances has led teachers to identify their malaise as "burnout" and others to describe it as such?

Two disciplinary perspectives on burnout included in this volume, such as psychological studies by Byrne and sociological analysis by Woods, help us understand this phenomenon. I wish to add another: a historical view. My observations are focused primarily on the United States, and I leave to others the applicability of the U.S. experience to other nations.

My query, fundamentally, is "Why burnout now?" To approach an

I am indebted to Ricardo Dobles for research assistance in the preparation of this chapter.

answer, I reviewed the elements that have changed in American teaching since World War II, specifically considering four changes:

1. The changing age and experience of teachers
2. The changing options for women professionals
3. The changing expectations for children's learning
4. The changing circumstances of childhood

Changing Age and Experience of Teachers

One finding that does seem to emerge from the literature on burnout and that is confirmed by my own experience is that burnout is directly related to time spent in teaching; teachers with longer service suffer from it more than do beginning ones. There seems to be an implicit conviction that burnout in both England and Wales as well as in North America is more severe now than it was in earlier years.

Although attrition is very high among beginning American teachers (about 50 percent leave during the first five years of teaching), their departure is not usually called burnout, but rather defined simply as an inability to cope with the demands of teaching or as a mistaken vocational choice on their part. However, a study of Houston, Texas, public school teachers, Dworkin (1987) attributes these early departures to burnout, finding less burnout among experienced teachers. One important distinction that we need to keep in mind, it seems to me, is the one between "burnout," which is a state of mind, and "attrition," which is an act. Burnout may cause attrition or attrition may be caused by any one of a number of other factors. More seriously, however, burnout may *not* cause attrition, and for the children who endure a teacher suffering acute burnout and for the colleagues who also endure a fellow teacher in such a state, the educational experience is severely damaged.

Any field in which half the professionals leave during the first five years and the ones who stay are acutely susceptible to burnout raises questions about the working conditions it entails. Such a phenomenon also provokes one to ask whether in such settings we should consider long teaching careers desirable. Perhaps, until working conditions improve, we would be wiser to anticipate shorter terms of teaching for all but the most exceptional teachers.

By 1950, schoolteaching in the United States was no longer dominated by the young. Professionalization had come to teaching, and for the three-quarters of U.S. teachers who were women, the combination of the financial needs of the Depression and the workplace shortages of World War II had kept a significant cohort of older women in that field. The distribution of women teachers was bimodal: the two peaks of age were the early twenties and the late forties. Men teachers were concentrated in their twenties. Women's professional mobility was limited to changing schools or changing grades as very few women were admitted to the career track of school administration, which remained heavily dominated by men. The exception was guidance counseling, which became widespread in the 1950s and which attracted both women and men.

The average age and experience of teachers that Byrne cites (this volume) in her study reveal that nearly three-quarters of her Canadian teacher sample was over forty; one-third of the teachers had thirteen to twenty years of experience, and between 40 and 50 percent of them had over twenty years of experience. Recent U.S. figures for public schoolteachers are similar; nearly 40 percent have ten to twenty years of experience, and 25 percent have over twenty years in the classroom. U.S. teachers are slightly younger than Byrne's Canadian sample, with 59 percent over age forty. The median age for U.S. teachers is now forty-two, up from thirty-three in 1976, and the median years of teaching experience is now fifteen, up from eight in 1976. Incidentally, the median age of U.S. teachers in 1900 was twenty-six, according to John Rury's (1989) analysis.

The effect on the schools, however, is this: Judging by Byrne's Canadian sample and figure for the United States, students today are taught by teachers who in large numbers have spent more than ten years teaching – about two-thirds of Canadian and three-quarters of American teachers. Are teachers in year seventeen of their career better or worse than in year seven?

Today there are more opportunities for both women and men to leave the classroom and to move on to various other administrative jobs than was true in earlier periods both because there are more administrative assignments and because there is less prejudice against women entering them. Nonetheless, many teachers do not seek administrative positions and remain in the classroom.

Doing the same thing year in and year out is burdensome to many. When one taught one's heart out for five or six years and then "retired" to bear and rear children or to seek a different career, acute burnout was unlikely. For the woman returning to teaching after such a time at home with children, her singular focus on her identity as a teacher that may have characterized the early years of her teaching now became more varied; she identified herself as a teacher but also as mother and often as wife. On the other hand, such returning teachers often faced both the turbulent adolescence of their children and the waning health of their parents and parents-in-law simultaneously, and as the presumed "nurturing" half of the marital dyad, they often faced additional responsibilities for both. Together these factors can certainly increase the likelihood of burnout.

Changing Options for Women Professionals

Women constitute nearly three-quarters of the teaching force, both public and private, in the United States. This female fraction has been relatively constant since 1900. What has changed, however, is the other options available to U.S. women who seek a professional career. In 1900, school teaching was one of the very few positions available to a woman with a baccalaureate degree. As late as 1960, the percentage of women receiving law or medical degrees was under 4 percent. Now many medical and law schools have classes that are half female. Similarly, fewer than 10 percent of the Ph.D.s went to women in 1960; today they receive nearly 40 percent. By 1972, 9 percent of high school girls said they wished to pursue graduate or professional education; today that figure is 35 percent.

The alumni rolls of the Harvard Graduate School of Education, for example, are sprinkled with women who came for a master's degree in the 1960s, when education seemed the only feasible course of study for a woman at Harvard, and who then transferred from the Education School to another faculty, often the Law School, as they (and the Law School) recognized the contributions and careers they could have as lawyers. Two specific examples are the former general counsel for Harvard University and current judge on the Massachusetts Supreme Judicial Court, Margaret Marshall, and the former Secretary of Labor and current president of the U.S. Red Cross, Elizabeth Dole.

In short, for a woman with education – either baccalaureate or normal school – in the first two-thirds of this century, almost her only option for employment consistent with her preparation was schoolteaching. In such circumstances, when she had no other professional alternatives, I suspect that she was more likely to consider its virtues and to ignore (or repress) its difficulties. Certainly in the society in which she moved, her appointment as a teacher was as prestigious a job as any woman was likely to have.

Today in the United States all this has changed. For a woman to be a teacher today is an indication either of her devotion to the calling or to her inability to become a lawyer, doctor, business executive, or some other more remunerative and highly regarded post. In this respect, of course, she is now subject to similar social scrutiny as the men who remain in teaching. What has changed is that for the vast majority of the teaching force in the

United States who are women, the options of their younger sisters and daughters are much greater than their own were at that age. A woman teacher of twenty-five years' experience, now approximately fifty years of age, graduated from college and presumably chose teaching just as the shift in professional opportunities for women occurred, and she may especially feel that her consignment to the classroom was an artifact of her age.

Changing Expectations for Children's Learning

During the first half of the twentieth century, the United States led the world in the percentage of its adolescent youth who completed secondary school – from 17 percent in 1920 to 50 percent in 1940. From 1940 to 1970 the growth in high school graduates continued and then stalled at 75 percent of the age group. In the 1990s, the rate has grown again, particularly when recipients of the GED or high school equivalency are included so that the present rate is 86 percent.

Although these are impressive figures, they obscure the meaning of the high school diploma. For much of this period there was no serious expectation that all graduates would actually learn academic subjects. Less than half the high school population for the past twenty years has been enrolled in an academic program, the majority of the remainder in a "general" track in which academic content was low and vocational training nonexistent (National Center for Education Statistics, 1994, 1995). In short, high school students, their families, and school people engaged in an accommodation: Children would enroll, little would be demanded of them, they would perform an absolute minimum without fuss, and they would graduate. The situation is very similar to the old Soviet anecdote about working: "We pretend to work and they pretend to pay us." The implicit pact between the educators and students is described most felicitously by Powell, Farrar, and Cohen in *The Shopping Mall High School* (1985).

In the last dozen years, this pact has disintegrated as the American public, inspired by their political leadership, has awakened to discover that their children are not performing at "world-class standards" in their academic work. Despite the many distractions of U.S. consumerist, entertainment-ridden society, adolescents are suddenly supposed to find enchantment in trigonometry. Not surprisingly, few do. The fault is often laid at the feet of the teachers, who are expected to overcome enormous counterpressures to awaken intellectual passions in their students, whose passions are more frequently stimulated by their hormones, their friends, and their music.

In short, an additional burden facing many U.S. teachers in recent years is the dramatic escalation of academic expectations for all students. There have always been high levels of academic expectations for some students, but never in U.S. history have we expected *all* our students to master complicated academic material. When students fail to do so, as many do, schools and their teachers are blamed. Many teachers rightly consider themselves to have taken the job under one set of expectations for what they were supposed to be able to accomplish with the children. The expectations changed, putting them under greater pressure to achieve the unachievable with children whose family and community supports do not include academic learning. Of course, this issue is aggravated for teachers who began work in schools twenty or thirty years ago when much less was expected either of them or their students.

Changing Circumstances of Childhood

The tragic truth about American children is that too many live in terrible circumstances. Nearly one-quarter of American children live in poverty, considerably more than twenty-five years ago when many of our experienced teachers began their service. Half of American children can expect to spend some fraction of their childhood in a single-parent home, still an excellent predictor of school difficulties regardless of income or class. In much of western Europe, between 85 percent and 98 percent of three- to five-year-olds attend early childhood programs; the figures for the United States are 29 percent for three-year-olds and 48 percent for four-year-olds, most of them in nonlicensed, poorly monitored, private facilities. A recent international study including leading industrialized nations revealed that U.S. children are more likely to be poor, to be in a single-parent family, and to be killed before they reach age twenty-five than children in any of the other countries. Only the former USSR had a higher rate of infant mortality. The only category in which the United States led was consumption of calories. More than 20 percent of all U.S. children have no health insurance, a profound disincentive for seeking preventive medical care, and more than 20 percent of all U.S. children are not fully immunized; polio immunization was down from 78 percent in 1970 to 55 percent in 1985. Meanwhile, American children average between three and four hours of television watching daily; they spend 200 more hours watching of television annually than they spend in school. Is it any wonder that teachers find instructing them difficult?

In sum, the teacher burnout phenomenon seems utterly plausible to me.

It is a quite reasonable response to the circumstances that the majority of U.S. teachers find themselves in. Many women entered education when teaching, along with nursing, was nearly the only professional option for them; they have seen the demands on them increase mightily just as they are reaching middle age. Not only are they now expected to help a much higher fraction of students learn much more demanding academic material, but they are also supposed to accomplish this instruction with many youngsters who have precious little academic reinforcement in their homes and communities. There is still much commitment for getting the diploma but much less to the learning that should be a concomitant of the diploma. The teachers' task is therefore to introduce the new element – rigorous academic accomplishment – without which the desired diploma will no longer be granted. An enormous shift in the rules of the academic game is going on now in the United States, and it is the teachers whose jobs are changing the most as a result of this shift. They are the enforcement squad, and as such, they are under immense pressure. No wonder many feel burnout.

PART THREE. Teacher Burnout: A Research and Intervention Agenda

19. Teacher Burnout:
A Research Agenda

CHRISTINA MASLACH AND MICHAEL P. LEITER

Burnout has long been recognized as an important stress-related problem for people who work in interpersonally oriented occupations, such as the human services. In these occupations, the relationship between providers and recipients is central to the job, and the nature of the work (whether it be service, treatment, or education) can be highly emotional. Unlike unidimensional models of stress, burnout has been conceptualized in terms of three interrelated components: emotional exhaustion, depersonalization, and reduced personal accomplishment (Maslach and Jackson, 1986). Emotional exhaustion refers to feelings of being emotionally overextended and depleted of one's emotional resources; depersonalization refers to a negative, callous, or excessively detached response to other people (often the recipients of one's service or care); and reduced personal accomplishment refers to a decline in one's feelings of competence and successful achievement in one's work. In terms of outcomes, burnout has been linked to decrements in both psychological and physical well-being, and it appears to be a factor in various problem behaviors, both on the job and in the home (see Cordes and Dougherty, 1993; Schaufeli, Maslach, and Marek, 1993).

Teaching shares with other human service professions the central role of working in a close relationship with recipients (i.e., students). However, teaching is unique in that these working relationships are dealt with en masse within a classroom ("batch processing"), unlike the more individual and sequential focus of other human services. The quality of the relationship between teacher and student is the basis for the most rewarding aspects of teaching, but it is also the point at which teachers are vulnerable

The development of this research agenda took place at the Johann Jacobs Conference on Teacher Burnout, Marbach Castle, Germany, November 2–4, 1995. The research development group, which was led by the co-authors, included Barry Farber, Isaac Friedman, Willy Lens, Richard Lerner, Peter Woods, and Isabelle Zuppiger. We thank all of them for their valuable contributions. We are also grateful to Judith Warren Little for her helpful comments on the manuscript.

to emotionally draining and discouraging experiences. Because burnout has considerable implications for teachers' performance in relation to students and colleagues (as well as for their own well-being), it is a problem with potentially serious consequences for both teachers' career and the learning outcomes of their students.

Burnout also has important implications for the extent to which teachers can pursue important values through their work. The opportunity to enact values pertaining to personal relationships, the learning process, or curriculum content is part of the teaching profession's attraction (Nias, 1988b). The enactment of values through work requires a commitment to the work itself, the prerogative to make consequential decisions about the work, and control over important aspects of the teaching process. If aspects of the job or organizational context make it difficult for teachers to pursue their values, then burnout is more likely to occur, and this experience leads readily to alienation from a specific job or even from teaching as a profession (Cherniss, 1980b, 1992).

A Working Model of Teacher Burnout

The top priority of the proposed research agenda is to gain a deeper understanding of both the impact of burnout on the teaching process and the key causal factors. To guide that agenda, we have developed a working model of teacher burnout that is presented in Figure 19.1. On the one hand, burnout is considered to be a factor contributing to both teachers' and students' behavior and experience. On the other hand, burnout is depicted as influenced by multiple factors, ranging from qualities inherent in the social environment and the school setting, to the nature of the work itself, to the personal characteristics of teachers and students. This pattern is consistent with a model of organizational health (Cox and Leiter, 1992) that explains personal distress of employees in terms of enduring conflicts of organizational processes and structures with personal needs and aspirations. This articulation of teacher burnout leads to a research program encompassing the quality and impact of the teaching relationship within the broad political and economic context of schools.

The model in Figure 19.1 maintains the three-component definition of burnout but does not specify the nature of the interrelationships between these three dimensions. Different hypotheses have been proposed and should be tested in future studies. So far, the empirical evidence in the teaching domain (Byrne, Chapter 1) is most supportive of the Leiter (1993) model in which emotional exhaustion occurs first and is linked sequentially

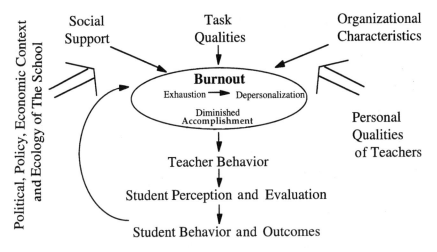

Figure 19.1. Proposed model of teacher burnout.

to the rise of depersonalization whereas reduced personal accomplishment develops separately. Presumably, the parallel (rather than sequential) development of the burnout components reflects their links to different factors in the work environment. This presumption is built into our model, although there has been no attempt to delineate the specific pattern of relationships of organizational conditions with each burnout component. However, prior research leads us to expect that certain work demands (work overload, personal conflict, role conflict) will be more predictive of emotional exhaustion and depersonalization whereas aspects of control and social support will be more strongly linked to personal accomplishment.

A variety of structural and demographic information may pertain to critical causal factors for burnout, such as work overload and role conflict. Thus, it is recommended that all research studies should report information on class level (elementary, middle school, secondary school), class size, number of classes (and thus overall number of students) per day, and the heterogeneity of the students in terms of ethnicity, gender, linguistic differences, academic abilities, and socioeconomic background. Part of the research agenda will be to identify issues that pertain specifically to a demographic group or teaching level (Byrne, 1994a).

Teacher–Student Interaction

The initial focus of the model is on the means through which burnout has an impact on the experience and behavior of students. It presumes a process in which the experience of emotional exhaustion, depersonalization, and reduced personal accomplishment shapes teachers' behavior. The nature and extent of these behavioral changes for teachers have not, as yet, been much studied, so this is clearly the central research question on which subsequent developments rest. Not only do these behavioral changes need to be identified, but their correspondence with the standard burnout measure, the Maslach Burnout Inventory (MBI; Maslach and Jackson, 1986), needs to be established.

Teachers' social behavior toward students is a likely area of impact. In general, burnout is predictive of "minimalist" responses in terms of teacher effort, involvement, and investment. Thus, burnout should be inversely related to the frequency with which teachers recognize and respond encouragingly to students' accomplishment, as is suggested by work in educational motivation (Lens and Schops, 1991). Both the thoroughness of classroom preparation and the involvement in classroom activities are also expected to decline as teacher burnout increases. In addition to a greater quantity (and perhaps lesser quality) of positive feedback, more criticism of students is likely to occur with greater teacher burnout. As suggested by Farber (1991a), there may be multiple manifestations or subtypes of burnout in addition to its "classic" form (e.g., being worn out, being chronically bored), and these subtypes may display different behavioral patterns. In all cases, the extent of the behavioral changes and the closeness of their relationship with scores on the MBI will clarify the extent to which burnout reflects a performance problem as well as an experiential problem for teachers.

In response to the teacher behaviors described above, students are likely to change their perception of the teacher, their feelings toward the teacher, and their behavior in the classroom. Consequently, the impact of teacher burnout should be evident in terms of student learning and performance. Students will have less of a sense of efficacy in school and will feel less competent as learners. They will have lower levels of intrinsic motivation, which may, in turn, influence their depth of learning. Student initiative and creativity are also expected to be inversely related to teacher burnout. In the long run, if students feel less competent in school, they may see less contingency between school and the rest of their lives, and eventually they may come to disidentify with school and the educational process.

Students are not depicted as passive recipients of teachers' influence in our model. As indicated by the arrow going from student behavior to teacher burnout, student behavior is an important contributor to teachers' subjective experience (Friedman, 1995b). Some student behaviors, such as disruptive actions in the classroom, disrespect, and inattentiveness, may aggravate teacher burnout whereas student successes and supportiveness toward teachers may prevent or alleviate the condition. Moreover, some student behaviors may be compensatory in response to teacher burnout, such as complaining to parents or engaging in attention-getting behaviors. As represented in our model, this reciprocal, bidirectional aspect of the teacher–student relationship acknowledges the centrality of this relationship for teacher burnout.

Personal Qualities of Teachers

The personal qualities of teachers are considered to be an interaction variable in the burnout model. That is, teachers with certain traits or characteristics (such as a low sense of intrinsic motivation) are expected to be more sensitive to the qualities of the school environment discussed below. Thus, teachers low in intrinsic motivation might experience greater increases in emotional exhaustion in response to only small increases in role conflict. In contrast, teachers highly motivated toward their teaching would be less likely to respond emotionally to minor variations in role conflict. There may be other qualities (such as sociability, personal initiative, and curiosity) that influence a teacher's responsiveness to a given teaching environment.

Another important set of personal variables is coping patterns or coping skills. Although it is recognized that some personal qualities may be directly related to one or more of the burnout components, research would benefit from examining the potential interaction or moderating effects of personal characteristics on the teacher's reaction to environmental conditions and events. The extent to which a given school environment encourages certain coping skills or other personal qualities is also relevant to the development of burnout. By encouraging or suppressing an action-oriented coping style among employees, an organization may have a significant impact on the development of personal qualities relevant to burnout (Leiter, 1991a). In a similar way, an organization may have an impact on other personal qualities, such as a teacher's capacity for intrinsic motivation.

School Environment

The context in which teaching takes place is assumed to be an important factor for burnout. This context includes both the classroom and the school as well as the other people and policies that affect teachers' work within that environment.

Task Qualities. Various aspects of the work task have been found in prior research to play a major role in the development of burnout among human service professionals. However, to understand teacher burnout, these generic task qualities need to be specified in terms of teachers' actual work within the school context. For example, the often found (but occasionally inconsistent) relationship of role conflict with emotional exhaustion (Byrne, 1994a; Leiter, 1993; Maslach, 1993) encompasses a wide range of potential conflict areas. Some of these occur within the school setting. Teachers may experience a conflict in purposes – that is, between educating students and maintaining order in the classroom (McNeil, 1986). Role conflict may also occur for teachers who occupy teacher leadership or mentor roles within what purports to be an egalitarian occupation (Little, 1990a; Wasley, 1991). In addition, as has been found in other professions, role conflicts can also occur between life domains, such as conflict between the job and family life, or management of the work–family boundary itself (Biklen, 1995; Burke and Greenglass, 1986; Leiter and Durup, 1996).

Another task quality that has been linked to burnout in prior research is role ambiguity. Again, this generic concept needs to be translated more specifically into relevant terms for teachers. "Endemic uncertainty" seems to be the popular term for ambiguity within the teaching occupation. Teachers may receive mixed messages about their work from different sources (e.g., school administrators and the district office). The general public may express their own goals with respect to the schools, and ambiguity may arise as to where teachers should be placing their priorities. A measure of role ambiguity that differentiates between these and other conditions of uncertainty would contribute more to the understanding of teacher burnout.

Work overload is a third task aspect that has been linked to burnout, but our understanding of teacher burnout would benefit from a more detailed specification of the nature of the overload for different teachers. In some school settings, the concern may be more with quantitative overload: total number of students, class size, or teaching contact hours. In other instances, the overload is more qualitative: demands on neglected academic skills, requirements for conflict management, or challenges in motivating students in the classroom. For teachers, both forms of work overload come together in the mass processing of students, especially within a school context in which teachers have very little control over determining which students they will teach, how many, and in what way.

All these task dimensions contribute to a negative classroom climate, which in turn is predictive of greater teacher burnout. However, there are other factors involved in classroom climate. The organization of the class, the extent of control or discipline, the task focus, the patterns of questions and answers, and the types of student behaviors described earlier are some of the additional variables that have an important impact at the level of the classroom.

Social Support. There is a wealth of research on social support in schools (Burke and Greenglass, 1989c, 1994; Byrne, 1994a; Jackson, Schwab, and Schuler, 1986; Thoits, 1982), as well as the relationship of social support with burnout (Leiter, 1993; Maslach, 1993). Thus, there is an existing base on which to develop future research. Numerous issues could be addressed by this new work. One of these concerns the distinctive aspects of collegial and supervisory networks in schools. In contrast with the teamwork and task interdependency of many health care workers, teachers conduct much of their work in isolation from everyone except their pupils. This difference introduces problems in conceptualizing the impact of social support and selecting measures that are relevant across human service occupations. For example, the use of a supervisor measure that pertains to the management of integrated workgroups would not address qualities of interactions between principals and teachers that influence teachers' experience. A thorough consideration of the existing literature on social support for teachers (Farber, 1991b; Sarros and Sarros, 1992) would bring needed clarity to this aspect of the model.

An important distinction in the social support literature is between desired and actual social support, whether it be provided by colleagues, the principal, or family and friends outside the school. Current research suggests that the discrepancy between desired and actual support is the critical issue rather than just the absolute amount of support; thus, a question for future study is whether a greater discrepancy would predict greater burnout. Other issues to consider are the impact of negative social support (rather than just its positive forms) and the effect of the time demands of social support (which may make it too costly a resource to provide).

Organizational Characteristics. The decision-making environment of the school determines the extent to which teachers can maintain sufficient control to enact their values through their work, and thus it affects the likelihood of teacher burnout. Teacher autonomy is based on recognition of teachers' professional prerogatives to exercise judgment over the teaching they do within their own classrooms. Policy decisions at the school or district level can constrain or enhance teachers' work, and schools vary in the extent to which such decisions arise through decree, consultation, or formally defined joint decision-making processes. An important distinction here is between teacher autonomy (control at the classroom level) and teacher influence (control at the school level). The type of decision-making process used in the school and teachers' satisfaction with its appropriateness to their work are relevant to burnout. Other organizational variables that might play a role are the adequacy of organizational communication networks and the level of burnout experienced by school administrators, such as principals (Friedman, 1995a).

Political, Economic, and Ecological Context

The larger social context in which the school functions is hypothesized to be an interaction variable in this model. If the environment is a socially "toxic" one (Garbarino, 1995) in which extreme conditions of violence, poverty, and/or alienation threaten the well-being of the community members, its impact will play a far greater role in predicting student learning and performance than will the process of teacher burnout as described in the model. On the other hand, when the larger political and economic context is not so powerful and threatening, it will have less of an intrusive impact on the school; in this situation, teacher burnout would account for a greater amount of the variance in student outcomes. The significance of this hypothesis lies in its implications for what kinds of interventions would be most effective in different environments to deal with student learning and motivation.

Research Issues

The research questions described here require a complex and extensive research program employing a variety of methods. In terms of priorities, the link between teacher burnout and student outcomes seems to be of paramount importance. More attention needs to be given to the teacher-student relationship in terms of theory, operationalization of variables, research paradigms, and appropriate measures. Determining the presumed impact of burnout must be an integral part of studies examining why and when it occurs. Better evidence about the effects of teacher burnout on students (as well as on other people) would lead to the next priority of linking the larger context variables to burnout. Following that, the next strategy would be to design intervention studies and determine whether these changes lead to different outcomes, or alternatively, to search for existing programs that work successfully and see whether they match the empirical model.

In terms of methodological issues, researchers hope to gain insight into the burnout process, its causes, and the impact of interventions through longitudinal designs. It is important to confirm whether the consistent patterns of relationships identified in cross-sectional studies hold up over varying study intervals, and to discover what relationships emerge in a longitudinal analysis. A design that relates assessments of specific teaching incidents with surveys would allow deeper insight into the development and alleviation of burnout. This information can help guide the design of effective interventions. In addition, burnout research would profit from a more interdisciplinary approach in which greater attention was given to a macro level of analysis.

A thorough examination of the correlates of burnout requires information from various sources: teachers, their students, colleagues, principals, parents, and outside observers. An action research model that included these participants as partners in the planning and implementation of the studies would not only facilitate the research but would open possibilities for intervention, as educators and researchers collaborate on a problem-solving approach to burnout.

In line with the multiple sources of information about burnout, greater efforts are needed to develop multiple measures (both of burnout and other variables) that are not simply self-reports. The large-scale survey methods currently available will permit examination of the overall model of relationships of organizational, task, and social characteristics with burnout. However, more qualitative research methods need to be integrated with these quantitative approaches. For example, interviews with teachers over an extended period of time, which were intensive, holistic, and more grounded in teachers' experience, would shed much needed light on the process of teacher burnout. Similarly, classroom observations would yield new understanding of the nature of teacher–student interactions as well as of the dimensions of classroom climate. Any new measures developed to be specific to the demands and resources of teaching would make subsequent research findings more useful in efforts to alleviate or prevent burnout.

Conclusion

The most valuable and most costly part of an educational system are the people who teach. Maintaining their well-being and their contribution to student education should be a primary objective of educational leaders. Research on burnout can contribute to this objective by identifying approaches for (a) preventing and alleviating severe breakdowns in teachers' engagement with their work, and (b) enhancing teachers' success at promoting student learning and achievement. Thus, the proposed research agenda provides a framework for improving the quality of the educational experience for both teachers and students.

20. Beyond Individual Burnout: A Perspective for Improved Schools. Guidelines for the Prevention of Burnout

GEERT KELCHTERMANS AND ANTON STRITTMATTER

Teacher burnout is not only an important issue on the agendas of educational research, as shown in the previous chapter. As an empirical phenomenon, it also has more immediate, practical consequences. Elsewhere in this volume are multiple studies showing that burnout affects the quality of teachers' professional performance, their level of commitment, and their job satisfaction. It also appears to affect pupils' learning negatively and places a heavy burden on the school as workplace – for example, in collegial relations, in the quality of the school climate. Even from a financial and economic point of view, there are consequences in terms of increased costs (Rudow).[1]

In this final chapter, we propose a set of *guidelines* that can help to redesign the school as a workplace so as to reduce or to minimize the risk of teacher burnout. These guidelines resulted from discussions of the papers presented at the international conference on "teacher stress and burnout," organized by the Johann Jacobs Foundation (November 2–4, 1995) in Marbach (Germany), of which several are incorporated in this volume.[2] As such, these guidelines constitute a school-specific complement to the research agenda proposed in the previous chapter. After providing some general assumptions in our approach, we present the guidelines at several levels of school organization and their relation to the wider sociocultural and political environment. Because the guidelines are closely connected to the perspective of teacher and school development, we address these issues in a final section.

1. Unless indicated otherwise, names in parentheses without dates refer to the authors of the chapters in this volume.
2. The first version of these guidelines was drafted during the conference in a working group consisting of Isaac Friedman (Israel), Geert Kelchtermans (Belgium), Lynne Miller (U.S.A.), Ralf Schwarzer (Germany), Anton Strittmatter (Switzerland), and Dorothee Widmer (Switzerland). In writing this chapter, we gratefully used the comments provided by Wolfgang Edelstein (Germany), Judith Warren Little (U.S.A.), and Michael Huberman (Schwitzerland).

Although our focus in the guidelines is clearly on the organizational level, we do not underestimate the individual affliction within the actual experience of burnout. It is clear that these teachers need specific and individualized help. An organizational approach, however, stems from the conviction that the more schools constitute supportive, collegial, and collaborative work environments, the less individual teachers run the risk of burnout. Or – as Maslach argues – teacher burnout not only asks for individual solutions but also demands social and organizational measures. The guidelines presented here are meant as a contribution to the latter.

A Contextualized Approach: Some Premises

As shown in the previous chapters, burnout results from the complex interplay of individual and contextual factors (see, e.g., Byrne; Leithwood et al.). The relevant *context* here, however, extends beyond the meso level of the local school as an organization to the more macro level (educational policy; administration) and even to societal issues in general (see, e.g., Smylie; Miller; Woods).

By acknowledging the contextualized nature of teacher burnout, we avoid an exclusive perspective in terms of a "disease" and thus as a purely individual problem (Maslach). Although the relative impact of personal and contextual determinants needs to be investigated further, the research presented in this book justifies the assumption that the actual working conditions of teachers in schools contribute to the risk of burnout. By improving those working conditions or – put negatively – by reducing their negative influence, it is then possible to lower the risk and heighten the prevention of teacher burnout. For example, developing uniquely individualized "anti-burnout" interventions might well be an inappropriate investment, given the complex and contextualized nature of the phenomenon.

Another aspect of a contextualized approach has to do with *values and norms* and turns around issues of "good teaching" and "educational quality." Preventing burnout should, in the end, be linked to school improvement. However, as argued by Smylie, Sergiovanni, and Miller, ambitious educational reforms can increase the endemic stress in teaching and thus might eventually contribute to teacher burnout. Studies (e.g., Friedman, 1991, 1995d) on the characteristics of schools with extremely high or low teacher burnout have shown that very often high performance by students is associated with a high degree of teacher burnout; the reverse is also often true. In other words, higher student performance may often be bought at the cost of excessive stress on teachers.

Theoretically, the classic burnout symptoms – emotional exhaustion, diminished personal accomplishment, and depersonalization – would be reduced in environments where teachers experience positive professional growth, self-efficacy, and success in their career progression; therefore, our guidelines focus on opportunities for individual teacher development as well as for improvement of the school as an organization. In this way we actually cover the entire matrix for intervention (individual-organization/direct action-palliative approaches) as developed notably by Friedman. A concern for educational efficacy is thereby linked to the well-being and commitment of both teachers and pupils. In our opinion, schools with high-performing and healthy teachers constitute the best guarantee for positive and lasting student results. Reflections about the working conditions for teachers should therefore parallel thinking about the environment for pupils. In other words, the needs of both groups have to be kept in mind; there is a real risk that support facilities for teachers might be created and eventually expanded without a direct concern for students' progression.

Keeping in mind that there are no simple solutions for complex educational phenomena, we believe that the guidelines following have a strong *heuristic potential* for those who want to develop interventions with the broad intention of making schools better places to live and learn for both teachers and pupils. As such, the guidelines are also in line with the projects of the so-called second and third reform wave, which urge teachers to "re-invent schools and re-invent themselves" (Miller).

Societal Influences and Teachers' Workplaces

Although the school and classroom constitute their primary workplace horizons, teachers are far from immune to wider socioeconomic, cultural, and political trends in society. The Exemplary analyses of educational policies in England and Wales reported by Woods and Nias in their chapters show how "intensification" and "deprofessionalization" negatively affect teachers' job satisfaction. These educational policies – such as reducing teachers' responsibilities for curriculum selection and at the same time extending bureaucratic control and central administrative prescriptions, threatening their professional, values and norms ("caring ethos"), their identity as professionals, and their self-esteem – contribute to increased stress and eventually to the actual risk of burnout. The impact of those measures is further reinforced by public criticism and depreciation in the media (see, e.g., Cole, 1997).

Public Recognition and a Balanced Media Image

As with other professionals, teachers need to have their commitment and efforts to perform well publicly acknowledged. The promotion of a positive image of teachers and, more broadly, of schools in the media, the recognition of the social importance of teaching, and more realistic expectations about the actual contribution of schooling in solving societal problems: All are important issues for educational policy makers and administrators (Woods). This legitimate expectation for a positive public image, however, does not replace the need for critical self-evaluation within the educational establishment itself, as discussed later in the chapter.

Balancing Central Policies and School Autonomy

The general guidelines from state agencies or other authoritative policy makers can and should provide the overall frame within which schools are to operate (goals, minimal performance expectations, overall standards of quality). Within this frame, however, schools should have sufficient autonomy to interpret, elaborate on, and even modify such guidelines according to the particularities of the local context (Miller). In general one can hope for fewer but clearer guidelines. Providing the teaching staff with more organizational autonomy and professional recognition as well as with clear expectations of minimal goals and norms of quality would theoretically heighten professional motivation and thus – indirectly – increase instructional quality while reducing the risk of burnout. However, as argued by Graham, Smylie, Miller, and Sergiovanni, such positive effects are uncertain and even unlikely when the necessary support and resources are not available. In such cases, decentralizing educational responsibilities might even increase teachers' vulnerability to burnout.

Providing Adequate and Readily Available Resources

Demanding expectations are hard to meet when the means to these ends are not available. Reduced teaching performance and increased burnout may be the result of such policy. To avoid this, a policy of resources that caters to occupational tasks and specific or local conditions and that reallocates resources when necessary seems advisable. The availability of resources at the right time presents another problem. Quite often, resources are made accessible only over the long term. In many systems of "forward" management, additional means are often not available when they are needed immediately for the resolution of an acute problem. Consider inservice training of teachers: Voluminous catalogues are often prepared months before the courses are actually due to take place. An important portion of these offers may never be used when a relevant domain appears for teachers or sets of schools. A solution might be to provide schools with a more general budget for a more flexible inservice facility, including the hiring of external consultants. Schools would get thereby more tailor-made training and assistance with local problems when required. The general rule would be "allocate time and means for things that matter now."

Career-Long Professional Learning

Analysts argue that future teachers should be supported to develop attitudes and skills for lifelong professional learning. The objective is not to attain ideals of perfection but to acquire an attitude of optimal problem solving. This implies that instead of a broad preparation with no areas of particular expertise, future teachers might do better to gain self-confidence and professional competence in specific aspects of their job – "starting competencies."

Apart from the technical aspects, the teacher education should also attend to the moral, emotional, and political dimensions of teaching (Hargreaves, 1995; Nias, 1996b). There may be a relationship between such factors and some aspects of burnout. Consider, for example, the development among trainees of a realistic but still motivating ethos of caring. Here, the scope of teacher education reaches beyond its knowledge base and technical skills to the level of the professional self and subjective educational theory (Kelchtermans).

Teachers need to parallel this agenda by developing an *attitude of inquiry* toward their work (Altrichter, Posch, and Somekh, 1993). Here, teaching is construed as a job that values searching, experimenting, and constant self-evaluation with the objective of professional pride and efficacy but also with the desire to take part in further professional development.

To stimulate such a process of professional development effectively, specific efforts must be made to provide support and guidance to teachers during their induction period and later on in their careers (see, e.g., Huberman, Grounauer, and Marti, 1993; Kelchtermans, 1993a; Sikes, Measor, and Woods, 1985). Ideally, then, the workplace becomes the location for ongoing professional learning, guided by principles of school-based development, adult education, cooperative planning, and evaluation and knowledge transfer within the school (see Miller, Nias, Smylie). In particular, providing a basic feeling of safety and trust is an important condition for achieving this professional learning process (Nias, 1996b).

Working Conditions at the Level of the Local School

How can schools become healthier places to work while assuring high-quality educational opportunities and performance for pupils? This is the central question in the next paragraphs. The guidelines presented below are structured into three categories: the mission of the school and a culture of inquiry; leadership; and professional relations among colleagues. It is obvious that these categories and their underlying guidelines are conceptually distinct but empirically related. In the perspective of burnout prevention, they constitute complementary fields of action.

The School's Mission and a Culture of Inquiry

Schein defines the organizational culture of schools as "the deeper level of basic assumptions and beliefs that are shared by members of an organization, that operate unconsciously, and that define in a basic 'taken-for-granted' fashion an organization's view of itself and its environment" (Schein, 1985, p. 6). In the organizational culture of schools, there is a corresponding set of values, norms, and goals that operates more or less explicitly as the "mission" of the school. Such a mission contributes to the sense of identity of the school members. It further serves as a normative point of reference in discussions about the legitimacy of certain decisions or actions. However, because not all members of a school share the same values, the "definition" of the collective mission, along with its norms and goals, is an important and ongoing organizational process. Often, teachers may feel excluded from this process of definition. Furthermore, because the process typically develops in an implicit, underground, or indirect way, team members often have feelings of role ambiguity or role uncertainty (Ball, 1987).

    Negotiation of Core Values and Goals. To reduce role ambiguity and role conflict – two important determinants of teacher burnout developed in this volume (Byrne; Smylie; Rudow) – teachers have to know what is expected of them and what counts as important in their school. Obviously, the school's principal goals should be clear to and accepted by the teachers. Such a set of goals, however, implies a focus on a limited number of components in the school curriculum that the school aims in particular to teach carefully and effectively. These are *explicit* commitments to pupils, school staff, administrators, and external constituencies.

    In fact, the establishment of core values, norms, and goals might best be conducted as a *public and collective enterprise,* in which the maximum number of members of the school organization can participate (Miller). Hypothetically, if these values and goals are not set by the school authorities but are developed by and agreed on by the school community (i.e., by the teaching staff in collaboration with students, parents, and local authorities), one could expect more positive effects on students' performance – even beyond the core objectives that were defined initially. With this approach, the outcomes of the process would be made public as well as the procedures for evaluation and eventual revisions. If such a mission is perceived by the teachers as meaningful and functional in conversations and decision making, it has the potential to enhance teachers' sense of personal accomplishment, as Leithwood et al. (1994) found in their recent study.

The public statement of a mission, in terms of core values and main goals, allows teachers to embed their own professional commitments in a larger enterprise at the organizational level of the school (e.g., Firestone and Pennell, 1993). It further clarifies individual responsibilities (the "psychological contract" – M. Leiter), provides clear points of reference for teachers' accountability (De Heus et al.; Smylie; Miller), and thus reduces outcome uncertainties. In more psychological terms, it can increase teachers' level of self-efficacy at different stages of the "self-regulatory goal attainment processes," as R. Schwarzer and E. Greenglass argue in this volume. Finally, we would claim that such a public mission will contribute to more supportive collegial relations and – as a "prophylactic" sense of purpose – to a decrease in levels of burnout. By setting goals for students over the course of their academic career in the school, the members of the teaching staff would logically become more interdependent organizational members, with a shared collective responsibility for student learning – this in contrast to individualistic, classroom-centered practitioners.

Nurturing a Culture of Formative Evaluation and Critical Self-Reflection. Schools are supposed to be result-oriented and effective. This implies not only agreement on binding, mutual core values and goals but also a commitment to their optimal implementation. As a consequence, "effective" schools tend to install procedures for permanent critical self-evaluation. Through systematic reflection on and assessment of teaching and the organizational functioning of the school, teachers and principals explicitly aim at a better understanding and an eventual improvement of the ongoing schooling practice. Professional self-evaluation thus encompasses more than a simple "technical effectiveness" approach. Rather, it results from a fundamental *inquiry orientation* (Miller; Woods; also Brubacher, Case, and Reagan, 1994; McGrath, 1995). In practice, such schools should develop systematic internal evaluation and forms of action research, aiming at "improving practice through better understanding it." Action research can be set up by individual teachers, small groups of colleagues, or the entire school team (see, e.g., Altrichter et al., 1993; Anderson, Herr, and Nihlen, 1994; Dadds, 1995).

Leadership

Leithwood et al. argue that the impact of school organizational and leadership factors on teacher burnout is often underestimated. Their own research suggests a stronger impact of leadership than of personality factors. They claim further that both organizational and leadership factors, as far as they influence teacher burnout, do so not by their "objective" condition but through the teachers' personal judgment of those conditions. This might account for Byrne's finding that the effect of support on teacher burnout is "provider specific." However, rather than discussing the differential impact of support by colleagues or by principals, the guidelines below concentrate on leadership as an organizational function.

Promoting Forms of Participative or "Democratic" Leadership. Educational leadership in schools is not simply a role or organizational position, occupied by a limited number of individuals (i.c. principal; headteacher; director; central office; administrator). Leadership is rather to be understood as a general organizational function, in which more members of the organization can play a part (e.g., perform tasks and responsibilities, for which they are accountable). Differentiated structures for decision-making in which also teachers and eventually pupils can participate – although they might increase teacher stress (Smylie) – guarantee that leading the organization becomes a shared process and task. Theoretically, decisions are then built on a broader base and are thus more likely to be acted on. The importance of genuine participation in decision making, teacher empowerment and democratic leadership, is underlined by several authors in this volume (see a.o. Byrne; Kelchtermans; Leiter; Leithwood et al.; Sleegers; Smylie).

Providing the Necessary Resources and Facilities. Those who take up such formal management or leadership positions should be willing and able to provide the time, money, and infrastructure necessary for improved performance. Facilities for inservice training by team members and for sharing their newly acquired knowledge with colleagues are also essential working conditions. Even specific assistance and counseling of teachers must be available if particular needs or problems make it necessary.

Professional Relations

The network of professional relations within a school constitutes an influential working condition. There is a good deal of research describing teachers' autonomy, or isolation, in the classroom (e.g., Bakkenes, 1996). At the same time, the research literature contains numerous studies in which collegiality and teacher collaboration is promoted as one of the most important factors in teacher development and school improvement. Recent studies, however, argue for a more balanced view (e.g., Hargreaves, 1993; Little, 1990b). Clement and Vandenberghe (1997), for example, analyze the impact of teacher autonomy and collegiality on professional development in terms of "a field of tension." Apart from differences in perspectives or priorities, one can easily imagine that the colleagues in a school can be either a very supportive or a very threatening and stress-inducing factor.

Different authors in this book, however, argue for the importance of a collegial and collaborative culture in the perspective of burnout prevention (Woods, Nias). Byrne's work further shows the positive effects of collegial support (see also De Heus et al.; Schwarzer and Greenglass). Nias emphasizes the role of colleagues as a moral reference group.

Both Miller and Leithwood et al. specifically argue that a collaborative and collegial culture in schools enhances the quality of teachers' professional learning. Our guidelines for intervention intersect here.

Functional, Teaching-oriented Structures for Teamwork. For many analysts, effective and efficient schools must learn how to put in place a variable work organization based on a broad and functional spectrum of collaboration (Little, 1990b). The guiding assumption here is that of a situation of isolation, in which each individual, with limited resources, reinvents the yearly replaced wheel. Inefficient, stereotypical conferences and team meetings are to be replaced by targeted interactive techniques – for lesson planning, for joint lessons and collective school development projects, for communication with parents and the public, for the organization of school-level inservice training, and so on. Hypothetically, teachers would thereby experience these forms of teamwork as instructively functional and effective for tackling authentic issues in their daily work (Smylie, 1994). Increased quality through the diversity of personal resources, economy through synergic effects, and professional satisfaction through social support and solidarity experienced among colleagues – these are the demands that this type of work organization are to be characterized and measured by.

Structures for Problem Stating and Problem Solving. In many staff rooms, this attitude prevails: "Things are just fine. As long as you don't talk to me about your problems, I don't have to expose mine to you." In addition, teachers often keep from colleagues their doubts or pertinent experiences when they enroll for an inservice course such as "the difficult student." Seeking advice is often considered an admission of failure, an indicator of one's own inadequacy. Laying it bare might not be a good idea. If a colleague does happen to talk about such a problem, it may be swiftly "solved" with consolation, with "tips," or by externalization ("oh well, the youth of today, you know. And the parents who neglect their children. There is no cure for stupidity! And then these preposterous directions from above!").

The guidelines in this chapter are designed to encourage teachers' sharing of experiences, to develop social supports, and to create a more transparent attitude toward problem solving. In addition, a set of processes and structures is needed to cope effectively with acute problems. This process implies first identifying the problem, then developing adequate solutions. Some examples are consulting hours with the principal, supervisionary, or consultancy groups; classroom observation; and peer-coaching. The idea of a "critical friend" could operate as the guiding principle in some problem-solving structures (Altrichter et al., 1993). It is important that teachers find a quick, functional path to helpful interactions before the problem takes on pathogenic proportions.

Conclusion: A Perspective on Teacher and School Development

In this final chapter, we have distilled from several contributions to this book a set of guidelines with the potential for both preventing teacher burnout and improving the quality of schooling. The core idea is simple: *Both teacher and school development should be closely intertwined.*

This development is perhaps best understood as an *active learning process,* with results at an individual and organizational level. Individual teachers would thereby develop more realistic professional ideals, more positive self-esteem, and a greater internal locus of control along with improved competencies to cope flexibly with the demands of day-to-day classroom practice.

At the school level, the developments would be guided by the images of "professional community" and "learning community." This not only implies emerging forms of organizational learning but also demands more participative structures of decision making. All members of the organization would be conceivably involved in the establishment, evaluation, and improvement of the working conditions each party considers crucial for its optimal job performance.

Ultimately, all these guidelines aim at making a difference at the *level of the classroom:* improving teachers' and students' performance and well-being. As Farber argues with pertinence, the direct teacher–pupil interactions in the classroom are at the same time a major source of satisfaction and of stress and frustration to teachers. Self-efficacy and positive self-esteem are first experienced by teachers at the classroom level (Smylie, Byrne, Sleegers). It follows that losing or lacking control over working conditions that affect one's work in the classroom would contribute to reduced satisfaction, lower levels of personal accomplishment, and frustration (Lens, Miller). The same is true for contrasting conditions and their classroom-level effects (Byrne, Woods). Still, we should bear in mind that the effects of any action undertaken at the school level will be codetermined by individual teachers' interpretations largely in terms of their perceptions of the classroom conditions they operate in (Kelchtermans).

There is *no guarantee for success* with these guidelines. As shown earlier, the complexities of individual and organizational functioning and the influences of the broader social, cultural, and economic environment are too strong for direct control locally. Given the specificity of a school's situation, we argue for an "inquiry orientation" within schools. Through thoughtful interventions following a general design of action research, both the research agenda in the previous chapter and the action agenda of the suggested guidelines could be forwarded, thereby providing a better understanding of burnout and its determinants, and at the same time revealing the results of actions and strategies to deal effectively with stress and burnout in the day-to-day practice of schools.

Through this approach, dealing with stress and preventing burnout in teaching becomes an integrated part of life and work in schools. Burnout is then no longer a "sword of Damocles" hanging above an individual teacher's head, threatening his or her health and inducing feelings of individual failure and guilt. In making teaching a "we-thing" rather than a "me-thing" – as Lens nicely puts it – we might make the most effective contribution to the prevention of teacher burnout.

References

Abercrombie, M. L. J. (1984). *Changing higher education by the application of some group analytic ideas.* Paper given at the 8th International Conference of Group Psychotherapy, Mexico City.

Acker, S. (1994). *Gendered education: Sociological reflections on women, teaching and feminism.* Milton Keynes, England: Open University Press.

Acker, S. (1995). Carry on caring: The work of women teachers. *British Journal of Sociology of Education, 16,* 21–36.

Adams, J. S. (1965). Inequity in social exchange. In L. Berkowitz (Ed.), *Advances in experimental social psychology* (Vol. 2, pp. 267–299). New York: Academic Press.

Adams, J. S., & Freedman, S. (1976). Equity theory revisited. Comments and annotated bibliography. In L. Berkowits & E. Walster (Eds.), *Advances in experimental social psychology* (Vol. 9, pp. 43–90). New York: Academic Press.

Ainscow, M., & Southworth, G. (1994, April). *The role of leaders in school improvement: Working with rather than working on.* Paper presented at the annual meeting of the American Educational Research Association, New Orleans.

Ajzen, I. (1991). The theory of planned behavior. *Organizational Behavior and Human Decision Processes, 50,* 179–211.

Alexander, R. (1984). *Primary teaching.* London: Cassell.

Altrichter, H., Posch, P., & Somekh, B. (1993). *Teachers investigate their work. An introduction to the methods of action research.* London: Routledge.

Anderson, G. L., Herr, K., & Nihlen, A. S. (1994). *Studying your own school. An educator's guide to qualitative practitioner research.* Thousand Oaks, CA: Corwin Press.

Anderson, M. B., & Iwanicki, E. F. (1984). Teacher motivation and its relationship to teacher burnout. *Educational Administration Quarterly, 20,* 94–132.

Apple, M. W. (1982). *Education and power.* New York: Routledge.

Apple, M. W. (1986). *Teachers and texts: A political economy of class and gender relations in education.* New York: Routledge and Kegan Paul.

Apple, M. W. (1988). Work, class and teaching. In J. Ozga (Ed.), *Schoolwork: Approaches to the labour process of teaching.* Milton Keynes, England: Open University Press.

Apple, M. W., & Jungck, S. (1992). You don't have to be a teacher to teach this unit: Teaching, technology and control in the curriculum. In A. Hargreaves & M. Fullan (Eds.), *Understanding teacher development.* London: Cassell.

Archibald, D. A., & Porter, A. C. (1994). Curriculum control and teachers' perceptions of autonomy and satisfaction. *Educational Evaluation and Policy Analysis, 16,* 21–39.

315

Argyris, C., & Schon, D. A. (1978). *Organizational learning: A theory of action perspective.* Reading, MA: Addison-Wesley.

Arrindell, W. A., & Ettema, J. H. M. (1986). *SCL-90 Symptom Checklist. Handleiding bij een multidimensionele psychopathologie* (SCL-90 Symptom Checklist. Manual for a multidimensional psychopathology). Lisse: Swets & Zeitlinger.

Bacharach, S. B., Bauer, S. C., & Conley, S. (1986). Organizational analysis of stress: The case of elementary and secondary schools. *Work and Occupations, 13,* 7–32.

Bakkenes, I. (1996). *Professional isolation of primary school teachers: A task-specific approach.* Leiden: DSWO Press.

Ball, S. (1987). *The micropolitics of the school: Toward a theory of school organization.* London: Methuen.

Ball, S. (1994, September 8). A shameful time for education. *The Guardian,* p. 21.

Ball, S. J. (1990). *Politics and policy making in education.* London: Routledge.

Ball, S. J. (1994). *Education reform: A critical and post-structural approach.* Buckingham: Open University Press.

Ball, S. J., & Bowe, R. (1992). Subject departments and the implementation of National Curriculum policy: An overview of the issues. *Journal of Curriculum Studies, 24,* 97–115.

Ball, S., & Goodson, I. (Eds.). (1985). *Teachers' lives and careers.* London-Philadelphia: Falmer Press.

Bandura, A. (1986). *The social foundations of thought and action: A social cognitive theory.* Englewood Cliffs, NJ: Prentice-Hall.

Bandura, A. (1989). Human agency in social cognitive theory. *American Psychologist, 44,* 1175–1184.

Bandura, A. (Ed.). (1995). *Self-efficacy in changing societies.* Cambridge, MA: Cambridge University Press.

Bandura, A. (1997). *Self-efficacy: The exercise of control.* New York: Freeman.

Barley, S. R., & Knight, D. B. (1992). Toward a cultural theory of stress complaints. In B. M. Staw & L. L. Cummings (Eds.), *Research in organizational behavior* (Vol. 14, pp. 1–48). Greenwich, CT: JAI Press.

Barth, A.-R. (1992). *Burnout bei Lehrern.* Göttingen: Hogrefe.

Bass, B. M. (1985). *Leadership and performance beyond expectations.* New York: Free Press.

Beck, C. L., & Gargiulo, R. M. (1983). Burnout in teachers of retarded and nonretarded children. *Journal of Educational Research, 76,* 169–173.

Becker, H. S. (1960). Notes on the concept of commitment. *American Journal of Sociology, 66,* 32–40.

Becker, H. S. (1977). Personal change in adult life. In B. Cosin et al. (Eds.), *School and society* (2nd ed.). London: Routledge and Kegan Paul.

Beehr, T. A., & Newman, J. E. (1978). Job stress, employee health, and organizational effectiveness: A facet analysis, model, and literature review. *Personnel Psychology, 31,* 665–699.

Beer, J., & Beer, J. (1992). Burnout and stress, depression, and self-esteem of teachers. *Psychological Reports, 71,* 1331–1336.

Begley, D. M. (1982, April). *Burnout among special education administrators.* Paper presented at the Annual International Convention of the Council for Exceptional Children, Houston, TX.

Bell, J. (1995). Teachers coping with change. In J. Bell (Ed.), *Teachers talk about teaching.* Buckingham: Open University Press.

Bensky, J. M., Shaw, S. F., Grouse, A. S., Bates, H., Dixon, B., & Beane, W. E. (1980). Public Law 94–142 and stress: A problem for educators. *Exceptional Children, 47,* 24–29.

Benson, N., & Malone, P. (1987). Teachers' beliefs about shared decision making and work alienation. *Education, 107,* 244–251.

Berger, P., & Luckman, T. (1966). *The social construction of reality: A treatise in the sociology of knowledge.* New York: Anchor Books.

Bernstein, B. (1975). *Class, codes and control: Vol. 3. Towards a theory of educational transmissions.* London: Routledge and Kegan Paul.

Bernstein, B., & Brannen, J. (Eds.). (1996). *Children, research and policy.* London: Taylor and Francis.

Best, R. (1995). *The caring teacher in the junior school.* London: Roehampton Institute.

Biener, K. (1988). *Streß: Epidemiologie und Prävention.* Bern: Huber.

Biklen, S. K. (1995). School work: *Gender and the cultural construction of teaching.* New York: Teachers College Press.

Bird, T., & Little, J. W. (1983, April). *Finding and founding of peer coaching: An interim report of the application of research on faculty relations to the implementation of two school improvement experiments.* Paper presented at the annual meeting of the American Educational Research Association, Montreal.

Black, P. J. (1994). Performance assessment and accountability: The experience in England and Wales. *Educational Evaluation and Policy Analysis, 16,* 191–203.

Blase, J. J. (1984). Teacher coping and school principal behaviors. *Contemporary Education, 22,* 173–191.

Blase, J. J. (1986). A quantitative analysis of sources of teacher stress: Consequences for performance. *American Educational Research Journal, 23,* 13–40.

Blase, J. J. (1988). The everyday political perspective of teachers. Vulnerability and conservatism. *International Journal of Qualitative Studies in Education, 1,* 125–141.

Blase, J. J., Dedrick, C., & Strathe, M. (1986). Leadership behavior of school principals in relation to teacher stress, satisfaction, and performance. *Journal of Humanistic Education & Development, 24,* 159–171.

Blase, J. J., & Greenfield, W. (1985). How teachers cope with stress: How administrators can help. *The Canadian Administrator, 25*(2), 1–5.

Blase, J. J., & Matthews, K. (1984) How principals stress teachers. *The Canadian School Executive, 4,* 8–11.

Blase, J. J., & Pajak, E. F. (1985). How discipline creates stress for teachers. *The Canadian School Executive, 4,* 8–10.

Blitz, T. (1988). *Female school principal burnout.* Unpublished master's thesis, Tel Aviv University, Faculty of Management.

Bloch, A. M. (1977). The battered teacher. *Today's Education, 66,* 58–62.

Bloome, D., & Willett, J. (1991). Towards a micropolitics of classroom interaction. In J. Blase (Ed.), *The politics of life in schools.* London: Sage.

Blumer, H. (1969). *Symbolic interactionism. Perspective and method.* Englewood Cliffs, NJ: Prentice-Hall.

Bolman, L. G., & Deal, T. E. (1991). *Reframing organizations.* San Francisco: Jossey-Bass.

Bönner, K. H., & Walenzik, M. (1982). Die Pulsfrequenz als physiologischer Parameter der Belastung von Lehrern durch den Unterricht in einer Sonderschule für Lernbehinderte. *Heilpädagogische Forschung, 9,* 375–385.

Borg, M. G. (1990). Occupational stress in British educational settings: A review. *Educational Psychology, 10,* 103–126.

Borg, M. G., & Falzon, J. M. (1989). Stress and job satisfaction among primary school teachers in Malta. *Educational Review, 41,* 271–279.

Borg, M. G., & Riding, R. J. (1991a). Towards a model for the determinants of occupational stress among schoolteachers. *European Journal of Psychology of Education, 6,* 355–373.

Borg, M. G., & Riding, R. J. (1991b). Occupational stress and satisfaction in teaching, *British Education Research Journal, 17,* 263–281.

Borg, M. G., & Riding, R. J. (1993). Occupational stress and job satisfaction among school administrators. *Journal of Educational Administration, 31,* 4–21.

Borg, M. G., Riding, R. J., & Falzon, J. M. (1991). Stress in teaching: A study of occupational stress and its determinants, job satisfaction and career commitment among primary schoolteachers. *Educational Psychology, 11,* 59–75.

Boyle, M., & Woods, P. (1995). *The composite head; coping with changes in the primary headteacher's role.* Paper presented at European Conference on Educational Research, Bath, September.

Brandt, R. (1989). On teacher empowerment: A conversation with Ann Liebermann. *Educational Leadership, 46,* 23–26.

Brenner, S. O. (1982). Work, health, and well-being for Swedish elementary school teachers. *Stress Research Reports No. 158.* Laboratory for Clinical Stress Research, Stockholm.

Brenner, S. O., Sörbom, D., & Wallius, E. (1985). The stress chain. A longitudinal confirmatory study of teacher stress, coping and social support. *Journal of Occupational Psychology, 58,* 1–13.

Brett, J. M. (1980). The effect of job transfer on employees and their families. In C. L. Cooper & R. Payne (Eds.), *Current concerns in occupational stress* (pp. 99–136). New York: Wiley.

Brissie, J. S., Hoover-Dempsey, K. V., & Bassler, O. C. (1988). Individual, situational contributors to teacher burnout. *Journal of Educational Research, 82,* 106–112.

Brookfield, S. D. (1991). *Understanding and facilitating adult learning.* San Francisco: Jossey-Bass.

Brubacher, J. W., Case, C. W., & Reagan, T. G. (1994). *Becoming a reflective educator. How to build a culture of inquiry in the schools.* Newbury Park, CA: Corwin Press.

Bryk, A. S., Easton, J. Q., Kerbow, D., Rollow, S. G., & Sebring, P. A. (1993, July). *A view from the elementary schools: The state of Chicago school reform.* Chicago: University of Chicago, Consortium on Chicago School Research.

Buhr, J., & Scheuch, K. (1991). Entwicklung des Gesundheitszustandes von Pädagogen eines Landkreises im Zeitraum von 1978–1988. In K. Scheuch (Ed.), *Einflußfaktoren auf den Gesundheitszustand von Pädagogen* (pp. 21–26). Berlin: VWB.

Burke, R. J., & Greenglass, E. R. (1986). Work and family conflict. In C. L. Cooper & I. Robertson (Eds.), *International review of industrial and organizational psychology.* New York: Wiley.

Burke, R. J., & Greenglass, E. R. (1989a). Sex differences in psychological burnout in teachers. *Psychological Reports, 65,* 55–63.

Burke, R. J., & Greenglass, E. R. (1989b). The clients' role in psychological burnout in teachers and administrators. *Psychological Reports, 64,* 1299–1306.

Burke, R. J., & Greenglass, E. (1989c). Psychological burnout among men and women in teaching: An examination of the Cherniss model. *Human Relations, 42,* 261–273.

Burke, R. J., & Greenglass, E. R. (1993). Work stress, role conflict, social support, and psychological burnout among teachers. *Psychological Reports, 73,* 371–380.

Burke, R., & Greenglass, E. (1994). Towards an understanding of work satisfactions and emotional well-being of school-based educators. *Stress Medicine, 10,* 177–184.

Burke, R. J., & Greenglass, E. R. (1995). A longitudinal study of psychological burnout in teachers. *Human Relations, 48,* 187–202.

Burke, R., & Leiter, M. P. (in press). Contemporary organizational realities and professional efficacy: Downsizing, reorganization and transition. In P. Dewe,

T. Cox, & M. P. Leiter (Eds.), *Stress, coping, & health in organizations* Washington, DC: Taylor & Francis.

Burns, J. M. (1978). *Leadership*. New York: Harper & Row.

Buunk, B. P., & Schaufeli, W. B. (1993). Burnout: A perspective from social comparison theory. In W. B. Schaufeli, C. Maslach, & T. Marek (Eds.), *Professional burnout: Recent developments in theory and research* (pp. 53–69). Washington, DC: Taylor & Francis.

Byrne, B. M. (1989). *A primer of LISREL: Basic applications and programming for confirmatory factor analytic models*. New York: Springer-Verlag.

Byrne, B. M. (1991a). Burnout: Investigating the impact of background variables for elementary, intermediate, secondary, and university educators. *Teaching and Teacher Education: An International Journal of Research, 7*, 197–209.

Byrne, B. M. (1991b). The Maslach Burnout Inventory: Validating factorial structure and invariance across intermediate, secondary, and university educators. *Multivariate Behavioral Research, 26*, 583–605.

Byrne, B. M. (1993). The Maslach Burnout Inventory: Testing for factorial validity and invariance across elementary, intermediate, and secondary teachers. *Journal of Occupational and Organizational Psychology, 66*, 197–212.

Byrne, B. M. (1994a). Burnout: Testing for the validity, replication, and invariance of causal structure across elementary, intermediate, and secondary teachers. *American Educational Research Journal, 31*, 645–673.

Byrne, B. M. (1994b). Testing for the factorial validity, replication, and invariance of a measuring instrument: A paradigmatic application based on the Maslach Burnout Inventory. *Multivariate Behavioral Research, 29*, 289–311.

Byrne, B. M. (1994c). *Structural equation modeling with EQS and EQS/Windows: Basic concepts, applications, and programming*. Newbury Park, CA: Sage.

Calderwood, D. (1989). Some implications of role conflict and role ambiguity as stressors in a comprehensive school. *School Organisation, 9*, 311–314.

Campbell, R. J. (1993). The National Curriculum in primary schools: A dream at conception, a nightmare at delivery. In C. Chitty & B. Simon (Eds.), *Education answers back: Critical responses to government policy*. London: Lawrence and Wishart.

Campbell, R. J., Evans, L., St. J. Neill, S. R., & Packwood, A. (1991a). *Workloads, achievements and stress: Two follow-up studies of teacher time in Key Stage 1*. Policy Analysis Unit, Department of Education, University of Warwick.

Campbell, R. J., Evans, L., St. J. Neill, S. R., & Packwood, A. (1991b, November). *The use and management of infant teachers time – some policy issues*. Paper presented at Policy Analysis Unit Seminar Warwick.

Campbell, R. J., & St. J. Neill, S. (1990). *Thirteen hundred and thirty days*. Final report of a pilot study of teacher time in Key Stage 1, commissioned by the Assistant Masters and Mistresses Association.

Campbell, R. J., & St. J. Neill, S. (1994a). *Curriculum at Key Stage 1: Teacher commitment and policy failure*. Harlow, Essex: Longman.

Campbell, R. J., & St. J. Neill, S. (1994b). *Primary teachers at work*. London: Routledge.

Capel, S. A. (1987). The incidence of and influences on stress and burnout in secondary school teachers. *British Journal of Educational Psychology, 57*, 279–288.

Capel, S. (1989). Stress and burnout in secondary school teachers: Some causal factors. In M. Cole & S. Walker (Eds.), *Teaching and stress* (pp. 36–48). Philadelphia: Open University Press.

Capel, S. A. (1992). Stress and burnout in teachers. *European Journal of Teacher Education, 15*, 197–211.

Capper, P. (1994). *Participation and partnership: Exploring shared decision making in twelve New Zealand secondary schools*. Wellington: New Zealand Post Primary Teachers' Association.

Carr, W., & Kemmis, S. (1986). *Becoming critical*. Lewes: Falmer Press.

Carter, K. (1993). The place of story in the study of teaching and teacher education. *Educational Researcher, 22*, 5–12, 18.

Cascio, W. (1993). Downsizing: What do we know? What have we learned? *Academy of Management Executive, 7*, 95–102.

Cecil, M. A., & Forman, S. G. (1990). Effects of stress inoculation training and coworker support groups on teachers' stress. *Journal of School Psychology, 28*, 105–118.

Cedoline, A. J. (1982). *Job burnout in public education: Symptoms, causes, and survival skills*. New York: Teachers College Press.

Chapman, J., & Boyd, W. L. (1986). Decentralization, devolution, and the school principal: Australian lessons on statewide educational reform. *Educational Administration Quarterly, 22*(4), 28–58.

Cherniss, C. (1980a). *Staff burnout: Job stress in the human services*. Beverly Hills, CA: Sage.

Cherniss, C. (1980b). *Professional burnout in human service organisations*. New York: Praeger.

Cherniss, C. (1988). Observed supervisory behavior and teacher burnout in special education. *Exceptional Children, 54*, 449–454.

Cherniss, C. (1989). Burnout in new professionals: A long-term follow-up study. *Journal of Health and Human Resources Administration, 12*, 14–24.

Cherniss, C. (1990). Natural recovery from burnout: Results from a 10-year follow-up study. *Journal of Health and Human Resources Administration, 13*, 132–154.

Cherniss, C. (1991, April). *Impact of stress on career adaptation in teachers: A long-term follow-up study*. Paper presented at the annual conference of the American Educational Research Association, Chicago, IL.

Cherniss, C. (1992). Long-term consequences of burnout: An exploratory study. *Journal of Organizational Behavior, 13*, 1–11.

Cherniss, C. (1993). Role of professional self-efficacy in the etiology and amelioration of burnout. In W. B. Schaufeli, C. Maslach, & T. Marek (Eds.), *Professional burnout* (pp. 135–150). Washington DC: Taylor & Francis.

Cherniss, C. (1995). *Beyond burnout: Helping teachers, nurses, therapists and lawyers recover from stress and disillusionment*. New York: Routledge.

Cichon, D. J., & Koff, R. H. (1980). Stress and teaching. *NASSP Bulletin, 64*, 91–104.

Clement, M. (1995). *De professionele ontwikkeling van leerkrachten Basisonderwijs. De spanning tussen autonomie en collegialiteit* [The professional development of primary school teachers: The tension between autonomy and collegiality]. Unpublished doctoral dissertation, K. U. Leuven, Center for Educational Policy and Innovation, Leuven, Belgium.

Clement, M., & Staessens, K. (1993). The professional development of primary school teachers and the tensions between autonomy and collegiality. In F. K. Kieviet & R. Vandenberghe (Eds.), *School culture, schoolimprovement and teacher development* (129–152). Leiden: DSWO Press.

Clement, M., & Vandenberghe, R. (1997). *Teachers' professional development: A solitary or collegial (ad)venture*. Paper presented at the annual meeting of the American Educational Research Association, Chicago.

Cohen, D. K. (1990). A revolution in one classroom: The case of Mrs. Oublier. *Educational Evaluation and Policy Analysis, 12*, 327–346.

Cohen, D. K., & Ball, D. L. (1990). Relations between policy and practice: A commentary. *Educational Evaluation and Policy Analysis, 12*, 331–338.

Cole, A. L. (1997). Impediments to reflective practice: Toward a new agenda for re-
search on teaching. *Teachers and Teaching: Theory and Practice, 3,* 7–27.
Conley, S. (1991). Review of research on teacher participation in school decision
making. In G. Grant (Ed.), *Review of research in education* (Vol. 17, pp. 225–266).
Washington, DC: American Educational Research Association.
Conley, D. T. (1993). *Roadmap to restructuring: Policies, practices and the emerging vi-
sions of schooling.* University of Oregon: ERIC Clearinghouse of Educational
Management.
Connors, L. J., & Epstein, J. L. (1994). *Taking stock: Views of teachers, parents, and stu-
dents on school, family, and community partnerships in high schools.* Center on Fam-
ilies, Communities, Schools, and Childrens' Learning: Report #25, August.
Cooper, C. L., & Kelly, M. (1993). Occupational stress in head teachers: A national
UK study. *British Journal of Educational Psychology, 63,* 130–143.
Cooper C. L., & Marshall, J. (1976). Occupational sources of stress: A review of the
literature relating to coronary heart disease and mental ill health. *Journal of
Occupational Psychology, 49,* 11–28.
Cooper, C. L., & Marshall, J. (1978a). *Understanding executive stress.* New York:
Macmillan.
Cooper, C. L., & Marshall, J. (1978b). Sources of managerial and white collar
stress. In C. L. Cooper & R. Payne (Eds.), *Stress at work* (pp. 81–105). New York:
Wiley.
Cooper, H. M. (1984). *The integrative research review: A systematic approach.* Beverly
Hills: Sage.
Cordes, C. L., & Dougherty, T. W. (1993). A review and integration of research on
job burnout. *Academy of Management Review, 18,* 621–656.
Cox, T. (1990). The recognition and measurement of stress: Conceptual and
methodological issues. In J. R. Wilson & N. Corlett (Eds.), *Evaluation of human
work* (pp. 628–647). London: Taylor & Francis.
Cox, T., Boot, N., Cox, S., & Hanson, S. (1988). Stress in schools: An organizational
perspective. *Work & Stress, 2,* 353–362.
Cox, T., Kuk, G., & Leiter, M. P. (1993). Burnout, health, work stress, and organizational healthiness. In W. B. Schaufeli, C. Maslach, & T. Marek (Eds.), *Professional
burnout: Recent developments in theory and research* (pp. 177–193). Washington,
DC: Taylor & Francis.
Cox, T., & Leiter, M. (1992). The health of health care organizations. *Work & Stress,
6,* 219–227.
Croall, J. (1995, February 7). Some of the children's problems were horrendous; the
stories they told made you want to weep. *The Guardian,* pp. 6–7.
Croll, P. (Ed.). (1996). *Teachers, pupils and primary schooling: Continuity and change.*
London: Cassell.
Cronbach, L. J., & Meehl, P. E. (1955). Construct validity in psychological tests. *Psy-
chological Bulletin, 52,* 281–302.
Cross, K. P. (1987). The adventures of education in wonderland: Implementing ed-
ucation reform. *Phi Delta Kappan, 68,* 496–502.
Csikszentmihaliy, M. (1985). *Das flow-Erlebnis.* Stuttgart: Klett.
Cummings, O. W., & Nall, R. L. (1983). Relationships of leadership style and burn-
out to counsellor's perceptions of their jobs, themselves, and their clients.
Counsellor Education and Supervision, 22, 227–234.
Cunningham, W. G. (1982). Teacher burnout: Stylish fad or profound problem.
Planning and Changing, 12, 219–244.
Cunningham, W. G. (1983). Teacher burnout – solutions for the 1980's: A review of
the literature. *The Urban Review, 15,* 37–51.

322   *References*

Cusack, I. (1993, January 8). Looking back in anger, aged 28. *The Times Educational Supplement*, p. 7.

Dadds, M. (1992). Monty Python and the three wise men. *Cambridge Journal of Education, 22,* 129–141.

Dadds, M. (1995). *Passionate enquiry and school development: A story about teacher action research.* London: Falmer Press.

Daily Telegraph, 1989, May 29.

Daniel, J., & Szabo, I. (1993). Psychological burnout in professions with permanent education. *Studia Psychologica, 35,* 412–414.

D'Arcy, J. (1990). Researching teacher stress: A methodological review. *Irish Educational Studies, 9,* 76–87.

Darling-Hammond, L., & Berry, B. (1988). *The evolution of teacher policy* (JRE-01). Santa Monica: Rand Corporation.

Darling-Hammond, L., & Wise, A. E. (1985). Beyond standardization: State standards and school improvement. *Elementary School Journal, 85,* 315–335.

Darwin, C. (1985). *The origin of species by means of natural selection.* Harmondsworth, England: Penguin.

David, J. L., & Peterson, S. M. (1984). *Can schools improve themselves? A study of school-based improvement programs.* Palo Alto, CA: Bay Area Research Group.

Dear Dad, no one can fight forever. (1993, September 17). *Times Educational Supplement,* p. 2.

Dearing, R. (1994). *Review of the National Curriculum: Final report.* London: School Curriculum and Assessment Authority (SCAA) Publications.

DeCharms, R. (1984). Motivation enhancement in educational settings. In R. E. Ames & C. Ames (Eds.), *Research on motivation in education: Vol. 1. Student motivation* (pp. 275–310). Orlando: Academic Press.

Deci, E. L., & Ryan, R. M. (1985). *Intrinsic motivation and self-determinism in human behavior.* New York: Plenum Press.

De Heus, P., Schaufeli, W. B., & Diekstra, R. F. W. (1996). *Specificity and epidemiology of burnout. Results from a large-scale omnibus survey.* Manuscript submitted for publication.

De Heus, P., Schouten, M. H., & Diekstra, R. F. W. (1994). *Werken onder druk. Technisch rapport* [Working under pressure. Technical report]. Department of Clinical, Health & Personality Psychology, University of Leiden.

Densmore, K. (1987). Professionalism, proletarianization and teachers' work. In T. Popkewitz (Ed.), *Critical studies in teacher education* (pp. 130–160). Lewes: Falmer Press.

Denzin, N. (1989). *Interpretive interactionism.* Newbury Park: Sage.

Depaepe, M., De Vroede, M., & Simon, F. (Eds.). (1993). *Geen trede meer om op te staan. De maatschappelijke positie van onderwijzers en onderwijzeressen tijdens de voorbije eeuw* [No place to stand on: The social position of primary school teachers during the last century]. Kapellen-Brussel: Pelckmans-Christen Onderwijzersverbond.

Derogatis, L. R., Lipman, R. S., & Covi, L. (1973). SCL-90: An outpatient psychiatric rating scale. Preliminary report. *Psychopharmalogical Bulletin, 9,* 13–28.

Der Spiegel. (1993). Horrorjob Lehrer. Nervenkrieg im Klassenzimmer. Nr. 24.

Dewe, P. J., & Guest, D. E. (1990). Methods of coping with stress at work: A conceptual analysis and empirical study of measurement issues. *Journal of Organizational Behavior, 11,* 135–150.

Diekstra, R. F. W., De Heus, P., Schouten, M. H., & Houtman, I. L. D. (1994). *Werken onder druk. Een onderzoek naar omvang en factoren van werkstress in Nederland* [Working under pressure. An investigation of dimensions and factors of work stress in the Netherlands]. Den Haag: VUGA.

Dirken, J. M. (1969). *Arbeid en stress. Het vaststellen van arbeidsproblemen in werksitu-aties* [Work and stress. Detecting problems in work situations]. Groningen: Wolters-Noordhof.

Doyle, W. (1986). Classroom organization and management. In M. Wittrock (Ed.), *Handbook of research on teaching* (3rd ed., pp. 392–431). New York: Macmillan.

Drummond, M. J. (1991). The child and the primary curriculum – from policy to practice. *The Curriculum Journal, 2,* 115–124.

Drummond, M. J. (1993). *Assessing children's learning,* London: Fulton.

Drummond, M. J. (1994). Personal communication.

Dubberley, W. (1988). Humour as resistance. *International Journal of Qualitative Studies in Education, 1,* 109–123.

Duke, D. (1994, April). *Drift, detachment, and the need for teacher leadership.* Paper presented at the annual meeting of the American Educational Research Association, New Orleans.

Dunham, J. (1983). Coping with organizational stress. In A. Paisey (Ed.), *The effective teacher.* London: Ward Lock Educational.

Dunham, J. (1992). *Stress in teaching* (2nd ed.). New York: Routledge.

Durkheim, E. (1970). *Suicide: A study in sociology.* London: Routledge.

Dworkin, A. G. (1987). *Teacher burnout in the public schools: Structural causes and consequences for children.* Albany: State University of New York Press.

Dworkin, A. G., Haney, C. A., Dworkin, R. J., & Telschow, R. L. (1990). Stress and illness behavior among urban public school teachers. *Educational Administration Quarterly, 26,* 60–72.

Edelwich, J., & Brodsky, A. (1980). *Burnout: Stages of disillusionment in the helping professions.* New York: Human Sciences Press.

Edgarton, S. K. (1977). Teachers in role conflict: The hidden dilemma. *Phi Delta Kappan, 59,* 120–122.

Eichenbaum, L., & Orbach, S. (1983). *What do women want?* London: Michael Joseph.

Einsiedel, A. A., & Tully, H. A. (1981). Methodological considerations in studying the burnout phenomenon. In J. W. Jones (Ed.), *The burnout syndrome: Current research, theory, interventions* (pp. 89–106). Park Ridge, IL: London House.

Elbing, E., & Dietrich, G. (1982). *Lehrerurteile zu Aspekten ihrer Berufssituation.* Universität München: Institut für Empirische Pädagogik.

Elchardus, M. (Ed.). (1994). *De school staat niet alleen. Verslag van de commissie Samenleving-Onderwijs aan de Koning Boudewijnstichting* [Schools don't stand alone. Report from the Commission "Society and Education to the Koning Boudewijn-Foundation"]. Brussel-Kappellen: Koning Boudewijnstichting-Pelckmans.

Elliott, J. (1991). *Action research for educational change.* Buckingham: Open University Press.

Elliott, J., Bridges D., Ebbutt D., Gibson R., & Nias J. (1981). *School accountability.* Oxford: Blackwell.

Elmore, R. (1995). Teaching, learning, and school organizations: Principles of practice and the regularities of schooling. *Educational Administration Quarterly, 31,* 355–374.

Elmore, R. F., & McLaughlin, M. W. (1988). *Steady work: Policy, practice, and the reform of American education* (R-3574-NIE/RC). Santa Monica, CA: Rand.

Elmore, R. F., Peterson, P. L., & McCarthey, S. J. (1996). *Restructuring in the classroom: Teaching, learning, and school organization.* San Francisco: Jossey-Bass.

Enzmann, D., & Kleiber, D. (1989). *Helfer-Leiden. Streß und Burnout in psychosozialen Berufen.* Heidelberg: Asanger.

Esteve, J. M. (1992). *Omal-estar docente.* Lisbon: Escher.

Etzion, D. (1984). The moderating effect of social support on the relationships of stress and burnout. *Journal of Applied Psychology, 69*, 615–622.

Evans, L., Packwood, A., Neill, S., & Campbell, R. J. (1994). *The meaning of infant teachers' work*. London: Routledge.

Evers, T. B. (1987). *Factors affecting teacher job satisfaction in a number of high schools in Michigan*. Paper presented at the American Educational Research Association Annual Meeting, Washington.

Evetts, J. (1994). *Becoming a secondary headteacher*. London: Cassell.

Ezrahi, Y., & Shirom, A. (1986, July). *Construct validation of burnout*. Paper presented at the 21st Congress of the International Association of Applied Psychology, Jerusalem, Israel.

Farber, B. A. (1984). Stress and burnout in suburban teachers. *Journal of Educational Research, 77*, 325–331.

Farber, B. A. (1991a). *Crisis in education: Stress and burnout in the American teacher*. San Francisco, CA: Jossey-Bass.

Farber, B. (1991b). Teacher burnout: A psycho-educational perspective. *Teachers College Record, 83*, 235–243.

Farber, B. A., & Miller, J. (1981). Teacher burnout: A psycho-educational perspective. *Teachers College Record, 83*, 235–243.

Fay, C. (1990, April). *Teaching and leading: In the teacher's voice*. Paper presented at the annual meeting of the American Educational Research Association, Boston.

Feiman-Nemser, S., & Parker, M. B. (1994). *Mentor teachers: Local guides or educational companions?* East Lansing: Michigan State University, National Center for Research on Teacher Learning.

Feitler, F. C., & Tokar, E. (1982). Getting a handle on teacher stress: How bad is the problem? *Educational Leadership, 39*, 456–458.

Fimian, M. J. (1988). The alpha and split-half reliability of the teacher stress inventory. *Psychology in the Schools, 25*, 110–118.

Filipp, S. H. (1990). *Kritische Lebensereignisse* [Critical experiences]. München: Psychologie Verlags Union.

Fiol, C., & Lyles, M. (1985). Organizational learning. *Academy of Management Review, 10*, 803–813.

Firestone, W. A. (1977). Participation and influence in the planning of educational change. *The Journal of Applied Behavioral Science, 13*, 167–183.

Firestone, W. A., & Bader, B. D. (1992) *Redesigning teaching: Professionalism or bureaucracy?* Albany: State University of New York Press.

Firestone, W. A., Bader, B. D., Massel, D., & Rosenblum, S. (1992). Recent trends in state educational reform: Assessing the prospects. *Teachers College Record, 94*, 254–277.

Firestone, W. A., & Pennell, J. R., (1993). Teacher commitment, working conditions, and differential incentive policies. *Review of Educational Research, 63*, 489–525.

Fishbein, M., & Ajzen, I. (1975). *Belief, attitude, intention, and behavior: An introduction to theory and research*. Reading, MA: Addison-Wesley.

Fisher, P. (1995, January 27). Conditions are the key to discontent. *The Times Educational Supplement*, p. 12.

Fiske, S. T., & Taylor, S. E. (1991). *Social cognition*. New York: McGraw-Hill.

Fletcher, B., & Payne, R. L. (1982). Levels or reported stressors and strains amongst schoolteachers: Some UK data. *Educational Review, 34*, 267–277.

Ford, M. (1992). *Motivating humans: Goals, emotions, and personal agency beliefs*. Newbury Park, CA: Sage.

Foucault, M. (1980). *Power/knowledge: Selected interviews and other writings* (C. Gordon, Ed.). New York: Pantheon.

French, J. R. P. (1973). Person-role fit. *Occupational Mental Health, 3,* 15–20.
French, J. R. P., & Caplan, R. D. (1972). Organizational stress and individual strain. In A. J. Marrow (Ed.), *The failure of success* (pp. 30–67). New York: Amacom.
French, J. R. P., Rodgers, W. L., & Cobb, S. (1974). Adjustment as person-environment fit. In G. Coelho, D. Hamburg, & J. Adams (Eds.), *Coping and adaptation* (pp. 316–333). New York: Basic Books.
Freudenberger, H. J. (1974). Staff burnout. *Journal of Social Issues, 30,* 159–165.
Freudenberger, H. J. (1975). The staff burnout syndrome in alternative institutions. *Psychotherapy: Theory, Research, & Practice, 12,* 72–83.
Freudenberger, H. J. (1977). Burn-out: Occupational hazard of the child care worker. *Child Care Quarterly, 6*(2), 90–99.
Freudenberger, H. J. (1983). Burnout: Contemporary issues, trends, and concerns. In B. A. Farber (Ed.), *Stress and burnout in the human service professions* (pp. 23–28). New York: Pergamon.
Freudenberger, H. J., & Richelson, G. (1980). *Burnout: The high cost of high achievement.* New York: Anchor Press.
Friedman, I. (1991). High- and low-burnout schools: School culture aspects of teacher burnout. *Journal of Educational Research, 84,* 325–333.
Friedman, I. A (1993). Burnout in teachers: The concept and its unique core meaning. *Educational and Psychological Measurement, 53,* 1035–1044.
Friedman, I. A. (1995a). School principal burnout: The concept and its components. *Journal of Organizational Behavior, 16,* 191–198.
Friedman, I. A. (1995b). Measuring school principal experienced burnout. *Educational and Psychological Measurement, 55,* 641–651.
Friedman, I. A. (1995c). *Being a school principal: The stress, the burnout and the coping* (Hebrew with English summary). Jerusalem: The Henrietta Szold Institute.
Friedman, I. A. (1995d). Student behavior patterns contributing to teacher burnout. *Journal of Educational Research, 88,* 281–289.
Friedman, I. A., & Farber, B. (1992). Professional self-concept as a predictor of teacher burnout. *Journal of Educational Research, 86,* 28–35.
Friedman, I. A., & Krongold, N. (1993). *Teacher-student relations: The student's point of view* (Hebrew). Jerusalem: The Henrietta Szold Institute.
Friedman, I. A., & Lotan, I. (1985). *Teacher burnout in Israel* (Hebrew with English summary). Jerusalem: The Henrietta Szold Institute.
Friedman, I. A., & Lotan, I. (1993). *Stress and burnout in teaching: Causes and prevention* (Hebrew). Jerusalem: The Henrietta Szold Institute.
Friesen, D., Prokop, C. M., & Sarros, J. C. (1988). Why teachers burn out. *Educational Research Quarterly, 12,* 9–19.
Friesen, D., & Sarros, J. C. (1989). Sources of burnout among educators. *Journal of Organizational Behavior, 10,* 179–188.
Fruytier, B. (1988). De resultaten van 18 gevalstudies (The results of 18 cases). *Meso, 38,* 3–12.
Fullan, M. (1991). *The new meaning of educational change.* New York: Teachers College Press.
Fullan, M. (1993). *Change forces: Probing the depths of educational reform.* London: Falmer.
Fullan, M., & Hargreaves, A. (1988). *What's worth fighting for in your school? Working together for improvement.* Buckingham: Open University Press.
Galloway, D., Panckhurst, F., Boswell, K., Boswell, C., & Green, K. (1987). Sources of stress for class teachers in New Zealand primary schools. *Pastoral Care in Education, 5,* 28–36.

326   *References*

Garbarino, J. (1995). *Raising children in a socially toxic environment.* San Francisco, CA: Jossey-Bass.

Garson, B. (1988). *The electronic sweatshop.* New York: Simon & Schuster.

Gehmacher, E. (1980). *Die Schule im Spannungsfeld von Schülern, Eltern und Lehrern.* Wien: Österreichischer Bundesverlag Jugend und Volk.

Geijsel, F., van den, Berg, R. & Sleegers, P. (in press). The innovative capacity of schools in primary education: A second qualitative study. *International Journal of Qualititative Studies in Education.*

Gerwing, Ch. (1994). Streß in der Schule – Belastungswahrnehmung von Lehrerinnen und Lehrern. *Zeitschrift für Pädagogische Psychologie, 8,* 41–53.

Giesbers, J. H. G. I., & Sleegers, P. (1994). The Marx-models as conceptual models in school effectiveness research. *School Organisation, 14,* 91–102.

Gilligan, C. (1982). *In a different voice.* Cambridge, MA: Harvard University Press.

Ginsberg, R., & Bennett, A. (1981). "I don't get no respect." *Vocational Education, 56,* 34–36.

Gitlin, A., & Margonis, F. (1995). The political aspect of reform: Teacher resistance as good sense. *American Journal of Education, 103,* 377–405.

Glaser, B. G., & Strauss, A. L. (1971). *Status passage.* Chicago: Aldine.

Glass, G. V., McGaw, B., & Smith, M. L. (1984). *Meta-analysis in social research.* Beverly Hills: Sage.

Gmelch, W. H. (1983). Stress, health and coping strategies of public school administrators. *Phi Delta Kappan, 64,* 512–514.

Goffman, E. (1968). *Asylums.* Harmondsworth, England: Penguin.

Gold, Y. (1984). Burnout: A major problem for the teaching profession. *Education, 104,* 271–274.

Golembiewski, R. T., & Munzenrider, R. (1984). Phases of psychological burnout and organizational covariants. *Journal of Health and Human Resources Administration, 7,* 264–289.

Golembiewski, R. T., Munzenrider, R., & Carter, D. (1983). Phases of progressive burnout and their worksite covariants. *Journal of Applied Behavioral Science, 13,* 461–482.

Golombiewski, R. T., Munzenrider, R. F., & Stevenson, J. (1986). *Stress in organizations.* New York: Praeger.

Gooding, D. (1990). *Experiment and meaning: Human agency and scientific observation and experiment.* London: Couwer Academic Publishers.

Goodson, I. (1984). The use of life histories in the study of teaching. In M. Hammersley (Ed.), *The ethnography of schooling* (pp. 129–154). Driffield: Nafferton Books.

Goodson, I. (1995). The story so far: Personal knowledge and the political. *International Journal of Qualitative Studies in Education, 8,* 89–98.

Gooren, W. A. J. (1989). Kwetsbare en weerbare scholen en het welbevinden van de leraar (Vulnerable and strong schools and teachers' well-being). In J. Scheerens, & J. Verhoeven (Eds.), *Schoolorganisatie, beleid en onderwijskwaliteit* (School organization, policy and educational quality) (pp. 89–98). Amsterdam: Swets & Zeitlinger.

Greenberg, S. F. (1984). *Stress and the teaching profession.* Baltimore: Paul H. Brookes.

Greenglass, E. R., & Burke, R. J. (1990). A gender-role perspective of coping and burnout. *Applied Psychology: An International Review, 39,* 5–27.

Greenglass, E. R., Fiksenbaum, L., & Burke, R. J. (1994). The relationship between social support and burnout over time in teachers. *Journal of Social Behavior and Personality, 9,* 219–230.

Griffin, G. A. (1995). Influences of shared decision making on school and classroom activity: Conversations with five teachers. *Elementary School Journal, 96,* 29–45.

Grimm, M. A. (1993). *Kognitive Landschaften von Lehrern.* Frankfurt: Lang.

Grumet, M. (1988). *Bitter milk: Women and teaching,* Amherst: University of Massachusetts Press.

Guskey, T. R. (1984). The influence of change in instructional effectiveness upon the affective characteristics of teachers. *American Educational Research Journal, 21,* 245–259.

Häbler, H., & Kunz, A. (1985). *Qualität der Arbeit und Verkürzung der Arbeitszeit in Schule und Hochschule.* München: IMU-Institut.

Hacker, W. (1986). *Arbeitspsychologie.* Bern: Huber.

Hacker, W., & Richter, P. (1984). *Psychische Fehlbeanspruchung: Psychische Ermüdung, Monotonie, Sättigung und Streß.* Berlin: Springer.

Hackman, J. R., & Oldham, G. R. (1980). *Work redesign.* Reading, MA: Addison-Wesley.

Haigh, G. (1995, February 10). To be handled with care. *The Times Educational Supplement,* pp. 3–4.

Hall, G. E., & Hord, S. M. (1984). *Change in schools: Facilitating the process.* Albany: State University of New York Press.

Hallinger, P., & Hausman, C. (1994). From Attila the Hun to Mary Had a Little Lamb. In J. Murphy & K. S. Louis (Eds.), *Reshaping the principalship* (pp. 154–176). Thousand Oaks, CA: Corwin.

Handy, J. A. (1988). Theoretical and methodological problems within occupational stress and burnout research. *Human Relations, 41,* 351–369.

Hanson, D., & Herrington, M. (1976). *From college to classroom: The probationary year.* London: Routledge and Kegan Paul.

Hargreaves, A. (1978). Towards a theory of classroom strategies. In L. Barton & R. Meighan (Eds.), *Sociological interpretations of schooling and classrooms.* Driffield: Nafferton Books.

Hargreaves, A. (1990). Teachers' work and the politics of time and space. *International Journal of Qualitative Studies in Education, 3,* 303–320.

Hargreaves, A. (1993). Individualism and individuality: Reinterpreting the teacher culture. In J. W. Little & M. W. McLaughlin (Eds.), *Teachers' work. Individuals, colleagues and contexts* (pp. 51–76). New York: Teachers College Press.

Hargreaves, A. (1994). *Changing teachers, changing times: Teachers' work and culture in the postmodern age.* London: Cassell.

Hargreaves, A. (1995). Development and desire: A postmodern perspective. In T. R. Guskey & M. Huberman (Eds.), *Professional development in education. New paradigms and practices* (pp. 9–34). New York–London: Teachers College Press.

Hargreaves, A., & Macmillan, R. (1995). The balkanization of secondary school teaching. In L. S. Siskin & J. W. Little (Eds.), *Subjects in question: Departmental organization and the high school.* New York: Teachers College Press.

Hargreaves, A., & Tucker, E. (1991). Teaching and guilt: Exploring the feelings of teaching. *Teaching and Teacher Education, 7,* 491–505.

Hargreaves, D. H. (1994). The new professionalism: The synthesis of professional and institutional development. *Teaching and Teacher Education, 10,* 423–438.

Harrison, W. D. (1983). A social competence model of burnout. In B. A. Farber (Ed.), *Stress and burnout in the human service professions* (pp. 29–39). New York: Pergamon.

Hart, A. W., & Murphy, M. J. (1990). New teachers react to redesigned teacher work. *American Journal of Education, 98,* 224–250.

Hawes, L. (1995, February 12). Teachers blamed for putting children first. *The Observer.*

Hayes, D. (1995). The primary heads' tale. *Educational Management and Administration, 23*, 233–244.

Heck, S. F., & Williams, C. R. (1984). *The complex roles of the teacher: An ecological perspective*. New York: Teachers College Press.

Heckhausen, H. (1991). *Motivation and action*. Berlin, Germany: Springer.

Henderson, P. (1995). *Eagles or boiled frogs: How the professional can cope with stress*. Unpublished paper, Cambridge.

Henson, B. E., & Hall, P. M. (1993). Linking performance evaluation and career ladder programs: Reactions of teachers and principals in one district. *Elementary School Journal, 93*, 323–345.

Hertog, P. den. (1990). *Persoonlijkheidskenmerken en causale attributies* (Personality characteristics and causal attributions). Amsterdam: Thesis Publishers.

Hiebert, B. (1985). *Stress and teachers: The Canadian scene*. Toronto, Canada: Canadian Education Association.

Hipp, K. A., & Bredeson, P. (1995). Exploring connections between teacher efficacy and principals' leadership behaviors. *Journal of School Leadership, 5*, 136–150.

Hobfoll, S. E. (1988). *The ecology of stress*. Washington, DC: Hemisphere.

Hobfoll, S. E. (1989). Conservation of resources: A new attempt at conceptualizing stress. *American Psychologist, 44*, 513–524.

Hoerr, W. A., & West, C. K. (1992, April). *Teacher burnout and school misbehavior: Differentiating sources of emotional exhaustion and depersonalization in the classroom*. Paper presented at the American Educational Research Association Annual Meeting, San Francisco.

Hofer, M. (1986). *Sozialpsychologie erzieherischen Handelns*. Göttingen: Hogrefe.

Hogan, R., & Hogan, J. C. (1982). Subjective correlates of stress and human performance. In E. A. Alluisi & E. A. Fleishman (Eds.), *Human performance and productivity: Stress and performance effectiveness* (pp. 141–163). Hillsdale, NJ: Erlbaum.

Holdaway, E. A. (1978). Facet and overall satisfaction of teachers. *Educational Administration Quarterly, 14*, 30–47.

Holland, R. P. (1982). Special educator burnout. *Educational Horizons, 60*, 58–64.

House, J. S., & Wells, J. A. (1978). Occupational stress, social support, and health. In A. McLean, G. Black, & M. Colligan (Eds.), *Reducing occupational stress: Proceedings of a conference* (publication 78–140, pp. 8–29). Washington, DC: National Institute of Occupational Safety and Health.

Hoyle, E. (1975). Leadership and decision-making in education. In M. G. Hughes (Ed.), *Administering education: International challenge*. London: Athlone Press.

Hoyle, E. (1989). The primary school teacher as professional. In M. Galton & A. Blyth (Eds.), *Handbook of primary education in Europe* (pp. 415–432). London: David Fulton (in association with the Council of Europe).

Huberman, M. (1989a). *La vie des enseignants*. Paris/Neuchâtel: Delachaux et Niestlé. (English translation, Teachers College Press, 1993).

Huberman, M. (1989b). The professional life cycle of teachers. *Teachers College Record, 91*, 31–57.

Huberman, M. (1990, April). *The social context of instruction in schools*. Paper presented at the annual meeting of the American Educational Research Association, Boston.

Huberman, M. (1993a). Professional careers and professional development: Some intersections. In R. T. Guskey & M. Huberman (Eds), *Professional development in education: New paradigms and practice* (pp. 193–224). New York: Teacher College Press.

Huberman, M. (1993b). Burnout in teaching careers. *European Education, 25*(3), 47–69.

Huberman, M., Grounauer, M., & Marti, J. (1993). *The lives of teachers.* London: Cassell.

Hubert, J. A., Gable, R. K., & Iwanicki, E. F. (1990). The relationship of teacher stress to school organizational health. In S. B. Bacharach (Ed.), *Advances in research and theories of school management and educational policy* (pp. 185–207). Greenwich: JAI.

Hughes, E. C. (1937). Institutional office and the person. In E. C. Hughes (Ed.), *Men and their work.* Glencoe: Free Press.

Hughes, M. (Ed.). (1995). *Teaching and learning in changing times.* Oxford: Blackwell.

Ianni, F. A., & Reuss-Ianni, E. (1983). "Take this job and shove it!": A comparison of organizational stress and burnout among teachers and police. In B. A. Farber (Ed.), *Stress and burnout in the human service profession* (pp. 82–96). New York: Pergamon.

Ilmarinen, J., Suurnäkki, T., Nygard, C.-H., & Landau, K. (1991). Classification of municipal occupations. *Scandinavian Journal of Work Environment & Health, 17,* Suppl. 1, 12–29.

Imants, J., & Bakkenes, I. (1993). Professional isolation of teachers, school culture and teachers' sense of efficacy. In F. K. Kieviet & R. Vandenberghe (Eds.), *School culture, schoolimprovement and teacher development* (pp. 153–160). Leiden: DSWO Press.

Imants, J., Tillema, H. H., & De Brabander, C. J. (1993). A dynamic view of teacher learning and school improvement. In F. K. Kieviet & R. Vandenberghe (Eds.), *School culture, schoolimprovement and teacher development* (pp. 109–128). Leiden: DSWO Press.

Innes, J. M., & Kitto, S. (1989). Neuroticism, self-consciousness and coping strategies, and occupational stress in high school teachers. *Personality & Individual Differences, 10,* 303–312.

Iwanicki, E. F. (1983). Toward understanding and alleviating teacher burnout. *Theory into Practice, 12,* 27–32.

Iwanicki, E. F., & Schwab, R. L. (1981). A cross validation study of the Maslach Burnout Inventory. *Educational and Psychological Measurement, 41,* 1167–1174.

Jackson, S. E., Schwab, R. L., & Schuler, R. S. (1986). Toward an understanding of the burnout phenomenon. *Journal of Applied Psychology, 71,* 630–640.

Jansen, Th., & Klaassen, C. (1994). Some reflections on individualisation, identity and socialisation. In P. Jarvis & F. Pöggeler (Eds.), *Developments in the education of adults in Europe.* Frankfurt/New York: Peter Lang.

Jantzen, W. (1987). *Allgemeine Behindertenpädagogik. Band 1.* Weinheim & Basel: Beltz.

Jantzi, D., & Leithwood, K. (1995, April). *Explaining variation in teachers' perceptions of transformational school leadership.* Paper presented at the annual meeting of the American Educational Research Association, San Francisco.

Jarvis, P. (1987). *Adult learning in social context.* London: Croom Helm.

Jehle, P., Lebkücher, A., & Seidel, G. (1994). Ursachen berufsbezogener Ängste von Lehrerinnen und Lehrern aus Lehrersicht. *Zeitschrift für Internationale Erziehungs- und Sozialwissenschaftliche Forschung, 11,* 141–164.

Jehle, P., & Nord-Rüdiger, D. (1989). Angst des Lehrers – Eine Literaturübersicht. *Zeitschrift für Internationale Erziehungs-und Sozialwissenschaftliche Forschung, 6,* 194–217.

Jenkins, S., & Calhoun, J. F. (1991). Teacher stress: Issues and intervention. *Psychology in the Schools, 28,* 60–70.

Jerusalem, M. (1990). *Persönliche Ressourcen, Vulnerabilität und Streßerleben* [Personal resources, vulnerability, and stress experience]. Göttingen, Germany: Hogrefe.

Jesus, S. N. (1993). As implicaçoes do projecto vocacional de futuros professores sobre a utilidade atribuida à sua formaçao. Um estudo exploratorio. In J. Tavares (Ed.), *Linhas de rumo em formaçao de professores* (pp. 229–236). Aveiro: University of Aveiro.

Jesus, S. N. (1995a). *A motivaçao para a profissao docente* [Teachers motivation]. Unpublished doctoral dissertation, University of Coïmbra, Coïmbra, Portugal.

Jesus, S. N. (1995b). Perspektivy d'alsieho vzdelavania ucitel'ov v zapadnej Europe [Perspectives on in-service teacher training in Western Europe]. *Pedagogicke Rozhl'ady, 2,* 16–19.

Jeurissen, R. (1992). *Taakbelasting en arbeidstevredenheid: een onderzoek bij leerkrachten secundair onderwijs* [Stress and job satisfaction among (junior)high school teachers]. Unpublished master's thesis, University of Leuven, Leuven, Belgium.

Joosten, J., & Drop, M. J. (1987). De betrouwbaarheid en vergelijkbaarheid van drie versies van de VOEG [Reliability and comparability of three versions of the VOEG]. *Gezondheid & Samenleving, 8,* 251–265.

Joreskog, K. G., & Sorbom, D. (1989). *LISREL 7: Users' reference guide.* Chicago: Scientific Software.

Kahn, R. L. (1970). Some propositions toward a researchable conceptualization of stress. In J. W. McGrath (Ed.), *Social and psychological factors of stress* (pp. 97–104). New York: Holt, Rinehart and Winston.

Kahn, R. L. (1974). Conflict, ambiguity and overload: Three elements in job stress. In A. McLean (Ed.), *Occupational stress* (pp. 47–61). Springfield, IL: Thomas.

Kahn, R. L., Wolfe, D. M., Quinn, R. P., Snoek, J. D., & Rosenthal, R. A. (1964). *Organizational stress: Studies in role conflict and ambiguity.* New York: Wiley.

Kannheiser, W. (1983). Theorie der Tätigkeit als Grundlage eines Modells von Arbeitsstreß. *Zeitschrift für Arbeits – und Organisationspsychologie, 27,* 102–110.

Karasek, R. A. (1981). Job socialization and job strain: The implications of two related psychosocial mechanisms for job redesign. In B. Gardell & G. Johansson (Eds.), *Working life. A social science contribution to work reform* (pp. 75–94). Chichester: Wiley.

Karasek, R. A. (1985). *Job Content Questionnaire and users guide. Revision 1. 1.* Department of Industrial and Systems Engineering, University of Southern California.

Karpenko, A. V. (1975). Excretion of 17-oxycorticosteroids and their relationships to the catecholamines over one year and over one day among middle schoolteachers. *Medical Field, 9,* 124–127 (Russian).

Katz, D., & Kahn, R. L. (1978). *The social psychology of organizations* (2nd ed.). New York: Wiley.

Kauchak, D., & Peterson, K. (1986, April). *Career ladders in Utah: Four district case studies.* Paper presented at the annual meeting of the American Educational Research Association, San Francisco.

Kelchtermans, G. (1993a). Getting the story, understanding the lives. From career stories to teachers' professional development. *Teaching and Teacher Education, 9,* 443–456.

Kelchtermans, G. (1993b). Teachers and their career story: A biographical perspective on professional development. In C. Day, J. Calderhead, & P. Denicolo (Eds.), *Research on teacher thinking: Understanding professional development* (pp. 198–220). London-Washington: Falmer Press.

Kelchtermans, G. (1993c). *De professionele ontwikkeling van leerkrachten basisonderwijs vanuit het biografisch perspectief* (The professional development of primary school teachers from a biographical point of view). Leuven: Centrum voor Onderwijsbeleid en-vernieuwing.

Kelchtermans, G. (1994). *Biographical methods in the study of teachers' professional development.* In I. Carlgren, G. Handal, & S. Vaage (Eds.), *Teacher thinking and action in varied contexts. Research on teachers' thinking and practice* (pp. 93–108). London: Falmer Press.

Kelchtermans, G. (1996). Teacher vulnerability: Understanding its moral and political roots [special issue: The Emotions in Teaching]. *Cambridge Journal of Education, 26*, 307–324.

Kelchtermans, G., & Vandenberghe, R., (1991). Leerkrachten over hun beroep: veelzeggende metaforen! [Teachers talking about their jobs: Telling metaphors!]. *Pedagogische Periodiek, 98* (27), 348–354.

Kelly, M. J. (1988). *The Manchester survey of occupational stress among head teachers and principals in the United Kingdom.* Manchester, England: Manchester Polytechnic.

Kievit, F., & Vandenberghe, R. (Eds.). (1993). *School culture, school improvement, and teacher development.* Leiden: DSWO Press.

Kilcher, C. A. (1992). Becoming a change facilitator: The first-year experience of five teacher leaders. In C. Livingston (Eds.), *Teachers as leaders* (pp. 91–113). Washington, DC: National Education Association.

King, M. B. (1993). Locking ourselves in: National standards for the teaching profession. *Teaching and Teacher Education, 10*, 95–108.

Kinnunen, U. (1988). Teacher stress during an autumn year in Finland: Four types of stress processes. *Work & Stress, 2*, 333–340.

Kinnunen, U. (1989). *Teacher stress over a school year.* Jyväskylä: University of Jyväskylä.

Kirby, P. C., & Colbert, R. (1992). *Principals who empower teachers.* Paper presented at the annual meeting of the American Educational Research Association, Chicago.

Kleiber, D., & Enzmann, D. (1986). Helfer-Leiden: Überlegungen zum Burnout in helfenden Berufen. In G. Feuser & W. Jantzen (Eds.), *Jahrbuch für Psychopathologie und Psychotherapie.* Köln: Pahl-Rugenstein.

Kleiber, D., & Enzmann, D. (1990). *Burnout: 15 years of research: An international bibliography.* Göttingen: Hogrefe.

Knight-Wegenstein-AG. (1973). *Die Arbeitszeit der Lehrer in der Bundesrepublik Deutschland.* Zürich: Antor.

Knothe, M., Scheuch, K., Misterek, M., Meyer, G., & Thümmler, D. (1991). Einflußfaktoren auf die psychische Beanspruchung von Lehrern im Unterricht. In K. Scheuch (Ed.), *Einflußfaktoren auf den Gesundheitszustand von Pädagogen* (pp. 34–44). Berlin: VWB.

Kohnen, R., & Barth, A. -R. (1990). Burnout bei Grund-und Hauptschullehrern – ein gesundheitliches Risiko? Lehrerjournal. *Grundschulmagazin, 10*, 41–44.

Koleva, N. W. (1985). Einige Ergebnisse einer sozialhygienischen Untersuchung von Lehrern in der VR Bulgarien. In W. Kessel, K. Scheuch, & B. Rudow (Eds.), *Lehrerpersönlichkeit, Lehrertätigkeit, Lehrergesundheit* (pp. 61–65). Universität Leipzig.

Korshavn, S. (1991, April). *Occupational stressors, organizational characteristics, teacher self-perceptions and teacher retention.* Paper presented at the annual conference of the American Educational Research Association, Chicago, IL.

Kreisberg, S. (1992), *Transforming power: Domination, empowerment and education.* Albany: State University of New York Press.

Krieger, R. et al. (1976). Erlebte Belastung des Lehrers durch verhattensauffallige *Zeitschrife für Entwicklungspsychologie und Pädagogische Psychologie, 8*, 245–251.

Kremer, L., & Hofman, J. E. (1985). Teachers' professional identity and burn-out. *Research in Education, 34,* 89–95.

Kuhl, J., & Beckmann, J. (Eds.). (1994). *Volition and personality: Action versus state orientation.* Göttingen, Germany/Toronto, Canada: Hogrefe.

Kuzsman, F. J., & Schnall, H. (1987). Managing teachers' stress: Improving discipline. *The Canadian School Executive, 6,* 3–10.

Kyriacou, C. (1980). Stress, health and schoolteachers: A comparison with other professions. *Cambridge Journal of Education, 10,* 154–158.

Kyriacou, C. (1981). Social support and occupational stress among schoolteachers. *Educational Studies, 7,* 55–60.

Kyriacou, C. (1987). Teacher stress and burnout: An international review. *Educational Research, 29,* 146–152.

Kyriacou, C., & Pratt, J. (1985). Teacher stress and psychoneurotic symptoms. *British Journal of Educational Psychology, 55,* 61–64.

Kyriacou, C., & Sutcliffe, J. (1977a). Teacher stress: A review. *Educational Review, 29,* 299–306.

Kyriacou, C., & Sutcliffe, J. (1977b). The prevalence of stress among teachers in medium-sized mixed comprehensive schools. *Research in Education, 18,* 75–79.

Kyriacou, C., & Sutcliffe, J. (1978a). A model of teacher stress. *Educational Studies, 4,* 1–6.

Kyriacou, C., & Sutcliffe, J. (1978b). Teacher stress: Prevalence, sources and symptoms. *British Journal of Educational Psychology, 48,* 159–167.

Kyriacou, C., & Sutcliffe, J. (1979). Teacher stress and satisfaction. *Educational Research, 21,* 89–96.

Kytaev-Smyk, I. A. (1983). *Psychology of stress* (Russian). Moskow: Science.

Lacey, C. (1977). *The socialization of teachers.* London: Methuen.

Larson, S. M. (1980). Proletarianisation and educated labour. *Theory and Society, 9,* 131–175.

Latack, J. C. (1989). Work, stress, and careers: A preventive approach to maintaining organizational health. In M. B. Arthur, D. T. Hall, & B. S. Lawrence (Eds.), *Handbook of career theory* (pp. 252–274). New York: Cambridge University Press.

Laughlin, A. (1984). Teacher stress in an Australian setting: The role of biographical mediators. *Educational Studies, 10,* 7–22.

Lazarus, R. S. (1966). *Psychological stress and the coping process.* New York: McGraw-Hill.

Lazarus, R. S. (1991). *Emotion and adaptation.* London: Oxford University Press.

Lazarus, R. S. (1993). From psychological stress to the emotions: A history of a changing outlook. *Annual Review of Psychology, 44,* 1–21.

Lazarus, R. S. (1995). Psychological stress in the workplace. In R. Crandall & P. L. Perrewé (Eds.), *Occupational stress* (pp. 3–14). Washington, DC: Taylor & Francis.

Lazarus, R. S., & DeLongis, A. (1983). Psychological stress and coping in aging. *American Psychologist, 38,* 245–254.

Lazarus, R. S., & Folkman, S. (1984). *Stress, appraisal, and coping.* New York: Springer.

Leach, D. J. (1984). A model of teacher stress and its implications for management. *Journal of Educational Administration, 22,* 157–172.

Leiter, M. P. (1988). Burnout as a function of communication patterns: A study of a multidisciplinary mental health team. *Group and Organizational Behavior, 13,* 111–128.

Leiter, M. P. (1991a). Coping patterns as predictors of burnout: The function of control and escapist coping patterns. *Journal of Organizational Behavior, 12,* 123–144.

Leiter, M. P. (1991b). The dream denied: Professional burnout and the constraints of service organizations. *Canadian Psychology, 32,* 547–558.

Leiter, M. P. (1993). Burnout as a developmental process: Consideration of models. In W. B. Schaufeli, C. Maslach, & T. Marek (Eds.), *Professional burnout: Recent developments in theory and research* (pp. 237–250). Washington, DC: Taylor & Francis.

Leiter, M. P. (1995, June). *Burnout in the 1990s: Research agenda and theory.* Invited Symposium, Canadian Society for Industrial/Organizational Psychology, Annual Convention of the Canadian Psychological Association, Charlotte-town, PEI.

Leiter, M. P., Clark, D., & Durup, J. (1994). Distinct models of burnout and commitment among men and women in the military. *Journal of Applied Behavioral Science, 30,* 63–82.

Leiter, M. P., & Durup, J. (1994). The discriminant validity of burnout and depression: A confirmatory factor analytic study. *Anxiety, Stress, & Coping, 7,* 357–373.

Leiter, M. P., & Durup, J. (1996). Work, home, and in-between: A longitudinal study of spillover. *Journal of Applied Behavioral Science, 32,* 29–47.

Leiter, M. P., & Durup, J. (in press). Work, home, and in – between: A longitudinal study of spillover. *Journal of Applied Behavioral Science.*

Leiter, M. P., & Maslach, C. (1988). The impact of interpersonal environment on burnout and organizational commitment. *Journal of Organizational Behavior, 9,* 297–308.

Leithwood, K. (1992). The move towards transformational leadership. *Educational Leadership, 49*(5), 8–12.

Leithwood, K. (1994). Leadership for school restructuring. *Educational Administration Quarterly, 30,* 498–518.

Leithwood, K., & Aitken, R. (1995). *Making schools smarter.* Thousand Oaks, CA: Corwin.

Leithwood, K., & Jantzi, D. (1990). Transformational leadership: How principals can help reform school culture. *School Effectiveness and School Improvement, 1,* 249–280.

Leithwood, K., Jantzi, D., & Fernandez, A. (1994). Transformational leadership and teachers' commitment to change. In J. Murphy & K. Louis (Eds.), *Reshaping the principalship: Insights from transformational reform efforts* (pp. 72–98). Newbury Park, CA: Corwin Press.

Leithwood, K., Jantzi, D., & Steinbach, R. (1995, April). *An organizational learning perspective on school responses to central policy initiatives.* Paper presented at the annual meeting of the American Educational Research Association, San Francisco.

Leithwood, K., & Steinbach, R. (1993). Total quality leadership: Expert thinking plus transformational practice. *Journal of Personnel Evaluation in Education, 7,* 311–338.

Leithwood K., Tomlinson, D., & Genge, M. (1996). Transformational school leadership. In K. Leithwood (Ed.), *International handbook of educational leadership and administration* (pp. 785–840). Boston/Dordrecht: Kluwer Press.

Lens, W., & Creten, H. (1995). *Motivatie van leerkrachten in het secundair onderwijs en van bedienden: een vergelijkende empirische studie* [Motivation of teachers in secondary education and of employees: A comparative study]. Leuven, Belgium: University of Leuven, Center for Research on Motivation and Time Perspective.

Lens, W., & Decruyenaere, M. (1991). Motivation and demotivation in secondary education: Student characteristics. *Learning and Instruction, 1,* 145–159.

Lens, W., & Schops, L. (1991). *Motivatie en demotivatie van leerkrachten in het secundair onderwijs: een exploratief onderzoek* [Motivation and demotivation among teachers in secondary education: an exploratory study]. FKFO-MIproject 89. 16. Leuven, Belgium: University of Leuven, Center for Research on Motivation and Time Perspective .

Leontjew, A. A. (1982). *Tätigkeit, Bewußtsein, Persönlichkeit*. Berlin: Volk und Wissen.

Leuschner, G. (1976). Zum Einfluß von Schulleitungs-und sozialen Bedingungen auf das Belastungserleben im Lehrerberuf. *Wissenschaftliche Zeitschrift der Universität Rostoch, 25,* 635–639.

Leuschner, G. (1979). Belastungsbedingungen im Lehrerberuf. *Zeitschrift für die Gesamte Hygiene, 25,* 18–21.

Lewin, K. (1935). *A dynamic theory of personality*. New York: McGraw-Hill.

Lieberman, A., & Miller, L. (1984). *Teachers: Their world and their work*. Alexandria, VA: Association for Supervision & Curriculum Development.

Lieberman, A., & Miller, L. (1990). Restructuring schools: What matters and what works. *Phi-Delta-Kappan, 71,* 759–764.

Lieberman, A., & Miller, L. (in press). *Teachers: Restructuring their world and their work*. New York: Teachers College Press.

Lieberman, A., Saxl, E., & Miles, M. (1988). Teacher leadership, ideology and practice. In A. Lieberman (Ed.), *Building a professional culture in schools* (pp. 148–166). New York: Teachers College Press.

Litt, M. D., & Turk, D. C. (1985). Sources of stress and dissatisfaction in experienced high school teachers. *Journal of Educational Research, 78,* 178–185.

Little, J. (1981). *School success and staff development in urban desegregated schools: A summary of recently completed research*. Paper presented at the annual meeting of the American Education Research Association, Los Angeles.

Little, J. W. (1990a). The mentor phenomenon and the social organization of teaching. *Review of Research in Education, 16,* 297–351.

Little, J. W. (1990b). The persistence of privacy: Autonomy and initiative in teachers' professional relations. *Teachers College Record, 91,* 509–536.

Little, J. W. (1993). Teachers' professional development in a climate of educational reform. *Educational Evaluation and Policy Analysis, 15,* 129–152.

Little, J., & McLaughlin, M. (Eds.). (1993). *Teachers' work: Individuals, colleagues, and contexts*. New York: Teachers College Press.

Littrel, P. C., Billingsley, B. S., & Cross, L. H. (1994). The effects of principal support on special and general educator's stress, job satisfaction, school commitment, health and intent to stay in teaching. *Remedial and Special Education, 15,* 297–310.

Lock, L. (1986, March 12). In M. Godfrey, Telling tales out of school. *The Guardian,* p. 22.

Locke, E. A. (1968). Toward a theory of task motivation and incentives. *Organizational Behavior and Human Performance, 3,* 157–189.

Long, B. C., & Gessaroli, M. E. (1989). The relationship between teacher stress and perceived coping effectiveness: Gender and marital differences. *Alberta Journal of Educational Research, 35,* 308–324.

Lortie, D. C. (1975). *Schoolteacher: A sociological study*. Chicago: University of Chicago Press.

Louis, M. R. (1990). Acculturation in the workplace: Newcomers as lay ethnographers. In B. Schneider (Ed.), *Organizational climate and culture* (pp. 85–129). Newbury Park, CA: Sage.

Louis, K. S., & King, J. (1993). Professional cultures and reforming schools: Does the myth of Sisyphus apply? In J. Murphy & P. Hallinger (Eds.), *Restructuring schooling: Learning from ongoing efforts* (pp. 216–250). Newbury Park, CA: Corwin Press.

Lunenburg, F. C., & Cadavid, V. (1992). Locus of control, pupil control ideology, and dimensions of teacher burnout. *Journal of Instructional Psychology, 19,* 13–22.

Lutz, F. W., & Maddirala, J. (1990). Stress, burnout in Texas teachers' and reform mandated accountability. *Educational Research Quarterly, 14,* 10–21.

Mac an Ghaill, M. (1992). Teachers' work: Curriculum restructuring, culture, power and comprehensive schooling. *British Journal of Sociology of Education, 13,* 177–199.

MacDonald, J. (1991). *Dilemmas of planning backwards: Rescuing a good idea.* Providence, RI: Coalition of Essential Schools.

MacFarlane, E. (1989, July 21). Down and out. *The Times Educational Supplement,* p. 19.

Macleod, D., & Meikle, J. (1994, September 1). Education changes "making heads quit." *The Guardian,* p. 6.

Madaus, G. F. (1988). The influence of testing on the curriculum. In A. N. Tanner (Ed.), *Critical issues in curriculum: 87th yearbook of the National Society for the Study of Education, Part 1* (pp. 83–121). Chicago: University of Chicago Press.

Maehr, M. L. (1984). Meaning and motivation. Toward a theory of personal investment. In R. E. Ames & C. Ames (Eds.), *Research on motivation in education: Vol. 1. Student motivation* (pp. 115–144). Orlando: Academic Press.

Mahoney, P. (1985). *Schools for the boys.* London: Hutchinson.

Mäkinen, R., & Kinnunen, U. (1986). Teacher stress over a school year. *Scandinavian Journal of Education Research, 30,* 55–70.

Malen, B. (1994). Enacting site-based management: A political utilities analysis. *Educational Evaluation and Policy Analysis, 16,* 249–267.

Malik, J. L., Mueller, R. O., & Meinke, D. L. (1991). The effects of teaching experience and grade level taught on teacher stress: A LISREL analysis. *Teaching & Teacher Education, 7,* 57–62.

Manthei, J. (1992). *The mentor teacher as leader: The motives, characteristics, and needs of seventy-three experienced teachers who seek a new leadership role.* [ERIC Document Reproduction Service No. ED 346 042]

Manthei, R., & Gilmore, A. (1994). Is stress among New Zealand teachers increasing? *New Zealand Journal of Educational Studies, 29,* 73–87.

Martin, W., & Willower, D. (1981). The managerial behavior of high school principals. *Educational Administration Quarterly, 17,* 69–70.

Maslach, C. (1976). Burned-out. *Human Behavior, 5,* 16–22.

Maslach, C. (1982a). *Burnout: The cost of caring.* Englewood Cliffs, NJ: Prentice-Hall.

Maslach, C. (1982b). Understanding burnout: Definitional issues in analyzing a complex phenomenon. In W. S. Paine (Ed.), *Job stress and burnout* (pp. 29–40). Beverly Hills, CA: Sage.

Maslach, C. (1993). Burnout: A multidimensional perspective. In W. B. Schaufeli, C. Maslach, & T. Marek (Eds.), *Professional burnout: Recent developments in theory and research* (pp. 19–32). Washington, DC: Taylor & Francis.

Maslach, C., & Jackson, S. E. (1981). The measurement of experienced burnout. *Journal of Occupational Behaviour, 2,* 99–113.

Maslach, C., & Jackson, S. E. (1984). Burnout in organizational settings. In S. Oskamp (Ed.), *Applied social psychology annual: Vol. 5. Applications in organizational settings* (pp. 133–153). Beverly Hills, CA: Sage.

Maslach, C., & Jackson, S. E. (1986). *MBI: Maslach Burnout Inventory; manual research edition.* Palo Alto: University of California, Consulting Psychologists Press.

Maslach, C., Jackson, S. E., & Leiter, M. P. (1996). *The Maslach Burnout Inventory* (3rd ed.). Palo Alto, CA: Consulting Psychologists Press.

Maslach, C., Jackson, S. E., & Schwab, R. L. (1986). The MBI-Educators Survey [originally Form Ed.]. In C. Maslach & S. E. Jackson, *The Maslach Burnout Inventory* (2nd ed.). Palo Alto, CA: Consulting Psychologists Press.

Maslach, C., & Pines, A. (1977). The burn-out syndrome in the day care setting. *Child Care Quarterly, 6*(2), 100–113.

Maslach, C., & Schaufeli, W. B. (1993). Historical and conceptual development of burnout. In W. B. Schaufeli, C. Maslach, & T. Marek (Eds.), *Professional burnout: Recent developments in theory and research* (pp. 1–18). Washington, DC: Taylor & Francis.

Mattingly, M. A. (1977). Sources of stress and burn-out in professional child care work. *Child Care Quarterly, 6*(2), 127–137.

Mayou, R. (1987). Burnout. *British Medical Journal, 295*, 284–285.

Mazur, P. J., & Lynch, M. D. (1989). Differential impact of administrative, organizational, and personality factors on teacher burnout. *Teaching and Teacher Education, 5*, 337–353.

McGrath, A., Houghton, D., & Reid, N. (1989). Occupational stress and teachers in Northern Ireland. *Work & Stress, 3*, 359–368.

McGrath, J. E. (1983). Stress and behavior in organizations. In M. D. Dunnette (Ed.), *Handbook of industrial and organizational psychology* (pp. 1351–1395). New York: Wiley.

McGrath, M. Z. (1995). *Teachers today. A guide to surviving creatively.* Newbury Park, CA: Corwin Press.

McLaughlin, M. W., Pfeifer, R. S., Swanson-Owens, D., & Yee, S. (1986). Why teachers won't teach. *Phi Delta Kappan, 67*, 420–426.

McLaughlin, M., & Talbert, J. (1993). *Contexts that matter for teaching and learning.* Palo Alto: Center for Research on the Context of Secondary School Teaching.

McNeil, L. M. (1986). *Contradictions of control: School structure and school knowledge.* New York: Routledge and Kegan Paul.

Mechanic, D. (1974). Social structure and personal adaptation: Some neglected dimensions. In G. V. Coelho, D. A. Hamburg, & J. E. Adams (Eds.), *Coping and adaptation* (pp. 32–44). New York: Basic Books.

Meier, S. T. (1983). Toward a theory of burnout. *Human Relations, 36*, 899–910.

Merriam, S. B., & Caffarella, R. S. (1991). *Learning in adulthood.* San Francisco: Jossey-Bass.

Mersh, C. (1991, February 13). Turning the tables on stress. *Northampton Chronicle and Echo.*

Merz, J. (1979). Wo drückt der Schuh am meisten? Empirische Befunde zur subjektiven Berufsbelastung von Lehrern. *Bayerische Schule, 32*, 13–16.

Meyer, J. W., & Rowan, B. (1977). Institutionalized organizations: Formal structure as myth and ceremony. *American Journal of Sociology, 83*, 340–363.

Menzies, T. V. (1995). *Teacher commitment in colleges of applied arts and technology: Sources, objects, practices and influences.* Unpublished Ph. D dissertation, University of Toronto.

Millard, A. (1995, February 10). Tired out from the weight of my armour. *The Times Educational Supplement*, p. 20.

Miller, G. A., Galanter, E., & Pribram, K. H. (1960). *Plans and structure of behavior.* New York: Holt.

Miller, L. (1993–1995). Unpublished field notes.

Milstein, M., & Golaszewski, T. (1985). Effects of organizationally based and individually based stress management efforts in elementary school settings. *Urban Education, 49*, 389–409.

Milstein, M. M., Golaszewski, T. J., & Duquette, R. D. (1984). Organizationally based stress: What bothers teachers. *Journal of Educational Research, 77,* 293–297.

Miskel, C., & Ogawa, R. T. (1988). Work motivation, job satisfaction, and climate. In N. Boyan (Ed.), *Handbook of research in educational administration* (pp. 279–304). New York: Longman.

Mitchell, D. E., Ortiz, F. I., & Mitchell, T. K. (1987). *Work orientation and job performance: The cultural basis of teaching rewards and incentives.* Albany: State University of New York Press.

Mortimore, P., Sammons, P., Lewis, L., & Ecob, R. (1988). *School matters: The junior years.* London: Open Books.

Motowidlo, S. J., Packard, J. S., & Manning, M. R. (1986). Occupational stress: Its causes and consequences for job performance. *Journal of Applied Psychology, 71,* 618–629.

Müller-Limmroth, W. (1980). *Arbeitszeit-Arbeitsbelastung im Lehrerberuf.* Frankfurt/M.: GEW.

Murphy, J. (1991). *Restructuring schools: Capturing and assessing the phenomena.* New York: Teachers College Press.

Murphy, K. (1995). *A case study of Central High School: Critical influences on the resilient nature of high schools.* Unpublished doctoral dissertation, Orono, Maine.

Murray, B. (1995, September). New Faculty get boost partnering with senior staff. *The A.P.A. Monitor,* pp. 50–51.

Natale, J. A. (1993). Why teachers leave. *The Executive Educator, 15,* 14–18.

National Center for Education Statistics. (1994). *Digest of Education Statistics.* Washington, DC: U.S. Department of Education, Office of Educational Research and Improvement.

National Center for Education Statistics. (1995). *Trends among high school seniors, 1972–1992: National education longitudinal study of 1988.* Washington, DC: U.S. Department of Education, Office of Educational Research and Improvement.

National Commission on Excellence in Education (1983). *A Nation at Risk. The Imperative for Educational Reform.* Washington: U.S. Department of Education.

National Education Association. (1992). *Status of the American public school teacher, 1990–1991.* Washington, DC: Author.

Naumann, H.-J., Rummel, U., Misterck, M., Scheuch, K., Naumann, W., & Meyer, G. (1985). Psychophysiologische Beanspruchungsuntersuchungen bei Heuisshutlehrem. In Kessel, W., Scheuch K. & Rudow, B. (Eds.), *Lehrertätigkeit, Lehrerpersönlichkeit, Lehrergesundheit* (II) Leipzig: Universität, 27–38.

Navakatikjan, A. O. (1980). Mechanism and criteria of neurological-emotional strain regarding mental work. *Working and Occupational Hygiene* (Russian), *6,* 5–15.

Neville, S. H. (1981). Job stress and burnout: Occupational hazards for service staff. *College and Research Libraries, 42,* 242–247.

Nias, J. (1981). Commitment and motivation in primary school teachers. *Educational Review, 33,* 181–190.

Nias, J. (1988a). Informal primary education in action: Teachers' accounts. In W. A. L. Blyth (Ed.), *Informal primary education today: Essays and studies.* London: Falmer.

Nias, J. (1988b). What it means to feel like a teacher: The subjective reality of primary school teaching. In J. Ozga (Ed.), *Schoolwork: Approaches to the labour process of teaching.* Milton Keynes, England: Open University Press.

Nias, J. (1989). *Primary teachers talking. A study of teaching as work.* London: Routledge.

Nias, J. (1991). Changing times, changing identities: Grieving for a lost self. In R. G. Burgess (Ed.), *Educational research and evaluation.* London: Falmer Press.

Nias, J. (Ed.). (1993a). *The human nature of learning: Selections from the work of M. L. J. Abercrombie.* Buckingham: Open University Press.

Nias, J. (1993b). Changing times, changing identities: Grieving for a lost self. In R. Burgess (Ed.), *Educational research and evaluation for policy and practice.* London: Falmer.

Nias, J. (1994). *Report on integration at Drybrook Lower School.* Plymouth, England: University of Plymouth.

Nias, J. (Ed.). (1996a). The emotions in teaching. *Cambridge Journal of Education, 26* (Special Issue).

Nias, J. (1996b). Thinking about feeling: The emotions in teaching. *Cambridge Journal of Education, 26,* 293–306.

Nias, J. (1997). Would schools improve if teachers cared less? *Education, 15*(3), 17–22.

Nias, J., Southworth, G., & Campbell, P. (1992). *Whole school curriculum development in primary schools.* London: Falmer.

Nias, J., Southworth, G., & Yeomans, R. (1989). *Staff relationships in the primary school: A study of organizational cultures.* London: Cassell.

Nicholson, N. (1984). A theory of work role transition. *Administrative Science Quarterly, 29,* 172–191.

Niemann, H.-J. (1970). *Der Lehrer und sein Beruf.* Weinheim: Beltz.

Nuding, A. (1984). Lehrerangst im Schulalltag. *Psychologie in Erziehung und Unterricht, 31,* 292–297.

O'Connor, P. R., & Clarke, V. A. (1990). Determinants of teacher stress. *Australian Journal of Education, 34,* 41–51.

Odden, A., & Odden, E. (1994, April). *Applying the high involvement framework to local management of schools in Victoria, Australia.* Paper presented at the annual meeting of the American Educational Research Association, New Orleans.

Offner, M. (1910). *Die geistige Ermüdung. Eine umfassende Darstellung des Wesens der geistigen Ermüdung, der Methoden der Ermüdungsforschung und ihrer Ergebnisse speziell für den Unterricht.* Berlin: Reuther & Rechard.

Ogus, E. D., Greenglass, E. R., & Burke, R. J. (1990). Gender-role differences, work stress and depersonalization. *Journal of Social Behavior and Personality, 5,* 387–398.

Okebukola, P. A., & Jegede, O. J. (1989). Determinants of occupational stress among teachers in Nigeria. *Educational Studies, 15,* 23–36.

Olson, J., & Matuskey, P. V. (1982). Causes of burnout in SLD teachers. *Journal of Learning Disabilities, 15,* 97–99.

Orpen, C., & King, G. (1987). Job stress, personality and individual strain. *Psychological Research Journal, 11,* 33–44.

Osborn, M. (1995, September). *Not a seamless robe: A tale of two teachers' responses to policy change.* Paper presented to European Conference on Educational Research, Bath.

Osborn, M., & Black, E. (1994). *Developing the National Curriculum at Key Stage 2: The changing nature of teachers' work.* Bristol: School of Education (for NASUWT).

Osborn, M., & Broadfoot, P. (1992). The impact of current changes in English primary schools on teacher professionalism. *Teachers College Record, 94,* 138–151.

Owen, M. (1990, May 1). School for scandal. *The Guardian,* p. 25.

Pallas, A. M., Natriello, G., & McDill, E. L. (1995). Changing students/changing needs. In E. Flaxman & A. H. Passow (Eds.), *Changing populations, changing schools, 94th yearbook of the National Society for the Study of Education, Part II* (pp. 30–58). Chicago: University of Chicago Press.

Payne, M. A., & Furnham, A. (1987). Dimensions of occupational stress in West Indian secondary school teachers. *British Journal of Educational Psychology, 57,* 141–150.

Pedrabissi, L., Rolland, J. P., & Santinello, M. (1993). Stress and burnout among teachers in Italy and France. *The Journal of Psychology, 127*, 529–535.

Peez, H. (1983). Angst als Begleiter im Lehereleben. *Bayerische Schule, 36*, 15–18.

Pelkmans, A., & Vrieze, G. (1987). *Meer over coördinatie en management* (More about co-ordination and management). Nijmegen: ITS.

Perlman, B., & Hartman, E. A. (1982). Burnout: Summary and future research. *Human Relations, 35*, 283–305.

Peters, T. J., & Waterman, R. H. (1982). *In search of excellence: Lessons from America's best-run corporations.* New York: Harper & Row.

Peterson, P. L. (1990). Doing more in the same amount of time: Cathy Swift. *Educational Evaluation and Policy Analysis, 12*, 261–280.

Pettegrew, L. S., & Wolf, G. E. (1982). Validating measures of teacher stress. *American Educational Research Journal, 19*, 373–396.

Phillips, B. N., & Lee, M. (1980). The changing role of the American teacher: Current and future sources of stress. In C. L. Cooper & J. Marshall (Eds.), *White collar and professional stress* (pp. 93–111). New York: Wiley.

Pierce, M. B., & Molloy, G. N. (1990). Psychological and biographical differences between secondary school teachers experiencing high and low levels of burnout. *British Journal of Educational Psychology, 60*, 37–51.

Pieren, F., & Schärer, A. (1992). *Lehrer-und Lehrerinnenbelastungen. Eine Untersuchung an Erst-und Viertklasslehrkräften.* Lizentiatsarbeit, Universität Fribourg (Schweiz).

Pines, A. M., Aronson, E., & Kafry, D. (1983, 1991). *Ausgebrannt. Vom Überdruß zur Selbstentfaltung.* Stuttgart: Klett-Cotta.

Pithers, R. T., & Fogarty, G. J. (1995). Occupational stress among vocational teachers. *British Journal of Educational Psychology, 65*, 3–14.

Plowden Report. (1967). *Children and their primary schools.* Report of the Central Advisory Council for Education in England. London: HMSO.

Podsakoff, P. M., MacKenzie, S. B., Moorman, R. H., & Fetter, R. (1990). Situational moderators of leader reward and punishment behavior: Fact or fiction? *Organizational Behavior and Human Performance, 34*, 21–63.

Pollard, A. (1982). A model of coping strategies. *British Journal of Sociology of Education, 3*, 19–37.

Pollard, A. (1985). *The social world of the primary school.* London: Cassell.

Pollard, A. (1991). *Learning in primary schools.* London: Cassell.

Pollard, A. (1992). Teachers' responses to the reshaping of primary education. In M. Arnot & L. Barton (Eds.), *Voicing concerns:* Sociological perspectives of contemporary education reforms (104–124). London: Triangle Books.

Pollard, A. (Ed.). (1994). *Look before you leap? Research evidence for the curriculum at Key Stage 2.* London: Tyrell Press.

Pollard, A., Broadfoot, P., Croll, P., Osborn, M., & Abbott, D. (1994). *Changing English primary schools? The impact of the Education Reform Act at Key Stage One.* London: Cassell.

Porter, A. C. (1993). School delivery standards. *Educational Researcher, 22*(5), 24–30.

Powell, A. G., Farrar, E., & Cohen, D. K. (1985). *The Shopping Mall High School.* Boston: Houghton Mifflin.

Power, S., Whitty, G., & Youdell, D., (1995). *No place to learn: Homelessness and education.* London: University of London, Institute of Education.

Prestine, N. (1993). Feeling the ripples, riding the waves: Making an essential school. In J. Murphy & P. Hallinger (Eds.), *Restructuring schooling* (pp. 32–62). Newbury Park, CA: Corwin Press.

Prochaska, J. O. (1994). Strong and weak principles for progressing from precontemplation to action on the basis of twelve problem behaviors. *Health Psychology, 13*(1), 47–51.

Proctor, J. L., & Alexander, D. A. (1992). Stress among primary teachers: Individuals in organizations. *Stress Medicine, 8,* 233–236.

Punch, K. F., & Tuettemann, E. (1990). Correlates of psychological distress among secondary school teachers. *British Educational Research Journal, 16,* 369–382.

Purnell, S., & Hill, P. (1992). *Time for reform* (R-4234-EMC). Santa Monica, CA: Rand.

Quicke, J. (1988). The New Right and education. *British Journal of Educational Studies, 26,* 5–20.

Rich, R. (1972). *The training of teachers in England and Wales during the nineteenth century.* Bath: Cedric Chivers.

Richardson, G. (1995). Leaving the profession. In J. Bell (Ed.), *Teachers coping with change.* Buckingham: Open University Press.

Ricken, R. (1980). Teacher burnout – A failure of the supervisory process. *NASSP Bulletin, 64,* 21–24.

Roberts, N. (1985). Transforming leadership: A process of collective action. *Human Relations, 38,* 1023–1046.

Rohmert, W. (1984). Das Belastungs-Beanspruchungs-Konzept. *Zeitschrift für Arbeitswissenschaften, 38* (10NF), 193–200.

Rohmert, W., & Landau, K. (1979). *Das arbeitswissenschaftliche Erhebungsverfahren zur Tätigkeitsanalyse (AET).* Bern: Huber.

Rose, A. M. (1962). A social-psychological theory of neurosis. In A. M. Rose (Ed.), *Human behaviour and social processes: An interactionist approach* (pp. 537–549). London: Routledge.

Rosenholtz, S. (1989). *Teachers' workplace: The social organization of schools.* New York: Longman.

Rossman, G. B., Corbett, H. D., & Firestone, W. A. (1988). *Change and effectiveness in schools: A cultural perspective.* Albany: State University of New York Press.

Rotter, J. B. (1966). Generalized expectancies for internal versus external control of reinforcement. *Psychological Monographs, 80,* 1–28.

Rousseau, D. M. (1995). *Psychological contracts in organizations: Understanding written and unwritten agreements.* Thousand Oaks, CA: Sage.

Rousseau, M. (1991). *Community, the tie that binds.* New York: New York University Press.

Rowan, B. (1990). Commitment and control: Alternative strategies for the organizational design of schools. In C. B. Cazden (Ed.), *Review of research in education* (Vol. 16, pp. 353–389). Washington, DC: American Educational Research Association.

Rudow, B. (1986). *Konzepte, Probleme und Ergebnisse psychologischer Belastungs-und Beanspruchungsforschung-dargestellt am Beispiel der Lehrertätigkeit und Lehrergesundheit.* Habilitationsschrift (Diss. B), Universität Leipzig.

Rudow, B. (1990a). Konzepte zur Belastungs-und Beanspruchungsanalyse im Lehrerberuf. *Zeitschrift für Pädagogische Psychologie, 4,* 1–12.

Rudow, B. (1990b). Empirische Untersuchungen zur Belastung und Beanspruchung im Lehrerberuf. *Zeitschrift für Pädagogische Psychologie, 4,* 75–85.

Rudow, B. (1992). Zur psychologischen Tätigkeitsanalyse im Lehrerberuf – Konzeption, Probleme und Ergebnisse. *Zeitschrift für Arbeits-und Organisationspsychologie, 36*(10), 137–143.

Rudow, B. (1995). *Die Arbeit des Lehrers. Zur Psychologie der Lehrertätigkeit, Lehrerbelastung und Lehrergesundheit.* Bern: Huber.

Rudow, B. (1996). *Stressmanagement bei Lehrerinnen und Lehrern in Rheinland-Pfalz.* Projektbericht. (In preparation)

Rudow, B., & Buhr, J. (1986). Beziehungen zwischen Tätigkeitsmerkmalen, personalen Eigenschaften und dem Belastungserleben sowie neurotisch-funktionellen Störungen bei Lehrern. In H. Schröder & K. Reschke (Eds.), *Beiträge zur Theorie und Praxis der Medizinischen Psychologie,* (Vol. 3, pp. 43–54). Universität Leipzig.

Rudow, B., & Scheuch, K. (1982). Konzepte und Begriffe in der psychologischen Streßforschung – eine kritische Betrachtung aus tätigkeitstheoretischer Sicht. *Nederlands Tijdschrift voor de Psychologie, 37,* 362–382.

Rury, J. (1989). Who became teachers? The social characteristics of teachers in American history. In D. Warren (Ed.), *American teachers: Histories of a profession at work* (pp. 9–48). New York: Macmillan.

Russell, D. W., Altmaier, E., & Van Velzen, D. (1987). Job-related stress, social support and burnout among classroom teachers. *Journal of Applied Psychology, 72,* 269–274.

Rutter, M., Maugham, B., Mortimore, P., & Ouston, J. (1979). *Fifteen thousand hours.* London: Open Books.

Sakharov, M., & Farber, B. A. (1983). A critical study of burnout in teachers. In B. A. Farber (Ed.), *Stress and burnout in the human service professions* (pp. 65–81). New York: Pergamon.

Sales, S. M. (1969). Organizational role as a risk factor in coronary heart disease. *Administrative Science Quarterly, 14,* 325–336.

Sammons, P., et al. (1995). *Key characteristics of effective schools: A review of school effectiveness research.* London: Office for Standards in Education.

Samuelson, P. (1947). *Foundations of economic analysis.* Cambridge: Harvard University Press.

Sarason, S. B. (1982). *The culture of the school and the problem of change* (2nd ed.). Boston: Allyn & Bacon.

Sarason, S. B. (1983). School psychology: An autobiographical fragment. *Journal of School Psychology, 21,* 285–295.

Sarason, S. B. (1985). *Caring and compassion in clinical practice.* San Francisco: Jossey-Bass.

Sarason, S. B. (1990). *The predictable failure of educational reform.* San Francisco: Jossey-Bass.

Sarason, S. (1995). *Parental involvement and the political principle: Why the existing governance structure of schools should be abolished.* San Francisco: Jossey-Bass.

Sarason, S., Levine, M., Goldenberg, I., Cherlin, D., & Bennett, E. (1966). *Psychology and community settings.* New York: John Wiley.

Sarros, J. C. (1988). Administrator burnout: Finding and future directions. *The Journal of Educational Administration, 26,* 184–196.

Sarros, J. C., & Sarros, A. M. (1992). Social support and teacher burnout. *Journal of Educational Administration, 30,* 55–69.

Saupe, R., & Möller, H. (1981). *Psychomentale Belastungen im Lehrerberuf.* Berlin: GEW.

Schaeffer, J. (1967). *The school as a center of inquiry.* New York: Harper & Row.

Schäfer, E. (1990). *Analyse der Arbeitszeiten von Lehrerinnen und Lehrern an Gymnasialabteilungen Bremer Schulen.* Hausarbeit für Lehramt. Universität Bremen.

Schaufeli, W. B. (1990). *Opgebrand. Achtergronden van werkstress bij contactuele beroepen: het burnout-syndroom* [Burned out. Determinants of work stress in the social professions: The burnout syndrome]. Rotterdam: Donker.

Schaufeli, W. B., Daamen, J., & Van Mierlo, H. (1994). Burnout among Dutch teachers: An MBI validation study. *Educational and Psychological Measurement, 54,* 803–812.

Schaufeli, W. B., & Dierendonck, D. van (1993). The construct validity of two burnout measures. *Journal of Organizational Behavior, 14,* 631–647.

Schaufeli, W. B., Leiter, M. P., Maslach, C., & Jackson, S. E. (1996). The Maslach Burnout Inventory – General Survey. In C. Maslach, S. E. Jackson, & M. P. Leiter (Eds.), *MBI Manual* (3rd ed.). Palo Alto, CA: Consulting Psychologists Press.

Schaufeli, W. B., Maslach, C., & Marek, T. (Eds.). (1993). *Professional burnout: Recent developments in theory and research.* Washington, DC: Taylor & Francis.

Schein, E. H. (1969). The mechanisms of change. In W. G. Bennis, K. D. Benne, & R. Chin (Eds.), *The planning of change* (2nd ed., pp. 98–107). New York: Holt, Rinehart, & Winston.

Schein, E. H. (1985). *Organizational culture and leadership: A dynamic view.* San Francisco: Jossey-Bass.

Scheuch, K., Navakatikjan, A. O., Tomaschevskaja, L. I., Karpenko, A. V., Michael, K., Rudow, B., Schreinicke, G., & Hüber, B. (1982). Neurotische Tendenzen und während eines Schuljahres auftretenden Herz-Kreislauf-Veränderungen bei Lehrern. *Zeitschrift für Ärztliche Fortbildung, 76,* 610–615.

Scheuch, K., Schreinicke, G., Leipnitz, B., & Rudow, B. (1978). Psychophysiologische Untersuchungen zur Beanspruchung von Lehrern. *Deutsches Gesundheitswesen, 33,* 2252–2256.

Schlansker, B. (1987). A principal's guide to teacher stress. *Principal, 66*(5), 32–34.

Schön, D. A. (1983). *The reflective practitioner: How professionals think in action.* New York: Basic Books.

Schönknecht, G. (1997). *Innovative Lehrerinnen und Lehrer. Berufliche Entwicklung und Berufsalltag* [Innovative teachers: professional development and their day-to-day jobs.]. Weinheim: Beltz – Deutscher Studien Verlag.

Schubert, R. (1983). *Feldstudie zur Phänomenologie von psychopathogen relevanten Belastungssituationen.* Diplomarbeit, Sektion Psychologie, Universität Leipzig.

Schuh, E. (1962). *Der Volksschullehrer. Störfaktoren im Berufsleben und ihre Rückwirkung auf die Einstellung im Beruf.* Hannover: Schroedel.

Schuit, H. (1993). *Organisatieproblemen in het voortgezet onderwijs* (Organizational problems in secondary education). Nijmegen: Katholieke Universiteit.

Schwab, R. L. (1983). Teacher burnout: Beyond psychobabble. *Theory into Practice, 21,* 27–33.

Schwab, R. L., & Iwanicki, E. F. (1982a). Who are our burned out teachers? *Educational Research Quarterly, 7,* 5–16.

Schwab, R. L., & Iwanicki, E. F. (1982b). Perceived role conflict, role ambiguity, and teacher burnout. *Educational Administration Quarterly, 18,* 60–74.

Schwab, R. L., Jackson, S. E., & Schuler, R. A. (1986). Educator burnout: Sources and consequences. *Educational Research Journal, 20*(3), 14–30.

Schwartz, B. (1994). *The costs of living.* New York: Norton.

Schwarzer, R. (1992). Self-efficacy in the adoption and maintenance of health behaviors: Theoretical approaches and a new model. In R. Schwarzer (Ed.), *Self-efficacy: Thought control of action* (pp. 217–242). Washington, DC: Hemisphere.

Schwarzer, R. (1996). Thought control of action: Interfering self-doubts. In I. G. Sarason, W. Pierce, & B. Sarason (Eds.), *Cognitive interference* (pp. 99–115). Hillsdale, NJ: Erlbaum.

Schwarzer, R., Dunkel-Schetter, C., & Kemeny, M. (1994). The multidimensional nature of received social support in gay men at risk of HIV infection and AIDS. *American Journal of Community Psychology, 22,* 319–339.

Schwarzer, R., & Jerusalem, M. (1992). Advances in anxiety theory: A cognitive process approach. In K. A. Hagtvet & T. B. Johnsen (Eds.), *Advances in test anxiety research* (Vol. 7, pp. 2–17). Lisse, The Netherlands: Swets & Zeitlinger.

Schwarzer, R., & Leppin, A. (1991). Social support and health: A theoretical and empirical overview. *Journal of Social and Personal Relationships, 8,* 99–127.

Schwarzer, R., & Wicklund, R. A. (Eds.). (1991). *Anxiety and self-focused attention.* Chur, Switzerland: Harwood.

Sederberg, C., & Clark, S. (1990). Motivation and organizational incentives for high vitality teachers: A qualitative perspective. *Journal of Research and Development in Education, 24,* 6–13.

Seidman, S. A., & Zager, J. (1991). A study of coping behaviours and teacher burnout. *Work & Stress, 5,* 205–216.

Selye, H. (1967). *Stress in health and disease.* Boston: Butterworth.

Selye, H. (1971). The evolution of the stress concept – stress and cardiovascular disease. In L. Levi (Ed.), *Society, stress and disease: Vol. 1. The psychosocial environment and psychosomatic diseases.* London: Oxford University Press.

Senge, P. M. (1990). *The fifth discipline: The art and practice of the learning organization.* New York: Doubleday.

Sergiovanni, T. (1985). Landscapes, mindscapes, and reflective practice in supervision. *Journal of Curriculum and Supervision, 1,* 5–17.

Sergiovanni, T. (1992). *Moral leadership: Getting to the heart of school improvement.* San Francisco: Jossey-Bass.

Sergiovanni, T. (1994a). The roots of school leadership. *Principal, 74,* 6–11.

Sergiovanni, T. (1994b). *Building community in schools.* San Francisco: Jossey-Bass.

Sergiovanni, T. (1995). Dimensions of professional virtue. *Journal for a Just and Caring Education, 1,* 27–29.

Sergiovanni, T. (1996). *Leadership for the school house: How is it different? Why is it important?* San Francisco: Jossey-Bass.

Shamir, B. (1991). The charismatic relationship: Alternative explanations and predictions. *Leadership Quarterly, 2,* 81–104.

Shinn, M., & Morch, H. (1984). A tripartite model of coping with burnout. In B. A. Farber (Ed.), *Stress and burnout in human service professionals* (pp. 227–210).

Shirom, A. (1989). Burnout in work organizations. In C. L. Cooper & I. T. Robertson (Eds.), *International review of industrial and organizational psychology 1989* (pp. 25–48). Chichester: Wiley.

Sikes, P. (1992). Imposed change and the experienced teacher. In M. Fullan & A. Hargreaves (Eds.), *Teacher development and educational change* (pp. 36–55). London-Washington: Falmer Press.

Sikes, P., Measor, L., & Woods, P. (1985). *Teacher careers. Crises and continuities.* London-Philadelphia: Falmer Press.

Silvernail, D. L. (1996). The impact of England's national curriculum and assessment system on classroom practice: Potential lessons for American reformers. *Educational Policy, 10,* 46–62.

Sizer, T. (1984). *Horace's compromise: The dilemma of the American high school.* Boston: Houghton Mifflin.

Skinner, B. (1953). *Science and human behavior.* New York: Macmillan.

Sleegers, P. J. C. (1991). *School en beleidsvoering* (School and policy making). Nijmegen: Katholieke Universiteit.

Sleegers, P., Bergen, Th., & Giesbers, J. (1994). The policy-making capacity of schools: Results of a Dutch study. *Educational Management & Administration, 22,* 147–160.

Sleegers, P., & Wesselingh, A. (1993). Decentralisation in education: A Dutch study. *International Studies in Sociology of Education, 3,* 49–67.

Sleegers, P., & Wesselingh, A. (1995). Dutch dilemmas: Decentralisation, school autonomy and professionalisation of teachers. *Educational Review, 47,* 199–209.

Smith, A. (1937). *An inquiry into the nature and causes of the wealth of nations.* New York: Modern Library.

Smith, H. (1995). *Rethinking America.* Random House: New York.

Smith, M. L. (1991). Put to the test: The effects of external testing on teachers. *Educational Researcher, 20*(5), 8–11.

Smith, M., & Bourke, S. (1992). Teacher stress: Examining a model based on context, workload, and satisfaction. *Teaching and Teacher Education, 8,* 31–46.

Smithers, A. (1989, May 12). Where have all the teachers gone? *The Times Educational Supplement,* p. A17.

Smylie, M. A. (1989). Teachers' view of the effectiveness of sources of learning to teach. *Elementary School Journal, 89,* 543–558.

Smylie, M. A. (1992). Teachers' reports of their interaction with teacher leaders concerning classroom instruction. *Elementary School Journal, 93,* 85–98.

Smylie, M. A. (1994). Redesigning teachers' work: Connections to the classroom. In L. Darling-Hammond (Ed.), *Review of research in education* (Vol. 20, pp. 129–177). Washington, DC: American Educational Research Association.

Smylie, M. A. (1995). Teacher learning in the workplace: Implications for school reform. In T. R. Guskey & M. Huberman (Eds.), *Professional development in education: New paradigms and practices* (pp. 92–113). New York: Teachers College Press.

Smylie, M. A. (in press). Research on teacher leadership: Assessing the state of the art. In B. J. Biddle, T. L., Good, & I. F. Goodson (Eds.), *International handbook of teachers and teaching.* Dordrecht: Kluwer.

Smylie, M. A., & Brownlee-Conyers, J. (1992). Teacher leaders and their principals: Exploring the development of new working relationships. *Educational Administration Quarterly, 28,* 150–184.

Smylie, M. A., Brownlee-Conyers, J., & Crowson, R. L. (1991, April). *When teachers make district-level decisions: A case study.* Paper presented at the annual meeting of the American Educational Research Association, Chicago.

Smylie, M. A., & Denny, J. W. (1990). Teacher leadership: Tensions and ambiguities in organizational perspective. *Educational Administration Quarterly, 26,* 235–259.

Smylie, M. A., Lazarus, V., & Brownlee-Conyers, J. (in press). Instructional outcomes of school-based participative decision making. *Educational Evaluation and Policy Analysis.*

Smylie, M. A., & Smart, J. C. (1990). Teacher support for career enhancement initiatives: Program characteristics and effects on work. *Educational Evaluation and Policy Analysis, 12,* 139–155.

Solman, R., & Feld, M. (1989). Occupational stress: Perceptions of teachers in Catholic schools. *Journal of Educational Administration, 27,* 55–68.

Sowell, T. (1987). *A conflict of visions.* New York: Morrow.

Staessens, K. (1993). The professional relationships among teachers as a core component of school culture. In F. K. Kieviet & R. Vandenberghe (Eds.), *School culture, schoolimprovement and teacher development* (pp. 39–54). Leiden: DSWO Press.

Starnaman, S. M., & Miller, K. I. (1992). A test of a causal model of communication and burnout in the teaching profession. *Communication Education, 41,* 40–53.

Stenhouse, L. (1975). *An introduction to curriculum research and development.* London: Heinemann.

Stenhouse, L. (1985). *Research as a basis for teaching* (J. Rudduck & D. Hopkins, Eds.). London: Heinemann.

Stern. (1994). Lehrer im Streß, Nr. 19.

Strassmeier, W. (1995). Wo drückt der Schuh am meisten? Teil II der Umfrage des vds vom Oktober 1993. *Zeitschrift für Heilpädagogik, 5,* 235–243.

Strelau, J. (1983). *Temperament, personality and activity.* London: Academic Press.

Sugrue, C. (1992). *Teachers' constructions of child-centred curricula.* Ph.D. thesis, OISE, University of Toronto.

Sutton, R. I., & Kahn, R. L. (1987). Prediction, understanding, and control as antidotes to organizational stress. In J. Lorsch (Ed.), *Handbook of organizational behavior* (pp. 272–285). Englewood Cliffs, NJ: Prentice-Hall.

Tang, C. S. K., & Lau, B. H. B. (1996). Gender role stress and burnout in Chinese human service professionals in Hong Kong. *Anxiety, Stress, and Coping, 9,* 217–227.

Temml, Ch. (1994). *Streß im Lehrberuf. Eine österreichweite Studie 1993.* Wien: GÖD.

Thoits, P. A. (1982). Conceptual, methodological, and theoretical problems in studying social support as a buffer against life stress. *Journal of Health and Social Behavior, 23,* 145–159.

Tomaschevskaja, L. I. (1978). *Influence of the working environment and scope of work on the heart-blood circulation system* (Russian). Kiew: Health.

Tonnies, F. (1957). *Gemeinschaft und Gesellschaft* [Community and society] (C. P. Loomis, Ed. and Trans.). New York: HarperCollins. (Original work published 1887)

Tosi, H., & Tosi, D. (1970). Some correlates of role conflict and role ambiguity among public school teachers. *Journal of Human Relations, 18,* 1068–1079.

Trachtman, R. (1991). Voices of empowerment: Teachers talk about leadership. In S. C. Conley & B. S. Cooper (Eds.), *The school as a work environment: Implications for reform* (pp. 222–235). Boston: Allyn & Bacon.

Trachtman, R., & Fauerbach, E. (1992, April). *Changing teachers, changing roles.* Paper presented at the annual meeting of the American Educational Research Association, San Francisco.

Travers, C. J., & Cooper, C. L. (1993). Mental health, job satisfaction and occupational stress among UK teachers. *Work & Stress, 7,* 203–219.

Troen, V., & Boles, K. (1992, April). *Leadership from the classroom: Women teachers as a key to school reform.* Paper presented at the annual meeting of the American Educational Research Association, San Francisco.

Troman, G. (1996). Models of the 'good' teacher: Defining and redefing. In P. Woods (Ed.), *Contemporary issues in teaching and learning* (pp. 20–32). London: Routledge.

Tropp, A. (1957). *The schoolteachers.* London: Heinemann.

Tuettemann, E., & Punch, K. F. (1992). Psychological distress in secondary teachers: Research findings and their implications. *Journal of Educational Administration, 30,* 42–54.

Turner, V. W. (1969). *The ritual process.* London: Routledge and Kegan Paul.

Ulich, D. (1987). *Krise und Entwicklung* [Crisis and development]. München: Psychologie Verlags Union.

Urban, W. (1985). *Berufszufriedenheit und Berufsbelastung bei österreichischen Hauptschullehrern.* Forschungsbericht, Pädagogische Akademie Wien.

Ursin, H., Mykletun, R., Tonder, O., Vaernes, R., Relling, G., & Murison, R. (1984). Psychological stress-factors and concentrations of immunglobulins and complement components in humans. *Scandinavian Journal of Psychology, 25,* 340–347.

U.S. Department of Education. (1993, May). *America's teachers: Profile of a profession* (NCES 93–025). Washington, DC: U.S. Government Printing Office.

Van den Berg, R. & Sleegers, P. (1996a). The innovative capacity of schools in secondary education: A qualitative study. *International Journal of Qualitative Studies in Education, 9,* 201–223.

Van den Berg, R. & Sleegers, P. (1996b). Building innovative capacity and leadership. In K. Leithwood et al. (Eds.). *International handbook of educational leadership and administration* (pp. 653–699). Boston/Dordrecht: Kluwer Academic Publishers.

Vandenberghe, R., & Vanoost, V. (1996). Waarom verlaten leerkrachten het Basisonderwijs? [Why do primary school teachers leave education?] *Nederlands Tijdschrift voor Opvoeding, Vorming en Onderwijs, 12,* 366–382.

Van Gennep, A. (1960). *The rites of passage.* London: Routledge and Kegan Paul.

Van Gennip, J., & Pouwels, J. (1993). *Loopbaanwensen van leraren in het voortgezet onderwijs* (Career wishes of teachers in secondary education). Nijmegen: ITS.

Van Gennip, J., & Sleegers, P. (1994). *Taakopvatting en taakuitvoering van leraren* (Task orientation and task performance of teachers). Nijmegen: ITS.

Van Ginkel, A. J. H. (1987). *Demotivatie bij leraren* [Demotivation of teachers]. Lisse: Swets & Zeitlinger.

Van Harrison, R. (1978). Person-environment fit and job stress. In C. L. Cooper & R. Payne (Eds.), *Stress at work* (pp. 175–205). New York: Wiley.

Vanoost, V. (1994). *Professionele biografie leerkrachten basisonderwijs: onderzoek van uitstappers* [The professional biography of primary school teachers. A study of teachers who left teaching] (Unpublished report). Leuven, Belgium: K.U. Leuven, Centrum voor Onderwijsbeleid en-vernieuwing.

Van Opdorp, C. A. W., (1991). *Problemen van docenten* (Problems of teachers). Nijmegen: Katholieke Universiteit.

Vasiljuk, F. E. (1984). *Psychology of mood* (Russian). Moskow: University Press.

Veninga, R., & Spradley, J. (1981). *The work-stress connection.* Boston: Little Brown.

Vogel, H., Scheuch, K., Naumann, W., & Koch, R. (1988). Einflußfaktoren auf den Gesundheitszustand von Pädagogen. *Zeitschrift für die gesamte Hygiene, 34,* 642–643.

Wallace, M. (1993). Discourse of derision: The role of the mass media within the education policy process. *Journal of Education Policy, 8,* 321–337.

Wallace, M., & Hall, V. (1994, April). *Team approaches to leadership in secondary schools.* Paper presented at the annual meeting of the American Educational Research Association, New Orleans.

Waller, W. (1932). *The sociology of teaching.* New York: Russell & Russell.

Walsh-Harrington, J. (1990, January 26). Out on a low note. *The Times Educational Supplement,* pp. 26–27.

Wasley, P. A. (1991). *Teachers who lead: The rhetoric of reform and the realities of practice.* New York: Teachers College Press.

Watkins, K. E., & Marsick, V. J. (1993). *Sculpting the learning organization.* San Francisco: Jossey-Bass.

Webb, R. (1993). *Eating the elephant bit by bit: The National Curriculum at Key Stage Two.* London: Association of Teachers and Lecturers.

Webb, R. (1994). *After the deluge: Changing roles and responsibilities in the primary school.* London: Association of Teachers and Lectures.

Weick, K. E. (1979). Cognitive processes in organizations. In B. M. Staw (Ed.), *Research in organizational behavior* (Vol. 1, pp. 41–74). Greenwich, CT: JAI Press.

Weick, K. E. (1993). The collapse of sensemaking in organizations: The Mann Gulch disaster. *Administrative Science Quarterly, 38,* 628–652.

Weiskopf, P. A. (1980). Burnout among teachers of exceptional children. *Exceptional Children, 47,* 18–23.

Weiss, C. H., Cambone, J., & Wyeth, A. (1992). Trouble in paradise: Teacher conflicts in shared decision making. *Educational Administration Quarterly, 28,* 350–367.

Welch, I. D., Meideros, D. C., & Tate, G. A. (1982). *Beyond burnout.* Englewood Cliffs, NJ: Prentice-Hall.

Wheatley, D. (1992). Environmental education – an instrument of change? In G. Hall (Ed.), *Themes and dimensions of the National Curriculum: Implications for policy and practice*. London: Kogan Page.

Whistler, T. (1988). *Rushavenn time*. Northamptonshire, England: Trixworth, Brixworth V.C. Primary School.

Whitaker, K. S. (1992, April). *Principal burnout and personality type: Do relationships exist?* Paper presented at the annual meeting of the American Educational Research Association, San Francisco.

Wiemers, N. J. (1990). Transformation and accommodation: A case study of Joe Scott. *Educational Evaluation and Policy Analysis, 12*, 281–292.

Williams, C. A. (1989). Empathy and burnout in male and female helping professionals. *Research in Nursing & Health, 12*, 169–178.

Wilson, D., & Mutero, C. (1989). Personality concomitants of teacher stress in Zimbabwe. *Personality & Individual Differences, 10*, 1195–1198.

Wilson, O., & Otto, R. (1988). Primary school administrators and occupational stress. *Sociology Papers, 12*, La Trobe University, Melbourne, Australia.

Wilson, S. M. (1990). A conflict of interests: The case of Mark Black. *Educational Evaluation and Policy Analysis, 12*, 293–310.

Winnubst, J. A. J. (1984). Stress in organizations. In P. J. D. Drenth, H. Thierry, P. J. Willems, & C. J. de Wolff (Eds.), *Handbook of work and organizational psychology* (Vol. 1, pp. 553–571). New York: Wiley.

Wise, A. E. (1979). *Legislated learning: The bureaucratization of the American classroom*. Berkeley, CA: University of California Press.

Wittern, O., & Tausch, A. (1980). Persönliche Beeinträchtigungen von Lehrern in ihrem beruflichen und privaten Leben. *Psychologie in Erziehung und Unterricht, 27*, 321–326.

Wolpin, J., Burke, R. J., & Greenglass, E. (1990). Golombiewski's phase model of psychological burnout: Some issues. *Psychological Reports, 66*, 451–457.

Wolpin, J., Burke, R. J., & Greenglass, E. (1994). A longitudinal study of psychological burnout and its effect on psychosomatic symptoms. *Journal of Health and Human Resources Administration, 17*, 286–303.

Woods, P. (1979). *The divided school*. London: Routledge and Kegan Paul.

Woods, P. (1981). Strategies, commitment and identity: Making and breaking the teacher role. In L. Barton & S. Walker (Eds.), *Schoolteachers and teaching*. London: Falmer.

Woods, P. (1989a). Stress and the teacher role. In M. Cole & S. Walker (Eds.), *Teaching and stress*. Buckingham, England: Open University Press.

Woods, P. (Ed.). (1989b). *Working for teacher development*. Cambridge: Peter Francis.

Woods, P. (1995). *Creative teachers in primary schools*. Buckingham, England: Open University Press.

Woods, P., & Jeffrey, R. J. (1996). *Teachable moments: The art of teaching in primary schools*. Buckingham, England: Open University Press.

Woods, P., & Wenham, P. (1994). Teaching, and researching the teaching of, a history topic: An experiment in collaboration. *The Curriculum Journal, 5*, 133–161.

Worrall, N., & May, D. (1989). Towards a person-situation model of teacher stress. *British Journal of Educational Psychology, 59*, 174–186.

Worsley, P. (1977). *Introducing sociology* (2nd ed.). Harmondsworth, England: Penguin.

Wulk, J. (1988). *Qualitative und quantitative Aspekte der psychischen und physischen Belastung von Lehrern. Eine arbeitspsychologische Untersuchung an Lehrern beruflicher Schulen*. Frankfurt: Lang.

Yee, S. M. (1991). *Careers in the classroom: When teaching is more than a job.* New York: Teachers College Press.

Zancanella, D. (1992). The influence of state-mandated testing on teachers of literature. *Educational Evaluation and Policy Analysis, 14,* 283–295.

Zaleznik, A. (1989). *The managerial mystique.* New York: Harper & Row.

Zeller, L. (1975). Arbeit der Lehrer auf dem Prüfstand: eine Pilotstudie über die psychophysische Beansprachung der Lehrer im Unterricht. *Schul- und Unterrichsorganisation, 2,* 18–25.

Index